Shakespeare For Dummies®

Mini Glossary

blank verse: Poetry in which the lines do not rhyme. Shakespeare used a mixture of prose, rhymed verse, and blank verse in his plays, but mostly he used blank verse.

comedy: A play in which the heroes do not die, but usually get married. Most comedies are lighthearted, but a few are somber until the final scene, when everyone is reconciled.

couplet: A pair of lines that rhyme. A couplet often marks the end of a scene or act.

exeunt ("eg-ZOONT"): Plural form of *exit,* used in stage directions when many people leave the stage at once.

flourish: A stage direction for a fanfare of drums and trumpets, usually announcing the entrance or exit of a king or queen.

history: A play that recounts historical events. Shakespeare's history plays are historical fiction. He altered time, people, and events.

iambic pentameter: A form of verse in which every other syllable is stressed (as in "dah-DUM") and each line contains five stressed syllables.

quatrain: A stanza of four lines, usually rhyming on alternate lines.

rhyme royal: A verse form of seven-line stanzas rhyming in the pattern *ababbcc.*

sennet: A stage direction for a trumpet fanfare, like a flourish.

soliloquy: A monologue that reveals a character's inner thoughts and feelings.

sonnet: A poem of 14 lines that follows a particular rhyme scheme. Shakespeare included sonnets in a few of his plays, and he wrote 154 sonnets as a series. Most of Shakespeare's sonnets rhyme in the pattern *abab cdcd efef gg.*

tragedy: A play in which the hero has a character flaw, such as pride, that leads to his death.

Shakespeare's Plays

If you can't quite remember what a particular play is about, this list can jog your memory. If not, you can find more detailed summaries in Chapters 13 through 15.

Comedies:

All's Well That Ends Well: Bertie runs away to avoid his new wife, Helena, but she follows him and tricks him into being her faithful husband.

As You Like It: A romp in the Forest of Arden, where everyone falls in love.

The Comedy of Errors: Two sets of twins turn the town of Ephesus upside down.

Cymbeline: A jealous husband believes a false story about his wife. She runs away and meets her long-lost brothers.

Love's Labour's Lost: The King of Navarre and his court try to study in seclusion but succumb to the temptations of love.

Measure for Measure: Power corrupts Angelo, the substitute duke, who tries to seduce the sister of a condemned man.

The Merchant of Venice: Moneylender Shylock tries to recover his "pound of flesh" collateral for a loan.

The Merry Wives of Windsor: Sir John Falstaff puts the moves on the Merry Wives, who turn the tables on him.

A Midsummer Night's Dream: Mix-and-match couples in the woods near Athens. "Lord, what fools these mortals be!"

Much Ado About Nothing: Claudio loves Hero. Benedick doesn't like Beatrice. Then Claudio hates Hero, and Benedick loves Beatrice. Eventually, everyone gets married.

Pericles: Pericles lives, loves, loses, and regains his family while touring the Mediterranean Sea.

Shakespeare's Plays (continued)

The Taming of the Shrew: Petruchio "tames" his wife, Katherina.

The Tempest: Prospero uses magic to reclaim his dukedom and find a husband for his daughter, Miranda.

Troilus and Cressida: In ancient Troy, Troilus and Cressida vow undying love, which dies all too quickly.

Twelfth Night: Orsino loves Olivia. Olivia loves Cesario. Cesario is really Viola, who loves Orsino.

The Two Gentlemen of Verona: Nothing can come between best friends Valentine and Proteus, except a girl, Sylvia.

The Two Noble Kinsmen: Two brothers fight for love in ancient Greece.

The Winter's Tale: Jealous husband Leontes drives away his wife, children, and best friend.

Histories:

King John: John turns over England to the Pope.

King Richard II: Henry Bolingbroke deposes King Richard and becomes King Henry IV.

King Henry IV, Part 1: Henry wonders why his son can't be more like that nice Hotspur boy, until Hotspur rebels against the king.

King Henry IV, Part 2: Henry's son Hal continues to act up, and rebels still threaten the throne, but Hal comes out all right in the end and becomes King Henry V.

King Henry V: Henry invades France.

King Henry VI, Part 1: Joan of Arc leads the French army against England. The Houses of York and Lancaster start a spat that lasts through the next three plays.

King Henry VI, Part 2: Peasants and the House of York rebel against King Henry.

King Henry VI, Part 3: The House of York deposes King Henry, despite help from France. Edward, son of the Duke of York, takes the throne as King Edward IV.

King Richard III: Edward's brother, Richard, kills everyone in his way and seizes the throne, only to lose it and his life.

King Henry VIII: King Henry divorces his wife, starts a new church, remarries, and fathers a daughter who becomes Queen Elizabeth I.

Tragedies:

Antony and Cleopatra: Antony tries to balance love and war but sacrifices everything for love.

Coriolanus: Rome's best general feels slighted, so he switches sides.

Hamlet: A young prince plans revenge against his murdering uncle.

Julius Caesar: Brutus and others kill Caesar to prevent him from becoming king.

King Lear: Lear gives up his kingdom to his daughters and then gives up his mind.

Macbeth: Witches' prophecies prompt Macbeth to seize the throne of Scotland.

Othello: Iago preys on Othello's jealousy and drives him to murder.

Romeo and Juliet: Forbidden love tempts and destroys a young couple.

Timon of Athens: Overgenerous Timon learns who his true friends are when he runs out of money.

Titus Andronicus: Bloody revenge in ancient Rome, with the emphasis on bloody.

The IDG Books Worldwide logo is a registered trademark under exclusive license to IDG Books Worldwide, Inc., from International Data Group, Inc. The ...For Dummies logo is a trademark, and For Dummies and ...For Dummies are registered trademarks of IDG Books Worldwide, Inc. All other trademarks are the property of their respective owners.

...For Dummies®: Bestselling Book Series for Beginners

TM

References for the Rest of Us!™

BESTSELLING BOOK SERIES

Do you find that traditional reference books are overloaded with technical details and advice you'll never use? Do you postpone important life decisions because you just don't want to deal with them? Then our *...For Dummies*® business and general reference book series is for you.

...For Dummies business and general reference books are written for those frustrated and hard-working souls who know they aren't dumb, but find that the myriad of personal and business issues and the accompanying horror stories make them feel helpless. *...For Dummies* books use a lighthearted approach, a down-to-earth style, and even cartoons and humorous icons to dispel fears and build confidence. Lighthearted but not lightweight, these books are perfect survival guides to solve your everyday personal and business problems.

> **"More than a publishing phenomenon, 'Dummies' is a sign of the times."**
>
> — **The New York Times**

> **"A world of detailed and authoritative information is packed into them..."**
>
> — **U.S. News and World Report**

> **"...you won't go wrong buying them."**
>
> — **Walter Mossberg, Wall Street Journal, on IDG Books' ...For Dummies books**

Already, millions of satisfied readers agree. They have made *...For Dummies* the #1 introductory level computer book series and a best-selling business book series. They have written asking for more. So, if you're looking for the best and easiest way to learn about business and other general reference topics, look to *...For Dummies* to give you a helping hand.

IDG BOOKS WORLDWIDE

1/99

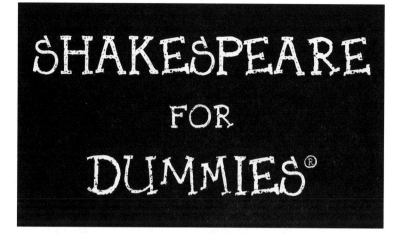

SHAKESPEARE FOR DUMMIES®

by John Doyle and Ray Lischner

Foreword by Dame Judi Dench

IDG BOOKS WORLDWIDE

IDG Books Worldwide, Inc.
An International Data Group Company

Foster City, CA ◆ Chicago, IL ◆ Indianapolis, IN ◆ New York, NY

Shakespeare For Dummies®

Published by
IDG Books Worldwide, Inc.
An International Data Group Company
919 E. Hillsdale Blvd.
Suite 400
Foster City, CA 94404
www.idgbooks.com (IDG Books Worldwide Web site)
www.dummies.com (Dummies Press Web site)

Library of Congress Catalog Card No.: 99-62259

ISBN: 0-7645-5135-3

Printed in the United States of America

10 9 8 7 6 5 4 3 2 1

1B/RU/QU/ZZ/IN

Distributed in the United States by IDG Books Worldwide, Inc.

Distributed by CDG Books Canada Inc. for Canada; by Transworld Publishers Limited in the United Kingdom; by IDG Norge Books for Norway; by IDG Sweden Books for Sweden; by Woodslane Pty. Ltd. for Australia; by Woodslane (NZ) Ltd. for New Zealand; by TransQuest Publishers Pte Ltd. for Singapore, Malaysia, Thailand, Indonesia, and Hong Kong; by ICG Muse, Inc. for Japan; by Norma Comunicaciones S.A. for Colombia; by Intersoft for South Africa; by Le Monde en Tique for France; by International Thomson Publishing for Germany, Austria and Switzerland; by Distribuidora Cuspide for Argentina; by Livraria Cultura for Brazil; by Ediciones ZETA S.C.R. Ltda. for Peru; by WS Computer Publishing Corporation, Inc., for the Philippines; by Contemporanea de Ediciones for Venezuela; by Express Computer Distributors for the Caribbean and West Indies; by Micronesia Media Distributor, Inc. for Micronesia; by Grupo Editorial Norma S.A. for Guatemala; by Chips Computadoras S.A. de C.V. for Mexico; by Editorial Norma de Panama S.A. for Panama; by American Bookshops for Finland. Authorized Sales Agent: Anthony Rudkin Associates for the Middle East and North Africa.

For general information on IDG Books Worldwide's books in the U.S., please call our Consumer Customer Service department at 800-762-2974. For reseller information, including discounts and premium sales, please call our Reseller Customer Service department at 800-434-3422.

For information on where to purchase IDG Books Worldwide's books outside the U.S., please contact our International Sales department at 317-596-5530 or fax 317-596-5692.

For consumer information on foreign language translations, please contact our Customer Service department at 1-800-434-3422, fax 317-596-5692, or e-mail rights@idgbooks.com.

For information on licensing foreign or domestic rights, please phone +1-650-655-3109.

For sales inquiries and special prices for bulk quantities, please contact our Sales department at 650-655-3200 or write to the address above.

For information on using IDG Books Worldwide's books in the classroom or for ordering examination copies, please contact our Educational Sales department at 800-434-2086 or fax 317-596-5499.

For press review copies, author interviews, or other publicity information, please contact our Public Relations department at 650-655-3000 or fax 650-655-3299.

For authorization to photocopy items for corporate, personal, or educational use, please contact Copyright Clearance Center, 222 Rosewood Drive, Danvers, MA 01923, or fax 978-750-4470.

About the Authors

John Doyle studied theater first at the Royal Scottish Academy of Music and Drama, and then on a scholarship as Junior Artist in Residence at the University of Georgia in the U.S. John staged his first professional production in 1974 at the tiny Ochtertyre Theatre in Perthshire, and now, 160 productions later, he has worked throughout the UK and abroad. He has been Artistic Director of the Swan Theatre, Worcester; the Everyman Theatre, Cheltenham; the Everyman Theatre, Liverpool; and the York Theatre Royal. Guest productions have been at Nottingham, Leatherhead, Perth, Edinburgh, Dublin, Vienna, Zurich, Glasgow, Salisbury, and Newbury — to name but a few. Awards include the British Theatre Award for Best Production of a Musical in 1995.

John's forays into Shakespeare include three productions of *Macbeth* (including one at Cawdor Castle), two productions of *A Midsummer Night's Dream* (one highly acclaimed production being at the famous Regent's Park Open Air Theatre in London), the repertory premiere of *Wars of the Roses,* which he adapted for the stage, two productions of *Twelfth Night* (one set 'round a swimming pool), *Romeo and Juliet* (also a production of *West Side Story*), two productions of *Much Ado About Nothing* (one set in Kentucky!), *As You Like It,* and *Othello*.

John has also enjoyed positions as Visiting Artist in Residence at Western Kentucky University and Visiting Artist to Oregon State University, as well as guest work at many UK theater schools.

John's adaptations for the theater include a musical of *Tom Jones* and stage versions of *A Tale of Two Cities* and *Dracula*.

John lives in Hastings on England's south coast. He enjoys his enormously varied career but still finds time for walks on the shore and visits to his beloved Italy! However, even though he was born in the Highlands of Scotland, he definitely feels that the U.S. is his second home.

Ray Lischner's day job involves a lot of mucking about with computers, but that hasn't blunted his interest in the theater. In college, he helped form TACIT (Theater Arts at the California Institute of Technology). He took time off from homework to participate in every theatrical production. While his fellow Caltech students engaged in scientific research, Ray's research project examined the influence of the Renaissance Italian theater on Shakespeare's *The Two Gentlemen of Verona*.

Ray has performed in *The Two Gentlemen of Verona, Titus Andronicus, Romeo and Juliet,* and other, non-Shakespearean plays. He also produced, directed, and helped translate the first English language production of Marivaux's 18th century French masterpiece, *La Dispute*. After college, he translated and directed the medieval French play *La Farce de Maistre Pierre Pathelin*.

When he's not working in the theater, Ray writes books about computer programming and teaches computer science at Oregon State University. You can reach Ray by sending e-mail to lischner@bardware.com.

ABOUT IDG BOOKS WORLDWIDE

Welcome to the world of IDG Books Worldwide.

IDG Books Worldwide, Inc., is a subsidiary of International Data Group, the world's largest publisher of computer-related information and the leading global provider of information services on information technology. IDG was founded more than 30 years ago by Patrick J. McGovern and now employs more than 9,000 people worldwide. IDG publishes more than 290 computer publications in over 75 countries. More than 90 million people read one or more IDG publications each month.

Launched in 1990, IDG Books Worldwide is today the #1 publisher of best-selling computer books in the United States. We are proud to have received eight awards from the Computer Press Association in recognition of editorial excellence and three from Computer Currents' First Annual Readers' Choice Awards. Our best-selling *...For Dummies*® series has more than 50 million copies in print with translations in 31 languages. IDG Books Worldwide, through a joint venture with IDG's Hi-Tech Beijing, became the first U.S. publisher to publish a computer book in the People's Republic of China. In record time, IDG Books Worldwide has become the first choice for millions of readers around the world who want to learn how to better manage their businesses.

Our mission is simple: Every one of our books is designed to bring extra value and skill-building instructions to the reader. Our books are written by experts who understand and care about our readers. The knowledge base of our editorial staff comes from years of experience in publishing, education, and journalism — experience we use to produce books to carry us into the new millennium. In short, we care about books, so we attract the best people. We devote special attention to details such as audience, interior design, use of icons, and illustrations. And because we use an efficient process of authoring, editing, and desktop publishing our books electronically, we can spend more time ensuring superior content and less time on the technicalities of making books.

You can count on our commitment to deliver high-quality books at competitive prices on topics you want to read about. At IDG Books Worldwide, we continue in the IDG tradition of delivering quality for more than 30 years. You'll find no better book on a subject than one from IDG Books Worldwide.

John Kilcullen
Chairman and CEO
IDG Books Worldwide, Inc.

Steven Berkowitz
President and Publisher
IDG Books Worldwide, Inc.

*Eighth Annual
Computer Press
Awards ≥1992*

WINNER

*Ninth Annual
Computer Press
Awards ≥1993*

*Tenth Annual
Computer Press
Awards ≥1994*

WINNER

WINNER

*Eleventh Annual
Computer Press
Awards ≥1995*

IDG is the world's leading IT media, research and exposition company. Founded in 1964, IDG had 1997 revenues of $2.05 billion and has more than 9,000 employees worldwide. IDG offers the widest range of media options that reach IT buyers in 75 countries representing 95% of worldwide IT spending. IDG's diverse product and services portfolio spans six key areas including print publishing, online publishing, expositions and conferences, market research, education and training, and global marketing services. More than 90 million people read one or more of IDG's 290 magazines and newspapers, including IDG's leading global brands — Computerworld, PC World, Network World, Macworld and the Channel World family of publications. IDG Books Worldwide is one of the fastest-growing computer book publishers in the world, with more than 700 titles in 36 languages. The "...For Dummies®" series alone has more than 50 million copies in print. IDG offers online users the largest network of technology-specific Web sites around the world through IDG.net (http://www.idg.net), which comprises more than 225 targeted Web sites in 55 countries worldwide. International Data Corporation (IDC) is the world's largest provider of information technology data, analysis and consulting, with research centers in over 41 countries and more than 400 research analysts worldwide. IDG World Expo is a leading producer of more than 168 globally branded conferences and expositions in 35 countries including E3 (Electronic Entertainment Expo), Macworld Expo, ComNet, Windows World Expo, ICE (Internet Commerce Expo), Agenda, DEMO, and Spotlight. IDG's training subsidiary, ExecuTrain, is the world's largest computer training company, with more than 230 locations worldwide and 785 training courses. IDG Marketing Services helps industry-leading IT companies build international brand recognition by developing global integrated marketing programs via IDG's print, online and exposition products worldwide. Further information about the company can be found at www.idg.com.   1/24/99

Authors' Acknowledgments

Our undying gratitude goes to Dr. Charlotte Headrick, who unwittingly made this book possible. When she directed *Titus Andronicus* at Oregon State University, she tapped Ray's passion for Shakespeare and renewed his involvement in the theater. She brought John, her friend and colleague, to OSU as an artist in residence, which is how we met and started our collaboration.

Many people contributed to our effort. Dr. Jenijoy La Belle, professor of Literature at the California Institute of Technology, reviewed our manuscript thoroughly, pointing our errors and suggesting improvements. We thank Dame Judi Dench for her support and encouragement. We also thank Jessica Hodge, editor for Arden Shakespeare, Kit Leary and Amy Richard of the Oregon Shakespeare Festival, and Mark Walton at the British Library for their help and research assistance. Thanks go to the organizations that provided photographs for use in this book: the British Museum, David Cooper Photo, Donald Cooper/Photostage, Everett Collection, Ronald Grant Archive, Henry S. Kranzler, the Shakespeare Centre Library, Shakespeare's Globe and Richard Kalina, Stratford-on-Avon P.C.C., Tate Gallery, and the V+A Picture Library. Pam Mourouzis, Mark Butler, Gwenette Gaddis, Diane Smith, Karen York, Janet Withers, and Shelley Lea of IDG Books did an outstanding job of turning our unpolished manuscript into a terrific book. Cheryl Klipp helped draw the maps in Chapter 12.

From Ray:

I especially thank Joseph Truitt, my high school English teacher who first showed me the joys and wonders of literature and Shakespeare. I also thank Shirley Marneus for proving that scientists and engineers can act and direct.

I thank my loving and unbelievably patient wife, Cheryl, for putting up with me this past year.

From John:

My unending thanks to Gordon Reid, Jacquie Crago, Karen Mann, Tina Gray, Terry Wale, and the hundreds of actors it has been my good fortune to work with, all of whom have helped me "cherish the words."

My eternal thanks to Robert Wilson — without whom it probably wouldn't have happened.

Publisher's Acknowledgments

We're proud of this book; please register your comments through our IDG Books Worldwide Online Registration Form located at http://my2cents.dummies.com.

Some of the people who helped bring this book to market include the following:

Acquisitions, Editorial, and Media Development

Senior Project Editor: Pamela Mourouzis

Senior Acquisitions Editor: Mark Butler

Copy Editors: Gwenette Gaddis, Susan Diane Smith

General Reviewer: Dr. Jenijoy La Belle

Associate Permissions Editor: Carmen Krikorian

Editorial Manager: Rev Mengle

Editorial Coordinator: Maureen F. Kelly

Production

Project Coordinator: Karen York

Layout and Graphics: Linda M. Boyer, Lisa Harrington, Angela F. Hunckler, Ted Pereda, Anna Rohrer, Brent Savage, Kathie Schutte, Janet Seib, Kate Snell, Michael A. Sullivan

Special Art: Cheryl Klipp

Proofreaders: Christine Berman, Jennifer Mahern, Nancy Price, Rebecca Senninger, Ethel M. Winslow, Janet M. Withers

Indexer: Sharon Hilgenberg

Special Help

Johnathon Malysiak, Allison Solomon

General and Administrative

IDG Books Worldwide, Inc.: John Kilcullen, CEO; Steven Berkowitz, President and Publisher

IDG Books Technology Publishing: Brenda McLaughlin, Senior Vice President and Group Publisher

Dummies Technology Press and Dummies Editorial: Diane Graves Steele, Vice President and Associate Publisher; Mary Bednarek, Director of Acquisitions and Product Development; Kristin A. Cocks, Editorial Director

Dummies Trade Press: Kathleen A. Welton, Vice President and Publisher; Kevin Thornton, Acquisitions Manager

IDG Books Production for Dummies Press: Michael R. Britton, Vice President of Production and Creative Services; Cindy L. Phipps, Manager of Project Coordination, Production Proofreading, and Indexing; Kathie S. Schutte, Supervisor of Page Layout; Shelley Lea, Supervisor of Graphics and Design; Debbie J. Gates, Production Systems Specialist; Robert Springer, Supervisor of Proofreading; Debbie Stailey, Special Projects Coordinator; Tony Augsburger, Supervisor of Reprints and Bluelines

Dummies Packaging and Book Design: Patty Page, Manager, Promotions Marketing

♦

The publisher would like to give special thanks to Patrick J. McGovern, without whom this book would not have been possible.

♦

Contents at a Glance

Cartoons at a Glance

By Rich Tennant

"I know you're all classically trained actors, but I don't think the public's ready for Titus Andronicus performed by the cast of Stomp."

page 329

"Oh, Will— such passion, such pathos, such despair and redemption. I've never read a more moving grocery list."

page 5

"I know it's a Furby, Ronald. Just work with it until we can get a skull."

page 69

"I enjoy Shakespeare as much as the next person, but not while I'm watching the weatherman."

page 121

"Excuse me! Witch number three, your line is also 'Hail,' not 'Whatever'."

page 37

page 311

Fax: 978-546-7747 • E-mail: the5wave@tiac.net

Table of Contents

Foreword

*W*hen I was asked to write a foreword for *Shakespeare For Dummies,* I balked at the idea because I was afraid I would not have time to give it my full attention and do the book justice. Having read it, this foreword has written itself.

Shakespeare For Dummies is exquisite. For those of us familiar with Shakespeare, it's terribly amusing. For those not so familiar, it brings the Bard to life and makes him easily understandable. I still remember schooldays when Shakespeare sounded like a foreign language. This book should be compulsory reading for everyone.

— Dame Judi Dench

Introduction

· ·

*W*illiam Shakespeare was the best English writer. Ever. Others might waffle and write "one of the best," but we wouldn't have written this book if we weren't firmly convinced that he was the absolute best, and we're not alone in that opinion.

Shakespeare suffers from an image problem, though. He lived about 400 years ago, and a lot has changed since then. In particular, the English language is different, and that's what makes his plays hard to read and understand — at least, that's what makes most people *think* that Shakespeare is hard to understand.

Despite Shakespeare's image problem, modern films of Shakespeare's plays are immensely popular. Baz Luhrmann's *Romeo+Juliet,* starring Leonardo DiCaprio and Claire Danes, is but one example of many recent hits. You've probably seen at least one of them: *Romeo+Juliet,* Kenneth Branagh's *Much Ado About Nothing,* Mel Gibson in *Hamlet,* and so on. One reason these films are so popular is that the audience can understand the language.

Baz Luhrmann updated *Romeo and Juliet,* but not as much as you might think. He moved Verona, Italy, to Verona Beach; he substituted guns for swords; and he added a modern soundtrack. But he didn't change the words. What you hear is what Shakespeare wrote. The modern screen-writers — for *Romeo+Juliet* and for the other films mentioned earlier — cut some lines to make the movies shorter, but they did not modernize or update Shakespeare's beautiful language.

In other words, you *can* understand Shakespeare.

About This Book

This book is your guide to help you get the most out of Shakespeare's works while watching, reading, or acting in them. It tells you what you need to know about Shakespeare's plays and poetry — without making you wade through a morass of literary jargon.

In everyday terms, this book guides you through Shakespeare's plays and poetry, as well as his life and world. Decode the mysteries of the sonnets, or take a tour of Elizabethan England through the plays and other poetry. In his day, Shakespeare wanted his audiences to enjoy themselves. Four hundred years later, you should, too, and this book gives you the tools to do so.

How This Book Is Organized

You don't need to read this book from cover to cover. Feel free to skip around from one part to another, picking out the topics that interest you. The parts are as follows:

- **Part I: What Makes Shakespeare Special** introduces William Shakespeare, discusses his life and times, and tells you about his influence in the modern world. To get the most from Shakespeare's plays, it often helps to understand a little about his culture and English society 400 years ago.

- **Part II: You Call That English?** helps you make sense of Shakespeare's language. If you find reading Shakespeare difficult, you're not alone. With a little help and some practice, though, you can read and understand Shakespeare's English almost as easily as you can modern English.

- **Part III: The Play's the Thing** tells you about the kinds of stories, characters, and settings that you find in Shakespeare's plays. Shakespeare lacked special effects and fancy sets, so he filled his plays with vivid images — images painted with words. In this part, you can unleash your imagination while reading or watching a play.

- **Part IV: Scorecards and Summaries** briefly describes the plot and key characters for every play. We also include a scorecard for each play so that you can keep track of who's winning and who's losing. Read the summary before you read or watch the play. You may find some important information in the summaries, such as a tip that you may not want to bring your young children to the latest film rendition of *Titus Andronicus*.

- **Part V: The Other Poems** tells you about Shakespeare's nondramatic poetry. We know Shakespeare best for his plays, which are a form of poetry, but he wrote other poems, too. He wrote many sonnets and a few longer poems, which you can read about in this part.

- **Part VI: The Part of Tens** completes the book. Here, you can read about Shakespeare's influence on modern language and society, find out where to go for the best of Shakespeare onstage, and more.

Conventions Used in This Book

All the quotes in this book come from *The Arden Shakespeare Complete Works* (Thomas Nelson and Sons Ltd, 1998). After each quote is a reference to the play, act, scene, and line number. For example, in the play *King Henry IV, Part 2*, the quote in Act 2, scene 1, at line 74 includes the following:

He hath eaten me out of house and home. (*2 Henry IV* 2.1.74)

For the sake of brevity and to avoid confusion with the act number, the plays with numbered parts are written with the number first. Other editions show the act number as capital Roman numerals and scene number as lowercase Roman numerals, in which case this quote would be marked II.i.74 or something similar.

If a quote uses an archaic or confusing word, a definition appears on the right-hand side of the page. For example, the Prince in *Romeo and Juliet* admonishes the lovers' parents as follows:

But I'll amerce* you with so strong a fine   *penalize

That you shall all repent the loss of mine. (191–92)

Every edition of Shakespeare's works has slightly different line numbers, and sometimes different scene numbers, too. Pages have different widths, causing line breaks to appear in different places. Editors might also disagree about where scene divisions belong. If you want to look up a particular quote in a different edition, the act, scene, and line number give you a starting point. Look around a little to find the exact location in your particular book. You can read more about these kinds of problems in Chapter 10.

Icons Used in This Book

This book uses icons to point out certain information that can make Shakespeare more interesting and enjoyable.

This icon marks a helpful hint for reading, viewing, or acting in Shakespeare's plays.

Shakespeare intended his plays to be performed, not read as literature. Therefore, he wrote the words so that they would sound good, not so that they would be easy to read. You can make the most sense from his plays and poetry by reading them aloud. This icon tells you when reading a certain passage aloud is particularly useful. If you can, find a friend to help you — one person speaks and the other listens. Then switch roles.

Most of Shakespeare's plays have made it to videotape, laser disc, or DVD, so you can enjoy your favorite plays from the comfort of your home. This icon marks information about notable performances, which you can see for yourself by renting or borrowing the tape or disc. If you don't have your own videotape player, you can introduce Shakespeare to a friend who does.

In the entertainment business, it pays to get the most out of a good idea. When Hollywood produces one alien-invasion film, it produces a dozen. Shakespeare did the same thing — not producing disaster films, but reusing ideas, characters, and themes. This icon points out the common elements that pop up in many different plays.

Where to Go from Here

Shakespeare's plays have entertained audiences over the past 400 years, and they will continue to do so for hundreds of years to come. We hope that this book will inspire you to read your favorite plays again, seek out performances of Shakespeare's plays at your local theaters, or get involved yourself.

Every year, you can find new movie releases. Some are straightforward performances of Shakespeare's plays, adapted to film. Some films retell or reshape the original story in significant ways. Both kinds of films can be fun to watch, especially when you're prepared with your scorecard and play summary.

If you want to acquire your own complete set of Shakespeare's plays, we believe that *The Arden Shakespeare Complete Works* is a good choice. If you prefer individual plays — which are more convenient to read — you have many choices. Visit a bookstore and choose the edition that you like best. There's no such thing as a "wrong" edition. And don't forget the local library, which should also have at least one copy of Shakespeare's complete works. Some libraries have videotapes, too.

If you have access to the Internet and the World Wide Web, you can find many Web sites about Shakespeare, the Globe Theatre, history, plays, acting, books, movies, videotapes, and more. To help find your way around these sites, visit www.bardware.com for an online guide to William Shakespeare and his works.

William Shakespeare is alive and well because his plays and poems live on — on the stage, on the screen, and in our hearts. We hope that this book brings Shakespeare to life for you.

Part I
What Makes Shakespeare Special

The 5th Wave   By Rich Tennant

"Oh, Will— such passion, such pathos, such despair and redemption. I've never read a more moving grocery list."

In this part . . .

This part tells you about William Shakespeare and his world. Don't worry; it's not a lesson in English literature, just a trip back about 400 years to drop in on an old friend. He's an actor and a writer — working in the Hollywood of his day — and he made quite a name for himself. Let us introduce you to our good friend, Will.

Chapter 1

Meet William Shakespeare

*A*bout 400 years ago, a small-town actor and writer made it big in the theaters of London. His plays were popular, and he earned his share of fame and fortune. He and his colleagues never suspected, though, that he would gain immortality as one of the great masters of English literature. After all, he wasn't writing literature, just popular entertainment. William Shakespeare (shown in Figure 1-1) was simply doing his job — as an actor, director, writer, and partner in a successful acting company.

Figure 1-1:
William Shakespeare — a woodcut from *The First Folio,* the first published collection of his plays.

Shakespeare Centre Library

It turns out that Shakespeare was good at his job. Really good. So good that he changed the face of drama, and that 400 years later, we still consider his plays to be among the best ever written. Shakespeare is also the most studied playwright in history. Book after book has analyzed and explored his life, his mind, and probably a lot of other things you don't want to know about.

Shakespeare's plays are a lot of fun to watch, read, and perform. Sometimes, the fun gets lost in pedantic analysis of Shakespeare and his plays, but don't let the scholars get in your way. Take a new look at his plays, putting aside the analysis and concentrating instead on having fun.

Ye Olde Hollywood

The scene is dark. The murderer unwisely sits with his back to the door. The hero walks by and sees the murderer — now's his chance to avenge his father's foul and unnatural murder. As the hero creeps forward, the audience members hold their breath, waiting to see what will happen next. Will the murderer turn around? Will the hero achieve his vengeance?

Is this scene from the latest Hollywood thriller?

The boy and girl are from different families, from different walks of life. He is destined to lead, and she to follow. Her father forbids her from seeing her love, but that's okay because her lover is going mad anyway. In his madness, he kills her father, which drives her to madness and then to suicide. Her brother returns from France and demands justice.

Is this just another soap opera?

The answer to both questions is "Yes," but the scenes are also from a play written 400 years ago — *Hamlet, Prince of Denmark* — the story of a young man (named Hamlet, naturally) and some really crazy goings-on in Denmark. You can read more about this play in Chapter 15.

Shakespeare's plays are full of lovers and warriors, heroes and villains, and even a wicked stepmother — all the ingredients for box office success. His plays quickly became big hits in his day, and they have remained popular ever since.

Shakespeare, the Man

William Shakespeare grew up in the small village of Stratford, on the banks of the Avon River, but we don't know much else about his early life. We don't even know when he was born — only that his christening took place on

April 26, 1564. He was probably born a few days before then, and the modern world conveniently uses April 23 as the anniversary of his birth for the somewhat macabre reason that he died on that day in 1616.

William was the third of eight children of John Shakespeare and Mary Arden. Three of his siblings died in infancy — an all-too-common fate in those days. We know almost nothing of William's childhood, but we do know that in November 1582, William married Anne Hathaway — who was eight years his senior — and they baptized their child, Susanna, on May 26, 1583. You do the math.

Anne later bore twins, a girl named Judith and a boy named Hamnet, both named after family friends. After that, William again drops out of the history books. Did he still live in Stratford? Did he move to London? We just don't know. All we know is that he surfaced seven years later, in 1592, as an actor and playwright living in London. E-mail hadn't been invented yet, so any aspiring playwright would have to live in London — that's where the theaters were. He was successful enough to draw the attention and ire of a competing playwright, Robert Greene, who called Shakespeare "an upstart crow."

Not everyone was so jealous of Shakespeare's success. Most of his other contemporaries recognized his genius. In a prefatory poem to *The First Folio*, which is the first published collection of Shakespeare's plays, Ben Jonson — also a well-regarded playwright — wrote:

Thou art a Monument without a tomb,

And art alive still while thy Book doth live,

And we have wits to read, and praise to give.

. . .

He was not of an age, but for all time!

Acting, writing, and directing paid the bills, but then as now, the real wealth came to the person in charge. Shakespeare didn't earn much money from writing plays, but from his share of the ticket receipts. He was part owner of an acting company and of the theater where that company performed: the Globe Theatre.

Shakespeare's plays at the Globe Theatre were so popular that he became a wealthy man. Shakespeare dutifully sent money back to Stratford, but we know little about his relationship with his family.

He purchased one of the largest houses in Stratford, where he and his family eventually lived until his daughters married and moved out. He invested in real estate around Stratford. He even purchased respectability in the form of a coat of arms. Pretty good for the son of a glove-maker.

Hamnet died in childhood, Shakespeare's his daughters grew up and had children of their own (Judith's children died young). Susanna's only child, Elizabeth, was the last of William Shakespeare's descendents.

Shakespeare, the Myth

Because we know so little about the true history of William Shakespeare, many stories have arisen surrounding his life. The most enduring myth is that Shakespeare did not write the plays that bear his name. Another interesting fable is that Shakespeare helped write the King James Bible.

Will the real William Shakespeare please stand up?

Some people claim that Shakespeare didn't actually write his plays. Instead, they say, someone else wrote the plays, and this mysterious person wanted or needed to remain anonymous. No one can prove these claims, and different people offer different mysterious candidates as the "real" William Shakespeare. Most of their arguments are similar, though:

- ✔ Shakespeare's education was limited, so he couldn't have had such an excellent command of English. Therefore, someone with a better education must have written his plays.

- ✔ Shakespeare didn't travel and see the world, so he couldn't have written plays that discuss such varied places as Egypt, Syracuse, and Italy.

- ✔ Shakespeare knew little of foreign languages, so he couldn't have written plays that contain passages of Latin and French.

- ✔ The plays often depict intimate details of the lives of kings and queens — a world unknown to the commoner Shakespeare.

The most popular contenders for Shakespeare's throne are Francis Bacon; Edward de Vere, 17th Earl of Oxford; and Christopher Marlowe — although the complete list of candidates is quite long, including such far-out suggestions as Queen Elizabeth and Anne Hathaway, Shakespeare's wife. Take a quick look at some of the facts.

The Earl of Oxford died in 1604, but some of Shakespeare's best plays were written later than that. For example, Shakespeare wrote *The Tempest* in 1611. You need to come up with some convoluted explanations to account for this little problem.

Christopher Marlowe was also an excellent playwright, but he was killed in 1593, before Shakespeare wrote most of his plays. If you don't believe that the Earl of Oxford wrote the plays, you won't accept Marlowe, either.

That leaves Francis Bacon, who was a prolific writer. His style is different from Shakespeare's, and we have no reason to believe that he wrote any plays using "Shakespeare" as a pseudonym.

Consider some additional facts. We don't know all the details of Shakespeare's life, but it's indeed likely that he never visited Italy, the setting for many of his plays. Therefore, he never visited the landlocked city of Milan, and he never knew his mistake when he wrote Prospero's lines that describe how he and his daughter, Miranda, were kidnapped one night:

. . . they hurried us aboard a bark,

Bore us some leagues to sea; where they prepared

A rotten carcass of a butt, not rigg'd,

Nor tackle, sail, nor mast; the very rats

Instinctively have quit it: there they hoist us,

To cry to th' sea that roar'd to us; to sigh

To th' winds, whose pity, sighing back again,

Did us but loving wrong. (*The Tempest* 1.2.144–51)

Milan is far from the sea, a major river, or anywhere a bark or other ship could land, but that didn't bother Shakespeare. He knew that the poetry of the moment was more important than getting the geographical details just right.

Similarly, an educated gentleman would know that church bells were a medieval invention, but Shakespeare has bells ringing in ancient Rome.

No funeral rite, nor man in mourning weed,

No mournful bell shall ring her burial. (*Titus Andronicus* 5.3.195–96)

Shakespeare's plays are full of similar mistakes. These little slips don't affect the plays, and you probably won't even notice most of them, but they reveal an author who lacked a college education. In other words, they tell us that William Shakespeare, not Francis Bacon and not the Earl of Oxford, wrote these plays. A few people will never be convinced that William Shakespeare, from the town of Stratford-upon-Avon, wrote the plays attributed to him. A few people believe that the Earth is flat, too.

If it were proved that a thousand monkeys, scrawling randomly with a quill, accidentally produced the works of Shakespeare, it would be a miracle, but one that does not in any way diminish the quality of the plays. They would remain masterpieces of entertainment and literature. When you settle into your seat in the theater and watch the armies of France and England march across the stage in *King Henry V,* you can enjoy the characters, the excitement, and the play, secure in the knowledge that William Shakespeare, the Bard of Stratford-upon-Avon, was the literary genius who wrote his plays.

Shakespeare as biblical scholar?

Shakespeare was a master of the English language; there's no question about that. King James ordered a new version of the Bible to be written in the common English tongue so that everyone could read and understand it. Somehow, someone mixed these two facts together and came up with the remarkable conclusion that Shakespeare must have participated in the creation of the King James Bible.

This wild rumor almost isn't worth taking the time to disprove, but it persists in pockets here and there. Today, we consider Shakespeare to be a master of the English language, but in his day, he was just an actor and a playwright. You can be certain that King James did not call for entertainers — no matter how famous — to aid this holy undertaking.

Entertaining the Masses

Shakespeare didn't have time to help translate the Bible, anyway. He was busy writing some of his best plays: *Othello, King Lear, Macbeth, The Tempest,* and more. Shakespeare and other entertainers had their own role to fulfill in early England: entertaining the masses. There was no cinema, no television, no football. If you were wealthy enough, you could bring the entertainment to your home by hiring musicians, actors, dancers, and fencers (precursors to the modern sport of fencing). Everyone else, however, had to find entertainment elsewhere, and in London, the theater was a favorite.

If you want to hang out with your friends today, you might go to a movie and then to a bar or nightclub. Four hundred years ago, you might have watched a play and then headed to a nearby tavern. Even the theater was a relatively modern invention. Traveling entertainers would visit the towns and taverns to perform music, dance, and plays, but the best plays were staged only in London. London was a small city by today's standards (London's population has grown to about 60 times what it was in Shakespeare's day), but it was big enough to propel a young playwright to stardom and immortality.

Shakespeare includes traveling and amateur actors in several of his plays. The rustics in *Midsummer Night's Dream* and the players in *Hamlet* are the best known, but the opening of *The Taming of the Shrew* best illustrates the traveling actors. They arrive at an inn and perform the play *The Taming of the Shrew*. (Read a complete summary of this wild play in Chapter 13.) Although the superficial trappings change — we have light bulbs and light beer, for example — people change much more slowly. We still enjoy a good show, a good drink, and the company of good friends. That's what Shakespeare's plays offered then and continue to offer now.

Sometimes, it's hard to believe that a play written four centuries ago can still be entertaining. If you don't believe it, watch Baz Lurhmann's version of *Romeo and Juliet,* starring Leonardo DiCaprio and Claire Danes. A modern setting, an ear-splitting soundtrack, rapid-fire editing, and Shakespeare's words all come together in this fast-paced, action-packed movie. When you leave the theater (or turn off the VCR), you may not realize that you were watching Shakespeare's play and hearing Shakespeare's words. Who said that Shakespeare has to be dull?

On the wrong side of the river

The western world has long had a curious attitude when it comes to entertainers. On the one hand, some of our greatest celebrities were and are entertainers — from Richard Burbage in Shakespeare's day to the popular stars of film, stage, and television today. On the other hand, the entertainment business has always had a seamy side.

Take a trip through any supermarket checkout lane, and you can see that the public never seems to get enough gossip about our stars. Their lives and loves are headline news, and their fans always want more, but not too much. The lifestyles of the rich and famous are fun to watch and read about. You might even imagine yourself living the high life, but then reality sets in — the divorces, affairs, and scandals. You wouldn't want your child to marry a star and join the notorious Hollywood scene. The glossy entertainment world is something to be admired from a distance.

Shakespeare's day wasn't much different. Theaters were disreputable and were banned from London. That didn't stop the actors — they merely built their theaters just outside of town. As shown in Figure 1-2, Shakespeare's theater, the Globe, was on the south side of town, across the Thames River, in Southwark (pronounced "SUH-therk"). It was the red-light district of London, populated by prostitutes, charlatans, and actors. The city leaders even prohibited women from acting in a misguided attempt to limit the "immorality" of actors and acting. This restriction meant that boys played women's roles, a fact that Shakespeare often used to his advantage by having the female characters disguise themselves as boys. Read more about boys playing girls playing boys in Chapter 8.

Figure 1-2:
London as it appeared in Shakespeare's day. Notice the theaters on the south side of the Thames River.

British Museum

The Globe Theatre

Until recently, we didn't know much about Shakespeare's theater. Historians have been able to assemble bits of information here and there to come up with some educated guesses about the appearance and use of Elizabethan stages. The most famous description of the Globe Theatre came from Shakespeare himself. In the prologue to *King Henry V,* he tells us about the circular theater that was the Globe when he asks:

. . . may we cram

Within this wooden O the very casques   **helmets

That did affright the air at Agincourt? (Prologue.12–14)

Suddenly, in 1989, everything changed when construction workers accidentally discovered the site of the original Globe Theatres. (Two Globe Theatres were built. Shakespeare used the first one, which burned down in 1613. It was rebuilt soon after in the same spot and used for several decades before being torn down in a fit of Puritanical excess in 1644.)

Special effects

Too bad Shakespeare didn't have a video camera. Some productions involved spectacular special effects, but all we have are words on paper. We have no idea what the audiences saw, but it must have been grand. For example, in *Cymbeline*, Jupiter didn't walk onstage the way mortals would. Instead, he descended from a loft above the stage. Naturally, this loft was often called the "heavens." A trap door in the stage led to "hell." Jupiter made his entrance by using elaborate machinery and special effects, according to Shakespeare's stage directions:

> Jupiter descends in thunder and lightning, sitting upon an eagle: he throws a thunderbolt. The Ghosts fall on their knees. (*Cymbeline* 5.4.93)

Stage directions of this sort are unusual in Shakespeare's plays. Most of the stage directions simply tell us when characters enter or leave the stage. A few plays have more complete stage directions, which tell us a lot about the special effects of Shakespeare's day.

We know that dogs occasionally appeared onstage. In *The Two Gentlemen of Verona,* for example, Launce steals the show with his dog, Crab. Larger animals were more difficult to manage. When Diomedes, in *Troilus and Cressida,* tells his servant, "Go, go, my servant, take thou Troilus' horse" (5.5.1), he probably didn't have an actual horse onstage. In *King Henry V,* the Prologue says, "Think, when we talk of horses, that you see them."

On the other hand, the most interesting animal is the one mentioned in *The Winter's Tale.* Antigonus meets his untimely end with the stage direction, "Exit, pursued by a bear" (3.3.58). Shakespeare's audience could watch bear-baiting close to the Globe Theatre, so they knew what real bears looked like. They wouldn't settle for an actor in a bear suit. The actor playing Antigonus may have been chased by a real bear. That would perk up any resume.

Archaeologists swooped onto the scene, but modern London isn't the most convenient site for archaeological digs. In particular, an existing building sits on top of most of the Globe's foundation, which makes it hard to study. Modern technology lets us examine the foundation from a distance, and a new Globe Theatre arose not far from the original. The new theater opened in 1997 and quickly became a major tourist destination. See Chapter 19 to find out more about this top-ten theater for seeing Shakespeare's plays.

The circular, outdoor theater — the "wooden O" — was about 100 feet (30 meters) across. The stage was about 50 x 25 feet (15 x 7 meters), and it jutted out into the audience, so the actors had spectators on three sides. Around the stage, spectators stood to watch the play. The spectators who stood on the ground — called *groundlings* — paid the least. For an extra fee, you got a seat in the galleries that formed the walls of the theater. Special box seats cost even more. The original Globe Theatre admitted about 3,000 attendees — much more than most theaters today.

Without artificial lights, plays took place outdoors during the day. We don't know what the sets and costumes looked like, but the sets were probably simple. An actor might have carried in an ornate chair for a throne, but that would be all to suggest the court of King Henry VI, for example. There were no intermissions or other interruptions for stagehands to change the scenery. Instead, one scene flowed into another without stopping. They spent a lot of money on costumes, though, and we have their financial records to prove it. It was important that the king look like a king.

Anyone who has read *Romeo and Juliet* knows that a balcony existed above the main stage. Underneath the balcony was a small curtained area used for dramatic revelations, such as Hermione's "statue" in *The Winter's Tale*. (See Chapter 13 for a description of the statue scene.)

The Blackfriars Theatre

The Globe wasn't the only theater that Shakespeare used. The Blackfriars was an indoor theater, smaller than the Globe, and tickets were much more expensive. Perhaps the exclusivity is why the city leaders allowed the theater to operate so close to the city center. Shakespeare started using the Blackfriars around 1608, late in his career, but the new theater was clearly important. He purchased a house nearby and probably lived there when he was in London.

The actors used the Globe during the summer and moved to Blackfriars for the rest of the year — when the weather wasn't amenable to outdoor performances. We know even less about the Blackfriars than we do about the Globe, but the stage was probably smaller than the Globe's, perhaps as small as 30 x 20 feet (about 9 x 6 meters).

To fully appreciate the size of Shakespeare's stage, try this experiment. The next time you're in a theater or even a cinema, try measuring 30 feet (about 10 large paces) across the front. (Most theaters won't let you onstage, but you can pace back and forth in front of it — if you don't mind the occasional odd stare.) You can visually estimate 20 feet of depth. In a professional theater, the stage in front of you will probably be larger, sometimes a lot larger. Schools and small theaters may use a space that's similar to what Shakespeare had in his theaters. Shakespeare and his fellow actors managed to fit a lot of play into a small space.

Chapter 2

Will's World

*T*here's nothing wrong with watching or reading Shakespeare's plays from a modern perspective. Several recent films have done so successfully, such as Baz Luhrmann's production of *Romeo+Juliet* starring Claire Danes and Leonardo DiCaprio (shown in Figure 2-1). Nonetheless, you can appreciate Shakespeare's plays more if you understand a little about his world. The central themes in most of the plays are universal and unchanging: lust, greed, ambition, jealousy, cowardice, and other basic human emotions. But some themes — attitudes about royalty and birthright, for example — are quite different today than they were in Shakespeare's day.

Figure 2-1: Harold Perrineau as Mercutio and Leonardo DiCaprio as Romeo in Baz Luhrmann's modern *Romeo+Juliet*.

Everett Collection

Religion

The concept of God and the role of religion in society have changed a lot over the centuries. A founding principle of the United States — the separation of Church and State — would have been a strange and unsavory concept in Shakespeare's England. The two could not easily have been separated because religion was an integral part of daily life. In the same way, religion plays an integral role in Shakespeare's plays as part of the background fabric.

Shakespeare brings religion to the foreground when it suits his purpose. For example, Shakespeare's audience knew that the Church had rules on burials in hallowed ground. Prostitutes and actors, for example, could not be buried in the Church grounds. People who committed suicide could not be buried in sanctified ground, either, because suicide demonstrated a lack of faith. You can see this in *Hamlet.* Ophelia drowns herself, and at her grave, the priest complains:

Her obsequies have been as far enlarg'd

As we have warranty. Her death was doubtful;

And but that great command o'ersways the order,

She should in ground unsanctified been lodg'd

Till the last trumpet. (5.1.224–28)

In other words, the king has to pull some strings to make sure that Ophelia receives a Christian burial. Shakespeare's audience understood the circumstances of her burial and the king's power to command more than she deserves.

The power of a king to shape religion wasn't new. A few decades before Shakespeare's birth, King Henry VIII pulled every string he could to secure a divorce from Katherine, his queen of 20 years. The Pope denied his demands, so Henry decreed that no one — not even the Pope — should have jurisdiction over the king. He broke from the Roman Catholic Church to found the Church of England. Shakespeare was therefore born in a Protestant country, but one that strongly remembered its Roman Catholic roots.

By the way, don't worry about Shakespeare's burial. If he had been just an actor, he could not have been buried in the Church grounds, but he was much more than that. His fame and fortune earned him a special place in Holy Trinity Church in Stratford-upon-Avon. The town even erected a monument in his honor, which still stands near his gravestone (see Figure 2-2).

Figure 2-2:
William
Shakespeare's
monument
in Stratford-
upon-Avon.

Stratford-on-Avon P.C.C.

Natural Order

Kings were kings. Peasants were peasants. In Shakespeare's day, everyone
had a place in the natural scheme of things. You were born into a particular
class, you married within your class, and you lived your life according to
your class. If you were unusually successful, you might move up the social
scale slightly, but your options were limited.

Social position was a natural consequence of birth. You don't expect a dog
to turn into a cat, and in Shakespeare's day, you wouldn't expect a peasant
to become a king or a king to become a cat. Every animal (people included)
fulfilled its natural position in the natural order.

So much for theory. In reality, people could change their positions. Kings
were deposed, the middle classes married up, and aristocrats married down
(usually for money). Even William Shakespeare himself moved up the social
ladder. His fame and fortune enabled him to acquire a coat of arms and
become a gentleman. But large-scale changes to the social order invited
disaster for the individual and for the greater society.

To help maintain the social order, marriages were usually arranged, especially among the upper classes. Kings and queens married for politics, not love. You can see this tendency best in *King Henry V.* King Philip of France offers his daughter, Katherine, to be Henry's wife, but he refuses:

Suppose th'ambassador from the French comes back,

Tells Harry that the King doth offer him

Katherine his daughter and with her, to dowry,

Some petty and unprofitable dukedoms.

The offer likes not. (3.0.28–34)

To King Henry, the land is more important than the wife. Philip's initial offer of "petty and unprofitable dukedoms" doesn't stop Henry from waging war on France. After the English triumph at Agincourt, Henry can dictate whatever terms he wants. His negotiators report:

The King hath granted every article:

His daughter first, and in the sequel all,

According to their firm proposed natures. (*Henry V* 5.2.324–26)

Don't mess with the boss

Scheming against your boss is always a bad idea. When your boss is a king, it's even worse because such an act attacks the natural order. Shakespeare has the most to say about natural order — or *degree* — with the character of Ulysses in *Troilus and Cressida.* He says it best when he points out:

The heavens themselves, the planets, and this centre

Observe degree, priority, and place,

Insisture*, course, proportion, season, form,   *regularity*

Office, and custom, in all line of order. (1.3.85–88)

He goes on to describe the terrible things that happen when the natural order is violated:

What plagues and what portents, what mutiny,

What raging of the sea, shaking of earth,

Commotion in the winds, frights, changes, horrors,

Divert and crack, rend and deracinate*   *uproot*

The unity and married calm of states

Quite from their fixure*! O, when degree is shak'd,   *fixed position*

Which is the ladder to all high designs,

Then enterprise is sick. How could communities,

Degrees in schools, and brotherhoods in cities,

Peaceful commerce from dividable shores,

The primogenity and the due of birth,

Prerogative of age, crowns, sceptres, laurels,

But by degree stand in authentic place?

Take but degree away, untune that string,

And hark what discord follows. (1.3.96–110)

In other words, if you mess around with the natural order too much, expect earthquakes, plagues, and storms. (Ulysses is a long-winded character, so he says a lot more. See Chapter 15 for more information about this play.)

The connection between natural disasters and disruption of the natural order is so strong that a violent storm in a Shakespeare play is often a harbinger of trouble to follow. In *Julius Caesar,* for example, Casca beholds a world in torment. Although he doesn't know it yet, the storms, winds, and lightning portend the assassination of Caesar:

I have seen tempests, when the scolding winds

Have riv'd the knotty oaks; and I have seen

Th' ambitious ocean swell and rage and foam,

To be exalted with the threat'ning clouds:

But never till to-night, never till now,

Did I go through a tempest dropping fire.

Either there is a civil strife in heaven,

Or else the world, too saucy with the gods,

Incenses them to send destruction. (1.3.5–13)

Behave yourself

The natural order also called for better behavior from people higher up the social scale. Kings were supposed to be wise and virtuous. Servants were not. You can see this in Shakespeare's plays, where servants are often saucy and impertinent. For example, in *The Two Gentlemen of Verona,* Proteus sends the servant Speed to deliver a love letter to Julia. Speed returns but answers Proteus in a roundabout way. Proteus keeps trying to get a straight answer from him, but Speed is quicker than Proteus, at least with his wit:

Speed. Sir, I could perceive nothing at all from her; no, not so much as a ducat for delivering your letter; and being so hard to me that brought your mind, I fear she'll prove as hard to you in telling your mind. Give her no token but stones, for she's as hard as steel.

Proteus. What said she? Nothing?

Speed. No, not so much as 'Take this for thy pains'. To testify your bounty, I thank you, you have testerned* me; in requital whereof, henceforth carry your letters yourself; and so, sir, I'll commend you to my master. (1.1.135–45)

*tipped

In real life, kings can be just as foolish as servants, but Shakespeare's plays describe a somewhat idealized world. When kings act foolishly, the heavens respond in kind. King Lear learns this lesson after he disinherits his only loyal daughter and gives up his kingdom to his two evil daughters. When they turn him out of his own house, he goes mad, and the world goes mad with him. Lear calls to the heavens:

Rumble thy bellyful! Spit fire, spout rain!

Nor rain, wind, thunder, fire are my daughters;

I tax not you, you elements, with unkindness.

I never gave you kingdom, called you children;

You owe me no subscription. Why then, let fall

Your horrible pleasure. Here I stand your slave,

A poor, infirm, weak and despised old man.

But yet I call you servile ministers

That will with two pernicious daughters join

Your high-engendered battles 'gainst a head

So old and white as this. O ho! 'tis foul. (*King Lear* 3.2.14–24)

Language is often a clue to social scale. Kings usually speak in blank verse, and servants speak in prose. Serious matters call for blank verse, romance for rhymed verse, and humor for prose. So a king might speak in prose when addressing a servant or behaving like a servant. You can read more about prose and verse in Chapter 6.

Moving on up

The natural order plays a role in many of Shakespeare's plays, but not always in momentous and earth-shattering ways. Sometimes, the natural order is upset in small ways — when a person aspires to a position above his natural station, for example. By the end of the play, natural order is always restored, and all the characters find their natural positions.

You can see how natural order affects everyone in *All's Well That Ends Well.* Helena loves the Count of Rossillion, a man well above her station. The count is young and foolish, but Helena is wise, virtuous, and patient. (She should win an award for patience. She gets married in Act 2 but doesn't get to settle down with her husband until the end of the play.) Shakespeare gives her the attributes of a person of a higher station, which tells you that her natural position is at the higher status, even though her birth places her at a lower level. According to her birth, she cannot marry the count, but her virtue places her in a natural position higher than that of her birth. (Read more about this play in Chapter 13.)

Birthright to the Crown

The natural order began at the very top: with God. Below God were the angels, below the angels came mankind, and then came the lower animals. Each level had sublevels, so mankind had different degrees: kings, princes, gentry, peasants, and so on. Sitting at the top of the spiritual food chain, kings received their right to rule directly from God. To oppose the king was to oppose God, which pretty much everyone agreed was a bad thing.

When Henry Bolingbroke challenges King Richard II, Richard responds:

. . . show us the hand of God

That hath dismiss'd us from our stewardship;

For well we know no hand of blood and bone

Can gripe the sacred handle of our sceptre,

Unless he do profane, steal, or usurp. (*Richard II* 3.3.77–81)

Never underestimate the power of greed and ambition, though. Kings often found themselves staring down the wrong end of a sword. To preserve some semblance of the natural order, Shakespeare's usurpers or would-be usurpers are from the ruling class: dukes, earls, and whatnot. Thus the step up to the throne is a small one. If a peasant revolts and tries to set himself up as king — such as Jack Cade in *King Henry VI, Part 2* — you can trust that the revolt will be stopped, lest the natural order be upset too much.

In Shakespeare's day, the threat of usurpation and civil war was very real. Queen Elizabeth faced assassination attempts, conspiracies to overthrow her, and threats from other countries, especially Spain. Although the events in the history plays (which we summarize in Chapter 14) took place many years before Shakespeare was born, they describe a world that was familiar to him and his audience. Today, however, the world is completely different. The monarch still reigns by divine right, and the eldest son (or eldest daughter if the monarch has no sons) inherits that right. The monarch's power, however, is symbolic, and the real government is the Parliament. Shakespeare's Queen Elizabeth had the power to tax her subjects, but the tables have turned 180 degrees, and the modern Queen Elizabeth must pay taxes.

The ruling class

The glass ceiling separating the upper and lower classes was strong in Shakespeare's day. The natural order made it difficult for a commoner to become an aristocrat, and almost as rare for an aristocrat to lose all titles. Within the aristocracy, though, people often moved up or down according to the whim of the king.

The ranks within the aristocracy usually corresponded to geographical areas within the kingdom. The exact divisions varied over time, and different countries used slightly different titles and conventions. Nonetheless, the English system of nobility affected all of Shakespeare's plays. He even added English-style aristocracies to Italian city-states that were actually ruled by democracy. As a result, you can get by with knowing how English titles and ranks work, as described here:

- **King/Queen:** A ruling king typically would marry someone from a nearly equal class, such as a foreign princess. Henry VI's decision to marry Margaret of Anjou was controversial partly because her station was not a match for the King of England.

- **Prince/Princess:** The children of the ruling monarchs were princes and princesses. Only the eldest prince (or if there were no male heir, the eldest princess) could succeed his father to become king (or queen).

- **Duke/Duchess:** The next highest title was duke, although just to confuse matters, a prince might be a duke, too. For example, in *King Henry IV,* King Henry's sons are all princes: Henry, Thomas, and Humphrey. Henry is the heir to the throne and therefore is Prince of Wales. Thomas is Duke of Clarence, and Humphrey is Duke of Gloucester. After Henry becomes King Henry V, his brothers are no longer princes — just dukes. After Edward seizes the throne in *King Henry VI, Part 3,* he names his brothers George and Richard as the Dukes of Clarence and Gloucester.

- **Marquess, Marquis/Marchioness, Marquise:** This title wasn't used often, but Henry VI elevates the Marquess of Suffolk to Duke of Suffolk in *King Henry VI, Part 2.*

- **Earl, Thane, Count/Countess:** The same title had different names in different regions: earl in England, thane in Scotland, and count in France. A count ruled a county. (Get it?)

- **Baron/Baroness:** The major political wheeling and dealing took place at the upper levels of the aristocracy, so barons don't appear often in Shakespeare's plays, and when they do, they usually have the title "Lord."

- **Knight:** A knight was a member of the lowest order of aristocracy. Every knight had an obligation to provide a certain number of soldiers for the king's wars.

Nature versus nurture

A side effect of the natural order was that a person's natural position was usually fixed at birth. If you removed the clothing of a king and a beggar (and cleaned up the beggar somewhat), you couldn't tell them apart. The natural order required some way to distinguish between the two, though, so Shakespeare and his contemporaries believed that some behavior was inborn. A royal changeling would still behave regally even if raised in the wilderness.

The royal children Arviragus and Guiderius in *Cymbeline* demonstrate this principle. Belarius, their kidnapper, observes:

How hard it is to hide the sparks of Nature!

These boys know little they are sons to th' King,

Nor Cymbeline dreams that they are alive.

They think they are mine, and though train'd up thus meanly

I'th' cave wherein they bow, their thoughts do hit

The roofs of palaces, and Nature prompts them

In simple and low things to prince it, much

Beyond the trick of others. (3.3.79–86)

Birth fixed your social status and also determined some of your character traits. Astrology was very much a part of everyday life, as you can see in Benedick's words in *Much Ado About Nothing*. He struggles to find rhymes for a love poem and finally concludes that he "was not born under a rhyming planet" (5.2.39–40). On the other hand, Shakespeare did not consign everything to fate. Cassius tells Brutus why some people rule while others serve — not because their destiny is predetermined but because they allow themselves to be led:

Men at some time are masters of their fates:

The fault, dear Brutus, is not in our stars,

But in ourselves, that we are underlings. (*Julius Caesar* 1.2.137–39)

Bastards

At one end of the behavior spectrum lie royal children who behave regally regardless of their upbringing. At the other end are the illegitimate offspring of royal parents. The Church condemned adultery and fornication, and the belief was that children born of an evil relationship were necessarily evil. Shunned by society, cut off from inheritances, and mistreated — no wonder the bastards in Shakespeare's plays turn to evil doings.

Edmund in *King Lear,* Don John in *Much Ado About Nothing,* and Thersites in *Troilus and Cressida* are the classic bastards. The first two are born into well-off families, but because they are illegitimate, they face lives of shame and scorn. They both deal with the problem in similar ways: by living up (or is that down?) to the stereotypes of bastards. Don John says of himself:

> I had rather be a canker in a hedge than a rose in his grace, and it better fits my blood to be disdained of all than to fashion a carriage to rob love from any: in this, though I cannot be said to be a flattering honest man, it must not be denied but I am a plain-dealing villain. (*Much Ado About Nothing* 1.3.25–30)

Thersites of *Troilus and Cressida* is the epitome of a bastard. He even lacks the benefit of noble parents, so he starts out low on the social ladder and goes down from there. He is rude, crude, and socially unacceptable. In battle, he is the biggest coward, so when he meets an illegitimate son of King Priam, he says:

> I am a bastard, too: I love bastards. I am bastard begot, bastard instructed, bastard in mind, bastard in valour, in everything illegitimate. One bear will not bite another, and wherefore should one bastard? Take heed: the quarrel's most ominous to us — if the son of a whore fight for a whore, he tempts judgement. Farewell, bastard. (*Troilus and Cressida* 5.7.16–22)

Shakespeare liked to bend the rules, so in *King John,* he has an honorable bastard. Philip is the illegitimate son of King Richard the Lion Heart. He gets royal treatment from King John, responds nobly, and turns out to be one of the few honest, honorable, and trustworthy characters in the play.

Body and Mind

Medicine in Shakespeare's day was simplistic compared to modern medical care. The Elizabethans believed that the body was governed by four fluids, called *humors*: black bile, phlegm, blood, and yellow bile. Small imbalances of the humors dictated one's personality and health: melancholic, phlegmatic (lethargic), sanguine (jovial), or choleric (angry). Good health — that is, good humor — required a balance of the four humors.

Lady Percy describes her late husband, Hotspur, in glowing terms. She uses "humours of blood" in this case to represent a balance of all the humors:

> In diet, in affections of delight,
>
> In military rules, humours of blood,
>
> He was the mark and glass, copy and book,
>
> That fashion'd others. (*2 Henry IV* 2.3.29–32)

In *Love's Labour's Lost,* the silly knight Don Armado writes about his sadness and how he treated this disease:

So it is, besieged with sable-coloured melancholy, I did commend the black oppressing humour to the most wholesome physic of thy health-giving air. (1.1.227–29)

In this case, the air restores his humor and his health, but the air can also be a source of problems. The night air, in particular, was considered bad for the health. In *Julius Caesar,* Portia asks her husband why he behaves so strangely:

Is Brutus sick, and is it physical

To walk unbraced* and suck up the humours   *undressed*

Of the dank morning? What, is Brutus sick?

And will he steal out of his wholesome bed

To dare the vile contagion of the night,

And tempt the rheumy and unpurged air

To add unto his sickness? (2.1.261–67)

An ingrained notion in Shakespeare's day was that an ugly body contained an ugly mind. In other words, beauty was way deeper than skin deep. The classic example of ugliness that extends to the soul is Caliban — "a savage and deformed slave" — in *The Tempest.* Before the play begins, Caliban attempts to rape Prospero's daughter, and during the play, he plots to murder Prospero.

Even Don John's looks betray him in *Much Ado About Nothing.* Beatrice comments:

How tartly that gentleman looks! I never can see him but I am heart-burned an hour after. (2.1.3–4)

Later in the play, he interferes with young lovers, even so far as upsetting their marriage. In the end he's caught, and everything is put right, but the warning is clear: Beware the man "whose spirits toil in frame of villainies" (4.1.188).

Racial Prejudice

Shakespeare's England was not politically correct by modern standards. Jews, blacks, and anyone else who didn't fit the English mold faced discrimination, restrictive laws, and sometimes open hostility. Shakespeare grew up in this environment, and his plays reflect the society in which he lived. In his plays, though, he managed to avoid simple stereotypes. He created complex characters with real lives and real problems.

For example, Othello faces racial discrimination. He's a Moor, which to Shakespeare meant that he is black, but he marries Desdemona, who is white. The way Desdemona's father sees it, the only way his daughter could love Othello is through witchcraft:

She is abused, stolen from me and corrupted

By spells and medicines bought of mountebanks,

For nature so preposterously to err

Being not deficient, blind, or lame of sense,

Sans witchcraft could not. (*Othello* 1.3.61–65)

The Nurse expresses a similar opinion in *Titus Andronicus.* Aaron the Moor fathers a child, which the Nurse describes as

A joyless, dismal, black and sorrowful issue.

Here is the babe, as loathsome as a toad. (4.2.68–79)

On the other hand, Othello does not use witchcraft. Desdemona truly and deeply loves him. Aaron the Moor is a thoroughly nasty character, but of all the characters in *Titus Andronicus,* he is the only one to have compassion for his child. Indeed, he sacrifices his own life to save the life of his baby, something even the protagonists won't do.

At first glance, Shylock — the Jewish moneylender in *The Merchant of Venice* — is cruel and greedy. When you take a closer look at the character, though, you see that he is not a stereotypical loan shark. He has been treated cruelly and has borne that cruelty with patience. When he sees an opportunity for revenge, he seizes it. Nothing can excuse his bloodthirsty demand for his "pound of flesh," but Shylock is a complicated person. Shakespeare wrote plays about people and their problems, not about racial stereotypes, and to see his characters in black and white is to miss the most interesting aspects of his plays.

Chapter 3

Shakespeare in the Modern World

· ·

In This Chapter

▶ Enjoying Shakespeare's plays on film, television, and your computer

▶ Understanding why schools still teach students about Shakespeare

· ·

Shakespeare is alive and well in the modern world. In comic books and textbooks, on the radio, in the cinema, and on the Internet, Shakespeare and his plays are everywhere. You can find his plays in every school and library. Although the English language has changed, many words and phrases that he invented are still part of our everyday speech. The more you look for him, the more you find him.

Shakespeare Meets Hollywood

Since the invention of the moving picture, Shakespeare's plays have been a staple of the cinema. It's difficult to imagine how a silent film could capture Shakespeare's rich language, but early directors did their best. At the 1900 Paris Exposition, Sarah Bernhardt played Hamlet in Clement Maurice's pioneering five-minute film of the duel scene with Laertes. Film assistants added live sound effects by banging kitchen knives together to enliven the sword fight.

One reel of film ran for only ten minutes, so most initial attempts to film Shakespeare's plays portrayed individual scenes. For example, Thomas Edison selected a scene from *As You Like It* to try an early experiment in adding sound to movies — synchronizing the motion picture with a phonograph.

Directors soon created feature-length silent films and then progressed to the talkies. In 1929, Douglas Fairbanks and Mary Pickford starred in *The Taming of the Shrew.* Originally filmed as a silent picture, a soundtrack was added later to keep up with advancing technology.

It wasn't long before Hollywood started to create budget-busting, star-studded productions. Leslie Howard played Romeo with Norma Shearer as Juliet in a 1936 production of *Romeo and Juliet.* This multimillion dollar movie featured a reproduction of a Renaissance Italian city. In today's dollars, this film would rank among the big-budget extravaganzas.

Other films soon followed. Laurence Olivier, Orson Welles, Franco Zeffirelli, and John Gielgud became household names in part because of their work on Shakespeare films. Even Mickey Rooney and James Cagney took on Shakespeare in Max Reinhardt's 1935 film of *A Midsummer Night's Dream.* Mickey Rooney played Puck, and James Cagney played Bottom. More recently, Kenneth Branagh has ushered in the latest age of Shakespeare on film, starting with *Henry V* in 1989. He also started the Shakespeare Film Company, devoted exclusively to producing Shakespeare's plays.

What's on the Telly?

Shakespeare's plays have also made it to broadcast and cable television. The British Broadcasting Corporation (BBC) took the lead with a scene from *As You Like It* in 1937. Not many people owned television sets at the time, but it was a start. The BBC aired recordings of several stage productions in the ensuing years and mounted its own productions for television.

The United States joined the Shakespeare-on-TV bandwagon in 1948 with a broadcast of Verdi's *Otello,* an opera based on Shakespeare's *Othello.* Since then, all of Shakespeare's plays have graced the television screen, sometimes in unexpected forms.

Shakespeare's plays have made it to radio as well. The BBC broadcasts radio performances and has those performances available as audio books. Other publishers also produce audio books of Shakespeare's plays. But the BBC is best known for its series of all of Shakespeare's plays (see the sidebar "The BBC's bold experiment" for details).

Here, There, and Everywhere

Shakespeare figures into a wide variety of films. Some films are based on Shakespeare's plays, and others incorporate scenes from his plays. Here are just a few examples of films that take advantage of Shakespeare's genius:

- ✔ Arnold Schwarzenegger as Hamlet? In *The Last Action Hero,* a boy dreams of how his action-film idol would handle Hamlet's problem: not with "rapier and dagger," but in a burst of gunfire. "To be or not to be? Not to be."

- ✔ Some books and films adapt Shakespeare's stories without using any of his lines. A recent example is the novel *A Thousand Acres* (and the film based on the Jane Smiley novel), which adapts *King Lear.* An American farmer, Larry Cook, divides his farm into three parts for his daughters, Rose, Ginny, and Caroline. The novel closely follows Shakespeare's plot and characters, but in a contemporary setting.

The BBC's bold experiment

In 1978, the BBC, with Time-Life Films, decided to produce all of Shakespeare's plays, at a rate of about six per year. The BBC had been producing Shakespeare's plays for decades, but this is the only series that includes every play. The shows were broadcast in the United Kingdom and on public television in the United States. Now they are available on videotape, and many libraries and schools have copies of the series.

Out of 37 plays (the BBC did not include *The Two Noble Kinsmen*), some of the productions are good, a few are excellent, and a few miss the mark completely. The BBC could not afford the lavish budgets of Hollywood films, so the sets are often simple and the casts are small. The intention was not to break new ground in finding novel interpretations of Shakespeare's plays, but to ensure that every one of Shakespeare's plays had a reliable production. For a few of his lesser-known plays, the BBC series is the only recording. For example, *Timon of Athens* has never been produced on film or videotape except in the BBC series. You might wait for years or even decades to catch a production of this play about flattery, misanthropy, and hypocrisy — but you can pop down to your local library and borrow the videotape.

The BBC took an innovative approach to the history plays by casting the same actor in the same role across multiple productions. Thus you get to see David Gwillim as the young Prince Hal in *King Henry IV* and as the grown-up King Henry V in the play of the same name.

- *Ran* is another adaptation of *King Lear*, this time in Japanese by the renowned filmmaker Akira Kurosawa. See Chapter 21 for a description of this and other plays that Kurosawa adapted for the Japanese cinema.

- One of the most famous adaptations is *West Side Story*, a musical reworking of *Romeo and Juliet*, which you can read more about in Chapter 21.

- Shakespeare is such a popular figure that he is the subject of stories that are not taken from his plays. *Shakespeare in Love* is a fictional comedy about a young Will Shakespeare who struggles over his script for *Romeo and Ethel, the Pirate's Daughter*. With inspiration from an actress masquerading as a boy, he manages to fix the title and finish his play.

Shakespeare's language, characters, and stories attract actors, writers, and directors of all sorts. Where you least expect him, Shakespeare shows up. For example:

- Shakespeare's fame spreads throughout the galaxy in the 24th century, thanks to the crew of the Starship *Enterprise*. Shakespearean allusions often crop up in the *Star Trek* series. For example, in "The Defector," Data plays King Henry in a scene from *King Henry V*.

- Shakespeare goes to the dogs. *Wishbone* is a children's show that encourages viewers to read. Each episode presents two parallel stories: One is a traditional adaptation of a book, and the other is a modern story that relates to the book. In "Shakespaw," the book is *The Tempest*, and Wishbone the dog portrays Ariel.

> ✔ In the cartoon *Pinky and the Brain,* the title characters — genetically altered laboratory mice — repeatedly try to take over the world. In "Melancholy Brain," the Brain plays the role of Old Hamlet's ghost and tries to sow discord between Hamlet and Claudius. As usual, the Brain's plan to take over the world fails. In this case, he fails to take over the Globe Theatre.

Shakespeare Goes High-Tech

You can even experience Shakespeare on your computer. Many companies sell CD-ROMs containing his complete works, often with additional notes, a glossary, and other information. Multimedia CD-ROMs of Shakespeare's plays are also available. If you don't want to spend money, use the Internet to find material about Shakespeare, the full text of his plays, and more. Point your Web browser to `www.bardware.com` to find links to many other Shakespeare sites on the World Wide Web.

The BBC also has a series of CD-ROMs. Each disc contains the text of the play, a complete audio recording, and video clips from the BBC productions. The CD-ROMs also include commentary about the plays, a glossary, and information about Shakespeare and his life.

Shakespeare Onstage

Modern technology can bring Shakespeare into our living rooms, but there's no substitute for seeing his plays onstage — live and in person. Shakespeare is a staple for school, community, and professional theaters around the world.

Almost every theater produces Shakespeare's plays occasionally. Some theatrical companies focus primarily or exclusively on Shakespeare. You can also find Shakespeare festivals in many countries.

A typical theatrical company performs one play at a time during a season. Each play may run for several weeks before being replaced. Schools and community theaters almost always work this way. For example, the theater might show *The Tempest* for two months, *King Richard III* for another two months, and then close with *Hamlet.*

A festival, on the other hand, performs many plays on a rotating schedule. That means that the company mounts all (or most of) its plays at the same time. The festival rotates the plays on different nights to encourage out-of-town visitors. For example, Friday night is *The Tempest;* Saturday matinee is *King Richard III,* followed by *Hamlet* on Saturday evening. The next weekend, the order will be slightly different so that every actor gets a chance to have a Saturday evening free.

Shakespeare's plays are sometimes performed with reduced casts. A small, local company may produce a play with a cast of five to ten actors. To work with a reduced cast, the play may be altered to eliminate minor characters, rearrange scenes, or shorten the play. An uncut, unmodified play can easily call for 20 actors, many taking on multiple roles.

If you want to see a traditional performance in historical costumes, your best bet is one of the major Shakespeare festivals: the Oregon Shakespeare Festival, the Stratford (Ontario) Shakespeare Festival, and so on. (See Chapter 18 for more information about these and other Shakespeare festivals.) Schools often choose traditional settings, too. Small, local theater companies are the most likely to experiment with novel settings, avant-garde productions, or off-the-wall interpretations. If you're tired of watching men in tights, take a look at the small, experimental theaters.

Shakespeare in School

If you're like most people, studying Shakespeare wasn't one of the high points of school. Maybe you were forced to memorize and recite lines that you didn't understand. Perhaps you had to read a different play every week and discuss its minutiae endlessly in class.

Shakespeare is a favorite of teachers everywhere because his plays are so good, even if students don't always feel the same way. Literature teachers see Shakespeare's plays as ideal vehicles for teaching about fiction for reasons that include the following:

- ✔ Shakespeare's best plots are masterpieces of story construction. He uses multiple plots to convey multiple, but related, messages. Each play has a theme that ties together the different subplots.

- ✔ Shakespeare's characters have depth and humanity. They express emotion, face problems, and make mistakes the way we all do. From Juliet's first love to Hamlet's indecision, we can identify with and understand his characters because they are so believable.

- ✔ The language in Shakespeare's plays is rich and evocative. He paints pictures with his words. (Chapter 9 has more to say on this topic.)

In short, Shakespeare's plays are masterpieces, and that's why teachers and scholars treat them as literature. They are also masterpieces of theater, and for most people, studying Shakespeare's plays in performance is more interesting that studying them as words on a page. Teachers have many films, videotapes, and even local theaters to help present Shakespeare as a dramatist, not a wordsmith. Once students get to see the excitement of

You're never too young for Shakespeare

Even young children can watch and understand Shakespeare's plays, often better than their elders. After all, children in Shakespeare's day didn't have any difficulty learning English as it was spoken then. We have difficulties now only because it is a little different from our everyday language. Young children, on the other hand, are still learning to speak, listen, read, and write. Picking up additional languages is far easier for a child than for an adult. Learning Shakespeare's English is also easier for a child.

Many teachers and parents find that children as young as 5 years old can watch, hear, and understand Shakespeare's plays. You don't need to simplify the language or the complex plots. Of course, young children won't understand every subtlety, but they will find enough jokes, interesting characters and situations, and plot twists to keep them entertained.

For the very youngest children, you can start with *The Animated Tales* — shortened, simplified, animated videotapes of some of Shakespeare's plays. Very quickly, however, you'll find that youngsters can handle Shakespeare's plays in their, unabridged glory.

Children like to play, so why not act out scenes from Shakespeare's plays? More and more elementary schools are mounting their own productions of Shakespeare's plays as part of the learning experience. Students get to play with Shakespeare's words firsthand and become familiar with his plays and his language at an early age.

Shakespeare's plays in performance, they can begin to unravel the plays and learn why they are so exciting, what makes the plays special, and how they remain important today.

Westward Ho! Shakespeare's Influence on the English Language

Shakespeare endures today not only in schools and theaters but also in familiar sayings from our everyday speech, although sometimes the context is a little different from what you may expect. For example, in *Twelfth Night,* Olivia tells Viola to leave:

Olivia. There lies your way, due west.

Viola.   Then westward ho! (3.1.135)

Shakespeare had a large vocabulary — most scholars agree that his vocabulary was around 30,000 words — and he freely extended it when he felt the need. From *anchovy* to *zany*, Shakespeare invented *countless* words, used old words in new ways, and had fun with the English language. (See Chapter 4 for more information about Shakespeare's language.) Our *reliance* on his *nerve* fills us with *amazement*.

Did you ever *dislocate* a joint and use *obscene* words, or were you *tranquil?* If so, thank Shakespeare because the italicized words are ones he invented or first used in a new way. He often used verbs as nouns and nouns as verbs. For example, when the Duke of Vienna takes a leave of absence in *Measure for Measure,* he appoints Angelo as his deputy. Angelo gets a little carried away with the job, and someone comments that "Lord Angelo dukes it well in his absence" (3.2.91). Before Shakespeare wrote "after dawn / Doth rise" (*Henry V* 4.1.270–71), the word *dawn* was used only as a verb, not as a noun.

A catalog of the words and phrases that appear first in Shakespeare's plays would go on for pages. Chapter 19 lists some of the phrases that he invented that are now part of everyday speech. Many other words and phrases that Shakespeare used may have been invented by others, but Shakespeare heard them, liked them, and used them in his plays. They survived in his plays, and we have Shakespeare to thank for preserving them.

Perhaps Shakespeare's greatest gift to the English language was his love of common speech. Latin was the language of scholarship and erudition. Shakespeare certainly studied Latin in school, and he frequently used Latin quotes and classical Latin stories and sources. Sometimes, his lovers use flowery, poetic speech of the educated English society, but he was also a master of the plain speech of the common person. The shepherd Corin describes his philosophy:

I know the more one sickens the worse at ease he is; and that he that wants money, means, and content is without three good friends; that the property of rain is to wet and fire to burn; that good pasture makes fat sheep; and that a great cause of the night is the lack of the sun. (*As You Like It* 3.2.22–27)

Corin's speech is as clear and simple today as it was 400 years ago. Shakespeare also enjoyed playing games with words. In *Love's Labour's Lost,* for example, Lord Berowne claims to reject elaborate speech in favor of simplicity, but he can't resist images of expensive cloth and other "figures pedantical":

Taffeta phrases, silken terms precise,

Three-pil'd hyperboles, spruce affection,

Figures pedantical; these summer flies

Have blown me full of maggot ostentation:

I do forswear them; and I here protest,

By this white glove (how white the hand, God knows),

Henceforth my wooing mind shall be express'd

In russet yeas and honest kersey noes. (5.2.406–13)

From "taffeta phrases" to everyday speech, Shakespeare continues to influence our language and our world. The more you watch for allusions to Shakespeare and his work, the more you will find them — in newspapers, books, films, and television shows and, of course, onstage.

Directing Shakespeare

At first glance, Shakespeare doesn't seem to give much help to the modern director. Except for *King Henry VIII,* the plays lack detailed stage directions. Most of the plays lack act and scene divisions, too. When stage directions exist, they rarely describe a scene's setting. As a result of the lack of specific directions, directors over the centuries have interpreted and reinterpreted the plays, bringing performances as varied as Franco Zeffirelli's traditional *Romeo and Juliet* and Baz Lurhmann's updated *Romeo+Juliet.*

Shakespeare's plays have been produced thousands of times, so directors often feel the urge to bring something new and different to their productions. The problem is that almost everything has been done before. From trapezes to trapdoors, Elizabethan costumes to nudity — few gimmicks are left untapped. A solution, therefore, is not to find a gimmick but to rediscover Shakespeare's words. If you read the text as if you have never read the story before — almost as if you were reading a new play — then you see things in the words that give you great directorial clues.

Shakespeare didn't have the benefit of fancy sets, so he used words to paint the scene. Words describe actions, moods, settings, and even hints about casting. Several plays mention a character's height, hair color, and other attributes. For example, Hermia compares herself with Helena in *A Midsummer Night's Dream:*

> Because I am so dwarfish and so low?
>
> How low am I, thou painted maypole? Speak:
>
> How low am I? I am not yet so low
>
> But that my nails can reach unto thine eyes. (3.2.295–98)

Shakespeare had to work without lighting for most of his plays (because the Globe Theatre was outdoors, and plays were performed during the daytime), but modern directors usually have more flexibility with lighting. Shakespeare describes the setting with words, and you can use those words as stage directions to determine the lighting. Romeo tells you everything you need to know:

> The grey-ey'd morn smiles on the frowning night,
>
> Chequering the eastern clouds with streaks of light;
>
> And darkness fleckled like a drunkard reels
>
> From forth day's pathway, made by Titan's wheels. (*Romeo and Juliet* 2.2.188–91)

Modern editors often insert light and sound cues where Shakespeare omitted them. For example, in *The Merry Wives of Windsor,* Master Ford says, "The clock gives me my cue" (3.2.40), and editors often insert a stage direction for the clock striking the hour.

Shakespeare tells you about sound effects in the same way that he tells you about lighting. The text often suggests when to play music, when to speak loudly, and when not to. *King Henry IV, Part 2* has an example of text directions when King Henry is weak and dying:

> *King Henry IV.* Let there be no noise made, my gentle friends,
>
> Unless some dull and favourable hand
>
> Will whisper music to my weary spirit.
>
> *Warwick.* Call for the music in the other room. (4.5.1–4)

Part II
You Call That English?

"Excuse me! Witch number three, your line is also 'Hail', not 'Whatever'."

In this part . . .

Sometimes, Shakespeare doesn't make any sense. Trying to sort out the *thees* and *thous* can make Shakespeare's English seem like a foreign language. Look a little more closely, and you'll see that the language really is English — just an older form of English. Your children seem to have a language all their own, and your parents have their own quaint, outdated phrases. Multiply that effect by a dozen or so generations, and you can see why Shakespeare is so difficult to understand. This part gives you a few tricks and tips to help you make sense of Shakespeare's language.

Chapter 4

Why Does Everyone Talk So Funny?

Zounds! Here will be an old abusing of patience and the king's English.

Sometimes, when you read Shakespeare's language, it doesn't seem like normal English. Four hundred years is a long time, and a language naturally changes over the years. Some words fall out of use, others take on new meanings, and the rules for assembling sentences change. Adding to the difficulty is that Shakespeare often wrote in verse, which can be harder to understand than prose. If you take it one step at a time, though, you'll find Shakespeare's language almost as easy to understand as your everyday English — and easier to understand than the lyrics of many popular songs.

Scholars recognize three historical languages called English: Old English, Middle English, and Modern English. They call Shakespeare's English "Modern" English to distinguish it from the Middle English of Chaucer, but the rest of us recognize that Shakespeare spoke and wrote a different, older form of English. This chapter uses the term *modern English* to refer to the language we use today.

New Words, Old Words

Groovy. Hep. Rad. Words come and words go. The nature of any spoken language is to change over time, and English has probably changed the most. Children shy away from their parents' old-fashioned phrases, and parents don't understand their children's newfangled speech. (*Newfangled* is an old word, much older than Shakespeare.)

Sometimes, you can understand Shakespeare without any difficulty. For example, when Beatrice complains about Benedick in *Much Ado About Nothing*, her speech is almost modern:

Why, he is the Prince's jester, a very dull fool; only his gift is in devising impossible slanders. None but libertines delight in him, and the commendation is not in his wit, but in his villainy; for he both pleases men and angers them, and then they laugh at him and beat him. (2.1.129–34)

The word order isn't quite right, though. Today, she would say, "His only gift is in devising impossible slanders." And no one would say, "The commendation is not in his wit." Words such as *commendation* are still used today, but slightly differently. The meanings of words change all the time.

Sometimes, you can understand old words, but they sound quaint and out of place in modern society. For example, we all know what *groovy* means, but you wouldn't use the word in public. Refer to a store as a *clip joint* today, and you're more likely to be met by confused looks than by an angry response. Many passages in Shakespeare's plays are similar. You can understand what they mean, but they are clearly out of date. For example, Benvolio encourages Romeo to join the Capulets' party (where he later meets Juliet for the first time) with these words:

Come, knock and enter, and no sooner in

But every man betake him to his legs. (*Romeo and Juliet* 1.4.33–34)

You don't always need to understand the exact meaning of a word to get the gist of the sentence. The Nurse tells Romeo about Juliet by saying

Her mother is the lady of the house,

And a good lady, and a wise and virtuous.

I nurs'd her daughter that you talk'd withal.

I tell you, he that can lay hold of her

Shall have the chinks. (*Romeo and Juliet* 1.5.113–17)

Even if you don't know what *chinks* means, you can tell that it's something desirable. The Nurse tells Romeo that whoever marries Juliet will have a good wife. In this case, *chinks* means "cash."

Formal or Familiar

One of the differences between Shakespeare's English and modern English is that Shakespeare had three different ways to say *you: you, thou,* and *ye.* Sometimes, the word he chose tells us something about the character who says the word or the relationship between characters. Briefly, here are the differences among the words:

> ✔ *Thou* is informal, used among friends, and to address a child or servant. *Thou* is also used in direct addresses to God.
>
> ✔ *You* is formal, used to address a stranger, or someone of a higher station.
>
> ✔ *Ye* is plural, or a synonym for *you*.

Most modern readers first meet the word *thou* in the King James Bible. The translators wrote the Bible for the common person, and they wanted to make the Bible friendly and approachable. They chose to use the informal *thou* as much as possible.

Although *you* is the same as the subject or object of a sentence, *thou* appears only as a subject. Use *thee* in the object of a sentence. For example,

dost thou know who speaks to thee? (*3 Henry VI* 2.6.61)

Thy and *thine* are the possessive forms of *thou* (like *your*). Use *thy* before a consonant and *thine* before a vowel or when used alone (equivalent to *yours*).

Lovers and friends refer to each other as *thou*. When Romeo and Juliet first meet, Romeo is forward and uses the familiar *thine*, but Juliet is more proper, so she uses the formal *you:*

Romeo. Then move not, while my prayer's effect I take.

Thus from my lips, by thine, my sin is purg'd.

Juliet. Then have my lips the sin that they have took.

Romeo. Sin from my lips? O trespass sweetly urg'd

Give me my sin again.

Juliet.　　　　　　　You kiss by th' book. (*Romeo and Juliet* 1.5.106–10)

But later, when they declare their love for each other in private, they both use the more intimate *thou:*

Romeo. O wilt thou leave me so unsatisfied?

Juliet. What satisfaction canst thou have tonight?

Romeo. Th'exchange of thy love's faithful vow for mine. (*Romeo and Juliet* 2.2.125–27)

Enemies might also use *thou* to refer to each other to show disrespect. For example, when Hamlet and Laertes grapple in Ophelia's grave, Shakespeare has them use *thou* to reflect the heat of the moment:

Laertes. The devil take thy soul!

Hamlet.　　　　　　　Thou pray'st not well.

I prithee, take thy fingers from my throat. (*Hamlet* 5.1.257–58)

Later, when they have calmed down, they politely use *you* to refer to each other. Even today, being overly polite is a subtle way of attacking an opponent.

Hamlet. Let my disclaiming from a purpos'd evil

Free me so far in your most generous thoughts

That I have shot my arrow o'er the house

And hurt my brother.

Laertes. . . .

I do receive your offer'd love like love

And will not wrong it. (*Hamlet* 5.2.240–51)

A parent typically says *thou* to children, but a child says *thou* to a parent only at certain, intimate times. In *The Tempest,* for example, Miranda uses the formal *you* when talking with her father, Prospero, but he uses *thou* to his daughter:

Miranda. Alack, what trouble

Was I then to you!

Prospero.   O, a cherubin

Thou wast that did preserve me. Thou didst smile,

Infused with a fortitude from heaven. (1.2.151–54)

A master often calls his servant *thou.* Servants use *thou* among themselves, but use *you* when talking to their masters. Lucetta is Julia's maid in *The Two Gentlemen of Verona.* They are discussing potential suitors and mates for Julia — in particular, Proteus, who recently sent a love letter to Julia:

Julia. And wouldst thou have me cast my love on him?

Lucetta. Ay; if you thought your love not cast away.

Julia. Why, he, of all the rest, hath never mov'd me.

Lucetta. Yet he, of all the rest, I think best loves ye. (1.2.25–28)

Lucetta also uses *ye* as a synonym for *you.* Shakespeare occasionally uses *ye* as a formal address. Sometimes, it just sounds better than *you,* as in the case of the rhyme in the preceding quote.

Ye can also be used as a plural form of *you,* a distinction that we don't have in modern English, except for *you all* or *y'all,* which you can hear in parts of the southern United States. In *King Henry VIII,* Queen Katherine is besieged by Cardinals Wolsey and Campeius as they urge her to submit to the king's divorce proceedings. She politely thanks the two of them. She uses "you both" and "ye" to address the two cardinals, saying

My lords, I thank you both for your good wills,

Ye speak like honest men (pray God ye prove so) (3.1.68–69)

As you can see in the examples, Shakespeare used the words that sound the best. Sometimes he mixed *ye* and *you* for plurals, or mixed *thou* and *you* for informal speech. A character might start using *thou* to talk to a servant and switch to *you* in the middle of the conversation.

If you have trouble with *thou* and *thee,* watch Richard Loncraine's *Richard III,* starring Ian McKellen. Loncraine and McKellen modernized Shakespeare's script, changing *thou* to *you* and substituting modern words for outdated ones. The result is a powerful film that captures the essence of Shakespeare's play, but in a more modern setting, and with words that are easier on modern ears.

Other directors take a different approach. Baz Lurhmann set *Romeo+Juliet* in a modern setting, substituting a modern, fictitious Verona Beach for Shakespeare's Verona, Italy. Within the updated setting, however, the characters — including Leonardo DiCaprio's Romeo — speak Shakespeare's original words. Watch both movies (available on videotape) and compare how different approaches to Shakespeare's plays can have different results. Which style do you prefer?

Verbs

One of the difficulties in reading the older *thou* and *ye* is that the verb forms are also different. To further complicate matters, *thou* has a couple of different forms. The third-person (*he, she,* and *it*) construction also has a different verb conjugation sometimes. Fortunately, *ye* works the same as *you,* so ye need not learn any other verb forms.

The most common verbs are *to be* and *to have,* so you see these constructions frequently: thou art and thou hast. On rare occasions, Shakespeare omitted *thou,* leaving just the verb. For example, in *Measure for Measure,* Lucio asks, "Art going to prison, Pompey?" (3.2.58).

To conjugate a verb with *thou,* add *t, st,* or *est,* depending on the verb — for example, *thou shalt, thou canst, thou dost,* and *thou knowest. Thou wilt* doesn't refer to drooping plants; it's the informal way of saying *you will.* To say *you wilt in the heat,* use *thou wiltest in the heat.*

Shakespeare mixed the old and new styles for *he, she,* or *it.* Sometimes, he wrote *he ist* or *he hath,* and other times, he wrote *he is* or *he has.* For other verbs, the conjugation usually requires that *eth* be added to the end of the verb, as in *she knoweth* or *he wanteth.* Shakespeare was at ease with both forms and freely used one or the other. In *The Merchant of Venice,* for example, Portia uses both forms in her speech to fit the meter of the verse:

The quality of mercy is not strain'd,

It **droppeth** as the gentle rain from heaven

Upon the place beneath: it is twice blest,

It **blesseth** him that **gives**, and him that **takes**,

'Tis mightiest in the mightiest, it **becomes**

The thronèd monarch better than his crown. (4.1.182–87)

Contractions

Contractions have been around as long as language has existed. Some of Shakespeare's contractions are familiar to the modern ear, and some aren't. You can see both the familiar and the unfamiliar in Cloten's observation, "It's almost morning, is't not?" (*Cymbeline* 2.3.9). *Is't* is a common contraction for *is it.* Many contractions, including the following, are the same as those we use today:

- ✔ "I'll be a brave judge!" (*1 Henry IV* 1.2.62).
- ✔ "I'm not their father" (*Cymbeline* 4.2.28).
- ✔ "Now he'll outstare the lightning" (*Antony and Cleopatra* 3.13.200).
- ✔ "That's not my fault, he's master of my state" (*Comedy of Errors* 2.1.96).

To make his verses come out right, with the correct number of syllables, Shakespeare also contracted some vowels and ran words together. For example, *the other,* with three syllables, becomes *th'other,* with only two. Any word that has a final syllable of *est* can also be contracted, as in *thou know'st* for *thou knowest.* Shakespeare used contractions anywhere he needed to adjust the number of syllables, or just to make a line sound better. He often used the following contractions, but they have since fallen into disuse:

Contraction	Expansion
't	it
'tis	it is
o'er	over
e'er	ever
ne'er	never

When reading Shakespeare's plays, you may also run into verbs that look like contractions, such as *alter'd* instead of *altered.* Just read the contracted verb the way you would read the expanded verb. Chapter 6 has more information about this kind of contraction.

Common Words

Shakespeare used many different words, some of which are no longer used. When you read a play, you can usually look up strange words in the footnotes. When you watch a play, however, the actors must understand the words and make their meaning clear to the audience. For example, Titus Andronicus holds his daughter and cries out:

She is the weeping welkin, I the earth.

Then must my sea be moved with her sighs,

Then must my earth with her continual tears

Become a deluge overflowed and drowned. (*Titus Andronicus* 3.1.227–30)

In this context, *welkin* means the sky. Titus compares his daughter to the sky, raining tears upon himself, the earth. It's a beautiful image, but one that's hard to grasp if you don't know what *welkin* means. The actor who plays Titus can help the audience by showing the distinction between the welkin and the earth, even if he just looks up and down.

Shakespeare didn't often use *welkin* (only 19 times in all of his plays and poetry, to be precise), so if you miss this one word, don't feel that you missed the whole point of the play. Some words he used repeatedly, and it pays to know what those words mean before you enter the theater. Keeping up with the action onstage is easier. The following pages list several words and phrases that you are likely to encounter in every play — words that are no longer used or that have different meanings.

A

A usually means *a* in the modern sense, but it also means *he* sometimes. When used to mean *he,* some editors write it as a contraction, *'a,* but some editors do not. For example, a night watchman recognizes one of Don John's nasty compatriots in *Much Ado About Nothing:*

I know that Deformed; a has been a vile thief this seven year; a goes up and down like a gentleman: I remember his name. (3.3.122–24)

An, And

An and *and* usually have their modern meanings, but they can also mean *if.* You can tell by context which meaning it has. A sentence that starts with *an* or *and* usually means *if.* For example, Benedick complains about a singer's voice:

And he had been a dog that should have howled thus, they would have hanged him, and I pray God his bad voice bode no mischief. (*Much Ado About Nothing* 2.3.78–80)

Anon

Anon means soon, as in "Get you gone, sir; I'll talk with you more anon" (*All's Well That Ends Well* 1.3.64).

Brave

Usually *brave* means courageous, but it can mean splendid or showy, as in:

Wrapp'd in sweet clothes, rings put upon his fingers,

A most delicious banquet by his bed,

And brave attendants near him when he wakes. (*Taming of the Shrew* Ind.1.37–39)

Conceit

Although *conceit* has the modern meaning of ego, Shakespeare used it in other ways, usually related to *conceit*'s common roots with *conceive*. In Shakespeare's plays, it has a number of different definitions, all related to the common meaning of conception, imagination, or thought.

In *The Comedy of Errors,* Adriana worries about her husband after learning that he was arrested. She lets her imagination get the best of her, saying

I am press'd down with conceit;

Conceit, my comfort and my injury. (4.2.64–65)

In *King Henry IV, Part 2,* Falstaff has a colorful way of saying that his friend is dimwitted:

He a good wit? Hang him, baboon! His wit's as thick as Tewkesbury mustard; there's no more conceit in him than is in a mallet. (2.4.240–42)

A servant uses *conceit* to mean *opinion* when he tells Anne Bullen that he will pass on a good word to King Henry VIII:

Lady,

I shall not fail t'approve the fair conceit

The king hath of you. (*Henry VIII* 2.3.73–75)

Cousin

Any relative or close friend may be called *cousin* or its abbreviation, *coz.* In *Measure for Measure,* for example, Isabella calls her friend Juliet *cousin:*

Isabella. Someone with child by him? My cousin Juliet?

Lucio. Is she your cousin?

Isabella. Adoptedly, as schoolmaids change their names

By vain though apt affection. (1.4.45–48)

Monarchs often referred to other monarchs as *cousin.* Indeed, they often were related. If a prince could marry only a princess, the pool of potential mates was small. The monarchs of Europe became one big, dysfunctional family, from a certain point of view. King Henry V uses *cousin* to address the crown prince of France, called the Dauphin, this way:

Now are we well prepared to know the pleasure

Of our fair cousin Dauphin; for we hear

Your greeting is from him, not from the King. (*Henry V* 1.2.235–37)

Cuckold

A *cuckold* is the husband of an unfaithful wife, and usually the brunt of jokes. The visual image of a cuckold is a man wearing two small horns. In *The Merry Wives of Windsor,* Falstaff thinks that he will seduce Mistress Ford and therefore make a cuckold of Master Ford. He says so to Master Brook (not knowing that Brook is really Ford in disguise):

Ford's a knave, and I will aggravate his style; thou, Master Brook, shalt know him for knave and cuckold. Come to me soon at night. (2.2.273–76)

Cur

A *cur* can be any dog, but Shakespeare often used the word as an insult. In *A Midsummer Night's Dream,* for example, Hermia yells at Demetrius:

Out, dog! Out, cur! Thou driv'st me past the bounds

Of maiden's patience. (3.2.65–66)

Fain

Fain means gladly, as in "Here is neither cheer, sir, nor welcome; we would fain have either" (*Comedy of Errors* 3.1.66).

Forsooth

Forsooth means in truth, and is mostly used to add strength to a statement, as in "Because the king, forsooth, will have it so" (*2 Henry VI* 1.3.115).

Gaol

Gaol means "jail" and is pronounced like *jail. Gaoler* is the same as *jailer.*

Hap, Haply

Hap or *haply* means perhaps. For example, when Juliet hopes that Romeo has some poison lingering on his lips to help her die, she says:

. . . I will kiss thy lips.

Haply some poison yet doth hang on them

To make me die with a restorative. (*Romeo and Juliet* 5.3.164–66)

Hence

Hence means away from here, and it can refer to place or time. *The Comedy of Errors* has examples of both uses. Dromio tells Antipholus of Syracuse:

I did not see you since you sent me hence,

Home to the Centaur with the gold you gave me. (2.2.15–16)

Angelo later tells the other Antipholus, "I'll meet you at that place some hour hence" (3.1.122).

Hither

Hither means here, as in "Come hither to me, Master Froth" (*Measure for Measure* 2.1.199).

Mistress

Mistress had a broader meaning in Shakespeare's day and could be applied to almost any woman. Typically, *mistress* meant the female head of a household, as in Mistress Ford and Mistress Page in *The Merry Wives of Windsor.* Other women could also have the same title, so Mistress Page's daughter is Mistress Anne Page. A mistress might also be a woman who has captured a man's heart, as in:

I give thee this

For thy sweet mistress' sake, because thou lov'st her. (*Two Gentlemen of Verona* 4.4.173–74)

The most common modern meaning — a woman in an illicit relationship — is less common in Shakespearean plays.

Sirrah

Sirrah is a term used to address a man or boy of low station — such as a servant — or a child. In *The Merry Wives of Windsor,* for example, Mistress Page uses *sirrah* when addressing her son:

Come on, sirrah, hold up your head. Answer your master, be not afraid. (4.1.18–19)

Master Ford uses *sirrah* as an insulting title for Sir John Falstaff:

Well said, brazen-face, hold it out. — Come forth, sirrah! (*Merry Wives of Windsor* 4.2.126).

Tarry

Tarry means to wait. In *A Midsummer Night's Dream,* for example, Lysander and Hermia get lost in the forest near Athens, and Lysander says:

We'll rest us, Hermia, if you think it good,

And tarry for the comfort of the day. (2.2.36–37)

Thence

Related to *hence, thence* means away from there. Rosencrantz asks Hamlet where he stowed the body of Polonius: "Tell us where 'tis, that we may take it thence and bear it to the chapel" (*Hamlet* 4.2.6).

Troth

Troth means faithfulness or faith. Shakespeare most commonly used it in *by my troth,* sometimes shortened to just *troth,* as in *Much Ado About Nothing:*

Margaret. Troth, I think your other rebato* were better.   *collar

Hero. No, pray thee good Meg, I'll wear this.

Margaret. By my troth 's not so good, and I warrant your cousin will say so.

(*Much Ado About Nothing* 3.4.6–9)

Sometimes, *troth* means truth, as in this example:

Fair love, you faint with wand'ring in the wood,

And, to speak troth, I have forgot our way. (*Midsummer Night's Dream* 2.2.34–35)

You may have heard the phrase *to plight troth*. Shakespeare rarely used it, but it has the same meaning — namely, to promise faith and loyalty:

I will remain

The loyal'st husband that did e'er plight troth. (*Cymbeline* 1.2.26–27)

Wench

A *wench* is a girl or young woman. The term is often used to address a daughter or female servant, as you can see when Queen Katherine addresses one of her attendants: "Take thy lute, wench, my soul grows sad with troubles" (*Henry VIII* 3.1.1).

Wherefore

Wherefore means why, which Dromio makes clear in this exchange from *The Comedy of Errors:*

Antipholus. Shall I tell you why?

Dromio. Ay, sir, and wherefore; for they say, every why hath a wherefore. (2.2.42–44)

But the most famous *wherefore* in Shakespeare is Juliet's question, "Why are you named Romeo?"

O Romeo, Romeo, wherefore art thou Romeo?

Deny thy father and refuse thy name.

Or if thou wilt not, be but sworn my love

And I'll no longer be a Capulet. (*Romeo and Juliet* 2.2.33–36)

Whither

Whither means "where to?" In *As You Like It,* for example, Celia asks her newly banished friend:

O my poor Rosalind, whither wilt thou go? (1.3.87)

Chapter 5

Did You Hear the One About . . . ?

In This Chapter

▶ Shakespeare wrote jokes into every play, even the most depressing and bloody tragedies

▶ Most jokes involve wordplay, but Shakespeare also used physical humor

▶ Many jokes are sexual in nature (and may not be suitable for all audiences)

*Y*ou may not realize it, but Shakespeare was a really funny guy. His plays are full of jokes — often bawdy and off-color. Some jokes involve physical slapstick, and others are side-splittingly funny, but most of his jokes are the kind that you have to think about for a second. Elizabethan audiences loved wordplay, and if you aren't accustomed to hearing this kind of joke, it may take you a moment to figure it out.

Some plays are funnier than others, but just because a play is called a *comedy* doesn't necessarily mean that it's funny. (In Shakespeare's day, *comedy* meant a play with a happy ending. You can read more about comedies and other kinds of plays in Chapter 7.) And often, his tragedies — the ones that end with dead bodies littering the stage — have funny scenes mixed in with the serious ones.

Explaining a joke is the surest way to kill it, so we want to let Shakespeare speak for himself. This chapter gives you some background information about the ways Shakespeare used humor in his plays, but it generally lets you figure out the jokes. If you have trouble understanding a joke when you read a play, try reading the passage out loud. Remember that Shakespeare wrote his jokes to be heard by an audience, and sometimes that's the only way to get the joke.

Playing with Words

Shakespeare loved words. He invented lots of new words, used old words in new ways, and created joke after joke after joke by playing with words in unexpected ways.

Puns and double meanings

A common theme in Shakespeare's plays was for characters to play games with words. All kinds of characters used puns — from kings to commoners — but the saucy servant was often the source of the best puns, sometimes with the master or mistress and sometimes with another servant. In *The Two Gentlemen of Verona,* for example, Launce is a clown who likes to play games with his master and with other servants. In the following exchange, Launce puns with *staff* and *stand*. Also note that his name means staff or lance. The phallic humor of "stands well" is also intentional:

Speed. Why then, how stands the matter with them?

Launce. Marry, thus: when it stands well with him, it stands well with her.

Speed. What an ass art thou, I understand thee not.

Launce. What a block art thou, that thou canst not! My staff understands me.

Speed. What thou say'st?

Launce. Ay, and what I do too: look thee, I'll but lean, and my staff understands me.

Speed. It stands under thee indeed.

Launce. Why, stand under and understand is all one. (2.5.19–29)

Most people today don't think of puns as being funny. More accurately, the person delivering the pun usually thinks that it's funny, but the listener often groans. We don't know whether people merely groaned 400 years ago, but Shakespeare used puns a lot, sometimes hundreds of puns in a single play. As Benedick puts it, "There's a double meaning in that" (*Much Ado About Nothing* 2.3.248). For example, Falstaff, the fat knight who appears in *King Henry IV* and *The Merry Wives of Windsor,* is often the brunt of fat jokes, and he sometimes makes such jokes himself. Here he puns on *waste* and *waist,* with the help of his friend, Pistol:

Falstaff. My honest lads, I will tell you what I am about.

Pistol. Two yards, and more.

Falstaff. No quips now, Pistol. Indeed, I am in the waist two yards about, but I am now about no waste: I am about thrift. (*Merry Wives of Windsor* 1.3.36–41)

A favorite game of young men with nothing better to do is to exchange puns and similar jokes. In this friendly duel of wits, the goal is to top each other in humor, as in this example from *Romeo and Juliet:*

Mercutio. Nay, gentle Romeo, we must have you dance.

Romeo. Not I, believe me. You have dancing shoes

With nimble soles, I have a soul of lead

So stakes me to the ground I cannot move.

Mercutio. You are a lover, borrow Cupid's wings

And soar with them above a common bound.

Romeo. I am too sore enpierced with his shaft

To soar with his light feathers, and so bound

I cannot bound a pitch above dull woe.

Under love's heavy burden do I sink. (1.4.13–22)

Malapropisms, or mistaken words

Another way of playing with words is to use words incorrectly on purpose. Usually a servant does this, but any character can jumble his or her words to reveal ignorance and stupidity. This form of wordplay is now called a *malapropism,* although Shakespeare didn't use that term.

Dogberry, the constable in *Much Ado About Nothing,* is one of Shakespeare's best-known manglers of words. When he chooses the most sensible person for the nightwatch, for example, he says, "You are thought here to be the most senseless and fit man for the constable of the watch" (3.3.22).

Constable Elbow has a similar problem in *Measure for Measure:*

Elbow. If it please your honour, I am the poor Duke's constable, and my name is Elbow. I do lean upon justice, sir, and do bring in here before your good honour two notorious benefactors.

Angelo. Benefactors? Well, what benefactors are they? Are they not malefactors? (2.1.46–51)

Slapstick

Shakespeare wasn't one to shy away from physical humor. Clowns and slapstick have played major roles in plays from the earliest days of the theater, so Shakespeare was just continuing a tradition, although we don't know all the details. Without stage directions to explain the physical actions, you must infer them from the text. In some cases, doing so is easy. For example, in *The Tempest,* Caliban fears Prospero's anger and hides on the ground. Trinculo tries to escape a storm and hides under Caliban's cloak. Stephano finds the two, but he can see only four feet emerging from a cloak. Stephano hears Caliban and Trinculo speak and responds with this comic outburst:

Four legs and two voices, — a most delicate monster! His forward voice, now, is to speak well of his friend; his backward voice is to utter foul speeches and to detract. If all the wine in my bottle will recover him, I will help his ague. Come: — Amen! I will pour some in thy other mouth. (2.2.89–94)

Poor Dromio gets caught between an irate master and an impatient mistress in *The Comedy of Errors*. Shakespeare doesn't give explicit stage directions, but you can imagine how Adriana treats her servant onstage:

Dromio. So that my errand due unto my tongue,

I thank him, I bare home upon my shoulders;

For in conclusion, he did beat me there.

Adriana. Go back again, thou slave, and fetch him home.

Dromio. Go back again, and be new beaten home?

For God's sake, send some other messenger.

Adriana. Back slave, or I will break thy pate across.

Dromio. And he will bless that cross with other beating;

Between you I shall have a holy head.

Adriana. Hence, prating peasant, fetch thy master home.

Dromio. Am I so round with you, as you with me,

That like a football you do spurn me thus?

You spurn me hence, and he will spurn me hither;

If I last in this service you must case me in leather. (2.1.73–86)

Shakespeare wrote many physical jokes into his plays, and you can be sure that actors and directors found other opportunities for slapstick that don't appear in the scripts. Will Kempe was a famous clown who played roles in Shakespeare's early comedies, such as Dogberry in *Much Ado About Nothing*. He probably found many chances to enhance his comic roles, and it's possible that Shakespeare had him in mind when he wrote Hamlet's advice to the players:

And let those that play your clowns speak no more than is set down for them — for there be of them that will themselves laugh, to set on some quantity of barren spectators to laugh too, though in the meantime some necessary question of the play be then to be considered. That's villainous, and shows a most pitiful ambition in the fool that uses it. (*Hamlet* 3.2.39–46)

Some things never change, and today, actors and directors often find opportunities to add humor where Shakespeare didn't write it. Sometimes, the additions are "villainous," but most often, they make the play more interesting and enjoyable for contemporary audiences.

Comic Interludes

Although comedies such as *The Comedy of Errors* and *A Midsummer Night's Dream* contain the most jokes and funny scenes, even Shakespeare's tragedies have their comic moments. Hamlet escapes an attempted execution, Ophelia commits suicide, and Shakespeare inserts the famous gravedigger scene to lighten the mood (see Chapter 8 to read how clowns, such as the gravedigger, filled other roles in a play):

Hamlet. I will speak to this fellow. — Whose grave's this, sirrah?

Clown. . . . Mine, sir.

Hamlet. I think it be thine indeed, for thou liest in't.

Clown. You lie out on't, sir, and therefore 'tis not yours. For my part, I do not lie in't, yet it is mine.

Hamlet. Thou dost lie in't, to be in't and say 'tis thine. 'Tis for the dead, not for the quick: therefore thou liest.

Clown. 'Tis a quick lie, sir, 'twill away again from me to you.

Hamlet. What man dost thou dig it for?

Clown. For no man, sir.

Hamlet. What woman then?

Clown. For none neither.

Hamlet. Who is to be buried in't?

Clown. One that was a woman, sir; but rest her soul, she's dead. (*Hamlet* 5.1.117–35)

Shakespeare also uses interludes to present different points of view, such as the reaction of the common folk to events that involve the main characters. Commoners and clowns often show wisdom when kings and queens do not. For example, a gardener compares the government of King Richard II to a neglected garden:

. . . Bolingbroke

Hath seiz'd the wasteful king. O, what pity is it

That he had not so trimm'd and dress'd his land

As we this garden! We at time of year

Do wound the bark, the skin of our fruit-trees,

Lest, being over-proud in sap and blood,

With too much riches it confound itself;

Had he done so to great and growing men,

They have liv'd to bear, and he to taste

Their fruits of duty. (*Richard II* 3.4.54–63)

Bawdiness

Many of Shakespeare's jokes are dirty jokes — scatology and other bathroom humor, sexual puns, anatomical jokes, and so on — but most of his jokes are about sex in its myriad forms.

Dirty but not filthy

Bathroom jokes have always been popular among some people. Shakespeare didn't often resort to such jokes, but coarse characters have coarse lines. Shakespeare used crude jokes to establish characters. Kings never make wisecracks about flatulence, but clowns and servants do. An example of a crude character is the porter in *Macbeth*. He is slow to answer the door in the middle of the night and makes his excuses:

Porter. Faith, Sir, we were carousing till the second cock; and drink, Sir, is a great provoker of three things.

Macduff. What three things does drink especially provoke?

Porter. Marry, Sir, nose-painting, sleep, and urine. Lechery, Sir, it provokes, and unprovokes: it provokes the desire, but it takes away the performance. Therefore, much drink may be said to be an equivocator with lechery: it makes him, and it mars him; it sets him on, and it takes him off; it persuades him, and disheartens him; makes him stand to, and not stand to: in conclusion, equivocates him in a sleep, and, giving him the lie, leaves him. (2.3.23–36)

Compared to modern television and movies, Shakespeare's crudest jokes are fairly tame. His jokes can be direct without being blatantly raw. The combination is refreshingly funny, as you can see in the following monologue from *The Two Gentlemen of Verona,* in which Launce chastises his dog:

I remember the trick you served me, when I took my leave of Madam Silvia: did not I bid thee still mark me, and do as I do? When didst thou see me heave up my leg, and make water against a gentlewoman's farthingale? Didst thou ever see me do such a trick? (4.4.33–38)

Just do it

Some jokes are just as understandable today as they were 400 years ago, and some are quite obscure. One thing is constant, however: sex. Sex hasn't changed, and jokes about sex haven't changed much, either. The vocabulary changes, but many jokes are just as clear today as they were in Shakespeare's day. In *Measure for Measure,* for example, the authorities arrest Pompey. He works as a pimp for Mistress Overdone, whose name is aptly chosen:

Escalus. Your mistress' name?

Pompey. Mistress Overdone.

Escalus. Hath she had any more than one husband?

Pompey. Nine, sir; Overdone by the last. (2.1.195–98)

In a more direct vein, Aaron the Moor delights in his illegitimate child, whose mother is Tamora, the Empress of Rome. If anyone else in Rome learned of the child's existence, Aaron, Tamora, and her sons would be in danger. Her sons, Demetrius and Chiron, confront Aaron:

Demetrius. Villain, what hast thou done?

Aaron. That which thou canst not undo.

Chiron. Thou hast undone our mother.

Aaron. Villain, I have done thy mother. (*Titus Andronicus* 4.2.75–78)

Innuendo

Shakespeare's favorite kind of joke was the sexual pun. Some of his jokes are evident to the modern playgoer, but others are a little harder to notice. You have to be quick to get these jokes, but don't worry if you miss a few — there are plenty more to come.

Jokes using the word *tail* — often punned with *tale* — are common, as in this contest of wits between Petruchio and Kate in *The Taming of the Shrew:*

Petruchio. Come, come, you wasp; i'faith, you are too angry.

Katherina. If I be waspish, best beware my sting.

Petruchio. My remedy is then to pluck it out.

Katherina. Ay, if the fool could find it where it lies.

Petruchio. Who knows not where a wasp does wear his sting?

In his tail.

Katherina. In his tongue.

Petruchio.   Whose tongue?

Katherina. Yours, if you talk of tales, and so farewell.

Petruchio. What, with my tongue in your tail? Nay, come again, Good Kate. I am a gentleman. (2.1.210–18)

Hamlet lets fly a barrage of sexual innuendo at the expense of Ophelia, who is naively innocent in this exchange:

Hamlet. Lady, shall I lie in your lap?

Ophelia. No, my lord.

Hamlet. I mean, my head upon your lap?

Ophelia. Ay, my lord.

Hamlet. Do you think I meant country matters?

Ophelia. I think nothing, my lord.

Hamlet. That's a fair thought to lie between maids' legs.

Ophelia. What is, my lord?

Hamlet. Nothing. (*Hamlet* 3.2.113–23)

As You Like It's Touchstone has his version of a love poem, in which every line has a double meaning. See if you can figure out the sexual innuendoes:

If a hart do lack a hind,

Let him seek out Rosalind.

If the cat will after kind,

So be sure will Rosalind.

Winter'd garments must be lin'd,

So must slender Rosalind.

They that reap must sheaf and bind,

Then to cart with Rosalind.

Sweetest nut hath sourest rind,

Such a nut is Rosalind.

He that sweetest rose will find

Must find love's prick, and Rosalind. (3.2.98–109)

Shakespeare's plays are full of jokes of all kinds. Every time you read or watch a play, you'll find flashes of wit that you missed the last time. That's one reason that watching a play over and over again can be fun. Don't worry if you miss some of the jokes; you're bound to get others. As you become more accustomed to Shakespeare's language and style, you'll amaze your friends by laughing at quips that no one else gets.

Chapter 6

How to Read Shakespeare's English

***

In This Chapter

▶ Getting the most out of Shakespeare's poetry

▶ Coping with archaic words

***

Shakespeare wrote his plays for performance — he never intended for people to read them as books. To fully appreciate his plays, therefore, you must watch them be performed. That doesn't mean that you can't read them, but also try reading the plays out loud. Speaking and hearing the words are very different from reading them to yourself.

When you read aloud, use your normal speaking voice. Don't feel that because Shakespeare is special, you must read his plays in a special way. Don't gesture or feel that you have to "act out" the plays. Just read normally — not too loud, not too soft, but just right. If you don't understand a word or phrase, don't worry — you're not alone. Just keep reading to get a feel for the entire line or speech.

For Better or Verse

Shakespeare was more than just the world's greatest playwright. He was also a poet. He wrote a number of poems, which you can read about in Chapters 16 and 17, and his plays were also poetry. Shakespeare usually wrote in verse. A few plays (especially his earlier work) are entirely in verse (such as *King John* and *King Richard II*), but most of his plays have some prose sections. *The Merry Wives of Windsor* is almost entirely prose, but even it contains some sections in verse. (Chapter 8 explains how prose and verse can tell you something about the character speaking the lines.) Reading Shakespeare's plays, therefore, is a lot like reading poetry. You might be surprised to find the poetry easier to read and understand than the prose. The rhyme and rhythm of verse gives you clues to help you understand what is important.

Why verse?

Shakespeare wrote his plays in verse for two reasons: tradition and memorization.

- ✔ Plays have been written in verse since the dawn of theater. The ancient Greeks used verse; Shakespeare's forerunners wrote in verse. However, Shakespeare bucked convention when it suited him, using prose instead of verse whenever he felt like it.

- ✔ Verse is easier to memorize than prose. Just like memorizing a song, you can use the rhythm to help you remember which word comes next. Shakespeare didn't usually make his lines rhyme, but when he did, that also aided in memorization. Professional actors — then and now — must learn a lot of lines in a short time. Remember that in Shakespeare's day, the plays were brand new. Modern actors have the benefit of knowing the plays before they need to learn the lines for a particular role.

Real people don't ordinarily speak in verse — they don't now and they didn't in Shakespeare's day — but having the characters speak in verse doesn't detract much from the reality being created onstage. The verse that Shakespeare used in his plays is similar to ordinary, spoken English.

I got rhythm

This section uses as an example the prologue to *Romeo and Juliet.* The prologue has the structure of a *sonnet,* which is a poem composed of 14 lines that rhyme a certain way. (You can read more about Shakespeare's sonnets in Chapter 16.)

Start by reading the prologue aloud. After you read it, hand it to someone else to read so that you can hear it, too.

Two households both alike in dignity

(In fair Verona, where we lay our scene)

From ancient grudge break to new mutiny,

Where civil blood makes civil hands unclean.

From forth the fatal loins of these two foes

A pair of star-cross'd lovers take their life,

Whose misadventur'd piteous overthrows

Doth with their death bury their parents' strife.

The fearful passage of their death-mark'd love

And the continuance of their parents' rage,

Which, but their children's end, nought could remove,

Is now the two hours' traffic of our stage;

The which, if you with patient ears attend,

What here shall miss, our toil shall strive to mend. (*Romeo and Juliet* Prologue.1–14)

Every line has a regular beat, like a heartbeat. You don't need to accentuate it when you read the lines, but the beat is inescapable, just as it is in music:

dah-DUM, dah-DUM, dah-DUM, dah-DUM, dah-DUM

Try beating the rhythm — by clapping, lightly hitting a table, or however you like — at about one beat per second or slightly faster. After you get a feel for the rhythm, read the prologue again. Time your reading so that the stressed syllables correspond to the beats. You should find yourself reading the lines as follows:

two HOUSEholds BOTH aLIKE in DIGniTY

(in FAIR veRONa, WHERE we LAY our SCENE)

from ANcient GRUDGE break TO new MUtiNY,

where CIvil BLOOD makes CIvil HANDS unCLEAN.

Finding the stress

Ordinarily, the last thing you want to find is more stress, but in this case, *stress* refers to the stressed syllables in the verse. Before reading a section from a Shakespeare play, you need to find which syllables are stressed. With practice, you can pick up any old play and read it the way a musician can sight-read music. Don't be discouraged if you need to take it slowly at first — even Laurence Olivier had to start at the beginning.

Go over every line of the prologue and write an accent mark over the stressed syllables. If you need to, you can find the stressed syllables by tapping out the rhythm while you read the text. As you get used to feeling the rhythm, you will be able to find the stressed syllables more easily just by reading the lines to yourself. When you're done, the text will look something like this:

Two hóuseholds bóth alíke in dígnitý

(In fáir Veróna, whére we láy our scéne)

From áncient grúdge break tó new mútiný,

Where cívil blóod makes cívil hánds uncléan.

Finish marking the rest of the prologue, and then read it out loud. Emphasize the stressed syllables to get a feel for the rhythm. Now read it again normally, but putting the stress on the right syllables.

Notice that every line has five stressed syllables. This verse form is called *iambic pentameter. Pentameter* means that the line has five stressed syllables. *Iambic* means that the line is made up of *iambs*. An iamb is a combination of an unstressed syllable followed by a stressed one, as in *aLIKE* or *our SCENE*.

Emphasizing the important syllables

If you want to know what's really important, discard all the unstressed syllable and read only the stressed ones.

HOUSE BOTH LIKE DIG TY

FAIR RON WHERE LAY SCENE

AN GRUDGE TO MU NY

CI BLOOD CI HANDS CLEAN

(You need to flesh out the syllables a little, as in "fair *Verona* where lay scene.")

When you read the verse, the last stress in the line is usually more important than the first one. Try reading the prologue again, this time starting each line quietly and getting louder toward the end of the line. You don't want to make a habit of speaking this way, but it's a good exercise for getting a feel for the verse.

Finally, read the prologue one last time comfortably and normally. Now ask someone else to read the prologue aloud while you listen. Let the stresses guide you to the important words. The meter of the verse should fade into the background so that the words don't sound like poetry. Instead, the iambic meter is like a constant heartbeat. As you grow more comfortable hearing the poetry, you will be better able to hear the important parts of the lines and will better understand what the actors are saying.

But it sounds wrong!

The first time you read the prologue, you probably emphasized the word *Two*. When you carefully mark the stressed syllables, though, you find out that *Two* is an unstressed word. One difference that you may have noticed is that if you stressed *Two*, you had to read the line as follows:

TWO HOUSEholds BOTH aLIKE in DIGniTY

If you try to read the subsequent two lines with the stress on the first syllable, it just sounds wrong. You can make the line sound a little better by pausing between *households* and *both,* but Shakespeare didn't write it that way. Look closely, and you see the absence of a comma or anything else to break the line. (Read more about punctuation later in this chapter.)

Without the stress on *Two,* you can read the text in one, smooth, even-flowing line. But some lines sound odd when you use a strict rhythm, such as this one:

doth WITH their DEATH buRY their PARents' STRIFE

Some of the differences are due merely to the evolution of language. We sometimes stress different syllables than Shakespeare and his contemporaries did. In these cases, it's best to stick with Shakespeare's verse, even though it sounds a little odd. Shakespeare had fewer rules about stressed syllables — he had no dictionary in which he could look up the rules, so he often fudged the words a little. Usually, *bury* is stressed on its first syllable, but the structure of the prologue calls for a stress on the second syllable, so you should read it that way.

In rare circumstances, a deliberate change to the rhythm can help draw attention to particular words. For example, you might add a stress on *break,* which emphasizes *grudge* and *break.* Instead of the original line:

from ANcient GRUDGE break TO new MUtiNY,

try swapping the stressed words *break* and *to:*

from ANcient GRUDGE BREAK to new MUtiNY,

The line is no longer iambic, but it emphasizes the important words. The interruption in the verse draws your attention to the word *break.*

Applying special verbal effects

Don't try the following except under the supervision of a trained expert. Without proper precaution, you could sprain your iambs or trip your tongue. You have been warned!

In a few situations, you can use an alternate rhythm to great effect. Consider the opening soliloquy of *King Richard III:*

Now is the winter of our discontent

Made glorious summer by this son of York;

And all the clouds that lour'd upon our House

In the deep bosom of the ocean buried.

Now are our brows bound with victorious wreaths,

Our bruised arms hung up for monuments,

Our stern alarums chang'd to merry meetings,

Our dreadful marches to delightful measures. (1.1.1–8)

(Pronounce *alarums* as "ah-LAHR-ums." It means calls to arms, usually on a trumpet.) You can read this passage normally, as in

now IS the WINter OF our DISconTENT

made GLOrious SUMmer BY this SON of YORK

Another way to read the lines is to disrupt the meter deliberately. Richard III is lame and so "deformed" that he says, "Dogs bark at me, as I halt by them" (1.1.23). He also has the use of only one arm; the other one is "like a blasted sapling wither'd up" (3.3.69). He is crippled and walks with a limp. You can read his lines in a way that emphasizes the limp. Try it. Read the same passage, but stand up and limp while you read it:

NOW is the WINter of our DISconTENT

MADE GLOrious SUMmer by this SON of YORK

You can use the irregular rhythm of the lines to accentuate the rhythm of the limp, or the other way around. We don't know how Shakespeare intended these lines to be read, but either way, they evoke a rich image of an evil, conniving villain whose sarcasm doesn't drip — it pours.

The alternate rhythm is effective in this case because most of the play follows the normal rhythm. Shakespeare uses iambic pentameter almost everywhere, with only a few exceptions. Always start by reading the line in straight iambic meter — dah-DUM, dah-DUM, dah-DUM, dah-DUM, dah-DUM. Don't just read the line, but listen to it. If you think that an alternate rhythm sounds better, feel free to try it. Shakespeare won't stop you.

Looking at other verse forms that Shakespeare used

Sometimes, Shakespeare used a different verse form to achieve a particular effect. If you consistently stress the first syllable of a line, for example, the verse sounds more like singing and less like speech. In *A Midsummer Night's Dream*, Puck speaks in lines of four stressed syllables, with the stress on the first syllable. Read the following passage aloud and notice the singsong quality of the lines.

If we shadows have offended,

Think but this, and all is mended,

That you have but slumber'd here

While these visions did appear.

And this weak and idle theme,

No more yielding but a dream,

Gentles do not reprehend:

If you pardon, we will mend. (5.1.417–24)

The songlike quality of these lines gives several choices for how to perform them. In some performances, Puck is a child, or childlike, and his lines are like nursery rhymes. A more mature Puck can lend a chantlike quality to the lines, giving them an otherworldliness.

The witches' lines in *Macbeth* have a similar verse structure. The witches are not childlike, but the verse makes their lines sound more like a spell or chant:

When shall we three meet again?

In thunder, lightning, or in rain?

When the hurlyburly's done,

When the battle's lost and won.

That will be ere the set of sun. (1.1.1–5)

Making the words fit the verse

In the previous examples, you may have noticed that you needed to cram big words into small spaces, such as *glorious* into two syllables. Shakespeare often exercised his poetic license to adjust words to fit the verse. If you have only two syllables, read *glorious* as "glor-yus."

Other times, you need to stretch a word to fit an extra syllable. For example, *bruised* is a two-syllable word, "broo-zed." Some editors help you by writing the full *-ed* ending when you need to pronounce it and using a '*d* contraction when you don't (as in *chang'd*). Other editors don't help you, so you need to read the lines carefully, find the stressed syllables, and decide whether you should pronounce the *-ed* endings.

Sometimes, a line has an extra, unstressed syllable at the end. For example, Claudius speaks with a mixture of stressed and unstressed endings when addressing the court. The unstressed line endings are shown in boldface. Read the passage out loud to hear the full effect of the unstressed endings:

Though yet of Hamlet our dear brother's death

The memory be green, and that it us befit**ted**

To bear our hearts in grief, and our whole king**dom**

To be contracted in one brow of woe,

Yet so far hath discretion fought with na**ture**

That we with wisest sorrow think on him

Together with remembrance of ourselves. (*Hamlet* 1.2.1–7)

A line that ends with a stressed syllable is said to have a *masculine* ending, and an unstressed final syllable is a *feminine* ending. As you can tell from the preceding passage, feminine endings can interrupt the flow of the verse. Instead of proceeding smoothly from one line to the next, you have to pause a little, as in though YET of HAMlet OUR dear BROther's DEATH

the MEMoRY be GREEN, and THAT it US beFITted *[pause]*

to BEAR our HEARTS in GRIEF, and OUR whole KINGdom *[pause]*

to BE conTRACted IN one BROW of WOE.

But it doesn't rhyme!

As we mentioned earlier in the chapter, most of Shakespeare's dramatic verse doesn't rhyme. The verse sounds more natural when the lines don't rhyme. Shakespeare usually used rhymed verse for songs, lovers, and fairies. For example, the lovers in *A Midsummer Night's Dream* often speak in rhymed verse, such as when Lysander spurns Hermia and woos Helena:

Content with Hermia? No. I do repent

The tedious minutes I with her have spent.

Not Hermia, but Helena I love:

Who will not change a raven for a dove?

The will of man is by his reason sway'd,

And reason says you are the worthier maid. (2.2.110–15)

The last two lines of an act or scene often rhyme. The two lines, called a *couplet,* help signal the end of the scene with dramatic finality. For example, at the end of Act 3, scene 3, Hamlet has a long soliloquy in which he chastises himself for his lack of action, but he ends with a couplet to announce his decision:

The play's the thing

Wherein I'll catch the conscience of the King. (*Hamlet* 2.2.606–7)

Using Punctuation as a Guide

Punctuation can also help you read and understand Shakespeare's verse. The punctuation tells you when to pause to breathe and how long each pause should be. Even in Shakespeare's day, printers added punctuation where they thought it fit best, and punctuation is where modern editions differ the most. Therefore, you shouldn't use punctuation as concrete rules, but as rough guidelines.

The punctuation marks that Shakespeare used are similar to those used in modern speech. A comma is the shortest pause. Semicolons are slightly longer, and colons are slightly longer than that. Periods denote the ends of sentences and call for the longest pauses. A long dash (—) is a pause that marks a separate thought. The length of the pause depends on the thoughts being separated. Usually it is short, similar to a semicolon; sometimes it is preceded by a punctuation mark, saving you the trouble of deciding how long the pause should be. Pause only at the punctuation marks, and not at the ends of lines that end in no punctuation. Try to breathe only at punctuation marks, preferably only at the ends of sentences.

Try reading the prologue to *Romeo and Juliet* again, paying particular attention to the punctuation marks. Change the parentheses to commas for the time being. To emphasize the punctuation, we reset the lines as though they were prose. Even without the verse structure, the punctuation alone helps you read the lines correctly:

Two households both alike in dignity, in fair Verona, where we lay our scene, from ancient grudge break to new mutiny, where civil blood makes civil hands unclean. From forth the fatal loins of these two foes a pair of star-cross'd lovers take their life, whose misadventur'd piteous overthrows doth with their death bury their parents' strife.

Were you able to make it through to end of each sentence in a single breath? You need to plan ahead where you will breathe so that you don't have to catch your breath in the wrong place. It's a shame to run out of breath and have to say "with their death bury *(gasp)* their parents' strife." The hesitation breaks the rhythm of the verse and robs the line of its strength. If you need to catch a quick, partial breath, do so at a comma. Then take a full breath at the period.

Here's how to breathe when reading the prologue to *Romeo and Juliet:*

Two households both alike in dignity, in fair Verona, where we lay our scene, *[quick breath]* from ancient grudge break to new mutiny, where civil blood makes civil hands unclean. *[full breath]* From forth the fatal loins of these two foes a pair of star-cross'd lovers take their life, *[quick breath]* whose misadventur'd piteous overthrows doth with their death bury their parents' strife. *[full breath]*

The next time you watch a play, pay attention to how the actors speak and breathe. If you have difficulty understanding what they're saying, it's likely that the actors are not following Shakespeare's verse properly or that they aren't breathing in the proper places.

Using the Glossary

When reading Shakespeare's plays, you might feel like Hermione in *The Winter's Tale,* when she tells her husband,

. . . Sir,

You speak a language that I understand not. (3.2.78–79)

The language is English, but an older form of English, and sometimes you must rely on a glossary to define the archaic words. The glossary is not Shakespeare's, but a modern addition written by a modern editor.

Most editions of Shakespeare's plays include a glossary or footnotes to explain the more difficult words. Sometimes, the glossary is in the back — this is common in large, complete works. If you have a paperback of an individual play, the notes are usually at the bottom of the page or on the facing page. Sometimes, the footnotes or endnotes tell you more than just the meanings of the words. Chapter 10 discusses these kinds of notes.

The first time you read a play, you may want to read it through without stopping. Just skip over the words that you don't understand and the phrases that don't make sense. You can still pick up the gist of the play. Then read the play again, this time stopping to check the glossary or notes for words that you don't understand.

Turning to the Mother of All Dictionaries

If a strange word is not in a footnote, you need to look it up in a dictionary. A fairly large, complete dictionary will have many words, including some obsolete words. You just can't find some 400-year-old words in modern dictionaries, though. In that case, consult the *Oxford English Dictionary* (OED). This behemoth is bigger than most encyclopedias, but it's a dictionary. Your public library may not have a copy of the OED, but most college and university libraries do. The OED also comes on CD-ROM, which your library may have. Ask for help at the reference or information desk.

The OED doesn't just define words; it also gives examples of how the word was used historically and when it was first used in literature. For some words that you look up, the first use may have been in one of Shakespeare's plays. For example, if you look up the word *obscenely,* the first entry you find is from *Love's Labour's Lost:*

O'my troth, most sweet jests! most incony* vulgar wit;   *delicate

When it comes so smoothly off, so obscenely as it were, so fit. (4.1.141–42)

Because the OED is so large, two compact editions have also been published. The first reduced each page by a quarter, packing the entire dictionary to two large volumes. The newer compact edition crams the entire dictionary into a single volume, with the pages reduced so that six original pages fit on one new page. You may find the compact editions in used bookstores, but make sure that you have a magnifying glass. Reading the tiny text without one is sure to make you go mad, blind, or both.

Part III
The Play's the Thing

The 5th Wave   By Rich Tennant

©RICHTENNANT

EXIT

"I know it's a Furby, Ronald. Just work with it until we can get a skull."

In this part . . .

"All the world's a stage" runs the quote from *As You Like It,* but to Shakespeare, the stage is all the world. A theater can hold "the vasty fields of France" from *King Henry V,* the far-flung journeys of Pericles as he crossed and recrossed the Mediterranean Sea, or the village of Windsor, England, and its Merry Wives. Through it all, Shakespeare created stories of kings, beggars, witches, saints, and ordinary people.

Explore the world of Shakespeare's plays — whether you read the plays, go to the theater, or watch videotapes in your living room. This part examines the stories, characters, and settings of Shakespeare's plays. No need to be intimidated. Just relax and enjoy the ride.

Chapter 7

Once Upon a Time . . .

In This Chapter

▶ Common themes in Shakespeare's plays

▶ What makes a comedy a comedy and a tragedy a tragedy

▶ A brief history of the English kings

▶ Where Shakespeare got his story ideas

A good story is a good story — in the 16th century, the 20th century, or the 21st century. Shakespeare's plays defy minor differences of a few hundred years. *Romeo and Juliet* appeals to readers of all ages, whether Leonardo DiCaprio plays a modern Romeo or Natalie Wood portrays Maria in *West Side Story*. The characters and plots are just as interesting and exciting today as they were 400 years ago.

Where did Shakespeare get the ideas for his stories? Mostly, he took his ideas from existing plays and books. He borrowed plots, characters, and entire speeches. He often mixed ideas from two stories into a single play. Always, though, he modified his sources and improved upon them. That's why most people have heard of *As You Like It,* but only literature majors know about Thomas Lodge's *Rosalynde.* Shakespeare based his play on Lodge's novel, which was based on the 14th-century *Tale of Gamelyn.* Reusing plots and characters from other stories was as common then as it is today.

To whet your appetite for Shakespeare's plays, this chapter tells you all about the different kinds of stories that Shakespeare wrote.

Five Acts

Every play has five acts, not necessarily because Shakespeare wrote them that way, but because modern editors always divide the plays that way. Many of Shakespeare's plays were divided into five acts when they were first printed. Some plays lack act or scene divisions, so editors enforce some uniformity by making up act divisions in those plays. Different editors might put the divisions in different places, but every modern edition has five acts:

- ✔ The first act introduces the characters and sets up the story. In most comedies, you meet the prospective lovers, who are usually at odds.

- ✔ The second act expands the story and tells you more about the characters. In a comedy, the situation usually involves some confusion: Most often the lovers don't love each other or they love the wrong person. In a tragedy, you've had a chance to meet the heroes and the villains. Modern writers sometimes hide the heroes and make them seem like villains, and vice versa, but Shakespeare usually makes the characters less ambiguous. By the end of the second act, you usually know who are the heroes and who are the villains. In some ways, this makes Shakespeare's plays easier to follow and understand.

- ✔ The third act is the pivotal act. In a comedy, the confusion is usually at its maximum, but you can see how the confusion will be resolved. In a tragedy, the villains have set their evil plans in motion, and the heroes must respond. The heroes make mistakes, though, and their decisions ultimately lead to their deaths. Scholars like to call the third act the *climax* of the play because it is the pivotal moment at which decisions are made and plans become clear. Nonetheless, you have to wait until the last act to see the full results of these decisions and plans, which is what most people consider to be the play's climax.

- ✔ The action unfolds in the fourth act, and the heroes' plans collide with the villains' plans. If this were a modern movie, you wouldn't be able to tell who will win, but this is Shakespeare. You know that the villains will be caught in the end and that the heroes will triumph, but, in a tragedy, at the cost of their lives.

- ✔ The fifth and final act brings all the pieces together. The villains are caught. The heroes learn their lessons. In a comedy, the lessons are light, and the lovers get married. In a tragedy, the heroes die to pay for their mistakes. The world is cruel to demand such a high payment for learning a lesson, but, hey, it's just a play. It's part of making the tragedy more grand than real life.

Think You've Got Problems?

Shakespeare wrote plays about people and their problems. The biggest reason his plays remain popular today is that people haven't changed much in 400 years, and we still have the same problems. The kings, tyrants, murderers, and lovers about whom Shakespeare wrote face the same issues that everyone else faces, more or less. You may never have to decide who will sit on England's throne, but you may have to help decide who will fill a job vacancy, which is much the same thing, albeit on a smaller scale.

The following sections describe the two problems that Shakespeare tackled most often in his plays: love and revenge.

Love

The most popular topic in Shakespeare's comedies is love: unrequited love, forbidden love, disguised love, misguided love. These same subjects are popular today in films, on television, and in the daily news. Do you admire someone who doesn't even notice you? Or perhaps someone you don't like is pestering you for love and attention. Shakespeare delighted in such situations, and he examined them in many plays.

Twelfth Night is a prime example. (See Chapter 13 for a summary of this play.) Orsino loves Olivia, but she ignores him. Viola loves Orsino, but she must hide her love because she is dressed as a man. Olivia falls in love with Viola (thinking that she is a man because of how she's dressed). The rule for comedy is that all the relationships must be straightened out by the end of the play. Shakespeare untangles this knot by means of Viola's twin brother, Sebastian. Once Viola is unmasked, Sebastian marries Olivia, Viola marries Orsino, and everyone lives happily ever after.

Shakespeare gives you lots of hints at the start of each play, so you can tell who will marry whom by the end. The first two acts introduce the characters and their relationships. If a couple is happy together when the play begins, you can be fairly sure that something will go wrong, but that matters will be patched up by the final act, and they will be together again at the end. If a play opens with a man pressing unwanted attention on a woman, Shakespeare is usually telling you that they don't belong together. In a comedy, the only solution to this kind of problem is to find a suitable mate for the misguided lover.

Even Shakespeare's tragedies examine some of the facets of love. King Lear, for example, disowns his daughter Cordelia because she doesn't love him enough, or so he thinks. Othello is never quite sure that he is worthy of Desdemona's love, so he readily believes Iago's lies about her. In both plays, you see how insecurity and low self-esteem can mar a relationship. (See Chapter 15 for summaries of *King Lear* and *Othello*.)

Revenge

It happens to everyone: Someone cuts in front of you in line or spills a double cappuccino on your best suit, or you get home from a hard day at work to find that your pet has been struck by a car whose driver never bothered to stop. Life just isn't fair. Sometimes life's trials and tribulations make you want to scream. Sometimes you really do scream, and on occasion you do more than scream. This is also true in the worlds that Shakespeare created.

Maybe your problems aren't quite a big as Hamlet's: His uncle murders his father, steals the throne of Denmark, and marries his mother; then his girlfriend kills herself, and her brother blames Hamlet and seeks revenge. But even if your problems don't measure up to Hamlet's, you can gain much from the play. Perhaps your rival for the big promotion stole your idea to sell as his own. You want to pop him one, but Hamlet doesn't do that. He watches and waits until just the right moment. Except that Hamlet gets it wrong — he waits too long; he plans and schemes his revenge too much. Hamlet is a planner, not a doer. So the lesson is to think and plan, but just the right amount. When you finish your plans, put them in action. (But don't assault your coworker. Or if you do, don't say that we told you to do so. Blame it on Shakespeare. You can read a summary of *Hamlet* in Chapter 15.)

Revenge is a popular theme in Shakespeare's plays, especially in his trag-edies. But revenge is usually just one element of a more complex story. As you read or watch the play, pay particular attention to *why* someone seeks revenge and *how* he or she carries out the plan. Inevitably, revenge begets revenge. In Shakespeare's plays, the barter rate is never an eye for an eye and a tooth for a tooth. Instead, revenge escalates until the final act, when villains and heroes alike face the consequences of their unbridled hatred.

Different plays have different lessons about revenge, so pay attention to what each play tells you. If Shakespeare had only one take on revenge, he would have written only one play. To see the limits of how far one can take revenge, read or watch *Titus Andronicus* (see Chapter 15 for a summary).

Tragedies, Comedies, and Histories — Oh My!

People like to put things into categories. Movie critics do so with films: slasher, buddy, western, war, and more. You can do the same with books: science fiction, gothic romance, *...For Dummies,* and so on. Shakespeare's plays also have categories: tragedies, comedies, and histories. But these terms don't mean exactly what you may think they mean.

A *tragedy* is a play in which the protagonist dies. In a *comedy,* on the other hand, the protagonist lives — and usually gets married, too. Shakespeare wrote the *history* plays about the kings of England. Sometimes the king dies, perhaps at the hands of his successor. In other history plays, the king lives to star in another play. Usually, a history play focuses on a significant event in a king's reign, such as an important war.

Some editors of Shakespeare's works choose different categories. For example, *The Two Noble Kinsmen,* instead of being a comedy, might be called a romance or a tragicomedy. Palamon and Emilia get married, as in a comedy, but Palamon's brother Arcite dies, adding a tragic element. Some of Shakespeare's later comedies have a dark and somber tone, such as *The Winter's Tale.* They are different from his earlier comedies, such as *As*

You Like It, so some modern editors call these plays *romances.* The most common categorization, though, is into comedies, histories, and tragedies, which is the grouping used when the plays were first published.

Shakespeare did not care about categories. Sometimes he labeled a play with a category title, such as *The Comedy of Errors* or *The Tragedy of Hamlet, Prince of Denmark.* Often, however, a play's title gives no hint about how Shakespeare thought of the play. It was up to the editors of *The First Folio,* seven years after Shakespeare's death, to group the plays into the three traditional categories of comedies, histories, and tragedies, and that is the categorization used in this book.

Aristole's rules for playwriting

In Shakespeare's day, playwrights had rules for writing plays. The rules didn't come from a Renaissance Writers' Guild (there was no such guild), but from an ancient Greek philosopher, Aristotle. He wrote the rules in *Poetics* about 2,000 years before Shakespeare was born. Europeans forgot about the great Greek and Roman philosophers and writers for hundreds of years but rediscovered their writings during the Renaissance. (That's one reason we call that era the *Renaissance,* or rebirth. It represented a rebirth of ancient knowledge.) The invention of the movable-type printing press made it easy to publish new translations of ancient classics, and soon everyone who was anyone had a copy of *Poetics* and was eager to discuss its merits. (See the sidebar "Aristotle's *Poetics*" to find out more.)

In the Renaissance, many people turned to ancient writings as sources of true knowledge and wisdom. Shakespeare's contemporaries were adamant about following Aristotle's rules, or at least their interpretations of the rules. These rules became the standard form of plays in Shakespeare's day. Shakespeare never followed the rules exactly, but his plays have the Renaissance mark about them.

The most important rule was the unity of action, namely — that a play should have a single plot line. Shakespeare followed this rule in a few plays, such as *The Comedy of Errors,* but usually he mixed multiple plots to make the plays more interesting.

The unity of time required that time onstage closely match real time. The rules allowed a play to stretch time a little bit and take as much as a day, but Shakespeare often folded, spindled, and mutilated time. He often let events sprawl over many days, weeks, or even years. Shakespeare followed the unity of time in *The Comedy of Errors* and *The Tempest,* but usually he let time pass as much or as little as he needed in order to write interesting, exciting plays, and he paid little heed to this particular rule.

Aristotle's *Poetics*

Aristotle wrote his *Poetics* almost 2,400 years ago. His work was rediscovered early in the 16th century and was translated into several languages. In *Poetics,* Aristotle lays out the rules for writing a good tragedy, comedy, or epic poem.

The most important rule is that a good play must have a single plot line. This is called the *unity of action.* The plot should tell a coherent story, with a beginning, a middle, and an end. Aristotle singles out as particularly bad the style of telling a story through a series of unrelated episodes.

A second rule is that the hero should be an illustrious person (such as a king, general, or other leader) but should have a character flaw (such as pride). The play should unfold around the hero's reversal of situation, brought about by his own frailty, and not through an accident of circumstance. This flaw is often called a *tragic flaw.*

Aristotle also stipulates that a tragedy should inspire pity and fear: pity for the tragic hero and his suffering, fear that the same might happen to you. A comedy, on the other hand, ends when enemies become friends, and no one is killed. Aristotle has many other rules concerning diction, language, and poetry. To find out more, visit www.bardware.com or visit your local library.

The unity of space rule dictated that a play should take place in one particular location. For example, *The Comedy of Errors* could be performed so that all the action takes place in the streets of Ephesus, or in houses adjacent to the street. *Pericles,* on the other hand, ranges all around the Mediterranean Sea, so it doesn't follow the unity of space rule. In many plays, the action simply takes place. Some scenes have a definite setting, but other scenes have no location more specific than a town name. The action just happens. Somewhere. You have to use your imagination (more in Chapter 9).

In other words, Shakespeare felt free to break the rules whenever he felt like it. After all, his audience didn't care whether the plays followed the rules, and Shakespeare wrote to please his audience, not to please neoclassical writers and scholars.

Tragedy

Shakespeare's most famous plays are his tragedies, such as *Hamlet, King Lear, Othello, Julius Caesar,* and *Macbeth.* These plays follow the standard rules for tragedies: The hero has a basic human frailty that brings about his downfall and death, but before he dies, he learns an important lesson about his frailty and how it destroyed his life (and usually the lives of those he loved). Shakespeare didn't write these plays to deliver a moral message, but that doesn't stop us from learning from his plays. He fills his plays with ordinary people, and we can see ourselves in their situations. They face when the heroes face their tragic ends, we can learn from their mistakes and ordinary problems (albeit exaggerated for dramatic emphasis), and we can see ourselves with the same problems. Thus, when the heroes face their tragic ends, we can learn from their mistakes and avoid similar ends in our own lives. At the same time, we can watch a play that is fun and entertaining, full of action, intrigue, and excitement.

The tragic hero

In some ways, all of Shakespeare's tragedies follow a similar course. Each tragedy has a central figure, the tragic hero. The hero is a person of high degree, often a king or prince. He is a good person, but not perfect. Like every human being, he has flaws. A tragic play takes one of those flaws and shows how it affects the hero's life. To make the play more thrilling, the action in a tragedy is magnified, so much so that the hero dies. Just as a modern film about police and criminals magnifies the conflict and action, Shakespeare's tragedies make everything seem grander than in real life.

In many plays, the protagonist is a true hero. Hamlet, for example, is clearly an honest, decent person who is wrongly cheated out of the throne of Denmark by his conniving uncle, Claudius. We root for Hamlet, cheer his triumphs, and pity his failures. The protagonist is not always a hero, though. Sometimes he is his own worst enemy. Coriolanus, for example, is too proud. He is a great Roman general — the best, and he knows it. His arrogance and conceit affect all around him and drive away those who would be his friends. In the end, you almost cheer when they conspire against him and he gets his due. (You can read a summary of *Coriolanus* in Chapter 15.)

Villains

Shakespeare's villains are often his most interesting characters. Although they seem at first to be pure evil, as you get to know them, you realize that they're human, too. They act in response to injury, although their response is out of proportion to the hurt. Othello passes over Iago and promotes Cassio to lieutenant. Iago considers Cassio to be less qualified, so Iago gets mad and plots revenge:

Iago. Why, there's no remedy, 'tis the curse of service:

Preferment goes by letter and affection

And not by old gradation, where each second

Stood heir to th' first. Now sir, be judge yourself

Whether I in any just term am affined

To love the Moor.

Rogerigo.　　　　I would not follow him then.

Iago. O sir, content you.

I follow him to serve my turn upon him. (*Othello* 1.1.34–40)

You can understand Iago's feelings, but you wouldn't respond in the same way if your boss promoted her friend instead of you, even though you're more qualified. *Othello* is a tragedy, so everyone's emotions are magnified, including Iago's. Instead of just getting mad or getting even, Iago goes overboard and takes an awful revenge. (See Chapter 15 for a summary of *Othello.*) The villain's role in a tragedy is to take advantage of the hero's flaw and bring it out into the open. The villain shows the audience how we all have a little bit of the villain in us.

The bastard is a common villain in Shakespeare's plays. Throughout much of European history, the children of unmarried parents had few rights. In Shakespeare's England, for example, the eldest son inherited his father's wealth, title, and land, but not if his parents weren't married at the time. Perhaps they were young and in love, and they started their family a little too soon before their wedding. Nonetheless, a son born out of wedlock was labeled a bastard and could not inherit. Such is Edmund's case in *King Lear:*

Edmund. Thou, Nature, art my goddess; to thy law

My services are bound. Wherefore should I

Stand in the plague of custom, and permit

The curiosity of nations to deprive me?

For that I am some twelve or fourteen moonshines

Lag of a brother? Why bastard? Wherefore base?

When my dimensions are as well compact,

My mind as generous and my shape as true

As honest madam's issue? Why brand they us

With base? With baseness, bastardy? Base, base? (1.2.1–10)

It isn't Edmund's fault that his parents were not married, but the law punished the son. Edmund points out that he is the same as anyone else whose parents were married. In other words, villains and heroes, kings and commoners, Nature's laws see no differences between legitimate and illegitimate children. The only differences are in the curious laws of nations. Because society's laws treat him unfairly, Edmund decides to turn down the path of villainy. (As you discover in the summary of *King Lear* in Chapter 15, Edmund's story is not the main plot, but he plays an important role.)

Shakespeare's plays contain numerous varieties of villains, from the merely disgruntled to the envious to those hell-bent on revenge. Conflict is a natural element to any dramatic story, and Shakespeare's villains usually provide all the conflict you could hope for. Not every play has a dastardly villain, though. Comedies may have villains, but some do not.

Comedy tonight

A Shakespearean comedy isn't the same as a modern comedy. In Shakespeare's day, a comedy was a play in which the protagonist didn't die.

The rules for comedies required that they be less grandiose than tragedies, and part of toning down the plays meant that the heroes might learn a lesson, but they wouldn't die. Similarly, the villains would get caught and face justice, but not the death penalty.

 Most comedies are love stories, and in the end, the hero and heroine get married. (Except in _Much Ado About Nothing,_ in which one of the heroines is named Hero. In that case, the hero and Hero get married. See Chapter 13 for more about this popular play.) Of course, a good comedy is more than a love story. Even in comedies, the characters grow and learn, although the lessons are simpler than in tragedies.

Comedies do not follow as strict a formula as tragedies. Sometimes, a villain causes the mix-up, and you know that by the end of the play, the villain will be caught and will get his just punishment (although this isn't a tragedy, so the villain rarely dies). Other times, the confusion is the result of honest circumstance, such as mistaken identity. Occasionally, the hero causes the mix-up, intentionally or accidentally.

In a tragedy, the action usually arises from the hero's character flaw. In a comedy, the action might originate with the hero, but just as likely, it arises from circumstances that are outside the hero's control. Perhaps a nasty relative has booted the hero out of his or her proper home. Sometimes, a wandering eye causes a would-be hero to fall in love with a woman other than his fiancée. Needless to say, that always causes trouble.

Although Shakespeare's comedies are not comedies in the modern sense, they can be funny nonetheless. Much of the hilarity comes from the situations his characters land in — Renaissance sitcoms. Chapter 5 explores Shakespeare's humor in more depth.

Historical fiction

Shakespeare based his histories on written accounts of the kings of England. His audience knew these stories well, so they knew when Shakespeare altered the past, moved events forward or backward by a few years, and so on. But they didn't care because he wrote such rip-roaring good plays. Sometimes, the truth is less interesting than a well-written story, but if you want to know more about the true history of England, we recommend _The Story of Britain,_ by Sir Roy Strong (1997, Fromm International).

Shakespeare also altered history to please England's reigning monarch, Queen Elizabeth, and her successor, King James. Shakespeare and his acting company depended on the good graces of the monarch, and pleasing the king or queen made good political and financial sense.

Holy war

Shakespeare's series of history plays starts with reign of King John, who took the throne in 1199, almost 400 years before Shakespeare wrote the play. *The Life and Death of King John* deals with a couple of key points in John's reign. You can read about the play in Chapter 14; to fully understand the play, though, you first need to know a little about English history.

Shortly before Shakespeare was born, King Henry VIII made the bold move of separating England from the Roman Catholic Church and the Pope. Henry's daughter, Elizabeth, eventually succeeded him to the throne, but the transition caused bloody fighting between Catholics and Protestants. By Shakespeare's day, matters had calmed down, but the conflict was still fresh in people's minds, and Shakespeare had to be careful how he treated this subject in his plays.

King John had his own altercation with the Pope. (Of course, in his day, it was a different Pope. Henry VIII confronted Pope Clement VII, and John dealt with Pope Innocent III.) At first, John resisted the Pope's intrusion into English political affairs, but when John faced defeat by the French army, he submitted to papal rule, so the Pope effectively became John's boss. This didn't sit well with the English people, so it made a fitting subject for a play. Shakespeare could show the Pope as an interfering foreign influence and depict John as a troublesome king who was a blot on England's past.

As the Globe Turns

After *King John,* the next history play jumps forward almost 200 years to Richard II, who became king in 1377. Richard was the son of Prince Edward, who was the eldest son of King Edward III. Unfortunately, Prince Edward died before his father did, so when Edward III died, Richard became king, following the line of the eldest sons. Never mind that he was only 9 years old. Edward III had other sons (Lionel, John of Gaunt, Edmund, and Thomas), and they were displeased by this arrangement. Richard's uncles tried to manipulate the young king, but with little success.

King Richard II eventually executed Thomas and exiled John's son, Henry. Richard II had other troubles in his reign, but Shakespeare wrote only one play about Richard, focusing on his relationship with Henry. Henry returned from exile and deposed Richard, taking the throne as Henry IV. Henry gets two plays of his own, dealing with his more rebellious and riotous son, Prince Hal. The young prince hangs out with the wrong crowd, but he grows up, shapes up, and succeeds his father to the throne, ruling as Henry V.

Henry V didn't have any serious problems in England, so he focused his attention outward, continuing England's long-running war with France. (It was called the Hundred Years War for good reason, starting in 1337 and ending in 1453, or later if you count minor skirmishes after that.)

Civil war

Henry VI succeeded his father, Henry V, but in troubled times in England. Three plays span the reign of Henry VI, depicting England's dealings with Joan of Arc and the war in France, plus the Wars of the Roses in England. The Wars of the Roses date back to the death of Edward III. Remember that he had several sons. Richard II was king, but John's son deposed him. John of Gaunt was Duke of Lancaster, and Edmund was Duke of York. Their children continued to bicker until the bickering turned to fighting. The House of York (White Rose) and the House of Lancaster (Red Rose) duked it out for several years. Edward of the House of York deposed Henry VI of the House of Lancaster and reigned as Edward IV. Henry reseized the throne, only to lose it again in 1471.

Edward IV takes over from Henry VI in Shakespeare's third play of Henry VI's reign, but he doesn't get a play of his own. After Edward IV's death, his brother Richard III seized the throne in 1483; he held the throne for two short years and warranted one play. His death marked the end of the civil war.

From Richard III to Henry VIII is a small jump, skipping the peaceful reign of Henry VII. Henry VIII's reign was tempestuous, and he is best known today for going through six wives, and known even more for divorcing or beheading most of them. His second daughter, Elizabeth, later became Queen of England, and Shakespeare was careful to paint Elizabeth and her mother, Anne Boleyn, in a good light when he wrote *King Henry VIII*.

If you find the family relationships hard to follow, peek ahead to Figure 14-1, which depicts a genealogy of the kings of England.

The politics are complicated, but one element always attracts interest: Who succeeds the king? Today, England retains its hereditary monarchy, where the current king or queen's child becomes the next king or queen. If a king dies without any children, though, matters get more complicated. It's hard to envision anyone going to war today over who will be king, but 600 years ago, the King of England had much more power than today's monarch. He could raise an army, tax his subjects, and even decide who could or could not marry whom.

Fairy Tales

Many of Shakespeare's tragedies and comedies are like fairy tales. Imogen's wicked stepmother in *Cymbeline* seems like she stepped out of *Cinderella*. Ferdinand in *The Tempest* is Miranda's Prince Charming. The stories are unreal or even outrageous. In Shakespeare's stories, magic, fairies, ghosts, and witches are as real as the people. To his audience, ghosts were real in a way that a modern audience finds hard to believe. On the other hand, modern audiences are more apt to believe in visitors from other planets than was Shakespeare's audience. If Shakespeare were writing plays today, he might have the three witches in *Macbeth* be space aliens who abduct and probe Macbeth before releasing him.

With or without magic, Shakespeare's plays stretch reality. To make sense of his plays, you must enter the theater believing in two things: love at first sight and divine justice.

Love at first sight

Especially in the comedies, two people might meet for the first time and fall immediately, desperately, and completely in love. This rarely happens in real life, but it's common in Shakespeare's plays. Sometimes, magic is involved, whether it's Prospero's magic to bring Ferdinand and Miranda together in *The Tempest* or a magic elixir that Oberon drops in Titania's eyes in *A Midsummer Night's Dream*. Sometimes, though, the lovers have no need of magic. When Romeo first sets eyes on Juliet and Juliet beholds Romeo, Shakespeare does not employ magic, spirits, or fairies. All he asks is that you, the audience, believe in love at first sight.

Shakespeare chose his themes well, and this particular one has remained popular throughout the ages. Books, films, television, advertisements — entire industries — spring from the fundamental notion that a boy and a girl can exchange glances and have their lives forever changed. It works in perfume commercials; why not plays, too?

Divine justice

In every one of Shakespeare's plays, the villains are always caught and punished. From the very beginning of any play, you can have faith that, even if the tragic heroes do not live happily ever after, they will see justice done on the villains. The characters always make mistakes, sometimes fatal mistakes. Often, the villains seem literally to get away with murder. But they are always caught in the end.

To a modern audience, believing in divine justice requires a bigger stretch of the imagination than does believing in love at first sight. More often, we believe that the Goddess Justice has left the Earth, as does Titus Andronicus (*"Terras Astraea reliquit" Titus Andronicus* 4.3.4). So it is that the most fairy tale-like element of Shakespeare's plays is Justice. You may not know how, but from the start of the play, you know that the villains will be unmasked. What was wrong will be put right. You can interpret this as divine justice. Even if the gods and goddesses do not intervene directly, you can have faith that justice will be served by the end of the play.

Fate and destiny

You may think that knowing how a play ends robs you of some of the excitement, but that isn't the case with Shakespeare's plays. Watching *Romeo and Juliet* may lack some suspense if you know that they both die in the end, but that doesn't make the play less interesting. Quite the opposite: Knowing the final fate of the characters can be comforting. Fate and destiny play important roles in many of Shakespeare's plays.

In every play, you know that justice always prevails on the villains. In the comedies, you also know that the heroes will come out okay in the end. An invisible hand seems to shape and order events so that everything comes out just right. In *Much Ado About Nothing,* for example, the nasty Don John tricks Claudio into denouncing Hero, his love and intended wife. By a stroke of luck, the night watchmen overhear Don John's accomplices discussing their dirty work, so all their plans unravel. In the end, Don John is captured, Claudio and Hero are reunited, and the lovers marry and live happily ever after.

As you can see, justice is not the only force at work behind the scenes. Every character has a destiny but also has a free will to make decisions that affect his or her life. These two forces seem to conflict, but Shakespeare offers a solution to this dilemma in Hamlet's lines:

Our indiscretion sometime serves us well

When our deep plots do pall; and that should learn us

There's a divinity that shapes our ends,

Rough-hew them how we will. (*Hamlet* 5.2.8–11)

In other words, characters are free to make some choices ("rough-hew" their ends), but they cannot escape their ultimate destiny. In Hamlet's case, he is the tragic hero, so you know his destiny from the start — to learn an important lesson but to die in the final act. Figure 7-1 shows Mel Gibson as Hamlet.

Figure 7-1:
Mel Gibson
in *Hamlet,*
directed by
Franco
Zeffirelli.

Everett Collection

Uncovering Shakespeare's Sources

It may seem as though every new movie is just a remake of an older movie, a sequel to an earlier hit, or a copy of someone else's blockbuster film. Things have changed little over the centuries. Shakespeare copied stories and characters from other plays and wrote sequels to successful plays. He even invented a new play *(The Merry Wives of Windsor)* centered around Sir John Falstaff because that character was so popular.

If you tried to make a new movie today by copying someone else's movie and just cleaning up the dialogue a little, you would find yourself on the losing end of a copyright lawsuit. Not so in Shakespeare's day, when copying was a form of flattery. Shakespeare borrowed his stories from mythology, ancient Greek and Roman plays and fables, and other plays and stories written by his contemporaries. He knew a good story when he saw one, and he felt free to take the good parts and leave behind the boring bits.

A favorite technique of Shakespeare's was to weave two stories into a single play. The rules for tragedy required a single plot, but Shakespeare knew that having multiple, intersecting plots often makes a better, more interesting play. Thus most of his plays — comedies, tragedies, and histories — feature multiple plots. *(The Comedy of Errors* is a counterexample. It is probably Shakespeare's first comedy, and the plot is simple. Read the summary in Chapter 13.) The first two acts set up the stories, which intersect in the middle of the play and come together in the final act.

For example, Shakespeare's main source for *The Two Gentlemen of Verona* is Jorge de Montemayor's *Diana Enamorada.* Montemayor's story unfolds around a young man who pledges his love to one girl only to fall in love with another. The other rejects his love, and eventually he returns to his former love.

To make the story more interesting, Shakespeare added another male character. The two men are friends. Proteus loves Julia, and Valentine loves Sylvia. But then Proteus falls in love with Sylvia. By adding Valentine to the story, Shakespeare improved it. The two boys feud over the girl, and Proteus plots against Valentine and even manages to turn the duke (Sylvia's father) against him, forcing Valentine into exile. Shakespeare picked up the second story from an Italian play, *Flavio Betrayed,* by Flaminio Scala. We will never know why Shakespeare decided to mix these two stories, but we can be thankful that he did. The resulting play is livelier than either of his sources, and the characters are more interesting.

For the history plays, Shakespeare usually followed Holinshed's *The Chronicles of England, Scotland, and Ireland* as his main historical source. Holinshed first published his chronicles in 1577, so they were fresh and new for Shakespeare's use. Holinshed included some mythological kings with his historical kings. They were not true kings of England, so *Cymbeline* and *King Lear* are not really histories, despite the fact that Holinshed thought they were true kings of ancient England.

Chapter 8

Shakespeare's People: Characters, Actors, and Audiences

- -

In This Chapter

▶ Shakespeare's characters are as varied as his plays

▶ In Shakespeare's day, boys played women's roles

▶ Shakespeare's audiences were also a mixed crowd

- -

Shakespeare usually followed the convention that great things happen only to great people, and therefore great leaders — kings, queens, and generals — were the proper subjects for his "great" plays. Nonetheless, he found ample opportunity to add servants, beggars, and ordinary people, as well as witches, monsters, fairies, and even the occasional god from classical mythology. In this chapter, you can find out about the people of Shakespeare's day: the characters who inhabit Shakespeare's plays, the actors who portrayed them, and the audiences who watched the plays.

Cabbages and Kings

In Shakespeare's day and today, the average playgoer doesn't usually get the chance to hobnob with the ruling king or queen. Then, as now, the average person lived the glamorous life vicariously through popular entertainment. Modern television shows take the viewer inside the boardroom and the bedroom; Shakespeare's plays take you inside the palace and show you what life is like on the other side.

King Henry V gives a telling glimpse of life as a king. He wants Princess Katherine of France to marry him and asks to kiss her. She demurs, saying that it is not the custom to kiss before marriage. But he responds:

O Kate, nice customs curtsy to great kings. Dear Kate, you and I cannot be confined within the weak list of a country's fashion. We are the makers of manners, Kate. (*Henry V* 5.2.266–69)

Attending the noble characters are lords and ladies, in accordance with the status of the nobility. Kings get dukes, earls, and barons as attendants. Dukes get a lesser number of knights and lords, and so on down the chain. (You can read about the natural pecking order in Chapter 2.) The history plays are especially crowded with dukes, duchesses, lords, and ladies of all shapes and sizes.

In the modern world, we believe that everyone is created equal, but in Shakespeare's day some people were "more equal than others." The natural order dictated that a person nobly born was inherently superior to a commoner. (You can find out more about the natural order in Chapter 2.) Although a king without his fancy clothes would look like anyone else, Shakespeare and his audience believed that an inborn quality separated the nobility from everyone else. For example, Belarius, a British lord who kidnaps the sons of King Cymbeline, notices that the noble sons behave nobly, even though they were raised as outlaws in the wild:

How hard it is to hide the sparks of Nature!

These boys know little they are sons to th' king,

Nor Cymbeline dreams that they are alive.

They think they are mine, and though train'd up thus meanly,

I'th' cave wherein they bow, their thoughts do hit

The roofs of palaces, and Nature prompts them

In simple and low things to prince it, much

Beyond the trick of others. (*Cymbeline* 3.3.79–86)

Common Folk

Shakespeare came from middle-class roots, and his depictions of middle-class and lower-class characters range from the sensitive to the outrageous. In *As You Like It,* for example, he portrays an old shepherd in an idealized light:

I am a true labourer: I earn that I eat, get that I wear; owe no man hate, envy no man's happiness; glad of other men's good, content with my harm; and the greatest of my pride is to see my ewes graze and my lambs suck. (3.1.70–74)

Shakespeare is less kind to crowds and mobs in *Coriolanus, Julius Caesar,* and other plays. For example, Jack Cade leads a peasant revolt in *King Henry VI, Part 2.* He makes absurd promises, such as:

there shall be no money; all shall eat and drink on my score (4.2.70–71)

The mob eagerly follows Cade and his ridiculous commands, even executing a clerk for the "crime" of knowing how to read and write. Shakespeare often depicts mobs as fickle and easily swayed by powerful — and sometimes unscrupulous — leaders. In *Coriolanus,* for example, the crowd praises Coriolanus and elects him Consul:

7th Citizen. Therefore let him be consul. The gods give him joy, and make him good friend to the people!

All citizens. Amen, amen. God save thee, noble consul! (2.3.133–35)

Two petty-minded officials who are jealous of Coriolanus work the crowd and try to change its collective mind. A short 70 lines later, they have done their job and turned the mob around:

3rd Citizen. . . . we may deny him yet.

2nd Citizen. And will deny him!

I'll have five hundred voices of that sound. (2.3.207–9)

Shakespeare goes even further and brings in beggars, thieves, and other lowlifes to brighten up his plays. For example, Autolycus, in *The Winter's Tale,* is a rogue, pickpocket, and thief. He discusses his profession as follows:

To have an open ear, a quick eye, and a nimble hand, is necessary for a cut-purse; a good nose is requisite also, to smell out work for the other senses. I see this is the time that the unjust man doth thrive. (4.4.672–76)

Autolycus is not a villain, but a colorful rogue. His antics contrast with the honest toiling of the country folk. In the end, he accidentally helps the lost Princess Perdita discover her heritage, so she can marry her true love and live happily ever after.

Fools and Clowns

The fool, or clown, holds a special position in Shakespeare's plays. The fool is an entertainer, singer, dancer, and musician, but mostly a master at word-play and verbal wit. Far from being foolish, the fool is intelligent and talented. Shakespeare's fools would do well in modern stand-up comedy acts. (See Chapter 5 for more information about the jokes and verbal games that fools often employed.)

Feste in *Twelfth Night* describes fools as follows:

Viola. Art not thou the Lady Olivia's fool?

Clown. No indeed sir, the Lady Olivia has no folly. She will keep no fool, sir, till she be married, and fools are as like husbands as pilchards are to herrings, the husband's the bigger. I am indeed not her fool, but her corrupter of words. (3.1.32–37)

Some of Shakespeare's most famous roles are the clowns and fools. For example, King Lear has a fool who is often wiser than the king, and the king more foolish than the fool. (Figure 8-1 shows Lear and the Fool in a performance by the Oregon Shakespeare Festival.)

Figure 8-1: Denis Arndt as King Lear and James Edmondson as the Fool.

Henry S. Kranzler

The fool also has special dispensation to poke fun at the king or queen and to dare to speak the truth. No one else can do that and get away with it. King Lear disinherits his loyal daughter Cordelia and divides his kingdom in two halves for his nasty daughters, against the advice of the Earl of Kent. Lear's Fool sees the truth and has this to say:

Fool. That lord that counselled thee to give away thy land,

Come place him here by me; do thou for him stand.

The sweet and bitter fool will presently appear,

The one in motley here, the other found out there.

Lear. Dost thou call me fool, boy?

Fool. All thy other titles thou hast given away; that thou wast born with.

Kent. This is not altogether fool, my lord.

Fool. No, faith, lords and great men will not let me; if I had a monopoly out, they would have part on't; and ladies too, they will not let me have all fool to myself, they'll be snatching. (*King Lear* 1.4.137–48)

Fools often provide social commentary, saying the truth that is so obvious but unsettling that no one else dares to mention it. Because the fool comments on human foibles, his comments are just as pertinent (or impertinent) today as they were 400 years ago. For example, Touchstone describes the seven degrees of quarreling as follows:

O sir, we quarrel in print, by the book; as you have books for good manners. I will name you the degrees. The first, the Retort Courteous; the second, the Quip Modest; the third, the Reply Churlish; the fourth, the Reproof Valiant; the fifth, the Countercheck Quarrelsome; the sixth, the Lie with Circumstance; the seventh, the Lie Direct. All these you may avoid but the Lie Direct; and you may avoid that too, with an If. I knew when seven justices could not take up a quarrel, but when the parties were met themselves, one of them thought but of an If, as, 'If you said so, then I said so'. And they shook hands and swore brothers. Your If is the only peacemaker: much virtue in If. (*As You Like It* 5.4.89–101)

The next time you watch a political debate, notice how the politicians never stop quarreling. Some things never change.

Fairies, Witches, and Magic — Oh My!

Not all of Shakespeare's characters are human. Witches, spirits, ghosts, magicians, and gods also populate his plays. The most interesting and enigmatic of Shakespeare's witches are the three weird sisters of *Macbeth*, who incite Macbeth to pursue the crown:

1 Witch. All hail, Macbeth! hail to thee, Thane of Glamis!

2 Witch. All hail, Macbeth! hail to thee, Thane of Cawdor!

3 Witch. All hail, Macbeth! that shalt be King hereafter.

. . .

Macbeth. Stay, you imperfect speakers, tell me more.

By Sinel's death I know I am Thane of Glamis;

But how of Cawdor? the Thane of Cawdor lives,

A prosperous gentleman; and to be King

Stands not within the prospect of belief,

No more than to be Cawdor. (1.3.48–75)

Immediately after the witches vanish, Macbeth learns that he has earned the title Thane of Cawdor. He and his wife decide that he should be king, too, at whatever cost. Did the witches merely predict the future, or did they cause the future to happen? Without the appearance of the witches, Macbeth would never have dreamt of murdering his king. Or would he have? Shakespeare doesn't give any easy answers.

Magic also plays a major role in *The Tempest,* but in a different way. Where the witches manipulate Macbeth indirectly, the magician Prospero takes direct control over his island. Although he is human, he moves and manipulates people and events with supernatural ease, like a grand master playing a game of chess. He conjures up a storm that sets the entire play in motion and keeps the play moving with his power:

. . . to the dread rattling thunder

Have I given fire, and rifted Jove's stout oak

With his own bolt; the strong-bas'd promontory

Have I made shake, and by the spurs pluck'd up

The pine and cedar: graves at my command

Have wak'd their sleepers, op'd, and let 'em forth

By my so potent Art. (5.1.44–50)

The fairies in *A Midsummer Night's Dream* represent yet another kind of magical character. A dispute between the King and Queen of the Fairies bubbles over into the real world. A mischievous sprite, Puck sows discord and chaos to his — and the audience's — amusement. Puck sums up the attitude of the fairies with his observation: "Lord, what fools these mortals be!" (3.2.115).

The ghost of Hamlet's father is a well-known character, but ghosts also play a role in the history plays. When Henry, Earl of Richmond, prepares to face King Richard III at Bosworth Field, the opposing leaders are visited by ghostly dreams. Richard is haunted by the ghosts of his victims, whereas the same ghosts offer words of comfort to Richmond. For example, the ghost of Clarence, Richard's brother, visits both leaders the night before the battle:

[to King Richard]

Let me sit heavy in thy soul tomorrow —

I, that was wash'd to death with fulsome wine,

Poor Clarence, by thy guile betray'd to death —

Tomorrow in the battle think on me,

And fall thy edgeless sword; despair and die.

[to Richmond] Thou offspring of the House of Lancaster,

The wronged heirs of York do pray for thee.

Good angels guard thy battle; live and flourish. (*Richard III* 5.3.132–39)

Richmond has supernatural reinforcements, so you know that he will win the battle the next day and become King Henry VII.

Ghosts also appear in *Cymbeline,* seeking to aid their still-living relative, Posthumus. Jupiter, king of the ancient Roman gods, makes a grand entrance to rebuke and pacify the ghosts.

Jupiter descends in thunder and lightning, sitting upon an eagle: he throws a thunderbolt. The Ghosts fall on their knees.

Jupiter. No more, you petty spirits of region low,

Offend our hearing: hush! How dare you ghosts

Accuse the thunderer, whose bolt (you know)

Sky-planted, batters all rebelling coasts? (5.4.93–96)

Although magic and fairies play major roles in a few plays, most of Shakespeare's plays don't need magic. Real life is weird enough. Instead of black magic and ghosts, the plays rely on everyday magic, such as love at first sight.

Lovers and Warriors

The most common character types are warriors and lovers, and sometimes one character is both.

Romeo and Juliet are probably Shakespeare's best-known lovers, but Shakespeare wrote many other plays about and for lovers. *The Winter's Tale,* for example, intertwines two stories of love against all odds. Florizel, a Prince of Bohemia, is in love with Perdita, a simple shepherdess. He would defy his father, the king, to be with his beloved:

. . . Or I'll be thine, my fair,

Or not my father's. For I cannot be

Mine own, nor anything to any, if

I be not thine. To this I am most constant,

Though destiny say no. (4.4.42–46)

It turns out that Perdita is actually the long-lost daughter of the King and Queen of Sicilia, Leontes and Hermione, so Perdita and Florizel can get married after all.

The other love story demonstrates the kinds of problems a married couple might have. Leontes' irrational, jealous rage overflows and kills his wife, or so it seems. She cannot live among her husband's lies, and she feigns death for 16 years. Her love is steadfast, though, and she waits patiently until her daughter is found, and her husband repents of his grave mistakes. (Read a summary of *The Winter's Tale* in Chapter 13.)

Modern audiences might prefer to give the scumbag the heave-ho, but in Shakespeare's world, love conquers all. Even soldiers can be passionate, tender lovers. For example, after defeating the French army, King Henry V undertakes his next conquest — Katherine, Princess of France — with words of love:

Henry. Fair Katherine, and most fair,

Will you vouchsafe to teach a soldier terms

Such as will enter at a lady's ear

And plead his love-suit to her gentle heart?

Katherine. Your majesty shall mock at me; I cannot speak your England.

Henry. O fair Katherine, if you will love me soundly with your French heart I will be glad to hear you confess it brokenly with your English tongue. Do you like me, Kate?

Katherine. Pardonnez-moi, I cannot tell vat is 'like me.'

Henry. An angel is like you, Kate, and you are like an angel. (*Henry V* 5.2.98–110)

Shakespeare also manages to arrange one of the most ironic relationships between the ever-feuding Beatrice and Benedick. *Much Ado About Nothing* opens with Beatrice's biting sarcasm directed against Benedick. Whenever they are onstage together, they engage in verbal battles. They are the least likely of lovers, but with the help of forged love letters, they give in to their love, in spite of themselves:

Benedick. Do not you love me?

Beatrice. Why, no, no more than reason.

Benedick. Why then, your uncle, and the Prince, and Claudio

Have been deceiv'd — they swore you did.

Beatrice. Do not you love me?

Benedick. Troth, no, no more than reason.

Beatrice. Why then, my cousin, Margaret, and Ursula

Are much deceiv'd, for they did swear you did.

Benedick. They swore that you were almost sick for me.

Beatrice. They swore that you were well-nigh dead for me.

Benedick. 'Tis no such matter. Then you do not love me?

Beatrice. No, truly, but in friendly recompense.

. . .

Benedick. Come, I will have thee, but by this light I take thee for pity.

Beatrice. I would not deny you, but by this good day I yield upon great persuasion, and partly to save your life, for I was told you were in a consumption. (*Much Ado About Nothing* 5.4.74–96)

Where Are the Women?

You may think that Shakespeare had talented actresses to play the roles of Juliet, Beatrice, and all the other lovers, queens, and madwomen who grace his plays. He didn't. Instead, talented, prepubescent boys played the women's roles.

In the modern world, the lack of female characters in Shakespeare's plays stands out. The problem for Shakespeare was that women were not allowed onstage. Actors and prostitutes were often treated similarly, so the restriction against actresses was considered a moral issue. Because of the ban against women, boys usually played the women's roles. For obvious reasons, a boy could play young women for a limited time before he would have to graduate to men's roles. Men possibly played some of the older women's roles, such as Juliet's nurse. Shakespeare brings up this point in a couple of his plays. For example, Hamlet welcomes the players and specifically greets the boy who plays the women's roles:

What, my young lady and mistress! By'r lady, your ladyship is nearer to heaven than when I saw you last by the altitude of a chopine*. Pray God your voice, like a piece of uncurrent gold, be not cracked within the ring. (*Hamlet* 2.2.425–30)

*elevated shoe

In *A Midsummer Night's Dream,* Peter Quince hands out the roles for a play and assigns the part of Thisbe to Francis Flute, whose name suggests that his voice is still high-pitched and unbroken:

Quince. Flute, you must take Thisbe on you.

Flute. What is Thisbe? A wandering knight?

Quince. It is the lady that Pyramus must love.

Flute. Nay, faith, let not me play a woman: I have a beard coming. (1.2.41–45)

Good acting requires experience and practice, so it was undoubtedly difficult to find boys who could act well. Thus Shakespeare's plays have few female roles. Nonetheless, he must have found at least one boy with tremendous talent. Some of Shakespeare's best roles are female roles, from Lady Macbeth to Queen Margaret in the *Henry VI* history plays. Some plays have two major women's roles, calling for two boys with acting talent, such as Beatrice and Hero in *Much Ado About Nothing* or Helena and Hermia in *A Midsummer Night's Dream*.

Shakespeare made life a little easier for boy actors by writing parts in which the female characters dress up as males. Here are some examples:

- ✔ Rosalind disguises herself as a boy, Ganymede, in *As You Like It*.

- ✔ Imogen disguises herself as a boy in *Cymbeline*.

- ✔ Viola dresses as a boy and calls herself Cesario in *Twelfth Night*.

- ✔ Julia dresses as a boy to follow Proteus in *The Two Gentlemen of Verona*.

- ✔ Jessica briefly disguises herself as a boy to escape from her father in *The Merchant of Venice*.

Unlike today — when a person's clothing does not necessarily tell you anything about that person's gender — in Shakespeare's day, women and men wore very different clothing. If a person wore a dress, that person was a woman. If the person wore tights, breeches, or something similar, that person was a man. Onstage, the same conventions applied: The audience accepted that any character wearing a dress was a woman, even if a boy played that character. When a female character dressed in men's clothing, "she" looked like a man, or at least like a boy.

In his plays, Shakespeare made the most of boys playing women playing boys. The fashion of Shakespeare's day was for men to wear beards — an accouterment that the female characters naturally lacked. Shakespeare used beards as the subject of jokes, such as Viola's lack of a beard when she is dressed as Cesario in *Twelfth Night:*

Clown. Now Jove, in his next commodity of hair, send thee a beard!

Viola. By my troth, I'll tell thee, I am almost sick for one, *[aside]* though I would not have it grow on my chin. (3.1.45–49)

Shakespeare on acting

When a traveling acting troupe visits Elsinore, Hamlet commissions a play that he hopes will trick the king into betraying his guilt. Before the play, Hamlet advises the actors on their trade. Over the centuries, scholars have debated whether Hamlet's advice is really Shakespeare's advice. We will never know Shakespeare's intent when he wrote these lines, but they remain excellent advice for aspiring actors:

> Suit the action to the word, the word to the action, with this special observance, that you o'erstep not the modesty of nature. For anything so o'erdone is from the purpose of playing, whose end, both at the first and now, was and is to hold as 'twere the mirror up to nature; to show virtue her feature, scorn her own image, and the very age and body of the time his form and pressure. (*Hamlet* 3.2.18–25)

Actors coming to Shakespeare for the first time have a tendency to overdo things. Modern society has an unfortunate stereotype of a man in black tights, exercising verbal acrobatics as he says, "To be, or not to be, that is the question." Shakespeare doesn't have to be that way. Instead, actors should heed Hamlet's advice:

> Speak the speech, I pray you, as I pronounced it to you, trippingly on the tongue; but if you mouth it as many of your players do, I had as lief the town-crier spoke my lines. Nor do not saw the air too much with your hand, thus, but use all gently. (*Hamlet* 3.2.1–5)

In other words, don't get carried away, but speak plainly and simply. Of course, you should also make sure that you understand the words and the verse, which you can read more about in Chapter 6.

The Audience

Shakespeare's audiences were as varied as his characters. In the Globe Theatre, the audiences ranged from poor commoners to wealthy aristocrats. Although women could not perform onstage, they were welcome in the audience. If you could afford the tickets, you could sit in the galleries around the edge of the theater. The cheap tickets (one penny) let you stand on the ground level, around the stage. The holders of the cheap tickets were called *groundlings,* as in this quotation from *Hamlet:*

O, it offends me to the soul to hear a robustious periwig-pated fellow tear a passion to tatters, to very rags, to split the ears of the groundlings, who for the most part are capable of nothing but inexplicable dumb-shows and noise. (3.2.8–13)

We don't know exactly what it was like to watch a play in the Globe Theatre of Shakespeare's day. The audience probably was livelier than today's theater-going crowd, but less rowdy than, say, the audience at a monster truck rally. Unlike the darkened theaters of today, the Globe Theatre was open to the air, and the performances took place during the day. The daylight certainly made it easier for the audience to be festive. The audience could buy concessions, not unlike what you find at a modern sporting event.

Shakespeare also wrote plays for indoor theater, the Blackfriars. Tickets cost more at the Blackfriars — 6 pence for the cheap seats, up to half a crown (30 pence) for a box seat — and everyone got to sit down. The indoor stage was lit by candlelight, and the theater was much smaller than the Globe. The expensive tickets and the indoor setting probably resulted in a more dignified audience at the Blackfriars than at the Globe.

Shakespeare and his company also performed for Queen Elizabeth and later for King James. Of course, the monarchs would not come to the theater; instead, the theater went to the monarchs. The king or queen regularly hired performers and entertainers of all sorts, even actors.

Performing for royalty or a noble patron was part of the normal work of an acting troupe in Shakespeare's day. Every troupe needed a patron to lend legitimacy to the actors and their work, and the troupes were known by their patrons' names. Shakespeare wrote for and acted in The Chamberlain's Men for most of his career. Their patron was the Lord Chamberlain, the highest-ranking nobleman of the royal court. After King James ascended the throne in 1603, he adopted the troupe and they became The King's Men. The patron did not pay the actors, but the patron's status reflected on the troupe's status. In exchange, a good acting troupe reflected well on the patron's taste in the arts, and the actors could provide entertainment on command. Even today, theaters depend on the support of wealthy patrons, but those patrons are corporations as well as individuals.

Chapter 9

Use Your Imagination

In This Chapter

▶ Understanding Shakespeare's verbal pictures

▶ Unleashing your imagination

A performance — in a film, on television, or onstage — brings together the collective imaginations of many people: the director; the actors; the designers of lighting, costumes, and sets; and others. When you *read* a play, though, you're on your own. Well, not entirely on your own; you have the companionship of the author. Shakespeare painted vivid pictures with his words, and you can use those words and pictures to bring the plays to life in your "mind's eye" (*Hamlet* 1.2.185).

This chapter helps you get the most out of reading or watching Shakespeare's plays by using the power of your imagination.

Getting a Picture from a Thousand (Or Fewer) Words

Shakespeare wrote scripts for the stage, not books to be read silently. Unlike plays, novels and short stories explicitly describe the characters and their settings. The narrative often takes you inside a character's mind, revealing inner thoughts and feelings. Reading Shakespeare's plays is different. A few stage directions may tell you the rudimentary actions, such as who enters or leaves the stage, but everything else comes from the words that the characters speak.

The words, therefore, must make visible what is otherwise invisible: They describe the setting and scenery, explain any action that preceded the start of the play, relate events that take place offstage, and tell you about thoughts and feelings. For example, in *A Midsummer Night's Dream,* the play's title and many of the lines invoke images of nighttime, sleep, and dreaming. In particular, near the end of the play, Puck says,

If we shadows have offended,

Think but this, and all is mended,

That you have but slumber'd here

While these visions did appear. (5.1.417–20)

A director can reinforce the words with sets and other visual elements that portray the same images. Figure 9-1 shows an example of such a production at the Oregon Shakespeare Festival.

Setting and scenery

Modern audiences expect films and television shows to have realistic settings, but Shakespeare's audience had no such expectations. Without elaborate sets and scenery, Shakespeare relied on the actors to establish the location for each scene. Thus when Rosalind and Celia escape to the forest, Rosalind states, "Well, this is the Forest of Arden" (*As You Like It* 2.4.13).

Shakespeare often used the convention of having characters mention their locale. Characters also greet each other by name, so the audience can easily tell who's who. When Petruchio arrives in Padua to find a wife, for example, he first visits his friend Hortensio:

Figure 9-1: *A Midsummer Night's Dream* invokes images of sleep and dreams. (Ray Porter plays Puck.)

A. Lanthier.

Verona, for a while I take my leave,

To see my friends in Padua, but of all

My best beloved and approved friend,

Hortensio; and I trow this is his house. (*The Taming of the Shrew* 1.2.1–4)

The exact setting isn't always important. The setting for most of *Julius Caesar* is the city of Rome. Different scenes take place at different times in different parts of Rome, but Shakespeare doesn't tell you exactly when or where — except when the setting is important. For example, the conspirators must ensure that Caesar goes to the Senate, where they plan to murder him. The reader and the audience must know when Caesar leaves home. The scenery onstage does not establish which scene takes place at his home and which scenes take place at the Senate, so the characters must establish the setting. Caesar's wife, Calphurnia, tells you that they are at home:

What mean you, Caesar? Think you to walk forth?

You shall not stir out of your house to-day. (2.2.8–9)

Then the action moves to the street between Caesar's home and the Senate. A character establishes the setting in a brief scene, saying, "Here will I stand till Caesar pass along" (2.3.1).

Other times, when the exact setting is not important, Shakespeare describes the environment without naming a particular place. For example, in *Henry VI, Part 3,* two hunters tell you where they are and what they're doing. Although they don't specify a particular location (which isn't relevant to the play), they do give you an important piece of information: that they're hiding. So when King Henry VI wanders onstage a few lines later, you aren't surprised that he doesn't see them.

Under this thick-grown brake we'll shroud ourselves,

For through his laund anon the deer will come;

And in this covert will we make our stand,

Culling the principal of all the deer. (3.1.1–4)

The time of day or night is sometimes part of the setting. If the time isn't important, Shakespeare doesn't mention it, and you usually can't tell whether a scene takes place in the morning or evening, during the day or at night. If the time is important to the scene, Shakespeare lets you know. When Romeo and Juliet must part company, for example, Shakespeare vividly describes the morning:

It was the lark, the herald of the morn,

No nightingale. Look, love, what envious streaks

Do lace the severing clouds in yonder east. (3.5.6–8)

Nothing more than feelings

Shakespeare's characters don't just tell you where they are; they also tell you how they feel. For example, Edward has chased King Henry VI out of England, but Henry can't stay away. He loves his land and his people too much to be parted from them, and he sneaks back, only to be captured. His captors ask him, if he is King, where is his crown, and he answers:

My crown is in my heart, not on my head;

Not deck'd with diamonds and Indian stones,

Nor to be seen: my crown is call'd content;

A crown it is that seldom kings enjoy. (*3 Henry VI* 3.1.62–65)

These lines tell you a lot about Henry's attitude toward his predicament. He's caught in a maelstrom of political intrigue and warfare, but through it all, he maintains his piety. He accepts the role God has given him, and so he remains "content." (To understand the political situation, read about *King Henry VI, Part 3* in Chapter 14.)

Characters often reveal their inner thoughts by talking directly to the audience, or at least to no one in particular onstage. Speaking one's thoughts aloud is a theatrical convention called a *soliloquy*. A soliloquy is similar to a novel's narrative that tells you how a character thinks or feels. In a film or television performance of a Shakespeare play, an actor might deliver a soliloquy as a voice-over, in which you hear the voice of the actor, but the character you see on-screen does not speak.

Shakespeare's most famous soliloquy is Hamlet's "To be, or not to be" speech (*Hamlet* 3.1.56–89). Hamlet has several soliloquies, and through his soliloquies, you can see how his inner character changes and grows throughout the play. Hamlet starts as a poster child for Prozac:

O that this too too sullied flesh would melt,

Thaw and resolve itself into a dew,

Or that the Everlasting had not fix'd

His canon 'gainst self-slaughter. O God! God!

How weary, stale, flat, and unprofitable

Seem to me all the uses of this world! (1.2.129–34)

By Act 3, Hamlet wonders, "To be, or not to be?" He still ponders suicide, but now he thinks that maybe living is better than dying, asking whether

the dread of something after death,

The undiscover'd country, from whose bourn

No traveller returns, puzzles the will,

And makes us rather bear those ills we have

Than fly to others that we know not of? (3.1.78–82)

Near the end of the play, Hamlet has changed his tune. He is ready to take revenge for his father's murder:

O, from this time forth

My thoughts be bloody or be nothing worth. (4.4.65–66)

The Power of Images

Shakespeare tells you what's going on in his characters' minds by letting the characters voice their thoughts, but he also paints pictures indirectly. For example, while Hamlet waits for his father's ghost to appear, he and Horatio fall to small talk and discuss the weather. Instead of just saying, "It is very cold," Shakespeare uses more graphic language:

Hamlet. The air bites shrewdly, it is very cold.

Horatio. It is a nipping and an eager air. (*Hamlet* 1.4.1–2)

When you enjoy the play, imagine that it's cold out, but more than cold; the air nips and bites. Shakespeare creates an image of an animal biting, which is much more interesting than just saying that it's cold out. Poetry uses images to convey ideas, and Shakespeare's plays are a form of poetry.

Richard II contains another great image. Henry Bolingbroke returns from exile to claim his rightful inheritance as Duke of Lancaster, and on the way, he heads

To Bristow castle, which they say is held

By Bushy, Bagot, and their complices,

The caterpillars of the commonwealth,

Which I have sworn to weed and pluck away. (2.3.163–66)

Henry wants to capture the knights Bushy and Bagot, but Shakespeare's words tell you more. Imagine caterpillars infesting your garden, eating the leaves off every plant. Shakespeare paints a picture of Henry the gardener, ridding the kingdom of thousands of caterpillars. Imagine how easy it is to pick up a caterpillar and fling it away. The language tells you that Henry thinks it will be just as easy to deal with Bushy and Bagot.

Shakespeare's plays are full of colorful images. Understanding the images helps you understand the characters, the plot, and the entire play. When you watch a play, the actors and director choose which images to emphasize and which to portray vividly in the lighting, scenery, costumes, and behavior of the actors. When you read a play, let your mind roam free.

Read Julius Caesar's description of Cassius, for example, and imagine what Cassius looks like. Caesar refers not only to Cassius's physical appearance but also to his behavior. He says that Cassius "has a lean and hungry look" (1.2.191), and that

Seldom he smiles, and smiles in such a sort

As if he mock'd himself, and scorn'd his spirit

That could be mov'd to smile at any thing. (*Julius Caesar* 1.2.202–4).

Sometimes, Shakespeare's images are more fanciful than real. For example, when the Earl of Salisbury sees the fate of King Richard II (who is about to be deposed by Henry Bolingbroke), he laments

Ah, Richard! with the eyes of heavy mind

I see thy glory like a shooting star

Fall to the base earth from the firmament.

Thy sun sets weeping in the lowly west,

Witnessing storms to come, woe, and unrest. (*Richard II* 2.4.18–22)

Do you see the night sky with a shooting star? The sunset? What do you imagine when you read the words "sun sets weeping"? Shakespeare paints pictures with his words, but everyone sees something slightly different. A literal-minded person doesn't ordinarily think of the sun weeping, but with a little practice, anyone can do it.

Drawing on Your Imagination

Roughly speaking, the left half of your brain understands words, and the right half of your brain interprets pictures. To get the most out of Shakespeare's plays — or any play — you need to get the two parts of your brain talking to each other. For some people, this is easy, but the rest of us need a little coaxing. The following sections give you some activities that can help you use your imagination to the fullest when reading Shakespeare.

Draw as a group or on your own

Here's an activity that you can use to unleash your artistic potential. This is a group activity, so you want to work with students in a class, actors in a play, or just some friends who want to have fun together. Each group should have about four to six people in it. If you're among seven friends, you might prefer to work in a single, large group.

Pick one person to read a short section from a play. Choose a passage that you can understand when hearing it. If you need to look up a few words, do so, and make sure that everyone understands the passage. To start, pick a passage that's about 10 to 20 lines long. For example, you may want to start with the prologue to *Romeo and Juliet.* If you're performing a play and want to examine it in more depth, pick a series of key sections from the play and work on them one at a time.

We'll use the opening speech from *Richard III* as an example. For brevity's sake, only the first four lines are shown below, but you should use at least the first thirteen lines:

Now is the winter of our discontent

Made glorious summer by this son of York;

And all the clouds that lour'd upon our House

In the deep bosom of the ocean buried. (1.1.1–4)

Give everyone a blank sheet of paper, the larger the better, and something to draw with. You can use a pencil, a pen, or even paintbrushes if you don't mind getting a little messy. You also need blindfolds for everyone (except the reader). Or if you don't want to use blindfolds, you can close your eyes.

Listen while the reader reads and repeats the passage. The reader should read quietly and simply, and let the words speak for themselves. Don't think about the words, but hear them and try to draw any image that comes to mind. Don't try to make a coherent picture, but draw each image that comes to you. Each time the reader repeats the passage, you may find a new image.

Keep the blindfold on or your eyes closed. It seems strange to draw while blindfolded, but there's a method to this madness. The purpose of this activity is not to create beautiful pictures, but to loosen up your imagination and let it run free. Visualize the words you hear, and then capture your visions on paper. If you can see what you're drawing, you'll be tempted to draw "correctly," to make sure that the picture matches what you can see in your mind. Fussing with the drawing inhibits your imagination and gets in the way. Keep your eyes closed and listen while the reader reads.

For an even more interesting experience, have one person hold the paintbrush or pencil and another person draw by guiding the first person's hand. Without talking, both people must try to draw the same image.

After the reader reads the passage 10 or 20 times over, you can stop. Now get into groups. In each group, compare your drawings — not the quality of your artistry, but the pictures you drew. No one can draw well without seeing the paper, but you should be able to recognize the objects that others were trying to draw. When you compare drawings, you will find that many people see the same images. For example, when hearing "A pair of star-cross'd lovers take their life," many people draw stars, but how do you draw "star-cross'd"? The phrase invokes different images for different people.

Find the common images and the interesting differences. What do you see when you hear the words "winter of our discontent"? In some, it conjures an image of a snowflake, in others an icicle; others might see a mountainous snowdrift, with only an aerial telling you where to dig to find your car.

Every word, phrase, and line can invoke different images. Some images are related, as in "winter of our discontent," "glorious summer," "clouds that lour'd," and so on. When you hear "son of York," in line 2, it sounds like "sun of York." Shakespeare plays such games throughout his plays. The son of York is King Edward IV, and Shakespeare puns *son* and *sun* to invoke an image of a bright sun melting away the "winter" of Richard's discontent.

You can work on your own, too, but obviously you can't read with your eyes closed. The best solution is to use a tape recorder. Read aloud and record the passage that you want to visualize. Then play back the tape while you draw the images that come to mind. You'll need to stop, rewind, and replay the tape many times, so you may find it more convenient to repeat the lines a few times when you first record them. That way, you won't have to interrupt the activity to rewind the tape so often. If you have a computer with a sound card, you can use the computer to record the speech, and the computer can repeat the lines as many times as you want it to.

Get on your feet!

Sometimes, imagination gets you only so far. There's no substitute for getting on your feet, reading the lines out loud, and using your body to interpret Shakespeare's words. The following exercise is especially helpful for actors. When acting, your body is just as important as your voice, and your body can help you create and understand the images in the plays.

Start with the pictures from the preceding exercise. (You can open your eyes now.) After each group shares its pictures, the next step is to bring the pictures to life. While the reader recites the passage, think about how you can use your body to give three-dimensional shape to the pictures you drew. Go ahead; try it. It seems silly, but it's painless. Once you open up your imagination, you'll be amazed at how much richer Shakespeare's plays will be to you.

Chapter 10

Reading a Play

In This Chapter

▶ Why the same play is usually different from different editors

▶ Tips and tricks to help you read Shakespeare's plays

Have you read it often enough yet? Shakespeare wrote plays for performance, not literature for reading. But don't let that prevent you from reading his plays. You can have fun reading, provided you remember that you are reading a script for a performance, which is different from reading a novel or other literary work.

When you read a play, you decide what the characters look like, how they behave, and how they interact. Your imagination sets the stage, and you become the director, the actors, the scenery painters, and everyone else. You also have the freedom to take as many intermissions as you like, which can last for as long as you like.

When you watch a performance, on the other hand, you are watching the interpretations of the director, the actors, and others. They decide for you how the play should look and sound. A film or television production even limits what you can see: The director may want a close-up just when you want to see all the action. Finding out how others see the play is always interesting, but sometimes you want to be in control.

Selecting a Book: Same Play, Different Scripts

The first difficulty in reading Shakespeare's plays is that every book is a little different, even for the same play. Go to a bookstore looking for *Hamlet*, and you'll probably find a half dozen books with that title shelved in the Shakespeare section. Compare the books, and you'll see that they are all different — usually just a little bit different, but sometimes entire scenes are in one version but not in another. They're all *Hamlet*, but each book is different, as though Shakespeare wrote many different versions of the play.

The problem is that we don't really know what Shakespeare wrote. He wrote scripts and gave the scripts to the acting company, but none of his original manuscripts survived. The acting company performed the plays but did not publish the scripts. In the modern film industry, publishing an official book version of a film is big business, but Shakespeare never bothered to publish official scripts of his plays.

Don't blame the poor guy. He didn't own the rights to the plays. The rights belonged to the acting company. Usually, the company didn't want to publish the script for fear that a rival company would steal it. Sometimes, people would steal a script just by watching a show and writing down the lines. A few surviving printed copies seem to have this heritage. Other printed copies were probably taken from actors' working scripts.

Several of Shakespeare's plays were published in his lifetime, but he took no interest in or notice of them. He never imagined that, 400 years later, we would admire him as a literary giant and would want to capture his words forever. From his point of view, he was just doing his job, which was to write scripts, not publish books.

The First Folio and Quarto editions

We are fortunate that in 1623, several years after Shakespeare died, two actors assembled 36 of Shakespeare's plays and published them in what is now called *The First Folio.* Some plays had been published individually, in Quarto form, but many were not. (*Folio* and *Quarto* refer to the page size. A Folio is a large sheet of paper, folded once to make two pages about the size of a tabloid newspaper. A Quarto is a Folio folded once more, making four pages. *The First Folio* is a large book; Quartos are much more manageable for individual plays.)

One of the challenges that modern editors face is untangling the different editions of Shakespeare's plays. The Folio and Quarto editions usually differ, often significantly. Some Quartos were bootleg copies, based on the recollections of actors and audience members. Modern editors try to determine which parts of the Quarto and Folio scripts are closest to what Shakespeare intended. Editors sometimes disagree, so they sometimes come up with very different plays. *Hamlet* is one of the more problematic plays, so you are likely to see differences from one edition of *Hamlet* to another. Most plays, however, have good original copies in *The First Folio,* and the differences among modern editions are slight.

In Shakespeare's day, English didn't have strict rules of grammar or spelling, so editors modernize the spelling of some words, modernize or otherwise change the punctuation, and correct obvious mistakes. Not every editor agrees on which mistakes are "obvious," though, which gives rise to more differences among modern editions. Almost every editor adds stage directions, too. Usually, an editor's additions are in brackets [like this], so you can clearly distinguish the original text from the editorial additions. Stage directions, corrections, interpretations, spelling, and punctuation all contribute to the differences among editions.

Deciding which book to buy

Modern scholars have learned a lot about Shakespeare, and recent editions tend to be more reliable than older ones. If you want a decent copy of Shakespeare's plays that doesn't cost too much, we believe that your best choice is *The Arden Shakespeare Complete Works* (Thomas Nelson and Sons Ltd.), which is the source we used for this book. We find *The Arden Shakespeare* to be the most readable edition, with good notes and a good glossary.

If you want copies of individual plays rather than an all-inclusive tome, you have many choices. *The Arden Shakespeare's* individual plays have copious notes, which you may enjoy or you may find intimidating. You can't go wrong with any of the modern editions, though, so don't be afraid that you are buying the "wrong" one.

Finding Shakespeare on the Net

If you really want to save money, you can find the complete text of Shakespeare's plays on the Internet, although the Internet versions have many typographical errors. These versions are fine for casual use, but you shouldn't use them as scripts for performance, at least not without checking for errors. To download the plays from the Internet, visit www.bardware.com. Several other sites have copies, too.

Knowing the Plot

Before you read a play, it helps to know the story, which you can find out by reading the play summary in Part IV. Shakespeare didn't write detective mysteries, so you aren't breaking any rules by discovering the ending before you start reading the play.

Even if you decide not to read the play summary, the nature of the play gives you some clues to the plot. If the play is a tragedy, for example, you know that the protagonist dies in the final act. (Read more about the rules of tragedies and comedies in Chapter 7.) If the play is a comedy, the protagonist doesn't die and most likely gets married. Before reading a history play, you may want to freshen up your understanding of the kings of England and the Wars of the Roses. Don't try to compare history too closely with the plays, though. Shakespeare's facts aren't always right, and he often moved events to different places and times to suit his dramatic purposes. Chapter 14 gives a bit of historical background for the history plays, but if you want to know what really went on, we recommend reading *The Story of Britain,* by Sir Roy Strong (Fromm International).

You may also know how the play ends because you know from where Shakespeare stole — or rather borrowed — the story. For example, the Roman plays come from the familiar history of ancient Rome. Perhaps you've seen films about Julius Caesar or Cleopatra. Some of these films are based on Shakespeare's plays, but other films depict other aspects of these famous ancient rulers' lives.

Reading the Notes

In addition to a glossary for difficult words, most editions include extensive notes that give you background information. Individual plays usually have more extensive notes than editions containing Shakespeare's complete works.

Introductory notes might discuss the play, its history, when Shakespeare probably wrote it, and what sources he used for the story and characters. Within the body of the play, explanatory notes explain difficult passages and provide background information. For example, plays often refer to characters from Greek and Roman mythology. If you — like us — haven't read much Ovid and don't know who Hero and Leander are, check the notes to find out that they were lovers separated by a river. Leander swam the river every night to be with Hero. One night, he drowned, and Hero threw herself into the sea. The two often pop up in Shakespeare's plays — either as examples of devoted lovers or as examples of love gone awry.

A few editions seem to have more explanatory notes than text, which makes the text hard to read. One way of coping with this problem is to put the short notes at the bottom of the page and the longer notes at the end of the book. When you read a play, you can glance down at the bottom of the page to see that *bodkin* can mean body — as in "God's bodkin" or God's little body (*Hamlet* 2.2.530) — or small dagger, as in "bare bodkin" (*Hamlet* 3.1.76). Then you can continue reading the play with only a minor interruption.

If a note makes you even more confused, ignore it and move on. Remember that Shakespeare wrote the *text,* not the notes.

Divvying Up the Plays: Acts and Scenes

In Shakespeare's day, plays were probably performed in one sitting, with no intermission. One scene flowed smoothly into the next, without any pause or division between scenes. Brief interludes may have separated the acts with singing and dancing, similar to the way the players in *A Midsummer Night's Dream* offer to finish their play with a dance (in Bottom's inimitable, confused style):

Will it please you to see the epilogue, or to hear a Bergomask dance between two of our company? (5.1.347–49)

Numbering acts and scenes is mostly a convenience for the reader and the actors. Scenes and acts often end with a pair of lines that rhyme — a *couplet* — which lends a sense of finality to the scene or act. Without set changes or other clues, the couplet lets the audience know that one scene is over and another is beginning, usually with a different setting.

Not all the printed plays have act and scene divisions. *Coriolanus,* for example, has five acts, but the acts are not divided into scenes. Modern editors usually add scene divisions. Thus, if you use the act, scene, and line numbers from this book to locate particular lines, you may have to hunt a little. Act, scene, and line numbering is one minor difference among various editions of Shakespeare's plays.

When an editor adds scene divisions, the scene usually changes when everyone leaves the stage. Typically, that means that the setting is changing, although you can't always tell from the script. Shakespeare often alternated between serious and humorous scenes, or scenes set in private and scenes set in public places. Think of a scene as a building block for assembling a play — Shakespeare built his plays with many different kinds of blocks, put together in interesting and varied patterns.

Shakespeare didn't give stage directions for each scene's setting; instead, he relied on the actors to establish the setting. Some modern editors add brief notes about the setting at the start of each scene. The notes are there to help you, but rely primarily on the characters' words. If the characters don't make it clear where they are, then their whereabouts are not important.

Keeping Track of the Characters

It's easy to lose track of the characters while reading a play — especially the history plays, in which the dukes, earls, and counts are identified by title more often than by name. When they are identified by name, usually more than one character has the same name. *King Henry IV, Part 1,* for example, has four characters named Henry:

- ✔ King Henry IV
- ✔ Henry, Prince of Wales, son of King Henry IV
- ✔ Henry Percy, Earl of Northumberland
- ✔ Henry Percy, called Hotspur, son of the Earl of Northumberland

Usually, the editor tries to keep the characters clear. For example, these four characters may be called King, Prince, Northumberland, and Hotspur.

Almost always, a play starts with a list of characters, sometimes called the *Dramatis Personae,* or its English translation, *People in the Play.* The list of characters is usually separated into male characters and female characters and is usually in order of rank: kings and queens first, then princes and princesses, and so on down the pecking order. (See Chapter 2 for a description of the English ranks of nobility.) The character list also tells you about relationships between the characters: which characters are friends, siblings, spouses, and so on. Figure 10-1 shows actress Ellen Terry portraying one of Shakespeare's most well-known female characters, Lady Macbeth.

You don't need to memorize the characters before you read a play, but you should read the list and familiarize yourself with the characters. Keep a bookmark on the page with the *Dramatis Personae* so that you can refer to it when you come upon an unfamiliar name in the play.

To help you keep track of who does what to whom, use the scorecards in Chapter 12.

Figure 10-1:
Ellen Terry
was one
of many
actresses
who
enjoyed the
role of Lady
Macbeth,
here shown
in an 1888
painting.

©*Tate Gallery, London, 1998*

Looking at the Prologue, Epilogue, or Chorus

Some plays start with a prologue to set the scene. In a few plays, a *Chorus* pops up between acts or scenes to move the story along. This is not the kind of chorus that sings, but a narrator who does not participate in the story's action. Shakespeare got the idea for the Chorus from classical Greek plays, but where the Greeks often used a group of men as the Chorus, Shakespeare always used an individual. Some plays don't have a Chorus; instead, a character in the play delivers a prologue or epilogue.

Think of the prologue as a short warm-up act. It can introduce the story, explain events that led up to the start of the play, or prepare the audience for the play to come.

The most famous Chorus in Shakespeare's plays is in *King Henry V*, probably the first play to grace the stage of the Globe Theatre, which opened in 1599. The play's prologue calls the Globe Theatre "this wooden O" (Prologue.13) and fires the audience's imagination to see the armies of England and France "on this unworthy scaffold" (Prologue.10).

For 'tis your thoughts that now must deck our kings,

Carry them here and there, jumping o'er times,

Turning th'accomplishment of many years

Into an hour-glass. (Prologue.28–31)

The prologue to *King Henry V* is a favorite of modern actors because it captures so powerfully the nature of theater and the imagination. The Chorus appears before the other acts in *King Henry V,* and as an epilogue, which apologizes for the author's shortcomings:

Thus far, with rough and all-unable pen,

Our bending author hath pursued the story,

In little room confining mighty men,

Mangling by starts the full course of their glory. (Epilogue.1–4)

The Chorus can fill in a variety of actions that you don't see onstage. In *The Winter's Tale,* for example, 16 years pass between the end of Act 3 and the start of Act 4. Shakespeare didn't want the audience to have to sit through that, so he added a Chorus in the figure of Time personified. The Chorus tells the audience what happened in those 16 years:

> . . . imagine me
>
> Gentle spectators, that I now may be
>
> In fair Bohemia, and remember well
>
> I mentioned a son o'th' king's, which Florizel
>
> I now name to you; and with speed so pace
>
> To speak of Perdita, now grown in grace
>
> Equal with wond'ring. (4.1.19–25)

The epilogue to a play can also be the last laugh, as in *As You Like It:*

> If it be true that good wine needs no bush, 'tis true that a good play needs no epilogue. Yet to good wine they do use good bushes; and good plays prove the better by the help of good epilogues. What a case am I in then, that am neither a good epilogue, nor cannot insinuate with you in the behalf of a good play? (5.4.199–204)

Doing It Again

Read the play twice. The first time, read it through without bothering to read the notes or look up obscure words. Even if you don't understand everything, you'll be able to understand enough to figure out what's going on, who the good guys and the bad guys are, and so on. You can get a feel for the play the first time through.

The second time you read the play, go a little slower and enjoy the words. Look up the words you don't know and read the explanatory notes. If you stumble over part of the play, read that part aloud. The words often make more sense when you hear them than when you read them. Chapter 6 has more information about reading Shakespeare's language.

Chapter 11

At the Theater

- -

- -

Time to repeat the litany one more time: Shakespeare wrote his plays as entertainment — to be performed, not read. This chapter helps you get the most from watching a performance, but don't take the chapter too seriously. If you enjoy the show, that's all that really matters.

Preparing to See a Play

With a Shakespeare play — unlike a modern thriller or mystery — you already know what happens and how the play ends, or at least you can if you want to. Before you head off to the theater or cinema, take a minute to read the play summary in Part IV of this book. The summary also tells you the names of some of the key characters, which helps you keep track of who's saying what to whom.

Shakespeare didn't always give his plays specific settings for place and time, so modern directors often use this freedom to create novel and inventive settings for their productions. For example, Shakespeare tells you that *A Midsummer Night's Dream* takes place in and near Athens, but he doesn't provide further details. One director might decide to set a scene in Theseus's palace, and another might set the same scene on a street. Other directors use unusual settings that have no particular identification, such as Peter Brook's circus-like production, shown in Figure 11-1. Even the history plays, which depict real events, often describe locations in general terms, no more specific than the name of a town. Depending on what the director wants to achieve, the results can be moving, interesting, exciting, or even shocking.

Figure 11-1:
Alan
Howard and
John Kane
in Peter
Brooks'
1970
production
of *A
Midsummer
Night's
Dream.*

A modern setting may be just the ticket to interest your children in Shakespeare. Some productions deliberately try to reach children and make the plays interesting and accessible to people of all ages. On the other hand, the performance might feature nudity, sex, extreme violence, seizure-inducing strobe lights, explosions, cigar smoke blown into the audience, or who knows what.

Before you get your tickets, find out what to expect. If you can, read a review before you see the show. If you aren't able to find reviews (for example, if you're attending opening night), ask before you purchase your tickets. Most theaters will not give you a refund after you pay for your tickets.

Purchasing tickets

Some shows are very popular, and you must get your tickets well in advance. This is especially true for the Shakespeare festivals, which are tourist destinations and theaters at the same time. (See Chapter 18 for a list of popular festivals.) The faithful, regular attendees plan their summer vacations around the theatrical performances and buy their tickets months in advance. If you just show up at the door, expect most shows to be sold out during the peak season.

If you want to visit Stratford-upon-Avon or one of the world-class Shakespeare festivals, a travel agent can often help you find a package that includes travel, lodging, and tickets.

Don't be discouraged from attending the popular Shakespeare festivals, though. If you can't or don't want to plan your vacations well ahead of time, visit the festivals during the off-peak season. The peak season is usually the summer, when children are out of school. Perhaps you can take an extended weekend holiday in the spring or autumn. Call ahead to find out which times typically have the most seats available. The advantage of not planning ahead is that theaters often sell tickets at a discount on the day of the performance.

Most theaters offer tickets at various prices. Usually, seats close to the stage, in the middle of the hall, are more expensive than seats farther away or on the sides. Unless you like being very close to the action onstage, the best seats are usually farther back, around the middle of the hall. The sound may be clearer in the front or the back, but you never know until you get there and watch a show. The most expensive seats are not always the best, so don't be afraid to ask for advice. Most ticket sellers are happy to offer suggestions.

At the other end of the festival spectrum are free performances. New York's Shakespeare in Central Park (hosted by the New York Shakespeare Festival) is the most well-known, but many communities offer free or inexpensive shows. Tickets are usually given away on a first-come, first-served basis, so show up early to get your free tickets.

If you have special needs, such as access for a wheelchair, be sure to mention that before you buy your tickets. Most theaters can accommodate wheelchairs and other special needs, but you need to tell the ticket seller ahead of time.

Many theaters offer special performances that feature signers for the hearing-impaired. Check with the theater to find out which shows are interpreted. Some theaters also have narration for the visually impaired. You wear a headset with a radio receiver, and a narrator describes the setting and the action between the characters' lines. This kind of interpretation is difficult with Shakespeare's plays: Because they contain so much dialogue, it's hard for the narrator to get in any extra words. With the narrative interpretation, though, you don't have to miss out on live performances just because you can't see the stage. Ask at the box office about interpretation and other special access.

Seeing a play inside or outside

The original Globe Theatre was exposed to the elements, and some modern productions also take place outdoors, in courtyards, or in open-air theaters. Outdoor productions may take place during the day under natural lighting or at night so that the production can incorporate modern theatrical lighting.

If it rains during an outdoor production, many shows go on. When you get your tickets, ask about the policy concerning inclement weather. You may be entitled to a refund or a ticket exchange, or you may have to bring a raincoat and tough it out.

Some outdoor productions take place in a park, where you need to bring your own seating. You can bring a blanket and sit on the ground, or you may be more comfortable on lawn chairs. If you bring chairs, consider others who are sitting on the ground, and set up your chairs on the sides or at the back of the audience area.

For an outdoor performance, you need to dress according to the weather. That may mean lots of sunscreen and a hat, or it may mean a raincoat or parka. Please put the umbrella away. Even though it may be pouring, the people behind you want to see the play, too.

For an indoor performance, wear what's comfortable. Theater is not the same as opera, and it's not a place to show off your sartorial elegance. If you're more comfortable wearing a suit or an evening dress, then by all means do so, but realize that you may be sitting next to someone wearing jeans and a T-shirt, even in the most expensive seats.

Going to the Theater

At a theater, the most important rule is to enjoy the show, but the next most important rule is to show up on time. Some theaters do not let you in the door if you arrive late, and if you can't see the show, you can't follow rule number one. Plan to arrive early so that you have time to use the facilities, find your seat, read the program, and settle down.

Finding your seat

In some theaters, all the even-numbered seats are on one side and all the odd-numbered seats are on the other. In other theaters, the numbers run in sequence from one side to the other. In other words, you can't tell from the seat number where the seat will be.

The ushers are there to help you find your seat. They know how the seats are numbered and can tell you the easiest way to get there. In a small theater, how you get to your seat may not matter, but in larger theaters, you may find yourself trooping up and down stairs, trying to find the right balcony. Unless you want to get some exercise before the show, show your tickets to an usher and let him or her direct you to your seat.

Getting your program

In a small, local theater, the program may be a single sheet of paper that lists only the actors, director, crew, and so on. In a large-scale professional show, you may get a Playbill or other commercially produced program. The commercial, glossy programs are mostly advertisements, but buried among the ads is the real program. You may have to pay for a program, or the theater may give you a small program for free and offer a larger, more interesting program for a fee.

Note: Festivals that produce many shows in one season often print a single program for all the shows. Make sure to find the right show in the program.

The program can tell you something about the performance. For example, the notes in the program might explain the director's reasons for choosing to set *Hamlet* in outer space. Knowing what to expect can prevent problems, such as thinking that you're in the wrong theater when the curtain rises on a spaceship instead of a Danish castle.

If you compare the characters in the program with the characters in the play (or on the scorecards in Chapters 13, 14, and 15), you might notice that the director has cut some characters from the play. If the program doesn't list Rosencrantz or Guildenstern as characters in *Hamlet,* for example, you know that the director removed those parts from the play and cut the scenes that feature those characters.

Shakespeare wrote his plays for relatively small companies of actors with the expectation that one actor might play several roles. Modern productions often do the same thing, which is called *doubling.* Usually, the principal actors are not doubled, but many of the servants, soldiers, and other minor characters are. The program tells you which actors play multiple roles, so you won't be surprised to see the same faces in different costumes. If your seat is at the back of a large theater, you may not be able to recognize some of the faces, anyway.

If the program has photographs of the actors, they might help you identify who's playing whom when the play begins, but makeup, wigs, and beards can dramatically alter the actors' appearances. Don't worry if the photographs don't seem to match the actors onstage.

Getting the characters straight

If you prepare yourself by reading the play summary, or even the entire play, beforehand, the first thing you should do when the play begins is to determine who's who. You know the major characters, so try to find them onstage.

Sometimes, the director mixes up the scenes, so the first scene you see is not necessarily Shakespeare's first scene. This makes your job a little harder, but you should still be able to spot the king and queen from the way they dress, act, and interact with the other characters. Dozens of people may be milling around onstage, so don't try to keep track of them all. Find the key characters first.

Check the program to find out which actors are playing multiple roles. Usually, the setting and costumes tell you which character the actor portrays in each scene, but knowing beforehand can help, too. Sometimes, several minor characters will be rolled into one. *Coriolanus,* for example, begins with a crowd scene, in which three different citizens have lines. A production can reduce the number of actors needed by giving all the lines to two people or — with a few modifications — to a single person.

Occasionally, a production deliberately doubles the major characters, too. If the program lists fewer than ten actors, you can be sure that all the actors will double their roles. With very few actors and lots of roles, the actors don't often have time to change costumes, so they need other ways to show you when they are playing one character or another. They may use hats, props, physical mannerisms and gestures, or style of speech. With lots of doubling, it can be hard to keep track of who's who, so make sure to study the list of characters and match them up with the actors early in the play.

Directors don't double the major roles deliberately to confuse you. Sometimes, a shoestring budget demands a minimum number of actors, but more often, a director wants to emphasize an artistic point. For example, in *A Midsummer Night's Dream,* the director can highlight the parallels between the fairy realm and the real world by doubling Theseus and Hippolyta with Oberon and Titania, rulers of their respective realms.

Showing your appreciation

As we mentioned earlier, the most important rule when watching a performance of one of Shakespeare's plays is to enjoy the show. Just do what everyone else does, and you'll be fine. As a general rule, you should save the applause for the end of the act (when the stage goes dark) and show your appreciation then. Interrupting the middle of a scene for applause, cheering, or booing makes the actors' jobs more difficult. It's harder to concentrate, and harder to make you believe in the characters. But feel free to laugh at the jokes during a scene.

The actors work best when the audience is lively and responsive. If you have fun, the actors have fun. If the actors have fun, they will perform better, and you will enjoy the show more. Remember that Shakespeare used humor in every play, even in his bloodiest tragedies, so don't be afraid to laugh while the blood runs off the stage. If Shakespeare didn't want the audience to laugh, he wouldn't have written so many jokes.

At the end of the show, applaud as much or as little as you think the show deserves. A truly outstanding performance will bring many audience members to their feet. Feel free to join them or not as you see fit. No one will think ill of you for sitting when everyone else is standing or standing when everyone else is sitting. Just remember the epilogue to *As You Like It*:

I charge you, O women, for the love you bear to men, to like as much of this play as please you. And I charge you, O men, for the love you bear to women — as I perceive by your simpering none of you hates them — that between you and the women the play may please. (5.4.207–12)

The New Globe Theatre in London and a few other theaters encourage the audience to participate in the performance: Cheer the heroes; boo the villains. Most theaters don't want quite so much enthusiasm from the audience, though. When in doubt, watch your fellow audience members and do what they do — don't boo or hiss when Iago takes the stage unless you know that's what the director and the theater management want.

Taking a break: Intermission

Most live performances have an intermission. In Shakespeare's day, plays probably did not have intermissions, and Shakespeare didn't write intermissions into his plays. With five acts, there is no simple division, so each director chooses when to have the intermission. Most directors seem to prefer a longer first half and place the intermission near the end of Act 3. A director may have artistic reasons for choosing a particular place for the intermission, and that place may not be too close to the middle of the play.

Most theaters serve refreshments during the intermission. The prices are high, but remember that ticket prices do not cover the full costs of producing most shows. Most Shakespeare festivals and other theatrical groups are nonprofit organizations that rely on donations and charity to survive. Refreshments, programs, and souvenirs are all ways to help them raise money to continue to produce their plays.

Intermissions are usually short, about 10 or 15 minutes. When the lights flash or the bell rings, follow the herd back to your seat. The show will begin soon, and if you're stuck outside, most theaters won't let you in after the play resumes.

Going to the Movies

As we discuss in Chapter 10, most film versions of Shakespeare's plays are shortened to be similar in length to other films. If a film is so long that a cinema can show it only twice in an evening, the cinema and the studio make less money. Therefore, moviemakers have a strong financial incentive to keep the films short.

That doesn't mean that you're missing anything, though. If the play is in good hands, you won't even notice the difference. If you're curious about what's been left out, rent a videotape and read the play while you watch the show.

Kenneth Branagh's film version of *Much Ado About Nothing* is an excellent example of how a good director can edit Shakespeare's plays for the cinema. The next time you see this film on cable television or rent the videotape, read the play at the same time. You'll see that Branagh cut long speeches down to short speeches, but the essence of the play remains intact. He didn't remove any major scenes and didn't detract from the spirit of Shakespeare's play.

Sometimes, though, a director may choose not to eliminate any lines or scenes. Branagh decided not to cut any of *Hamlet,* and the result is a film that runs for more than four hours. If you go to the cinema to watch a film that runs for more than three hours, ask whether it has an intermission. If not, make sure to visit the bathroom before the show. After all, you can't freeze-frame the movie.

Part IV
Scorecards and Summaries

The 5th Wave — By Rich Tennant

"I enjoy Shakespeare as much as the next person, but not while I'm watching the weatherman."

In this part . . .

The Play! The Play! Before watching a play, it helps to know the story and the characters. This part contains brief summaries of Shakespeare's plays. Each summary starts with a list of the key characters — not so many that you forget who's who, but enough so that you don't get entirely lost. The plays are grouped in their traditional categories of comedies, histories, and tragedies. If you aren't sure which category a play falls into, just look up the play's title in the table of contents or the index. The scorecards, explained in Chapter 12 and found at the ends of Chapters 13, 14, and 15, help you keep track of what's going on: who's winning, who's losing, and who's in love.

Chapter 12
Keeping Score

In This Chapter

▶ About the play summaries

▶ How to use the scorecards

A theatrical program may give you a list of characters and perhaps a short description of the play you're about to see. After the play begins, though, it's up to you to keep track of the characters, especially who's in love or who's at war. What you need is a scorecard, where you can make notes and keep track of changing lovers and changing loyalties. This chapter explains how to use the scorecards and summaries that appear in the subsequent chapters.

Using the Play Summaries

Chapters 13, 14, and 15 contain summaries of Shakespeare's plays, divided into three categories: comedies, histories, and tragedies. The first collection of Shakespeare's plays, published in 1623, uses these three categories, and most modern editions follow suit.

Each summary is short enough to read just before you head to the theater to watch a play, but long enough to give you a feel for the action and the characters in the play. Some performances leave out scenes, rearrange scenes, omit characters, add characters, and otherwise modify Shakespeare's plays. But even with large-scale modifications, the summaries will help you understand the action as it unfolds onstage.

You can also read the corresponding summary before reading a play. Keeping track of two dozen characters, strange place names, and outdated language all contribute to difficulties in reading Shakespeare's plays. If you know what to expect and which characters to pay particular attention to, you'll have an easier time.

Amaze your friends with your erudition. When the next film version of one of Shakespeare's plays is released, you can read the summary before you head to the cinema and impress your friends with your knowledge of the plot and the major characters.

Location, location, location

Shakespeare set his plays throughout Europe and the Mediterranean, shown in Figure 12-1. The history plays, for the most part, take place in England and Scotland. Because the details are hard to see on the map of Europe, Figure 12-2 shows only Great Britain.

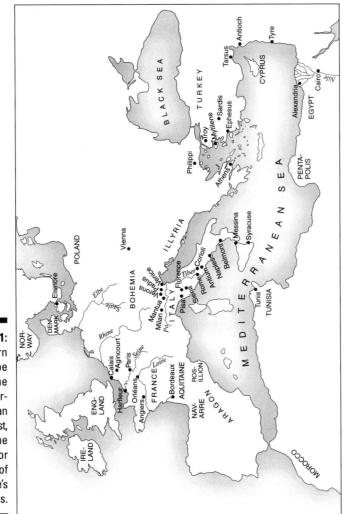

Figure 12-1: Modern Europe and the Mediterranean coast, showing the settings for most of Shakespeare's plays.

Figure 12-2:
Modern
Great
Britain,
showing
landmarks
and
settings for
some of
Shakespeare's
plays.

Shakespeare particularly liked Italy as a setting, prompting some scholars to suppose that he visited Italy sometime before he started writing plays. If you look closely at Shakespeare's geography, though, it becomes clear that he never left England. His local geography is excellent, even down to the great oak tree in Windsor, known as Herne's Oak, which figures into *The Merry Wives of Windsor*. When he sets his plays farther afield, however, the geographical accuracy starts to suffer.

Characters regularly travel by ship, which is a convenient way to move characters from one locale to another. Sometimes, though, Shakespeare has seafaring ships pulling up to ports in landlocked cities or countries. For example, in *The Winter's Tale,* ships dock at the nonexistent port of Bohemia. You can see Bohemia's nonexistent coast in Figure 12-1.

The play settings suit Shakespeare's artistic needs. He wrote about people and their passions. He needed places where the people could live, but the places serve his artistic requirements, not geographical reality. Use the maps to satisfy your curiosity about Pericles' journey, for example, but don't try to analyze the distance from Verona to Mantua to try to determine how quickly a message from Friar Laurence would reach Romeo in exile.

Using the Scorecards

Most plays don't have winners and losers per se, but keeping score is a great way to help you keep track of what goes on during a play. At the ends of Chapters 13, 14, and 15, you can find the scorecards for the plays in those chapters.

The Shakespeare scorecards look like sports scorecards. Instead of innings, these scorecards use act and scene divisions. Instead of players, they list characters. Both "teams" appear on a single scorecard, so you can easily compare, say, the Montagues and the Capulets.

Note: Most editions agree on the act divisions, but different editions have different scene divisions for some of the plays. If you have an edition with different scene divisions, just leave the boxes for the extra scenes blank, and do your best to squeeze in any scenes that are missing from the scorecard.

You can use a scorecard in one of three ways:

- ✔ Try to fill in the scorecard while you watch the play. Doing so is difficult in a dark theater, but it's easy at an outdoor, afternoon production. Be careful not to annoy your neighbor who is trying to enjoy the play.

- ✔ Fill in the scorecard while you read the play, and then take the card with you for reference while you watch the play. The scorecard can remind you of the parts of the story that you forgot after reading the summary.

- ✔ Fill in the scorecard while you read the play, but leave the scorecard at home when you watch the play. Just enjoy the show. When you watch the play, you will remember more, but you won't have to fuss with the scorecard or reading in the dark, which lets you pay more attention to the play.

Before you use a scorecard, we recommend making a photocopy. You may want to see a particular play many times. Each time you watch the play, it will be a little different, and you can record these differences on your copies of the scorecard.

Read the play summary first to become familiar with the key characters and the plot. Then read the play while you record the action on the scorecard. Note that the summaries list only a few key characters, so you don't have to memorize too many names when reading the summary. The scorecard lists additional characters because you can use it to help keep track of them. Not all the characters fit on the scorecard, though, so the scorecards omit minor servants, attendants, and so on.

The action symbols

Like you do with a scorecard in sports, fill in each character's box for each scene with a special symbol, denoting what that character did in the scene. Not every player gets to play in every inning of baseball, and not every character gets to appear in every scene. If a character doesn't appear, leave the box blank. Table 12-1 lists all the symbols that you might want to use when completing a scorecard. In addition, each scorecard has a smaller table that lists additional symbols you're likely to use for that specific play. Feel free to use different symbols or invent new ones.

Table 12-1	Scorecard Symbols
Symbol	*Description*
.	Appears in scene: If a character appears in a scene but doesn't do anything special, put a dot in the middle of that character's box. Doing so reminds you who appears when.
"	Famous quote: When a character says something you recognize as a famous quote, mark the scorecard with quotation marks. Doing so will help you find the quote if you decide to look it up.
①⟩	Woos a lover
②⟩	Meets a lover in private
③⟩	Gets engaged
④⟩	Home run: Marries
K	Strikeout: Rejected in love
!	Consummates a marriage
E	Elopes

(continued)

Table 12-1 *(continued)*

Symbol	Description
♥	Falls in love
💔	Falls in love with the wrong person
◉	Falls out of love
→	Sent to penalty box: Banished
←	Returns to game: Returns from banishment
F	Foul: Attacks someone
S	Sacked: Victim of an attack
X	Ejected from game: Dies
⊗	Commits suicide
A	Arrested
Ⓐ	Pardoned
+	Reunited with long-lost kin
R	Rescues or saves someone's life
☹	Defeated in battle
☺	Victorious in battle
♕	Crowned king or queen
⊜	Deposed
M	Goes mad
⚡	Visited by supernatural beings
C	Involved in a conspiracy
↺	Gets lost
?	Mistaken for someone else
T	Plays a trick (fakes own death, for example)
TT	Plays a counter-trick
☠	Uses a potion or poison
⌒	Dons a disguise
⊘	Removes a disguise
⚔	Challenges to a duel
B	Betrays a friend or country
J	Jealous rage

Symbol	Description
✚	Heals a sick person
➜✉	Sends a letter or message
✉⬅	Receives a letter or message
P	Makes a prophecy or prediction
①	Seeks help
②	Rejects help
⚓	Shipwrecked

If an event takes place offstage but is described by someone onstage, you can put the symbol in parentheses. Sometimes, a director will choose to show these events. If the events are on the scorecard, you can follow them as they happen onstage. The parentheses tell you not to expect to see them.

On a scorecard, each character has a number, which you can use to denote actions that involve other characters. For example, when Romeo marries Juliet, you can mark Romeo's symbol as ◈8, where Juliet is number 8. Similarly, mark Juliet's symbol as ◈13, because Romeo is number 13.

If multiple events occur in a single scene, write small. When you photocopy a scorecard, you may want to enlarge it slightly to allow more room to write your notations.

The scorecards

For your convenience, the scorecards are at the ends of Chapters 13, 14, and 15. Comedies are in Chapter 13, histories are in Chapter 14, and tragedies are in Chapter 15.

The following page shows you the scorecard for *Romeo and Juliet* already filled out. Use this example to see how a Shakespeare scorecard works. We haven't taken the fun away from you — Chapter 15 has a blank scorecard that you can fill in the next time you read or watch *Romeo and Juliet.*

Romeo and Juliet

Legend

Symbol	Meaning	Symbol	Meaning	Symbol	Meaning
♠	Falls in love	⊗	Sent to penalty box: Banished		Own goal: Commits suicide
↑	Home run: Marries	X	Ejected from game: Dies	•	Appears in scene
!	Consummates a marriage	T	Plays a trick: Fakes own death	"	Famous quote

Characters, in order of appearance

	Character	A1 S1	S2	S3	S4	S5	A2 S1	S2	S3	S4	S5	S6	A3 S1	S2	S3	S4	S5	A4 S1	S2	S3	S4	S5	A5 S1	S2	S3
Capulets																									
1	Sampson, a servant	F9																							
2	Gregory, a servant	F9																							
3	Tybalt, nephew of wife of Capulet	F10				•							FX												
4	OldCapulet	•	•			•										•	•		•		•	•			
5	Wife of Capulet	•		•		•							•			•	•		•		•	•			•
6	Paris, kinsman of the Prince		•													↗8		•				•			X
7	Nurse to Juliet			•		•				•	•			•	•		•				•	•			
8	Juliet, daughter of Capulet	♥		•		♥8 13		↓13 "			♥8	◇		•"			!"	!"		↗6 ♀T					⊗"
Montagues																									
9	Abram, servant to Montague	F1,2																							
10	Benvolio, nephew of Montague	F3 •	•		•	•	•			•			•												
11	Old Montague	•											•												•
12	Wife of Montague	•											•												
13	Romeo, son of Montague	♥	•			↗8	↗8	↗8	•		♥8	◇8 F↑	↗8 F↑	•	!		•						•		↗8⊗"
14	Mercutio, friend of Romeo				"	•	X"			•			X"												
15	Escalus, Prince of Verona	•											•												•"
16	Friar Laurence								•			•			•		•	•				•		↑⊠	↓⊠

Chapter 13
Comedies

In This Chapter

▶ Summaries of Shakespeare's comedies

▶ Interesting performances on videotape

*T*his chapter begins the summaries of Shakespeare's plays, in alphabetical order. It's a long chapter because Shakespeare wrote more comedies than other kinds of plays.

A Shakespearean "comedy" is not necessarily the same as a modern comedy. A classical comedy is a play in which the protagonists live and usually get married. (Chapter 7 tells you more about the different kinds of plays that Shakespeare wrote.) Regardless of the official meaning of "comedy," most of Shakespeare's comedies are fun and funny, full of zany goings-on from mistaken identity to cross-dressing to practical and impractical jokes.

All's Well That Ends Well

Key characters:

✔ Bertram, the spoiled Count of Rossillion

✔ Helena, daughter of a famous doctor, later wife of Bertram

✔ Lafew, an old lord

✔ Diana, an impoverished lady, later friend to Helena

✔ Parolles, a cowardly follower of Bertram

Bertie is a bad boy. He disregards his wife, disobeys his king, and hangs out with a disreputable scoundrel. Lucky for him, the play is a comedy, so you know that everything will work out in the end. He returns to his wife, obeys his king's orders, gives up on his companion, and all's well that ends well.

Act 1

Bertie is all grown up. His father is dead, and he is now man of the castle. His first duty as the new Count of Rossillion is to attend his king. He heads out into the big world with his friend Parolles. Parolles is a liar and a coward, puffed up by his own words, but Bertie doesn't realize this. Yet.

The king is gravely ill and has called all his courtiers to his deathbed. Despite his illness, the king must still attend to matters of state. A war brews between Florence and Sienna. France is a friend to both sides, so he does not intervene. Instead, he lets his courtiers join the fight on either side — a prospect that pleases the young lords who are eager to prove their mettle.

Helena is an orphan living in the Rossillion household. She secretly loves Bertram, but his station is so far above hers that she cannot reveal her love to anyone. Bertram's mother is no fool, and she can see Helena's love for her son. She knows that Helena is virtuous and wise, and she agrees that Helena would be a good match for Bertram.

Helena is the daughter of the world's greatest doctor, now deceased. While he was alive, her father could easily have cured the king. She has some of her late father's medicines and knows how to use them, so she travels to Paris, confident that she can help the king.

Act 2

The king sends his lords to war, warning them not to dally with the young girls of Italy — some things never change. He keeps Bertram in France, telling him that he is still too young to go. Bertie wants to go play with the big boys, and he chafes at the restriction.

Helena arrives in the French court and offers to cure the king. At first, he refuses her help because he is fed up with all doctors. Helena insists that she can help and offers a bargain to back up her claim. Should she fail to cure the king, she will yield her life as recompense. If she succeeds, the king will give her the husband of her choice. They strike the bargain.

The play is a comedy, so of course Helena heals the king. Long Live the King! The king fulfills his side of the bargain: He calls all his bachelor lords before him. Helena surveys the lot and questions and rejects Bachelor Number 1. She checks out Bachelor Number 2, but she never seriously considers any of the lords except Bertram, the Count of Rossillion. The other lords would be happy to marry a beautiful, virtuous young woman, especially one who has the love of the king. Bertie, however, thinks of her as a "poor physician's daughter" (2.3.124) who is beneath his station and unworthy of his high estate. The king orders Bertram to marry her, and he reluctantly agrees to the match.

After the wedding, Bertram sends Helena back to his mother's house, promising to follow shortly, but in truth he packs up to go fight in Italy. Lafew, a lord in the French court, warns Bertram about Parolles, but Bertie can't see past the flashy clothes and words. Bertie continues to trust him, and they head off to Italy together. They are meant for each other.

Act 3

Bertram's mother welcomes Helena, who left as a ward and returns as a daughter-in-law. By now, they know that Bertram is not returning. He has not consummated the marriage with Helena. He even makes an outrageous proposition: If Helena can get the ring he always wears, and if she will bear his child — though they will never share a bed — he will accept her as his wife. Helena realizes the futility of staying put and packs up to go on a pilgrimage.

With Helena out of the way, Bertie is now free to return home, but he stays in Italy, where he distinguishes himself in battle. Off the battlefield, he also tries to distinguish himself, especially with a young maid, Diana.

Helena makes her way to Italy as a pilgrim and lodges with an old widow and her daughter, who is — guess who? — the same Diana who is the object of Bertram's lust. Helena reveals her situation to the widow and asks for help. When Helena hears about Bertie's solicitation, she hatches a plan.

Helena asks Diana to agree to Bertram's suit. Diana must demand his ring, and when they meet at night, she will give him a ring in exchange. Helena will take Diana's place, so this arrangement is above board because it allows a husband and wife to sleep together. The widow and Diana agree to "this deceit so lawful" (3.7.38).

Act 4

Bertram's companions secretly capture Parolles and pretend to be the enemy. He immediately bargains for his life, offering to betray his comrades in exchange. He eagerly tells his captors the size and strength of the army, and he berates the French lords. He even has a letter to Diana, warning her against Bertram. Bertram finally sees firsthand what kind of man Parolles is. The French abandon Parolles, leaving him alone with his shame and humiliation.

Bertie has to finish his business with Diana. He gives up his ring, which he claims to be a family heirloom, as a token of his professed love. He promises to marry Diana when his wife, Helena, dies. The French lords hear news that Helena died of grief while on her pilgrimage, so that leaves Bertie free and clear. If you expect him to keep his promise to Diana, you haven't been paying attention to the first three acts.

On video

1980, British Broadcasting Company (BBC): Elijah Moshinsky director, Ian Charleson as Bertram, Michael Hordern as Lafeu, Angela Down as Helena, and Peter Jeffrey as Parolles

Act 5

Lord Lafew hears the news of Helena's death and wants his daughter to marry Bertram. Bertie also hears the news, and he happily accepts Lafew's daughter as his new wife. He offers a ring for Lafew to take to his daughter, but Lafew recognizes it as one that Helena wore. The king also recognizes it, and well he should because he gave it to Helena. If she ever needed help, she was to send him the ring and he would come to her aid. Bertie claims that he never saw Helena with the ring — that a woman threw the ring to him from a window. The king isn't the fool Bertie takes him for, and he orders Bertram to be taken prisoner.

Helena, Diana, and the widow must finish what they started by seeking justice from the King of France. Diana demands that Bertram make good on his promise to marry her after Helena dies. Bertie still hasn't grown up and lies about his relationship with Diana. He tries to put her off as a "common gamester to the camp" (5.3.188), but then she shows the king Bertram's ring. Would he give such a valuable ring to a camp follower?

Caught in his web of lies, Bertie tries yet another. He agrees that he slept with her and gave her the ring, but that was all. She then demands the return of her ring and points to Helena's ring (the ring that Bertram tried to give to Lafew). The king asks where Diana procured the ring, and her mother fetches Helena to reveal the truth. Helena has fulfilled Bertram's ridiculous demands: She has his ring and carries his child. Bertram asks for pardon and promises to "love her dearly, ever, ever dearly" (5.3.315). Order is restored in Rossillion.

As You Like It

Key characters:

- ✔ Orlando, lover of Rosalind
- ✔ Oliver, nasty brother of Orlando
- ✔ Rosalind/Ganymede, daughter of the banished duke

✔ Celia/Aliena, daughter of Duke Frederick, and Rosalind's friend

✔ Duke Senior, the banished duke

✔ Duke Frederick, brother of Duke Senior

✔ Touchstone, a clown

✔ Silvius, a lovesick shepherd

✔ Phebe, a shepherdess

As You Like It takes sibling rivalry past the usual bickering to new depths, but at the same time, Shakespeare sprinkles love affairs liberally throughout the play. Throw in a contrived, artificial ending, and you have one of Shakespeare's most popular plays.

Act 1

Brothers just can't seem to get along in this play. In the de Boys family, Oliver abuses his younger brother, Orlando, treating him worse that an animal, forcing him to live "rustically" (1.1.7) despite being a gentleman. Just as bad is the relationship between Duke Senior and his younger brother, Frederick. Frederick usurped his older brother's position as Duke and banished him to the Forest of Arden. The only people who do get along are Rosalind and Celia, the daughters of the banished Duke Senior and the new Duke Frederick, respectively.

Oliver's relationship with his brother is most clear when Orlando wants to enter a wrestling match. Oliver asks Orlando's opponent, a champion wrestler, to injure Orlando, even to "break his neck" (1.1.141). Rustic living must have done some good for Orlando, for he beats the odds and wins. He wins not only the wrestling match but also Rosalind's heart.

While Rosalind muses on her new love, the new Duke decides that he doesn't like the daughter of the old Duke hanging around the court, and he banishes her, too. Celia will not be parted from her friend, and they agree to face exile together. Shakespeare trots out his favorite plot device: Rosalind dresses as a boy, under the name Ganymede. (Chapter 8 tells you more about cross-dressing and why Shakespeare and his contemporaries used this trick so often.) Celia plays the part of Ganymede's sister, Aliena; Touchstone, a clown, also accompanies them on their trip into exile.

Act 2

The banished Duke Senior takes an unofficial position with the Forest of Arden tourist bureau. He extols the virtues of the natural life: no courtiers and their false flattery, no envy — just plain honest living. Life is better in the forest than it was at court, or so he says.

The forest attracts many people. A servant overhears Oliver plotting against Orlando's life, and Orlando and the servant escape to the forest. Orlando finds the Duke's camp and demands food, which the Duke freely offers. The Duke sees that he is "not all alone unhappy" (2.7.136) and that his tragedy is but one scene in a multitude of tragic plays in "this wide and universal theatre" (2.7.137). A companion continues the metaphor and philosophizes that

All the world's a stage,

And all the men and women merely players. (2.7.139–40)

Ganymede, Aliena, and Touchstone also find a new home in the forest. They had the foresight to bring money and jewels, so they are able to buy a flock of sheep and a pasture. They also promise to raise the pay of the poor old shepherd who tends the flock.

Act 3

Orlando settles into a life of exile, but he misses Rosalind dearly. Everyone in the forest knows this because Orlando carves her name into the bark of trees and posts love poems throughout the forest. Rosalind is touched, but she wants to sound out the depth and honesty of Orlando's professed love. In the guise of Ganymede, she promises to "cure" Orlando of his love for Rosalind by play-acting. Orlando must woo Ganymede in the name of Rosalind. It's not clear how this is supposed to help Orlando, but the disguised Rosalind sure gets her kicks out of the deal.

Ganymede also tries to help a shepherd, Silvius, win the heart of a shepherdess, Phebe, but her plan backfires. Instead, Phebe falls in love with Ganymede, Rosalind's alter ego.

Act 4

Rosalind continues her "cure" of Orlando by encouraging him to woo Ganymede acting as Rosalind. Orlando promises to love her "for ever, and a day" (4.1.138). Orlando has an appointment with Rosalind and Celia, but he's late. His brother Oliver arrives with a bloody cloth and a strange story: The new Duke thinks that Orlando absconded with Celia and Rosalind, and he blamed Oliver. Oliver needed to escape the Duke's wrath, so he went to the popular tourist destination, the Forest of Arden. Orlando found him asleep at the foot of a tree, but he also saw a lion nearby, ready to pounce. At first, Orlando wanted to leave his evil brother to his fate, but virtue is in Orlando's blood, and he fought the lion and rescued his brother. Orlando suffered an injury in the rescue, though, so he sent his brother to deliver his message to Ganymede (Rosalind in disguise).

SEE IT

On video

- ✔ 1992, Sands: Christine Edzard director, Celia Bannerman as Celia, Emma Croft as Rosalind, and Andrew Tiernan as Orlando and Oliver

- ✔ 1978, BBC: Basil Coleman director, Helen Mirren as Rosalind, and Brian Stirner as Orlando

- ✔ 1936, Inter-Allied: Paul Czinner director, Laurence Olivier as Orlando, Sophie Stewart as Celia, Mackenzie Ward as Touchstone, and Elisabeth Bergner as Rosalind

---

Act 5

There must be something in the water. Oliver and Celia have fallen in love at first sight. The exiled Duke is set to marry them the next day. Even Touchstone has fallen in love with a local girl and will marry her. Ganymede promises that Orlando, too, will marry Rosalind on the same day.

Silvius longs for Phebe, but she professes her love for Ganymede. Rosalind, still disguised as Ganymede, strikes a deal with Phebe. Ganymede convinces Phebe to agree to marry Silvius as her second choice, should she not want to marry Ganymede for any reason. Phebe agrees to the deal, and Ganymede leaves to return in her normal clothing as Rosalind.

Phebe sees that she cannot marry Ganymede, so she agrees to marry Silvius. Orlando and Rosalind are to be married. Finally, to restore order in all matters, Jaques de Boy, brother of Oliver and Orlando, arrives with news: Duke Frederick was out to hunt down Duke Senior, but on the way, he met an old religious man and repented of his evil life. He restored the title and lands to the banished Duke, so all the couples can return to their rightful places and live happily ever after.

The Comedy of Errors

Key characters:

- ✔ Antipholus of Syracuse
- ✔ Antipholus of Ephesus
- ✔ Dromio of Syracuse, servant to Antipholus of Syracuse

- Dromio of Ephesus, servant to Antipholus of Ephesus

- Adriana, wife of Antipholus of Ephesus

- Luciana, sister of Adriana

- Egeon, father of the Antipholus brothers

- Emilia, an abbess, long-lost wife of Egeon, and mother of the Antipholus brothers

- Angelo, a goldsmith

The Comedy of Errors has a simple plot: Antipholus of Syracuse is looking for his long-lost twin brother. Through a quirk of parental ingenuity, both twins have the same name: Antipholus. Each Antipholus is accompanied by a servant, and the servants also happen to be twins and happen to have the same name, Dromio. Antipholus of Syracuse grew up with his father, Egeon, but upon reaching adulthood ventured into the world to seek his brother. He has been gone for seven years, and now Egeon is looking for him. They arrive separately in Ephesus, where the other Antipholus and Dromio just happen to live.

No complicated, interwining plots. No politics, no wars — just good, old-fashioned slapstick humor. Everyone mistakes one Antipholus for the other. Even the Antipholi can't tell their Dromios apart. The confusion builds throughout the play until the final act, when the two Antipholi and Dromios finally meet each other. The entire family is reunited, and everyone lives happily ever after. That said, there's little left to discuss about the play, other than to point out some of the interesting errors, which give the play its title.

To keep the characters straight, Antipholus of Syracuse (the visitor in town) is called A1 here. His servant, Dromio, is D1. The local Antipholus and Dromio are A2 and D2. Dromio's android is R2D2, but he never appears in the play.

Act 1

Egeon is condemned to death because he comes from Syracuse, an enemy of Ephesus. He has one day to pay a hefty fine or he faces the death penalty.

A1 and D1 arrive in Ephesus. They are strangers and know no one in town. Nonetheless, D2 meets A1 and bids him come home to dinner.

A1 thinks that D2 is joking around and beats D2 for his foolishness. D2 goes home and explains to Adriana, A2's wife, what took place.

Act 2

A1 meets up with D1 again and berates him for his games. D1, having not met D2, is confused by what A1 has to say.

Adriana and her sister Luciana find A1 and D1. They mistake them for A2 and D2. Adriana demands that they return home for dinner. A1 doesn't know the women, but how can he turn down an insistent request from two beautiful women?

Act 3

You finally get to meet A2, who knows that he's late for dinner. He finds himself locked out of his own house and guesses that his wife is mad because he's so late. To spite his wife, he decides to dine with a courtesan and give her a gold chain that he commissioned for his wife.

Meanwhile, inside A2's home, A1 has the hots for Luciana. She still thinks that he is A2, married to Adriana, so she scolds him for being unfaithful. Life in Ephesus is just too weird, so A1 decides to leave on the next boat out of town. He sends D1 to discover whether any ship is leaving soon.

While A1 waits for D1 to return, Angelo delivers the gold chain to A1. Angelo promises to come to Antipholus's home later to receive payment (except that it's really A2's home).

Act 4

A2 sends D2 to buy a rope, which he intends to use on his apparently wayward wife. Angelo accosts A2 and demands payment for the gold chain, but he's got the wrong Antipholus. A2 refuses to pay, so Angelo has him arrested. D1 arrives and tells A2 about a ship that will leave that very night. Naturally, A2 thinks that he's talking to D2, doesn't understand why D1 would care about ships, and sends D1 home to fetch money for his bail.

D1 gets the bail money from Adriana and Luciana but then runs into A1. This Antipholus was never arrested, so D1's talk about arrests and bail confuses him.

A2 convinces the jailer to let him go home for the bail money, but on the way he meets D2 and demands the money. D2 doesn't know what he's talking about. He does have the rope, though.

Adriana and Luciana have decided that A2 and D2 are mentally unhinged. Several people help them tie up and drag off A2 and D2 to be cured and exorcised by a dubious doctor.

SEE IT

On video

- 1983, BBC: James Cellan Jones director, Michael Kitchen as the Antipholi, and Roger Daltrey as the Dromios. The magic of videotape lets one person play two roles, which is harder to pull off in a live performance.

- 1974, Royal Shakespeare Company (RSC): Philip Casson and Trevor Nunn directors, Roger Rees as Antipholus of Syracuse, Mike Gwilym as Antipholus of Ephesus, Judi Dench as Adriana, and Francesca Annis as Luciana. This excellent production is not currently available in the U.S.

Act 5

A1 and D1 argue with Angelo and another merchant. Adriana sees them and thinks that they must have escaped from the doctor. The argument turns nasty, and A1 and D1 escape into a nearby abbey.

A2 and D2 do indeed escape from the doctor. A2 tells his version of recent events to the Duke of Ephesus. Angelo, D2, the courtesan, and others chime in with their accounts. Just as everything seems to be as confused as possible, the abbess, A1, and D1 emerge from the abbey.

The two Antipholi and the two Dromios sort out who did what, when, and with whom. The Antipholi also find their father, Egeon, who has been searching for them. To make matters even more wondrous, the abbess turns out to be their long-lost mother, Emilia.

Egeon is released from his death sentence, the family is reunited, A1 is free to marry Luciana, Angelo is paid for his gold chain, matters are all put back to right, and the audience members leave the theater with their heads whirling.

Cymbeline

Key characters:

- Cymbeline, King of Britain
- Queen of Britain, Imogen's wicked stepmother
- Imogen, daughter of Cymbeline, wife of Posthumus
- Posthumus, husband of Imogen

> ✔ Pisanio, servant to Posthumus
>
> ✔ Cloten, son of the queen by a former husband
>
> ✔ Belarius, called Morgan, a banished lord
>
> ✔ Guiderius, called Polydore, long-lost son of Cymbeline
>
> ✔ Arviragus, called Cadwal, long-lost son of Cymbeline
>
> ✔ Iachimo, an Italian gentleman

Look! Up on the stage! It's a history. It's a tragedy. It's a comedy. No, it's *Cymbeline!* This play was first published as *The Tragedy of Cymbeline,* but it's more like a comedy than a tragedy. Toting a severed head across the stage is not the usual comedic fare, though. Shakespeare probably thought of the play as a history about an ancient King of Britain, although we now know that Cymbeline is a king of myth, not history. We list it as a comedy because of its happy ending, but this play defies easy categorization. To make matters worse, this is Shakespeare's most complicated play, with several interwoven plots. So don't worry if you get confused — that's normal when watching this play.

Act 1

One of the key villains in this play is Imogen's evil stepmother. Imogen's real mother died, and her father, King Cymbeline, remarried and named his stepson Cloten as the heir to the throne. Cymbeline wants Imogen to marry Cloten, but she refuses because Cloten is a fool and a coward. A courtier describes him as "too bad for bad report" (1.1.17). Instead, she secretly marries Posthumus, who is a good, honorable man. When the king learns of his daughter's secret marriage, he banishes Posthumus from the kingdom. Before the couple separate, they exchange gifts: Imogen gives Posthumus a ring, and he gives her a bracelet.

The queen is secretly pleased with the banishment, but she pretends to side with Imogen and Posthumus. She gives a box of potions to Pisanio, Posthumus's servant, saying that they are healing medicines, but they are actually poisons. At least she thinks that they're poisons, but the doctor who gave them to her doesn't trust her, so he substituted sleeping potions for the poisons. They bring on the semblance of death, but only temporarily.

The banished Posthumus makes his way to a friend's home in Rome, where he brags about the beauty and faithfulness of the wife he left in Britain. Iachimo, the other key villain, doesn't believe that any woman can be so faithful. They cannot agree, so they do what any immature boys would do under the circumstances: They bet on Imogen's honor. If Iachimo can seduce Imogen, Posthumus will turn over Imogen's ring. If Iachimo loses, he will pay a small fortune in gold.

Iachimo goes to Britain and tries to seduce Imogen, but he fails. He then tells her that his advances were merely to test her faithfulness, and that she passed the test. Imogen is pacified, but Iachimo sees that he lost the bet. If at first you don't succeed, cheat. He asks Imogen for a safe place to store a trunk full of precious treasure and jewels for the night. She offers her own bedchamber, where she will personally vouch for the trunk's safety.

Act 2

In Imogen's bedroom, Iachimo climbs out of the trunk. (Did you really think that the trunk contained treasure?) He takes notes about the room, the bed, the decorations, and so on. He steals the bracelet from the sleeping Imogen's wrist, and finally notices a mole on her breast, which he knows will certify his false report. He climbs back into the trunk so that his servants can recover it the next morning.

In the morning, Imogen cannot find the bracelet. She knows that she had it the night before, but now it is missing. The bracelet was a parting gift from Posthumus, and she doesn't want to lose it.

Iachimo returns to Rome in triumph. He tells Posthumus about Imogen's room, but that doesn't persuade Posthumus. He shows her bracelet, which Posthumus claims that he stole. Finally, he describes certain distinguishing features about the mole on Imogen's breast, which convinces Posthumus that Iachimo must have slept with her. Posthumus concedes the bet, delivers the ring, and curses his wife and all womankind.

Act 3

In Britain, Cymbeline has new problems. Britain has not been paying its tribute to Rome. Caesar sends an ambassador to demand that Cymbeline pay the tribute or face open war. At the queen's insistence, Cymbeline chooses war.

Posthumus writes a letter to Imogen, telling her that he is returning to Britain and asking her to meet him in Wales. He also sends a letter to Pisanio, asking him to go with Imogen and then kill her. Pisanio and Imogen travel together and stop in the forest along the way, where he tells her the truth.

His master's letter troubled him so much that Pisanio has "not slept one wink" (3.4.100). He refuses to carry out his master's orders. Instead, he counsels Imogen to follow the Roman ambassador when he returns to Rome. Pisanio helps Imogen disguise herself as a boy (one of Shakespeare's favorite plot devices), and he also gives her the potions from the queen.

(Remember that he thinks that they are healing medicines, and the queen thinks that they are poisons, but they're really just sleeping potions. We told you that this play is complex.)

Three characters pop up out of nowhere: an old man, called Morgan, and his two sons, Polydore and Cadwal. They live as outlaws in the wilds because many years ago Morgan was wrongfully banished from Cymbeline's court. You learn that the two young men are the king's long-lost sons, Guiderius and Arviragus. The old man, whose real name is Belarius, kidnapped the sons out of anger for his mistreatment. He raised them as his own sons without telling them the truth. Imogen gets lost in the forest and meets Belarius/Morgan and his "sons." They have an instinctual recognition of the noble character in each other and become fast friends. (See Chapter 2 for the Elizabethan take on the nature-versus-nurture debate.)

The court is in an uproar over Imogen's disappearance. Cloten suspects that Pisanio is involved and threatens him. When Pisanio tells Cloten where Imogen is going, Cloten hatches a plan of his own: He will dress in Posthumus's clothing, kill Posthumus, and then surprise Imogen.

Act 4

Imogen stays with Belarius and the king's sons, but because she is feeling ill, she takes some of the "medicine" that Pisanio gave her. Cloten arrives on the scene looking for Posthumus and Imogen, but he finds Guiderius/Polydore instead. Cloten insults and attacks Guiderius, who has no choice but to defend himself. He kills and beheads Cloten.

Arviragus/Cadwal finds Imogen, apparently dead (because of the queen's potion). The three outlaws lay the bodies of Imogen and Cloten next to each other.

Imogen soon wakes up and sees Cloten's headless body, dressed in Posthumus's clothing. She thinks the worst — that the corpse is Posthumus — and swoons in despair. The Roman ambassador finds Imogen mourning over Cloten's body. She makes up a story about bandits attacking them. The Romans offer to take Imogen with them, and she accepts.

Act 5

Posthumus marches with the Roman army, but he sides with Britain. He discards his Roman outfit and disguises himself as a British peasant, expecting to die fighting for Britain. He fights against Iachimo (who is with the Roman army) and wins, but he leaves Iachimo alive and unharmed.

On video

1983, BBC: Elijah Moshinsky director, Richard Johnson as Cymbeline, Claire Bloom as Queen, Helen Mirren as Imogen, and Michael Pennington as Posthumus

The battle swings against Britain, and Cymbeline is captured. Belarius and his "sons" remain loyal to Britain and try to rally the British army. Posthumus joins them, and together they rescue the king and turn the tide against the Romans. The British win the day.

Cymbeline is sorting out the aftermath of the war when he hears that the queen is dead. On her deathbed, she conveniently confessed to her many crimes.

Imogen is among the Roman captives, still disguised as a boy. She sees her ring on Iachimo's finger and demands to know where he got it. Iachimo, racked by guilt, tells the truth, the whole truth, and nothing but the truth. Posthumus hears the story and reveals himself. He, too, is consumed by guilt because he thinks that he caused Imogen's death. Imogen reveals herself and is reconciled with her father and Posthumus. Finally, Belarius reveals himself and the king's long-lost sons.

So the soap opera ends: Guiderius is found and is now heir to the throne. The evil queen and her son are dead — and good riddance. Imogen and Posthumus are happily reunited. Britain and Rome are at peace. Posthumus forgives Iachimo for his villainy. And everyone lives happily ever after.

Love's Labour's Lost

Key characters:

- ✔ King of Navarre
- ✔ Princess of France
- ✔ Berowne, a lord attending Navarre
- ✔ Rosaline, a lady attending the princess
- ✔ Longaville, a lord attending Navarre
- ✔ Maria, a lady attending the princess

- ✔ Dumain, a lord attending Navarre
- ✔ Katherine, a lady attending the princess
- ✔ Boyet ("bo-YAY"), advisor to the princess
- ✔ Don Armado, a Spanish gentleman
- ✔ Jaquenetta, a country girl
- ✔ Costard, a clown

Love's Labour's Lost is an unusual comedy because no one gets married. Instead, the protagonists defer their weddings (four of them!) until one year after the play ends.

Act 1

The King of Navarre longs for the contemplative life, so he wants to isolate himself from the world to study for three years. Joining him will be his lords, Berowne, Longaville, and Dumain. To study most effectively, they must avoid all distractions — in particular, that most distracting of influences: women. Therefore, the king declares that no woman shall come within a mile of his court. In a bit of foreshadowing, Berowne predicts that they will not be able to keep their commitments.

A clown, Costard, breaks the king's commandment by seeing the servant, Jaquenetta. A visiting gentleman, Don Armado of Spain, catches the two together and reports this to the king. Costard is playing "fast and loose" (1.2.153), so the king orders a punishment — that Costard eat nothing but bran and water for a week — and gives Don Armado custody of the wayward Costard. Don Armado, however, is himself smitten with Jaquenetta.

Act 2

The Princess of France and three attending ladies (Rosaline, Katherine, and Maria) pay a visit to Navarre, but the new laws do not permit the women to enter the court. Instead, they camp out on the front steps, which does not make a favorable first impression.

The ladies already know the lords who attend Navarre and report them in esteem. Maria knows Longaville, Katherine knows Dumain, and Rosaline knows Berowne. The Lord Berowne likewise recognizes Rosaline, Longaville inquires after Maria, and Dumain asks about Katherine. The princess's advisor, Boyet, remarks how the king could not take his eyes off the princess. He tells her that she can win over the king with just "one loving kiss" (2.1.249). Now you know how everyone will pair off, but what about the men's earlier resolutions?

Act 3

Don Armado remits Costard's punishment if he will carry a letter to Jaquenetta. Costard quickly agrees. Berowne also asks Costard to deliver a letter to Rosaline. Before you can blink, Act 3 is over.

Act 4

Costard gives to the princess Don Armado's letter for Jaquenetta. Costard doesn't realize that he delivered the wrong letter and says that it is Berowne's letter for Rosaline. Jaquenetta receives the letter intended for Rosaline, but she cannot read, so she brings the letter to a schoolmaster. The letter is hot stuff, so the schoolmaster takes it directly to the king.

Berowne is composing another love poem for Rosaline when he spies someone approaching, so he hides himself. The newcomer is the king, composing verses for the princess. He hides when someone approaches: Longaville. Longaville is hard at work on his own sonnet, and he hides when Dumain enters. Dumain wishes that he were not alone in breaking his oath against visiting a woman. Longaville emerges and chides Dumain. The king emerges and chastises the two lords for breaking their oaths. Berowne reveals himself and upbraids the king for committing the same fault. Berowne paints himself as the only one to resist temptation, but then Jaquenetta shows up with Berowne's letter for Rosaline. All the men realize that their oaths were just plain silly.

Act 5

The lords send gifts and letters to the ladies. Then Boyet brings news that the lords will visit them, disguised as foreign visitors. The guys don't want others to know that they are breaking their vows, hence the disguises. The ladies decide to play a trick. They, too, will wear masks, so the lords cannot tell who is who. The lords will need to identify the ladies by finding the gifts of gloves and jewels that they sent. The ladies will swap gifts, so the men will woo the wrong women.

In their disguises, the lords woo the ladies and swear their love and affection. After the men leave, the women share stories, laughing at the men's folly. The men return in their true forms, but the women continue to sport with them.

The king invites the ladies into the court, but the princess refuses. She wants nothing to do with oath-breakers. The men try to swear their love, but the women confound and confuse them. Berowne swears his love to Rosaline, but he earlier confessed his love to the princess because they swapped favors. Similarly, the king had sworn his love to Rosaline instead of to the princess.

SEE IT

On video

1985, BBC: Elijah Moshinsky director, Jonathan Kent as King of Navarre, Clifford Rose as Boyet, and Maureen Lipman as Princess of France

It is time for the princess and her ladies to leave, but the king once again entreats them to stay. She makes a deal: He must retire to a remote hermitage for a full year, and if, at the end of the year, he still professes his love, she will marry him. Each of the ladies imposes the same burden on the lord who would love her. So ends the play: No one gets married, but after a year's penance, everyone will probably live happily ever after.

Measure for Measure

Key characters:

- ✔ Duke of Vienna

- ✔ Angelo, regent for the duke

- ✔ Claudio, a young man in love with Juliet

- ✔ Juliet, a young woman carrying Claudio's child

- ✔ Isabella, sister of Claudio

- ✔ Escalus ("ESS-kah-luss"), advisor to the duke

- ✔ Lucio ("LOO-chee-o"), a rogue

- ✔ Mariana, a lady who was jilted by Angelo

A leading politician gets caught in a sex scandal — some things never change. *Measure for Measure* is often called a "dark comedy," but that doesn't refer to the lighting. With talk of executions, rape, diseases, and fornication, you're not sure how the play will end, but it turns out to be a comedy after all.

Act 1

The Duke of Vienna is packing up and leaving town, and he appoints Angelo as his replacement. By all reports, Angelo is an upright kind of guy and is well-suited to fill in for the duke.

The duke knows that the populace is getting randy and wanton because he has not enforced the laws against fornication and prostitution. He doesn't want to be the tyrant, though, so he lets Angelo play the fall guy. He knows that Angelo will be strict with the law in a way that the duke never was. The duke plans to return to Vienna after Angelo has cleaned up the town. Until then, the duke will watch the proceedings privately, disguised as a friar.

Angelo loses no time in asserting himself as the new ruler of Vienna. To demonstrate his strict adherence to the law, he arrests Claudio and condemns him to death for the crime of fornication. Claudio consummated his marriage a bit prematurely, and for that he must die. This particular law has not been enforced for many years, but suddenly Angelo enforces all the laws strictly. He even tears down the brothels, thereby increasing the unemployment rate among the city's lowlife.

Lucio is a rogue, a scamp, a trickster — a "fantastic," in Shakespeare's words. He wants to help Claudio out of his predicament, so he visits Claudio's sister, Isabella. Lucio explains the situation and asks her to visit Angelo and plead for mercy. She is about to take her vows in a convent but puts her plans on hold so that she can try to rescue her brother.

Act 2

Escalus, one of the duke's advisors, is taken aback by Angelo's sudden and severe enforcement of the law. He agrees that the law is clear and that Claudio broke the law, but still he counsels mercy. Escalus asks Angelo whether he ever entertained similar thoughts. Foreshadowing subsequent scenes, Angelo argues that thought and action are different, and that had he ever acted on improper thoughts, he would expect the same severity of law.

Isabella pleads with Angelo to pardon her brother, but Angelo is adamant. When she asks for pity, he replies, "I show it most of all when I show justice" (2.2.101) by enforcing the law. She persists, saying,

It is excellent

To have a giant's strength, but it is tyrannous

To use it like a giant. (2.2.107–9)

She starts to wear down Angelo's stern position, but he doesn't relent. Instead, he invites her to come again tomorrow. The next day, Angelo lays plain his devices. Isabella can save her brother's life, but at the cost of her virginity. Angelo would commit the same offense for which he condemned Claudio. Isabella is outraged. She would do almost anything to save her brother, but she will not sacrifice her honor.

Act 3

Isabella tells her brother about Angelo's perfidy. At first, Claudio agrees that his sister should not debase herself, but then he thinks about his own life and death and changes his mind. He fears death and begs his sister to reconsider. He argues that sinning to save a brother's life is not a sin at all, but a virtue. Isabella is horrified and leaves.

The duke overhears everything and quickly concocts a plan. Angelo was once engaged to Mariana but left her at the altar. She still loves Angelo, so the duke wants to substitute Mariana for Isabella. He counsels Isabella to agree to Angelo's demands. In her place, though, Mariana will sleep with Angelo and, in a way, consummate the marriage that never quite happened.

Lucio is caught in the web of newly enforced laws, and he, too, is arrested for fathering an illegitimate child. He also makes up tales about the duke, unwittingly telling them to the disguised duke.

The duke has learned a great lesson. He wanted Angelo to be the strict enforcer of the law, but he now sees that severity alone is not enough. A severe enforcer must be honest:

He who the sword of heaven will bear

Should be as holy as severe. (3.2.254–55)

Now the duke must work his plan to restore order and justice.

Act 4

The duke, still in disguise, tells Mariana about his plan. He emphasizes that because Angelo and Mariana were contracted in marriage, his plan is just. Mariana agrees and goes to meet with Angelo "i'th' dark" (4.1.43).

The duke waits for news from Angelo. By now, Mariana has had her assignation with Angelo. According to the agreement, Angelo should now pardon Claudio. Finally, a letter arrives, hastening the execution time. Angelo demands Claudio's head. Apparently, Angelo isn't just a little underhanded with Isabella, but extremely underhanded.

The duke, still disguised as a friar, convinces the jailer to pretend to execute Claudio. The jailer agrees to substitute another condemned prisoner for Claudio.

The duke does not tell Isabella about the substitution, but instead reports Angelo's double-cross. He tells Isabella to ask for justice from the duke, who will be returning shortly. Angelo and Escalus go out to meet the returning duke, but Angelo is guilty and nervous.

On video

1978, BBC: Desmond Davis director, Kenneth Colley as the duke, Kate Nelligan as Isabella, Tim Pigott-Smith as Angelo, Christopher Strauli as Claudio, John McEnery as Lucio, and Jacqueline Pearce as Mariana

Act 5

The duke, no longer disguised, "returns" to Vienna. Isabella and Mariana sue for justice, laying out Angelo's deeds and misdeeds. Until now, Angelo thought that he slept with Isabella, but now he learns that he was wrong. Nonetheless, he puts on a brave face and charges Isabella with lying. Everyone agrees that the new friar (that is, the disguised duke) was the prime instigator, so the duke demands his presence. Like a superhero hiding his secret identity, he leaves and asks Angelo and Escalus to sort things out.

The duke returns in his friar disguise. Escalus orders the friar to prison, and Lucio seizes the opportunity to abuse the arrested friar. All the stories he concocted about the duke he now ascribes to the friar. He pulls off the friar's hood only to discover that the friar is really the duke.

Seeing the duke and realizing that he knows everything, Angelo repents and agrees to marry Mariana. The duke reveals that Claudio is safe and orders him and Juliet to be married immediately. He pardons Lucio for his slanders but forces him to marry the mother of his child. Finally, the duke, not to be left out of the marriage-fest, asks for Isabella's hand in marriage.

The Merchant of Venice

Key characters:

- ✔ Antonio, a merchant
- ✔ Bassanio ("bah-SAHN-ee-o"), friend to Antonio and suitor to Portia
- ✔ Shylock, a moneylender
- ✔ Jessica, daughter of Shylock
- ✔ Lorenzo, lover of Jessica
- ✔ Portia ("POR-sha"), a rich heiress
- ✔ Launcelot, servant to Shylock

The Merchant of Venice is one of Shakespeare's "problem" plays. The villain is Shylock, a Jewish moneylender. In Shakespeare's day, Jews faced much discrimination in England and Europe and were often the victims of racial stereotyping. Shylock suffers the imprint of Elizabethan society, but if you read the play closely, you will see that some Christians don't fare any better.

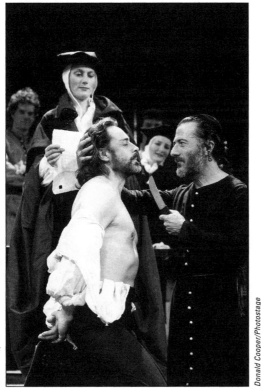

Figure 13-1:
Dustin Hoffman as Shylock in *The Merchant of Venice.*

Donald Cooper/Photostage

Act 1

Bassanio has been living beyond his means, but his best friend, Antonio, a successful merchant, is willing to pay Bassanio's debts, if needed. Bassanio hopes to see his way clear of his financial burdens: He is in love with Portia, whose wealth matches her beauty. For these reasons, she is beset by suitors, and Bassanio needs a little extra cash so that he can woo her in a style suitable to her station. All of Antonio's cash is tied up in ongoing ventures, but his credit is good in Venice, and he will raise the money that Bassanio needs.

Even if Portia returns Bassanio's love, she is not free to choose her husband. Her father, when he died, bequeathed her an unusual inheritance. He left three caskets — of gold, silver, and lead — and every suitor must choose one of the three. The first one to choose correctly wins Portia's hand. While her maid lists the suitors to date, Portia has little to recommend any of them except Bassanio.

Bassanio will borrow 3,000 ducats for three months from Shylock, a Jewish moneylender. Antonio will provide the surety for the loan. Shylock knows Antonio well. Antonio has often cursed and insulted Shylock, spat on him, and kicked him. Even now, when he asks for money, Antonio does not repent of his vicious behavior, but promises to do it again. No wonder Shylock hates Antonio, but his hatred clouds his judgment. Shylock agrees to lend the 3,000 ducats, and if the full amount is not repaid in three months' time, the surety will be a pound of Antonio's flesh. Bassanio is horrified at the prospect, but proud Antonio accepts the bizarre conditions. He expects to receive the money that he needs a month before the loan is due, so he doesn't fear the penalty.

Act 2

Portia's latest suitor agrees to the terms imposed by Portia's father: If he chooses the right casket, he marries Portia, but if he chooses wrong, he promises never to woo or marry another woman. This suitor chooses the gold casket, which is the wrong one, and so goes on his way.

Bassanio has his money and prepares to leave for Belmont, where Portia lives. Before he goes, he hosts a feast for his friends. A friend, Lorenzo, will dine at the feast, but first he has to pick up his date, Jessica, Shylock's daughter. They plan to elope that night. To help her escape, Lorenzo and his friends dress in fancy dress and masks and disguise Jessica similarly. She mixes into the party, but first she helps herself to some of her father's jewels and money.

Shylock learns that his daughter eloped with a Christian and, moreover, robbed him of precious jewels and cash. Naturally, he is distraught, but it is unclear which bothers him most: that his daughter eloped, that she will marry out of her faith, or that she robbed him before she left. Bad tidings come for Antonio, too. One of his ships was wrecked in the English Channel. Antonio has other ships, though. He is too wise to put all his wealth in a single venture.

Portia has yet another suitor to deal with. This one chooses silver, which is also wrong. Portia receives news that Bassanio has arrived. She hopes that he will choose more wisely than the others. (If you've been paying attention, you know which casket is the right one.)

Act 3

Bad news continues to mount for Antonio. Another of his ships wrecked near Genoa. His creditors are demanding payment, and Shylock is certain that Antonio will not be able to repay the loan. Shylock loves money so much; why would he rather have Antonio's pound of flesh? The answer is simple: revenge. Antonio has disgraced Shylock repeatedly, interferes with his business, mocks his religion and race, insults him, sets others against him, and incites his enemies — not for anything that Shylock has done, but just because Shylock is Jewish. But Jews and Christians are more alike than Antonio can imagine. In particular, Jews seek revenge just as much as Christians, and so Shylock does.

Portia wants Bassanio to wait before choosing a casket. If he chooses wrong, he must leave immediately, and Portia wants to spend time with him. Nonetheless, he wants to proceed, and naturally, he chooses the right casket, the lead one, with the inscription that he "must give and hazard all he hath" (2.9.21). Portia and Bassanio are elated and will marry that very night. Portia generously offers to repay the loan, many times over if needed to prevent Shylock from exacting his payment.

Lorenzo and Jessica have made their way to Belmont, and the newlyweds welcome each other. Portia invites the newly arrived couple to stay at her home while Bassanio hastily returns to Venice. After Bassanio leaves, Portia has ideas of her own and follows after him.

Act 4

The loan papers are all in order. No one can see any way out of Antonio's predicament. By the letter of the agreement, the loan is in forfeiture, and Antonio must pay a pound of flesh. The duke will not intercede, lest everyone else with unfavorable terms seeks to evade his bonds. Even when Bassanio offers treble payment, Shylock, consumed by hatred and revenge, would rather have the pound of flesh.

The duke has called for a learned doctor of law to make the final pronouncement of the legality of the loan. That doctor sends a letter that he is ill and recommends a replacement, who happens to be Portia, dressed as a lawyer.

Portia first asks for mercy, not justice. "The quality of mercy is not strain'd" (4.1.182), and mercy blesses the giver and receiver, but Shylock will settle for nothing less than his pound of flesh. Bassanio again offers to repay the loan amount ten times over, and Shylock refuses. Portia pronounces her judgment: The loan is sound, and Shylock is entitled to a pound of flesh. But she also notes that the document does not mention blood, so Shylock is not entitled to any blood, only flesh. Should he also draw any blood, his life would be forfeit and all his goods confiscated.

SEE IT

On video

- 1980, BBC: Jack Gold director, Gemma Jones as Portia, Warren Mitchell as Shylock, and John Rhys-Davies as Salerio

- 1973, Associated TV: Jonathan Miller and John Sichel directors, Laurence Olivier as Shylock, Joan Plowright as Portia, and Jeremy Brett as Bassanio

The tables have turned, and Shylock is now willing to accept treble payment, but Portia will not let him. He demanded justice, and justice he will have. Shylock would accept repayment of the principal only, but Portia is adamant. Shylock forgives the loan entirely and drops his suit against Antonio, but still he cannot escape. For plotting the death of Antonio, his goods and wealth are forfeit, half to the duke and half to Antonio.

Antonio will forgive his half of the fine, provided that Shylock bequeath it to Jessica and Lorenzo. Moreover, Antonio demands that Shylock convert to Christianity. Shylock has no choice but to accept the terms.

Act 5

Bassanio and Antonio arrive in Belmont and deliver their happy news. Portia reveals that she was the lawyer who saved Antonio and, in a most improbable ending to an improbable play, delivers a letter to Antonio, which reveals that some of the ships he thought were lost actually returned to harbor safely.

The Merry Wives of Windsor

Key characters:

- Falstaff, a fat, cowardly knight
- Mistress Ford, friend to Mistress Page
- Mistress Page, friend to Mistress Ford
- Master Ford, husband of Mistress Ford
- Master Page, husband of Mistress Page
- Anne Page, daughter of Mistress and Master Page

✔ Fenton, a young gentleman, suitor to Anne

✔ Doctor Caius, suitor to Anne

✔ Slender, a foolish young man, suitor to Anne

✔ Hugh Evans, a schoolmaster

The character Falstaff was so popular in *Henry IV* (both parts) that Shakespeare spun off a play just to highlight the fat knight. Unlike most of Shakespeare's other plays, *The Merry Wives of Windsor* portrays country life, without kings and queens. The character of highest station is a knight, Sir John Falstaff, who is also the biggest buffoon. The most levelheaded, reasonable, and worthy characters are the merry wives: Mistress Ford and Mistress Page.

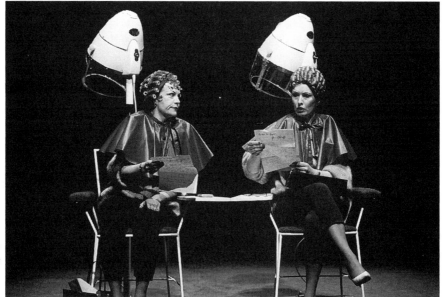

Figure 13-2:
Janet Dale and Lindsay Duncan compare letters in *The Merry Wives of Windsor.*

Donald Cooper/Photostage

Act 1

Anne Page, the daughter of Master and Mistress Page, is the object of much attention. A country justice wants his cousin Slender to marry her, or rather the 700 pounds that she will inherit on her 17th birthday. The other suitors are Doctor Caius and a young gentleman named Fenton.

Sir John Falstaff is the center of the main story. His followers are unruly, in part because Falstaff is out of money and cannot afford to pay them. He must find a way to cut expenses and increase his revenue. First he fires one of his followers, and then he devises a plan to raise money: He will woo Mistress Ford and Mistress Page. As their lover, he will try to gain access to their husbands' purses. His remaining followers refuse to carry his illicit love letters, though, and he fires them, too. That reduces his payroll but leaves him with a boy as his only messenger.

Act 2

Falstaff is a little out of touch with reality. Rather than being flattered by his attentions, Mistress Page is repulsed. To make matters worse, she and her friend Mistress Ford compare their letters and discover that they are identical except for the names. They won't get mad, though; they'll get even.

Falstaff's former employees turn on their ex-boss and reveal his plans to Masters Ford and Page. Page knows his wife to be virtuous and laughs off the matter. Ford is jealous and suspicious and thinks that his wife might fall for the suit. He decides to question Falstaff directly.

Mistress Ford sends a message to Falstaff, saying that she will meet him at ten o'clock, when her husband is away. Mistress Page also sends a message: Her husband is never away, so they cannot meet, but perhaps Falstaff can send his page so that they can easily exchange messages. Falstaff is loath to do so — the page is his sole remaining follower — but he relents, thinking that Mistress Page is warming to his suit.

Master Ford, in disguise and going by the name of Brook, meets with Falstaff. Brook wants to woo Mistress Ford, or so he says, but he is timid. Instead, he offers to pay Falstaff to pave the way. Falstaff reveals that he already has an assignation planned and accepts the payment for what he was about to do anyway. Ford thinks that his wife is false to him and plans to catch her in the act.

Act 3

Master Ford asks Mistress Page where she hired her new page. She pretends that she cannot remember Falstaff's name: "I cannot tell what the dickens his name is" (3.2.17–18). Ford thinks that Mistress Page is fooling around with Falstaff, which further incites his jealousy toward his wife.

It's ten o'clock — time for his wife's rendezvous with Falstaff — so Master Ford rounds up some friends to come to his house. But Mistress Ford is ready for him. She lets Falstaff enter her home, but Mistress Page soon arrives with news that Master Ford is coming. Falstaff hides in a laundry basket, which the servants unload into the Thames River for washing. Ford searches the house from top to bottom but cannot find Falstaff. Nonetheless, he remains convinced that his wife is unfaithful.

Fenton and Anne find some time together, and it becomes clear that her heart belongs to Fenton. Her father wants her to marry Slender, and her mother prefers Doctor Caius.

Falstaff didn't particularly like being dumped in the Thames with a load of dirty laundry, but he has another chance to meet with Mistress Ford. The next morning, at eight o'clock, Master Ford will be out hunting. Falstaff can meet her then. After some initial reluctance, he agrees.

Master Ford, disguised as Brook, approaches Falstaff and asks for the news. Falstaff tells the truth, more or less, and so Ford learns about the laundry basket and the meeting scheduled for the next morning.

Act 4

Mistress Ford lets Falstaff into her home. Once again, Mistress Page comes with an alarm that Master Ford approaches in a jealous rage. There is nowhere for Falstaff to hide, and they can't play the laundry basket trick again. This time, they put Falstaff in a dress and pretend that "she" is the maid's aunt, also called the Witch of Brainford. The only hitch is that Master Ford doesn't like the witch, doesn't allow her in the house, and promised to beat her should she enter the house again. That's exactly what Ford does when he comes in to search for Falstaff. He beats the person he thinks is the witch, and then searches in vain for Falstaff.

The merry wives finally reveal their merry plans to their husbands and friends. Master Ford apologizes to his wife for doubting her. Everyone enjoys a good laugh at Falstaff's expense, and they plan one last humiliation for him. They will ask him to meet the wives at the big oak, called Herne's Oak, named after an ancient legend of Herne the hunter. They ask Falstaff to dress up as Herne and wear antlers. Their secret plan calls for the town's children to dress as fairies and scare Falstaff.

Anne Page will lead the fairies. Amid the confusion, Master Page tells Slender to lead Anne away and secretly marry her. Mistress Page tells the same thing to Doctor Caius. Everyone will be wearing masks, so they will identify Anne by the color of her dress. Fenton and Anne make their own plans to slip away during the midnight Falstaff-bash.

On video

1982, BBC: David Hugh Jones director, Richard Griffiths as Sir John Falstaff, Miranda Foster as Anne Page, Judy Davis as Mistress Ford, and Prunella Scales as Mistress Page

Act 5

The townsfolk play their trick. Falstaff is bewildered and thinks that he sees real fairies. The "fairies" must test Falstaff: If fire cannot burn him, his heart is true, but if he feels the heat, he is corrupt and tainted. The fairies burn him with candles, and of course, he feels the heat and fails the test. For punishment, they pinch him black and blue. Slender slips away with someone wearing a white dress, and Caius takes off with someone in a green dress.

Finally, the Pages, Fords, and all reveal their identities, and Falstaff realizes his position. Everyone forgives Falstaff, who is remorseful, to say the least. Slender and Caius return, extremely upset. Each thought that he was to marry Anne, but slipped into the night with a boy instead. Fenton arrives with the real Anne, after they have married. It's too late to undo the marriage, so Anne's parents accept the inevitable.

A Midsummer Night's Dream

Key characters:

- Theseus, Duke of Athens
- Hippolyta, Queen of the Amazons, betrothed to Theseus
- Lysander, in love with Hermia, then Helena, and then Hermia
- Hermia, in love with Lysander
- Demetrius, in love with Hermia and then Helena
- Helena, in love with Demetrius
- Oberon, King of the Fairies
- Titania, Queen of the Fairies
- Puck, a fairy
- Bottom, a weaver

A Midsummer Night's Dream is one of Shakespeare's most popular and widely performed plays. It is a quintessential comedy, full of confusion and misguided affection. Sit back and enjoy the ride, because you know that everything will turn out okay in the end.

Act 1

Hermia and Lysander are in love. Demetrius and Helena were once in love, but he strayed and fell in love with Hermia. Hermia's father prefers Demetrius and orders her to marry him. If she will not, she must be shut up in a cloister, away from the society of men. She would rather face such a sentence than marry Demetrius.

Lysander acknowledges that "the course of true love never did run smooth" (1.1.134). He and Hermia will elope that very night. They confide their plan to Helena, trying to give her hope of regaining Demetrius.

Meanwhile, in another plot, a band of craftsmen will present a play in honor of Theseus's upcoming wedding to Hippolyta, Queen of the Amazons. Bottom, the weaver, will portray Pyramus, the famous lover of Thisbe.

Act 2

In a wood near Athens, the fairies are active. It seems that the King of the Fairies, Oberon, has his own problems in love. The queen, Titania, has adopted a human boy and spends all her time with the boy, making Oberon jealous. When the King and Queen of the Fairies have a row, it affects everyone around them, disrupting the land, seas, and air.

Oberon asks his servant Puck to find a special flower that yields a love potion. He will put the potion in Titania's eyes to cause her to love the first creature she sees. Oberon has the antidote but won't give it unless Titania turns over the boy. Puck brings the flower to Oberon. They find Titania, and while she sleeps, Oberon squeezes the flower on her eyes.

Lysander and Hermia escape Athens into the forest, but they aren't alone. Helena revealed their plans to Demetrius, who follows, trying to catch up with Hermia. In desperation, Helena follows, pleading with Demetrius.

Oberon wants to help Helena. He tells Puck to put the love potion in Demetrius's eyes so that he will fall in love with Helena and leave Hermia alone. Puck searches the forest for the Athenian couple but finds Lysander and Hermia. He mistakes them for the couple Oberon told him to find and puts the love potion in Lysander's eyes.

Helena searches for Demetrius but stumbles over Lysander instead. He wakes up, and when he sees her, the love potion takes effect and he falls in love with her on the spot. He spurns Hermia and declares his total love for Helena. She resists, trying to remind him of his love for Hermia, finally running away. He runs after her, leaving Hermia alone.

Act 3

The players meet in the woods to rehearse their play. Just for the fun of it, Puck gives Bottom the head of an ass. The others run away in fear, but Bottom doesn't understand what they are afraid of. Titania wakes up and sees Bottom, and the love potion makes her fall in love with him, ass's head and all. Puck brings the news to Oberon, who enjoys the sport. He then asks whether Puck succeeded in applying the love potion to the Athenian lord's eyes (meaning Demetrius), and Puck affirms that he did.

Demetrius finds Hermia, but she has lost Lysander. She doesn't know that he is chasing Helena, and she accuses Demetrius of foul play. Oberon realizes that Puck goofed, and he wants to put matters right. He administers the love potion to Demetrius's eyes and commands Puck to find Helena and bring her before Demetrius. Puck's commentary sums up the play neatly, "Lord, what fools these mortals be!" (3.2.115).

Lysander doggedly pursues Helena. Demetrius wakes up and sees her, and the potion causes him to fall in love with her. She thinks that it is just a cruel trick to mock her.

Oberon and Puck clearly have more work to finish that night. Puck leads the lovers astray in the woods until they fall asleep. Then he puts the antidote in Lysander's eyes to restore his love for Hermia.

Act 4

Titania still fawns over Bottom. Oberon has found her in the woods and has taken the changeling child that he wanted. Now he is content and restores Titania's eyes to normal. She wakes up, and the two are reconciled.

In the woods, Theseus and Hippolyta stumble upon the sleeping forms of Lysander, Demetrius, Hermia, and Helena. They wake the lovers, who try to explain their presence. The past goings-on seem like a dream to them. Lysander confesses to eloping with Hermia. Demetrius, however, now loves only Helena and no longer desires to marry Hermia. They all return to Athens to sort out the strange matters.

On film and video

SEE IT

- 1999, Fox Searchlight: Michael Hoffman director, Kevin Kline as Bottom, Michelle Pfeiffer as Titania, and Calista Flockhart as Helena.

- 1996, RSC: Adrian Noble director, Alex Jennings as Oberon and Theseus, and Lindsay Duncan as Titania and Hippolyta. Not available in the U.S.

- 1981, BBC: Elijah Moshinsky director, Pippa Guard as Hermia, Nicky Henson as Demetrius, Robert Lindsay as Lysander,

Cherith Mellor as Helena, and Geoffrey Palmer as Quince.

- 1968, RSC: Peter Hall director, Diana Rigg as Helena, Ian Richardson as Oberon, Judi Dench as Titania, Helen Mirren as Hermia, and Ian Holm as Puck.

- 1935, Warner Brothers: William Dieterle and Max Reinhardt directors, James Cagney as Bottom, Dick Powell as Lysander, Mickey Rooney as Puck, and Olivia De Havilland as Hermia.

The players wonder what happened to Bottom. Without him, the play cannot go on. He returns, normal head intact. He won't tell them what happened in the forest. He just says that it's show time.

Act 5

The lovers have sorted out their affairs, and everyone is happy with the current arrangements. Demetrius and Helena love each other; Lysander and Hermia love each other. Everyone enjoys the play of Pyramus and Thisbe.

Pyramus and Thisbe are in love, but their parents keep them separated by a wall. They promise to elope, but a lion chases away Thisbe. Pyramus cannot find Thisbe, only her mantle (or cloak), stained by the lion's bloody mouth. He thinks the worst and kills himself. She finds his body and kills herself. The rustic players make sure that the audience understands that it's just a play, that no one is truly hurt, and that it's not a real lion.

A dance follows, and the party draws to a close. The fairies bless the bridal beds so that all the couples and their future children can live happily ever after.

Much Ado About Nothing

Key characters:

- ✔ Don Pedro, Prince of Arragon
- ✔ Benedick, a young lord
- ✔ Beatrice, niece of Leonato
- ✔ Claudio, a young lord, in love with Hero
- ✔ Hero, daughter of Leonato
- ✔ Leonato, Governor of Messina
- ✔ Don John, bastard brother of Don Pedro
- ✔ Dogberry, a silly constable

Much Ado About Nothing intertwines two very different love stories. The story of Hero and Claudio is a classic tale of love won, lost, and regained, with a twist of dastardly doings by Don John. The other story is the unlikely pairing of Beatrice and Benedick, who fight with each other to hide their true feelings.

Act 1

Don Pedro returns triumphantly from war and drops in on the local governor, Leonato. With him come the young gentlemen Claudio and Benedick. Immediately, you are treated to verbal fireworks between Beatrice and Benedick. They fight with words the way soldiers fight with swords. Claudio, on the other hand, has a softer side. He is enamored of Hero, the daughter of Leonato.

Don Pedro, Claudio, and the gang are all staying at Leonato's home while in town, and Leonato is throwing a party in celebration. Don Pedro offers to arrange the marriage between Claudio and Hero that very night.

Don John is Pedro's nasty brother. He's a bastard, so his only goal is life is to cause trouble and mischief. (Read more about bastardy in Shakespeare's plays in Chapter 2.)

Act 2

Don John tries to ruin Leonato's party by telling Claudio that Don Pedro wants Hero for himself. Claudio rushes to judgment and condemns Pedro as a false friend. In truth, Pedro has secured Hero's and Leonato's agreement for the match with Claudio. Fortunately, they straighten matters out, and the wedding day is set for one week hence. Claudio is speechless with delight, managing to say only, "Silence is the perfectest herald of joy. I were but little happy if I could say how much" (2.1.288–89).

Beatrice is of a different mind than her cousin. She and the bachelors will be "as merry as the day is long" (2.1.45). She prefers words of spite to words of love, especially when Benedick is the target. This gives Don Pedro an idea: He will play Cupid and make Beatrice and Benedick fall in love. For this Herculean task, he enlists the aid of Leonato, Claudio, and Hero.

Don Pedro, Leonato, and Claudio tell Benedick that Beatrice is completely, head-over-heels in love with him. They don't tell him to his face, though. They pretend to hold a private discussion where Benedick can overhear them. Benedick hears this, believes it, and falls in love with her. It's more a case of love-at-first-praise than love-at-first-sight.

Act 3

Hero and her waiting woman lay the same trap for Beatrice. They pretend not to notice Beatrice and tell each other how Benedick is completely in love with her. Beatrice also falls for the gambit and professes love for Benedick.

Figure 13-3: Kenneth Branagh and Emma Thompson in Branagh's film of *Much Ado About Nothing*.

Everett Collection

Don John also has plans, but to a different end. He leads Claudio and Don Pedro to a window, where they see a man and woman together. The man calls the woman Hero, and that's all the evidence Claudio and Don Pedro need to believe that Hero is unfaithful.

Rising (or is that descending?) to new levels of silliness, Shakespeare introduces the constable Dogberry. His is a classic role, a master of the malapropism. (See Chapter 5 to find out more about malapropisms and other word games.) Dogberry is a fool in every way. He lets the night watch sleep because he "cannot see how sleeping should offend" (3.3.40–41). Nonetheless, the night watchmen overhear Don John's henchmen talking. One explains that he was the man in the window, calling a servant "Hero" and so fooling Claudio and Don Pedro. For his prank, Don John paid him 1,000 ducats. The watchmen fall upon the pair and arrest them.

Dogberry tells Leonato that he has arrested two villains and asks Leonato to question them. Leonato is busy arranging the marriage of his daughter, Hero, and doesn't want to be bothered by the foolish Dogberry. He asks Dogberry to conduct the examination himself.

Act 4

The wedding ceremony begins, but Claudio refuses to marry Hero. In the midst of the ceremony, he accuses her of infidelity. Don Pedro backs up his accusation, and they storm out of the wedding. Of course, Hero is baffled, Leonato is upset, and Beatrice is angry. They pretend that Hero died from the shame of the accusation. (See *The Winter's Tale* for another example of how Shakespeare uses this plot device.) After everyone believes that she is dead, they can seek to uncover the truth. It's a familiar gambit: From Juliet's drugged sleep in *Romeo and Juliet* to Hermione's fake death in *The Winter's Tale,* Shakespeare often reused his favorite plot elements.

Benedick witnesses the whole affair. He recognizes that Claudio and Don Pedro are honest men, so if they have been misled, it must be Don John's doing. After Leonato leads away his daughter, only Benedick and Beatrice remain. In the past, Benedick might have supported his friends, but he serves a greater purpose now. Grudgingly, Benedick and Beatrice reveal their hearts to each other, professing their mutual love.

Meanwhile, Dogberry tries to interrogate the prisoners. He believes that they are thieves who have stolen 1,000 ducats from Don John and have falsely accused him of knavery. Fortunately, the sexton is recording the testimony and recognizes the truth in what they say. He hastens to Leonato to present the results of the examination.

SEE IT

On video

- 1993, Renaissance Films: Kenneth Branagh director and as Benedick, Emma Thompson as Beatrice, Denzel Washington as Don Pedro, Keanu Reeves as Don John, and Michael Keaton as Dogberry. This film is a wonderful production in a fairy-tale setting.

- 1984, BBC, Stuart Burge director, Cherie Lunghi as Beatrice, Katharine Levy as Hero, Jon Finch as Don Pedro, and Robert Lindsay as Benedick. Lunghi gives an excellent performance.

- 1978, BBC, Donald McWhinnie director, Nigel Davenport as Don Pedro, Penelope Keith as Beatrice, Ian Richardson as Don John, and Michael York as Benedick.

- 1967, BBC: Alan Cooke and Franco Zeffirelli directors, Derek Jacobi as Don Pedro, Maggie Smith as Beatrice, and Robert Stephens as Benedick.

Act 5

Leonato finally gets to hear the sexton's report and goes to confront Don John's henchmen. In front of Claudio and Don Pedro, the ringleader reveals the full story of how Don John paid him handsomely to carry out their plan. Claudio, needless to say, is full of remorse. Leonato offers a substitute: His daughter is "dead," but Claudio can marry his niece instead. But first, Claudio must publicly apologize.

The next day, Claudio arrives as scheduled, where he finds that Hero is alive after all. "She died . . . but whiles her slander liv'd" (5.4.66). Benedick admits his love for Beatrice, and they, too, will get married. News arrives that Don John has been captured. All the villains have been arrested, and all the lovers are getting married, so the play can end.

Pericles, Prince of Tyre

Key characters:

- Pericles, Prince of Tyre
- Thaisa, Princess of Pentapolis, later married to Pericles
- Marina, daughter of Pericles and Thaisa

  - Cleon, Governor of Tarsus
  - Cerimon, a lord of Ephesus
  - Helicanus, a lord of Tyre

Pericles, Prince of Tyre wins the Improbable Plot Award. To help you keep track of the sometimes disjointed action, a Chorus sets the scene and fills in missing details, starting with King Antiochus and his beautiful daughter — so beautiful that he cannot resist her charms and commits incest with her. To prevent someone from taking away his bedfellow, the king passes a law: Anyone who would marry his daughter must answer a riddle correctly. If the suitor answers incorrectly, he dies. That doesn't sound much like a comedy, but don't worry; it gets better, or at least weirder.

Act 1

Pericles arrives in Antioch to try his luck with the riddle. He is willing to take the risk because the prize is so beautiful. The riddle asks who can be "father, son, and husband" (1.1.69) and who "mother, wife, and yet his child" (1.1.70). Pericles correctly discerns the matter of the riddle, namely Antiochus's incest with his daughter. Pericles would die if he answered incorrectly, but to answer correctly would reveal the incestuous relationship to the world, which Antiochus would not allow. Pericles faces death either way, so he flees from Antioch and returns home to Tyre.

His counselor Helicanus suggests that Pericles travel abroad. Antiochus will not allow Pericles to live in possession of the answer to the riddle, so his life is in jeopardy if he remains in Tyre. Pericles embarks for Tarsus, just in time to escape an assassin sent by Antiochus. The assassin assumes that Pericles will surely perish at sea, so he gives up and goes home.

Pericles chooses Tarsus because it is beset by famine, and he brings ships full of grain. He wins the favor of the people and their governor, Cleon.

Act 2

Pericles hears about the assassin's arrival in Tyre but doesn't know that the assassin is no longer in pursuit. Unsure of his safety in Tarsus, Pericles flees again. This time he is shipwrecked near Pentapolis. Three fishermen rescue him and also pull up a suit of armor — wreckage from his ship. In an amazing stroke of luck, the local king is hosting a tournament in honor of his daughter Thaisa. Pericles, suited with the rescued, rusty armor, competes and wins. This is a romantic comedy, so Pericles and Thaisa fall in love and get married.

Back in Tyre, the people want their prince back. Helicanus has 12 months to find out where Pericles is before the people choose a new leader.

Act 3

Pericles learns that Antiochus is dead, and that he must return to Tyre soon. He and his wife embark for Tyre, but again his ship founders, this time with his new wife, who is pregnant, on board. She gives birth at sea but dies in childbirth. The superstitious mariners demand that Pericles dump the body overboard or else they believe that they will never reach port safely. Coincidentally, they have a watertight coffin on board. With rich jewels and an epitaph, Pericles bids his wife farewell. He names his daughter Marina in honor of her birth at sea.

The coffin washes ashore at Ephesus, which is ruled by the learned Cerimon. He realizes — in case your credulity has not been stretched enough yet — that Thaisa is not completely dead and, with his art, he revives her. She thinks that Pericles perished at sea and retires to a nearby convent.

Pericles lands at the nearest port, which is Tarsus, and asks his friend Cleon and his wife to raise Marina as befits a princess. He continues to Tyre to satisfy his subjects that he still lives.

Act 4

Marina grows to womanhood and is by all reports a gentle, virtuous, educated young lady, perfect in every way, much to the annoyance of the queen, whose own daughter is eclipsed by Marina's virtue. The queen hires a murderer to do away with Marina, but pirates seize the girl before the murderer can complete his plan. He tells the queen that Marina is dead. Cleon is angry at the queen's betrayal of Pericles's trust, but Pericles is far away. They build a monument in Marina's memory and hope that Pericles never learns the truth.

Their wishes don't come true. Pericles wants to see his daughter, so he travels to Tarsus, only to learn of her supposed death. He falls into deep despair and withdraws from the world.

The pirates sell Marina into slavery as a prostitute. The bawds expect to earn a huge profit from her beauty and charm, but they underestimate her. In true fairy tale fashion, every time they try to sell her virginity, she convinces the would-be customers, including the local governor, to turn from a life of vice. Finally, she convinces her purchasers that her abilities are of more use in teaching gentle skills, such as singing and dancing, than working in a brothel.

SEE IT

Act 5

Pericles's ship wanders the sea aimlessly. The crew's leader speaks to no one, does nothing, eats next to nothing, and pines for his lost wife and daughter. By chance, the ship arrives at Mitylene, where Marina lives. The governor visits the ship, but Pericles will speak to no one. The governor suggests that they ask a gentlewoman of Mitylene to talk to him. She is renowned for her fair speech and soothing words of comfort. They bring her on board. When she sees Pericles in his pitiful state, she challenges his woes with her own.

Marina (you knew it would be Marina, didn't you?) relates her story, from her watery birth and the loss of her mother to the attempted murder to being almost forced into prostitution. As she unfolds her tale, Pericles perks up and slowly discovers his daughter, whom he had given up for dead. Marina finds the father she never knew, and to add to the good news, the governor asks to marry Marina.

One last outrageous scene ends the play. Pericles has a dream in which the goddess Diana visits him and asks that he go to her temple in Ephesus. He does, bringing his newly discovered daughter and her new husband. Before the altar, Pericles recounts his tale of woe, and the head priestess recognizes her long-lost husband. The family is reunited. Pericles and Thaisa will return to her country, where Pericles will reign as king, and Marina and her husband will rule in Tyre.

The Taming of the Shrew

Key characters:

- Petruchio, a gentleman of Verona, later married to Katherina
- Katherina, a shrewish daughter of Baptista
- Bianca, daughter of Baptista
- Lucentio, suitor to Bianca
- Baptista, a rich gentleman of Padua

The Taming of the Shrew is unusual in how it presents a play-within-a-play. A common theatrical convention is for the play onstage to contain another play. *Hamlet* (see Chapter 15) gives an excellent example of this. *The Taming of the Shrew* is different. The first two scenes introduce one story, where itinerant actors will perform a play, and the rest of Shakespeare's play is that play-within-a-play. The original play disappears. Most modern productions of *The Taming of the Shrew* omit the first two scenes and present only the inner play.

Act 1

The first two scenes start the outer story. A man refuses to leave a bar, saying, "I'll not budge an inch" (Induction.1.14), and falls into a drunken sleep. A lord and his hunting party stop at the inn, and the lord decides to have some fun with the poor man. He asks his servants to dress him up in fine clothing, put him in the lord's bedroom, and pretend that he is the lord. When the poor man wakes up, he is confused. The servants pretend that he suffers from an illness and has forgotten who he is. For his entertainment, a traveling acting troupe will present a play.

The inner play begins, which is *The Taming of the Shrew*. Baptista is the wealthy father to two daughters: Katherina and Bianca. Bianca is as beautiful as she is kind, but her elder sister, Katherina, is mean, spiteful, and shrewish. Guess which one all the men in Padua want to marry? The father desperately wants to unload Katherina, so he will not let Bianca marry until Katherina marries first.

A visitor from Pisa, Lucentio, is also captivated by Bianca's beauty and joins the ranks of her panting, restless suitors. He hatches a plan: He will approach one of the other suitors and offer his services as a tutor for Bianca. Thus he will get to spend some private time with Bianca to press his own suit. To disguise his station, he trades clothing with his servant. His servant will claim to be Lucentio of Pisa.

Another visitor arrives in Padua: Petruchio comes from Verona to visit his friend, who happens to be one of Bianca's suitors. Petruchio wants to find a wife and settle down. Any wife will do, provided that she is rich. His needs are simple: He plans to marry, and "if wealthily, then happily" (1.2.75).

Act 2

Petruchio introduces himself to Baptista and asks for Katherina's hand in marriage. At first, Baptista is incredulous, but Petruchio is in earnest. Her reputation doesn't faze him, because he can be as proud, curt, and rough as she. When Petruchio and Katherina meet, they engage immediately in a war of wits — trading barbs and insults. Nonetheless, he insists on marrying her. She resists, but Petruchio tells the others that she secretly agreed and keeps up her shrewish front in public.

Now that Baptista has arranged Katherina's marriage, Bianca's suitors line up to claim her. Baptista offers his daughter's hand to the highest bidder. (You can see how Baptista earned his wealth.) Lucentio's servant — still pretending to be his master — bids the highest, boasting of several homes, much land, and a fleet of merchant ships. Another suitor points out that this wealth belongs to Lucentio's father, and if Lucentio were to die young, Bianca might be left penniless. Baptista requires a pledge from Lucentio's father to support Bianca.

Act 3

Petruchio arrives late to his own wedding. Worse, he shows up in a pathetic state, wearing tattered clothing. Naturally, Baptista is put off by this dismal show from his new son-in-law, but Petruchio insists that Katherina is marrying the man, not the clothes. The wedding ceremony takes place offstage, and then Petruchio hustles his bride home, not even stopping for the wedding feast that Baptista has arranged.

Petruchio is out to tame his wife by being more of a shrew than she. He yells, curses, and insults the servants worse than Katherina ever did. When a servant brings water for washing, Petruchio strikes him for letting some of the water spill. When the servants bring food, Petruchio turns it away, saying the meat is overcooked. Katherina finds herself in a new position — defending the servants and asking for patience and forgiveness. Petruchio goes further, preventing Katherina from sleeping. He throws off the sheets and bedcovers, saying that the bed was not made properly. Thus, Katherina doesn't eat, sleep, or get any rest from her abusive husband.

Act 4

Bianca has chosen Lucentio (the real Lucentio, dressed as a teacher), but his servant must keep up the pretense as the fake Lucentio to keep Baptista off the track. The servant finds a traveler, whom he solicits as a substitute for Lucentio's father. The fake Lucentio needs the fake father to sign the pledge to support Bianca.

Petruchio's taming of Katherina continues. A tailor brings a dress for Katherina, but Petruchio sends it away because it's the wrong fashion. Whatever she says or wants, Petruchio says the opposite. If the time is two o'clock but Petruchio says that it is seven, Katherina must agree that it is seven or provoke his wrath. Now she knows what it's like to be the receiver of shrewish fury.

The pretend Lucentio and his pretend father discuss the final arrangements for Bianca's marriage. At the same time, the real Lucentio elopes with Bianca.

SEE IT

On video

- 1980, BBC: Jonathan Miller director, Sarah Badel as Kate, Susan Penhaligon as Bianca, and John Cleese as Petruchio. A disappointing performance by John Cleese.

- 1967, Columbia Pictures: Franco Zeffirelli director, Elizabeth Taylor as Katherine, and Richard Burton as Petruchio. A delightful film. Elizabeth Taylor at her best.

- 1929, United Artists: Sam Taylor director, Douglas Fairbanks as Petruchio, Dorothy Jordan as Bianca, and Mary Pickford as Katherine.

The next time you meet Petruchio and Katherina, they are on the road to Padua for Bianca's wedding. He has tamed the wild shrew. They meet an old man on the road, and when Petruchio says that the old man is a young girl, Katherina greets the man as a "young budding virgin" (4.5.36).

It turns out that the man is Lucentio's real father, on his way to visit his son in Padua. They arrive, but the pretend father berates the real father until no one knows who is who, at least until Lucentio returns from the church. He sees his real father and knows that the game is up.

Act 5

Baptista thinks that he just arranged a marriage with Lucentio, only to learn that the suitor is actually Lucentio's servant. He also learns that his daughter has secretly married someone else, although that person turns out to be the real Lucentio. It will take time and lots of explaining to straighten everything out.

Lucentio has appeased Baptista, and now all that's left is to celebrate the various weddings that have taken place. Petruchio and Katherina are happily married, much to everyone's surprise. Lucentio and Bianca are married, and a local widow agrees to marry another of Bianca's suitors.

To convince everyone that Katherina is no longer a forward shrew, Petruchio proposes a wager. Each husband will call for his wife, and the first wife to respond wins the bet. Both the other bridegrooms ask for their wives, who respond that they are busy and cannot come. Petruchio calls for Katherina, who obediently comes and asks what his will is.

Katherina lectures the other wives on a woman's place: subservient to her husband. It's a message that may not sit well with a modern audience, but remember that in the Elizabethan world, everyone had a place in the natural order of the universe (which can you read more about in Chapter 2). Just as a gentleman was subject to his lord, so a lady was subject to her husband:

Such duty as the subject owes the prince

Even such a woman oweth to her husband. (5.2.156–157)

The Tempest

Key characters:

- ✔ Prospero, rightful Duke of Milan
- ✔ Miranda, daughter of Prospero
- ✔ Ferdinand, son of Alonso
- ✔ Alonso, King of Naples
- ✔ Antonio, brother of Prospero and usurping Duke of Milan
- ✔ Sebastian, traitorous brother of Alonso
- ✔ Ariel, a spirit, servant to Prospero
- ✔ Caliban, a deformed, savage creature, slave to Prospero

The Tempest is a play of wonder and magic. The entire play takes place on an island inhabited by spirits, where people are just visitors. It is the perfect setting for a play about the trials and triumphs of humanity and human relationships in particular: love, hate, and fear.

Act 1

The Tempest opens, fittingly enough, with a tempest. On a ship are Alonso, the King of Naples, his brother Sebastian and son Ferdinand, plus Antonio, the Duke of Milan, and their servants. The ship apparently sinks in the storm, but this is a comedy, so you know that no one dies.

Meanwhile, on an island, you meet the heroes of the story: Prospero and his daughter, Miranda. Prospero raised Miranda on this island, and she has had no other human contact since her infancy. You learn that Prospero is the rightful Duke of Milan, and that his brother, Antonio, usurped his position with some help from Alonso, King of Naples.

Prospero, a man of learning, is a powerful magician. In Milan, he was too busy reading, learning, and studying to bother with affairs of state, so he let his dukedom slip through his unwary fingers. He learned his lesson, though, and is now ready to resume his proper place. Therefore, he raised the storm to bring the ship to his island. Through his magic, Prospero is master of the island and has arranged everything to his liking. Watch the play and his plan unfold.

The king's son, Ferdinand, washes ashore separately from the rest of the ship's company. Thinking that he is the sole survivor of the shipwreck, he mourns his father's death. Ariel, Prospero's spirit servant, leads Ferdinand to where he meets Miranda. For the first time in her life, she sees a man other than her father, so of course they fall in love immediately. (It's a comedy, after all.)

Act 2

On another part of the island, Alonso thinks that his son died when the ship foundered. He and the rest of the ship's passengers have survived, but magic is clearly at work because their clothing is clean, dry, and fresh.

If the king's son is dead, the heir to the throne apparently becomes Alonso's daughter, Claribel, who recently married the King of Tunis. (Claribel does not appear in the play.) The king's brother, Sebastian, would much rather have the throne all to himself. Antonio agrees to help him. After all, he has experience in stealing titles: He usurped Milan from his brother Prospero.

By now, you know who the heroes are (Prospero, Miranda, and Ferdinand) and who the major villains are (Alonso, Sebastian, and Antonio). But this is a comedy, so the villains are merely nasty, not evil, and justice will prevail in the end.

Act 3

Like any father, Prospero is wary of the man wooing his daughter, so he requires Ferdinand to prove his love through burdensome tasks. Ferdinand is unaccustomed to manual labor, but he willingly undertakes his work if it will bring him closer to Miranda. Together, they pledge their love and promise to marry each other.

Prospero has much to manage on his island. His slave, Caliban, happens upon two servants from the ship. Caliban has lived around spirits all his life, and he mistakes the two drunken servants for gods, and their bottle of wine for "celestial liquor" (2.2.116).

Together, they fall to drinking and fighting. Caliban, however, has evil plans in mind, and he recruits the two silly servants to help him kill Prospero. He promises Miranda as a prize. Ariel witnesses their plotting and reports back to Prospero.

Act 4

Ferdinand finishes his tasks, and at last Prospero gives him permission to marry Miranda. He prepares a magical entertainment but suddenly remembers Caliban and his cronies. The entertainment ends, the spirit actors disappear, and Prospero compares humans' brief lives to those of the spirits: "We are such stuff / As dreams are made on" (4.1.156–57).

A magician's work is never done. Prospero conjures spirit hounds that rouse Caliban and the drunks and give them chase. Prospero exults in his triumphs. All his plans are succeeding, and it is time to bring them to a close.

Act 5

In the final act, Prospero brings together the various parties who have been wandering the island. He confronts Sebastian and Antonio and chastises them for plotting against the king's life and for stealing Prospero's rightful position in Milan. Were Prospero to reveal their treason to the king, their lives would be in jeopardy, but instead he forgives them. All he asks for is the return of his dukedom.

Prospero reunites Ferdinand with his father, and Miranda marvels at meeting so many people after a lifetime of seclusion, exclaiming,

O brave new world,

That has such people in 't. (5.1.183–84)

Ariel leads the ship's crew to reunite them with their passengers. The ship is safely harbored, and the crew has slept in enchantment. Finally, Prospero brings forth the drunken servants and publicly accuses them of plotting against his life. He turns them over to their masters, again showing forgiveness.

Prospero is master of his island world, but he gives it all up to return to the natural world, where he belongs. He holds the lives of Antonio and Sebastian in his hands, but he forgives them for deeds that most people find unforgivable. He arranges events to ensure that Ferdinand and Miranda will fall in love, but he still feels a fatherly care to be sure that Miranda chooses her husband well. In the end, he gives up his island and his power; frees his servant, Ariel; and returns home to an ordinary dukedom, in an ordinary life, but one more fitting for an ordinary man.

SEE IT

Troilus and Cressida

Key characters:

✔ Pandarus, a meddler, uncle of Cressida

✔ Troilus, son of King Priam of Troy, lover of Cressida

✔ Cressida, daughter of a Trojan priest, lover of Troilus

✔ Hector, son of King Priam, Troy's war hero

✔ Paris, son of King Priam, abductor of Helen

✔ Ulysses, a Grecian commander

✔ Achilles, a Grecian war hero

✔ Ajax, a Grecian war hero

✔ Diomedes, a Grecian commander

✔ Thersites, servant to Ajax and scurrilous rogue

It all started with Helen, whose beauty was famous throughout the world. Paris seduced her and brought her to his home, Troy. Naturally, this upset her husband, who launched an enormous navy of a thousand ships to retrieve Helen. This is not their story.

The Trojan War is merely the backdrop for *Troilus and Cressida,* a play that warns against meddling and interfering with the natural order (which you can read about in Chapter 2). The first of two plots centers on Pandarus, a busybody who interferes in matters of the heart. The second plot involves Ulysses, a Greek commander, who meddles in matters of the mind. Both their plans backfire, but in different ways. Like *Cymbeline* and *Two Noble*

Kinsmen, this play is difficult to classify. The title characters don't die, so the play isn't a tragedy, so of the three categories, comedy is the best fit. Don't expect the love match to end happily, though. For a comedy, this play is a real downer.

Figure 13-4:
Peter
O'Toole in
*Troilus and
Cressida.*

Shakespeare Centre Library

Act 1

Pandarus plays matchmaker between his niece, Cressida, and Troilus. He has already succeeded in winning over Troilus, who now pines for Cressida. Pandarus also works on Cressida and reminds her of Troilus's virtues. Pandarus goes overboard and praises Troilus above his brother Hector, the greatest Trojan hero. His exaggerations pay off, and Cressida falls in love with Troilus.

Just outside Troy, the other plot unfolds. The Greek army has been camped outside Troy for seven years, and they are no closer to success than when they started. The Greek commanders lament their poor performance in the war and try to figure out what went wrong. Ulysses offers his theory: They have not followed the natural order, or the chain of command, as we might call it today. "Untune that string, / And hark what discord follows" (1.3.109–10). The natural order requires soldiers to obey their commanders, but Achilles disdains and mocks the Greek generals. Achilles and his servant stay in their tent "upon a lazy bed" (1.3.147) and refuse to fight, which sets a bad example for the rest of the army. The other generals agree with Ulysses and his assessment of the problem.

A Trojan messenger brings a challenge to the Greek army. Hector is bored and wants to have some fun. He challenges any Greek to a sporting fight over the honor of their lovers. Ulysses sees the challenge as an opportunity. He will offer Ajax, not Achilles, as the Greek challenger. Choosing Ajax instead of Achilles just might gall Achilles enough to rouse him from his tent and join the army once more.

Act 2

Further evidence that the natural order is upset in the Greek camp comes in the form of Thersites, who is such an arrogant slave that he mocks and insults his master, Ajax. Ajax tries to learn about the proclamation concerning Hector's challenge, but Thersites refuses to cooperate. Finally, Ajax learns from Achilles that a lottery will determine Hector's challenger. Ulysses revealed his plan in Act 1, so you know that the lottery is fixed, but of course, Ajax and Achilles don't know this.

Hector — Troy's bravest, greatest soldier — counsels Paris to "let Helen go" (2.2.17) and return her to the Greeks rather than continue the war. He argues that the Trojans are violating the natural law by keeping Helen from her rightful husband. Troilus disagrees, and the brothers debate the point. In the end, Hector relents and agrees with his brothers, Troilus and Paris, to keep Helen. This decision violates the natural order, so you know that rack and ruin are the inevitable results, but you have three acts to go before you see exactly how matters pan out.

The Greek commanders manipulate Ajax to do their will. Achilles is still proud and disdainful, refusing even to talk with the Greek generals. The generals scorn Achilles for his treatment of them, and at the same time commend Ajax because he is so unlike Achilles. Privately, however, they see the two as similar as two can be.

Act 3

Pandarus finally succeeds in bringing Troilus and Cressida together. He isn't merely a go-between, but much more. He encourages them, pushes them, and entreats them to consummate their relationship. The lovers swear their eternal love and faith to each other. In a heavy-handed bit of foreshadowing, Pandarus takes credit for bringing the lovers together; therefore, should they ever prove false:

Let all pitiful goers-between be called to the world's end after my name: call them all Pandars. (3.2.197–99)

And so we do.

Cressida's father defects from the Trojans to the Greeks. In exchange for secrets about the Trojan army, he wants his daughter, Cressida, to join him, so he asks the Greeks to trade a prisoner for Cressida. Agamemnon agrees to the deal and asks Diomedes to effect the exchange. Disloyalty violates the natural law, so expect the worst to come of this exchange.

Act 4

Diomedes exchanges prisoners, brings Cressida to the Greek encampment, and shows her off to the Greek generals. The first general salutes her "with a kiss" (4.5.19), as do the other generals while she flirts with them. Almost instantly, she seems to forget about Troilus and her promises. That's what comes of the love that Pandarus manufactured, rather than one that comes from the heart.

Trumpets call forth the armies. Hector and Ajax are ready to fight. They fight for a while, with neither gaining the upper hand, but Hector stops the fight. The two are cousins, and he doesn't want to carry the fight any further, lest he harm his close relation.

Act 5

Achilles invites the Trojan warriors and Greek generals to a party in his tent. Diomedes bows out, saying that he has other affairs to attend to.

It turns out that his affair is with Cressida. Ulysses brings Troilus to the tent, where they hide and watch Cressida break faith with Troilus and agree to meet with Diomedes. She hasn't forgotten about Troilus, but absence makes the heart go wander, and she falls for the lover in front of her.

The next day, the warriors prepare for battle. Hector and Troilus perform heroic feats, and the Greeks are in trouble. Achilles still keeps from the field, but now Ajax is so puffed up by the Greek generals that he acts like Achilles and is too proud to fight. So much for their brilliant plan to get Achilles onto the battlefield.

Then Hector kills Achilles's servant. This finally rouses the great Achilles to don his armor and enter the battle. Ajax, too, loses a friend and enters the fight. All the meddling in the world doesn't get the warriors onto the battlefield. What finally succeeds is injury to their friends. To restore order, the warriors must fight and support their friends. After order is restored in the Greek army, Achilles and his followers find Hector and kill him.

On video

1981, BBC: Jonathan Miller director, Anton Lesser as Troilus, Suzanne Burden as Cressida, and Charles Gray as Pandarus. A decent production.

With the natural order restored on the battlefield, Shakespeare needs to finish the other plot line. Troilus turns all this thoughts to battle and hatred. As he leaves the stage, he directs his last barbs at Pandarus, who remains alone. He bemoans his fate and the fate of all panders and peddlers of flesh.

Twelfth Night

Key characters:

- ✔ Olivia, a rich, beautiful countess
- ✔ Orsino, Duke of Illyria, in love with Olivia
- ✔ Viola/Cesario, in love with the duke, sister of Sebastian
- ✔ Toby Belch, Olivia's drunk uncle who sponges off her
- ✔ Malvolio, Olivia's humorless steward
- ✔ Andrew Aguecheek, a silly knight, suitor to Olivia
- ✔ Maria, Olivia's gentlewoman
- ✔ Feste, Olivia's clown
- ✔ Sebastian, twin brother of Viola

Twelfth Night gets its name from the date of its first performance, on Twelfth Night — that is, January 6. The alternate title for this play is *What You Will.*

Act 1

Orsino, the Duke of Illyria, is madly in love with the Countess Olivia, but she has different ideas. She is mourning the death of her father and brother and will not speak with Orsino, nor will she accept letters or messages from him.

In plot number 2, Viola was shipwrecked and rescued, and finds herself stuck in Illyria. She mourns the loss of her twin brother, Sebastian, who drowned in the shipwreck, but the ship's captain saw her brother clinging bravely to a mast, so there is hope.

Alone in a strange country, Viola decides that it would be most prudent to disguise herself as a boy — a favorite plot device of Shakespeare, and one you can read more about in Chapter 8 — and enter the employment of Orsino. She adopts the name Cesario and gets the job of delivering Orsino's love letters to Olivia.

Another of Olivia's suitors is Sir Andrew Aguecheek, a silly, stupid man. He drinks often with a kinsman of Olivia, the aptly named Sir Toby Belch. Olivia will no more speak with Andrew than with Orsino. She keeps to her household, including her steward, Malvolio. True to his name, he has only ill will toward others, but he has an eye for his mistress (plot number 3).

Viola, as Cesario, shows up at Olivia's door and refuses to leave. Her impudence intrigues Olivia, who finally agrees to see the "boy." Viola/Cesario tries to woo Olivia in Orsino's name, but Olivia will not listen. She is more interested in the messenger than the message. After Viola leaves, Olivia thinks of a trick to get Cesario to return — she makes up a story that Cesario left a ring as a gift and she wants to return the ring. She sends Malvolio to find Cesario and return the ring.

Act 2

Plot number 4 introduces Viola's twin brother, Sebastian. He thinks that his sister drowned in the shipwreck and that he is the sole survivor. Coincidentally, he comes ashore in Illyria and heads for Duke Orsino's home.

Malvolio tracks down Viola/Cesario and delivers Olivia's ring and her message. Viola recognizes the device that Olivia uses to woo Cesario, and the plots start to thicken. Viola has fallen in love with Orsino, who loves Olivia, who loves Cesario, who is really Viola. Got that straight?

Malvolio scolds Toby and Andrew because they were out drinking, as usual. He also scolds Maria, Olivia's gentlewoman, for joining the two carousers. He's good at scolding, which doesn't make him very popular among the other members of Olivia's household. Maria hatches a plan to get even with Malvolio. She will send a love letter to Malvolio and make it seem as though Olivia wrote the letter.

Malvolio finds the letter and takes the bait. In the letter, he reads that "some are born great, some achieve greatness, and some have greatness thrust upon 'em" (2.5.140–41).

He assumes that the latter applies to him and pictures himself elevated to the status of count. He would become Toby's master, and instead of merely scolding him, Malvolio could command him.

The letter tells Malvolio to dress and act outrageously, to wear bright yellow stockings, and to smile always. Maria chooses the color and styles knowing that they will annoy her mistress.

Act 3

The man who rescued Sebastian still wants to help him, and even lends him money. He must be careful, though: He fought against Orsino some time back and is a wanted man in Illyria. Nonetheless, he will help Sebastian as best he can.

Malvolio dresses as commanded in the false letter. Seeing the yellow stockings and Malvolio's other affectations (as recommended in the forged letter), Olivia thinks that Malvolio is mentally unhinged. She asks Toby to take care of the poor, sick man. One of Toby's friends watches Malvolio's peculiar behavior and says, "If this were played upon a stage now, I would condemn it as an improbable fiction" (3.4.127–28).

Toby isn't content in mischievously toying with Malvolio. He also encourages Sir Andrew to woo Olivia, even though she refuses to see him. Toby urges Andrew to challenge Cesario to a duel and eliminate his rival.

Olivia can't restrain herself anymore. She confesses her love for Cesario, which puts Viola in an uncomfortable position. Viola/Cesario continues to plead for Orsino's love, but Olivia swears that she loves Cesario and so cannot requite Orsino's love. Cesario says that no woman shall ever be mistress of "his" heart.

After Olivia leaves, Toby delivers Andrew's challenge to Cesario. Of course, Cesario, who is really Viola, doesn't want a fight. She asks Toby to dissuade Andrew. Instead, Toby tells Andrew that Cesario is spoiling for the match.

Sebastian's friend sees the fight and draws his sword to intervene because he thinks that Viola is Sebastian. The tumult draws the attention of the local police, who break up the fray. The officers recognize and arrest Sebastian's friend. He asks for help from the person he thinks is Sebastian, who everyone else thinks is Cesario, but who is really Viola.

Act 4

Toby continues to egg on Andrew, who wants to renew the duel with Cesario. To his misfortune, he finds Sebastian instead, who beats Andrew soundly. Toby tries to stop Sebastian, but then Olivia intervenes. She mistakes Sebastian for Cesario. He's confused, but when a beautiful woman asks him to follow her, he happily obeys.

Toby and Maria continue to play with Malvolio's mind. They have imprisoned him and bring in Feste, Olivia's clown, to pose as Sir Topas, the parson. Malvolio asks "Sir Topas" to deliver a message to Olivia, but Feste persists in calling Malvolio mad or possessed by the devil. Matters are finally over the edge for Toby, who realizes how deep in hot water he is. Olivia is displeased over the dueling matter, and the Malvolio trick will just make things worse.

Sebastian is bewildered by Olivia's professed love and the riches she bestows on him. He tried to find his friend but couldn't. He isn't sure what's going on, but when Olivia appears with a priest, he still follows her.

Act 5

The officers lead Sebastian's friend to Duke Orsino, where Viola recognizes him and reports how he sided with her in the duel. The friend tells the story of how he rescued Sebastian from the shipwreck. Before anyone can start to make sense of the different stories, Olivia enters. She is looking for Cesario, whom she thinks is her husband. Andrew and Toby complain that Cesario attacked and hurt them.

Viola denies that she married Olivia, denies that she attacked Andrew and Toby, and is just as confused as everyone. Finally, Sebastian enters and apologizes to Olivia for hurting her kinsman and his friend, but says that they started the fights, and he merely ended them.

Now that Sebastian and Viola are onstage together, it's time to sort things out. Sebastian doesn't have a brother, but with a little discussion, he recognizes his sister, Viola, dressed as a boy: "One face, one voice, one habit, and two persons" (5.1.212).

So Olivia is happily married to Sebastian. Cesario is free to become Viola again, and she will marry Duke Orsino. Malvolio eventually gains his freedom and shows the letter to Olivia, who recognizes her maid's handwriting. Toby repents of the trick and marries Maria as recompense for urging her to write the letter. With three weddings and a happy reunion, everyone can live happily ever after. Well, almost everyone. Malvolio doesn't fare so well, and he promises that he will "be reveng'd on the whole pack of you" (5.1.370).

SEE IT

On video

✔ 1996, Renaissance Films: Trevor Nunn director, Helena Bonham Carter as Olivia, Ben Kingsley as Feste, and Imogen Stubbs as Viola. An excellent production.

✔ 1980, BBC: Alan Shallcross director, Felicity Kendal as Viola, Annette Crosbie as Maria, and Sinéad Cusack as Olivia.

✔ 1969, ITC: John Sichel director, Alec Guinness as Malvolio, Joan Plowright as Viola and Sebastian, and Ralph Richardson as Sir Toby Belch.

The Two Gentlemen of Verona

Key characters:

✔ Valentine, a young lover

✔ Proteus, unfaithful friend to Valentine

✔ Duke of Milan, father of Silvia

✔ Silvia, daughter of the Duke of Milan, in love with Valentine

✔ Julia, in love with Proteus

✔ Speed, servant to Valentine

✔ Thurio, suitor to Silvia

✔ Launce, clownish servant to Proteus

✔ Crab, Launce's dog

The characters' names tell you much in *The Two Gentlemen of Verona*. The gentlemen in question are Valentine, the lover, and Proteus, named after the shape-changing god of ancient mythology. Valentine loves Silvia, who runs off to the woods to follow Valentine. Her name comes from the Latin for forest: *silva*. Valentine's servant is Speed. You can judge for yourself whether his name is accurate or ironic.

Act 1

Valentine and Proteus are the best of friends, but they will part company when Valentine heads off to Milan while Proteus remains in Verona so that he can be close to his beloved Julia.

Proteus's father decides that travel would be good for his son. Knowing how close Proteus and Valentine are, his father arranges for Proteus to follow Valentine and take a position in the court of the Duke of Milan. Proteus protests because he doesn't want to leave Julia, but he cannot defy his father's wishes.

Act 2

In Milan, Valentine is true to his name and falls in love with Silvia, daughter of the Duke. Unfortunately, the duke wants Silvia to marry Thurio, who has lots of money. Valentine is unsure whether Silvia prefers him or Thurio. She tries to tell him, but he is too thick to understand her subtle message, leaving his servant, Speed, to interpret her message that she loves Valentine.

Meanwhile, back in Verona, Proteus and Julia have pledged their undying love for each other. They exchange rings as tokens of their vows. Then Proteus must depart for Milan. Launce, Proteus's servant, steals the show in a comic scene with his dog, Crab.

Shakespeare takes you back to Milan, where Thurio and Valentine joust with words. Valentine is on the verge of victory when the duke interrupts, bringing news of Proteus's unexpected arrival. Valentine confides in his friend and reveals that he and Silvia plan to elope that very night.

Proteus sees Silvia and falls for her immediately, completely forgetting about what's-her-name in Verona. His lust for Silvia drives him to betray his best friend, and he decides to reveal Valentine's plan to the duke.

Julia can't live without Proteus, so she follows him to Milan. This was a day when young women did not travel alone, so she hatches a plan. With her servant's help, she will disguise herself as a boy. There's that familiar plot device — a woman disguised as a boy!

Act 3

Proteus tells the duke about Valentine's plan to elope with Silvia. He concocts an excuse for betraying his friend, saying that his care for the duke outweighs friendship. The duke then banishes Valentine from Milan.

Proteus pretends to be upset at the news of Valentine's banishment. Silvia pleads with the duke on Valentine's behalf, which only makes him angrier, and he locks her away, in prison as it were.

Proteus's treachery reaps a second reward. The duke trusts Proteus and seeks his advice for advancing Thurio's suit with Silvia. Proteus provides advice to Thurio and promises to speak with Silvia on Thurio's behalf. The duke gives Proteus access to Silvia, which he intends to use for his own selfish gain.

Act 4

A band of outlaws accosts Valentine in the forest. The outlaws are no ruffians, though. They are gentlemen who have been banished for faults great and small and now must "make a virtue of necessity" (4.1.62). They elect Valentine as their leader.

Julia arrives in Milan dressed as a boy. She just wants to be near her love, so she gets a job as his page. Ironically, she must deliver his entreaties of love to Silvia. Julia is reassured, though, when she sees that Silvia rebukes Proteus for being unfaithful to his first love. Silvia even refuses to accept a ring that he sends her because she knows that Julia gave it to him.

Silvia cannot live without her Valentine, so she decides to follow him into banishment. She enlists the aid of a gentleman to accompany her on her trip into the unknown.

Act 5

Silvia and her companion leave Milan. The duke soon learns of this and hastens to follow her, as do Thurio and Proteus. In true soap-opera fashion, the same outlaws who captured Valentine also capture Silvia. Her companion tries to run away. Maybe traveling alone wasn't such a bad idea after all.

Before the outlaws can bring their prize to Valentine, though, Proteus rescues Silvia. He still presses his suit, but this time Valentine, hiding in the woods, overhears him. Valentine reveals himself and confronts his friend. Proteus, ever true to his name, immediately repents of his past behavior. The friends reconcile, and to show that he has no hard feelings, Valentine offers Silvia to Proteus. (Valentine doesn't seem to realize that he is doing exactly what the duke was trying to do — dispose of Silvia without considering her wishes — but let that pass. Things will turn out fine in the end.) Julia, in the guise of Proteus's page, swoons in response.

Trying to recover, Julia says that she forgot to return Proteus's ring. She "accidentally" gives Proteus her own ring, the ring that Proteus gave her in Verona. He recognizes the ring and demands to know where she got it. She reveals herself, and Proteus is covered again in shame, guilt, and repentance.

On video

1983, BBC: Don Taylor director, Tessa Peake-Jones as Julia, Tyler Butterworth as Proteus, John Hudson as Valentine, Nicholas Kaby as Speed, Joanne Pearce as Silvia, and Tony Haygarth as Launce

The outlaws have captured the duke and Thurio. Thurio bravely claims Silvia as his own, but he backs down when Valentine challenges him. The duke is chagrined at Thurio's cowardice and realizes that Valentine is the better match for Silvia. Valentine also extracts from the duke a pardon for his band of outlaws. Thus, everyone (except Thurio) lives happily ever after.

The Two Noble Kinsmen

Key characters:

- Theseus, Duke of Athens

- Hippolyta, Queen of the Amazons, bride of Theseus

- Emilia, sister of Hippolyta

- Palamon, Arcite's bother, nephew to Creon, King of Thebes

- Arcite, Palamon's brother, nephew to Creon, King of Thebes

- Jailer's daughter, in love with Palamon

The "noble" kinsmen are brothers, and they behave nobly except when it comes to love. Nothing can resolve their dispute over their love for Emilia — nothing, that is, except the random chances of fate.

This play was a collaboration between John Fletcher and William Shakespeare. Fletcher was the primary author, and Shakespeare probably had a hand in writing parts of the first and last acts. This play has not been filmed, and until recently was rarely performed. The general recognition that Shakespeare contributed some of the writing has sparked renewed interest in the play.

Act 1

Theseus and Hippolyta are about to be married, but three queens arrive unexpectedly and interrupt the ceremony. (The same wedding begins *A Midsummer Night's Dream*. Both plays feature people running around in the woods, getting lost, and falling in love, but the similarities end there.) The queens beg Theseus to intervene in a dispute with Creon, King of Thebes (who does not appear in the play). Creon recently put down a revolt, but he refuses to bury the bodies of the opposing army. The queens ask Theseus to force Creon to let them bury their husbands' bodies. After some persuading, Theseus relents and agrees to force Creon to permit the burials.

In Thebes, the brothers Palamon and Arcite also complain about their uncle Creon's base behavior and how it is bringing down all of Thebes. He is "a most unbounded tyrant" (1.2.63). Nonetheless, when Theseus threatens Creon, the brothers choose to defend Thebes — but not Creon — from Theseus's threat. Theseus wins the battle and captures Arcite and Palamon.

Act 2

Palamon and Arcite share their woes in prison. They vow eternal friendship:

I do not think it possible our friendship

Should ever leave us. (2.2.114–15)

But then Palamon spies Emilia, Theseus's sister-in-law, in the garden outside the prison. He falls instantly in love. Arcite also falls in love with her, and they forget about their friendship and argue over who can love her. The jailer interrupts the brothers' dispute. Theseus has called for Arcite, leaving Palamon to wonder whether Arcite will gain his freedom and therefore be able to woo and wed Emilia.

Theseus frees Arcite but banishes him from Athens. He envies Palamon, who is still imprisoned but at least is free to see Emilia from afar. Arcite doesn't leave Athens, instead disguising himself as a peasant. The town celebrates May Day, and he joins the festivities in disguise. He enters races and wrestling matches and wins, drawing the notice of Theseus and Emilia. They don't see through his disguise but recognize his inherent nobility.

The jailer's daughter is engaged to marry a local man, but she falls in love with Palamon and secretly frees him from jail. She hides him in the woods while she fetches food and a file to cut off his shackles.

Act 3

Arcite recounts his fortune: He is free, he is in love with Emilia, and Emilia "takes strong note" (3.1.17) of him. He thinks that he is alone, but Palamon, hiding in the woods, overhears him. Palamon accuses Arcite of stealing Emilia. They argue and agree to an honorable duel that evening.

Later that night, Arcite brings food to Palamon and a file to cut off his chains. While Palamon eats, they remember the women and girls they have known, at one time reminiscing as best of friends and then in an instant threatening each other over Emilia.

The jailer's daughter cannot find Palamon (because he wandered off after Arcite). Letting Palamon escape will probably cost her father his life. Her love for Palamon, distress over her misbehavior, and worry about her father's fate take their toll on her and her sanity. She wanders the woods lost and raving in madness.

Arcite brings swords and armor for the fight with Palamon. They bandy congratulatory words and treat each other as the brothers they are. Their love for each other is deep and true, except for the small, insurmountable problem of their mutual love for Emilia.

Before they can begin the fight, Theseus finds them. After learning their identities, he condemns the brothers to death. Hippolyta and Emilia ask for mercy, suggesting that the two be banished instead. Palamon and Arcite refuse to accept banishment, saying that they would rather die than be parted from Emilia.

Theseus suggests that Emilia choose one of the princes as her husband, and Theseus will condemn the other to death. The brothers accept the bargain, but Emilia cannot choose. Theseus declares a martial contest in a month's time. The winner of the feat of arms will marry Emilia, and the loser will die.

Act 4

The jailer is in the clear: Palamon told Theseus the exact circumstances of his escape, so Theseus knows that the jailer is not to blame. Theseus also pardons the jailer's daughter for her youthful indiscretion. Nonetheless, the daughter is out of her mind. She pines for Palamon. A doctor prescribes a solution: Her former betrothed must pretend to be Palamon. She wants Palamon, so give her Palamon, and slowly try to coax her back to her wits.

Act 5

Arcite wins the contest and Emilia's hand. Just as Palamon is about to be executed, a messenger arrives with strange news. Arcite was riding a horse when the horse ran amok. Arcite wasn't thrown, but the horse reared and fell on top of him. With his dying breath, Arcite gives Emilia to Palamon. Theseus remarks:

Never Fortune

Did play a subtler game. (5.4.112–13)

It's a strange ending to a strange play.

The Winter's Tale

Key characters:

- ✔ Leontes, King of Sicilia
- ✔ Polixenes ("pol-ICK-senn-eez"), King of Bohemia
- ✔ Hermione ("her-MY-oh-nee"), Queen of Sicilia, suspected unjustly of infidelity
- ✔ Camillo ("ka-MILL-oh"), Lord of Sicilia
- ✔ Perdita, daughter of Leontes and Hermione, in love with Florizel
- ✔ Florizel, son of Polixenes, in love with Perdita
- ✔ Paulina, wife of Antigonus
- ✔ Antigonus, a lord of Sicilia

On the surface, both *The Winter's Tale* and *Othello* deal with the subject of insane jealousy. But *The Winter's Tale* treats the subject quite differently. Remember that this play is a comedy, so no matter how desperate the situation seems, everything will work out for the best by the end of the play.

Act 1

Nine months is a long time to visit a friend, but it's not long enough for Leontes, the King of Sicilia. He wants his friend, Polixenes, the King of Bohemia, to stay longer. Finally, Hermione, Leontes's wife, convinces Polixenes to stay just one more week.

In a bizarre state of mind, Leontes muses why Polixenes would give in to Hermione but not to him. He decides that the only possible reason is that they are lovers. Suddenly, Leontes interprets everything Hermione and Polixenes say in a new light, and he goes so far as to doubt the parentage of his son and of the unborn child that Hermione carries.

Leontes reveals his irrational beliefs to his trusted councilor, Camillo. Camillo defends the queen, but to no avail. Leontes is adamant and demands that Camillo kill Polixenes. Camillo owes his loyalty to his king, so he pretends to agree.

Fortunately for Polixenes, Camillo is wiser than the king. Instead of carrying out the heinous deed, he helps Polixenes escape in the middle of the night. Knowing that he cannot return to Sicilia, Camillo accompanies Polixenes to Bohemia.

Act 2

To Leontes's twisted mind, Polixenes's midnight escape is proof of his guilt. Leontes confronts Hermione, who protests (of course). Leontes's advisors try to argue with him, but without success, and he orders Hermione to prison. To appease his court, Leontes agrees to ask the Oracle at Delphi for the truth. Everyone is satisfied that the Oracle will reveal all.

The stress of the false accusation and imprisonment causes Hermione to give birth early, but the new baby is healthy. Hermione's lady, Paulina, brings the child to the king, hoping that the sight of the newborn will soften the king's heart. It doesn't. Instead, he orders a lord, Antigonus — Paulina's husband — to kill the baby. All the lords protest, and finally Leontes gives way a little (very little) bit: He orders Antigonus to take the baby to a remote location and leave it. Antigonus must obey his king but thinks that a quick death might have been more merciful to the baby.

Act 3

Leontes calls Hermione to trial. She protests that he lacks evidence against her. Two lords return from the Oracle, which Leontes and Hermione agree will be objective evidence. The report from Shakespeare's Oracle is much clearer than what you find in classical Greek mythology: "Hermione is chaste; Polixenes blameless; . . . Leontes a jealous tyrant" (3.2.131–32). That isn't what Leontes wants to hear, and he chooses not to believe the Oracle. The shock is too much for the family. Leontes's son and wife die from the shock and shame of the false accusations.

Faced with the terrible results of his jealousy and the implacable truth, Leontes repents, but too late. His fearsome jealousy has also consumed Paulina's husband, Antigonus. He has taken the newborn princess far away, and Paulina knows that he will never return.

This is a comedy, isn't it?

Antigonus takes the princess to Bohemia and names her Perdita (Latin for lost) because she is lost forever. By her side, he leaves money and tokens to identify her, but a bear chases him away before he can see whether she is rescued. A shepherd and his son find the child (and the remains of Antigonus, after the bear finishes its meal). The shepherd can tell from the rich clothing that Perdita comes from noble stock, but they can't return her to her parents, so they will raise her themselves.

Act 4

Sixteen years pass, and Camillo is homesick for Sicilia. King Polixenes pleads with him to stay in Bohemia. Finally, he succeeds by asking Camillo to look in on his son, Florizel, who has been acting strangely of late. Rumors abound that Florizel has been spending time with a lowly shepherd. Camillo and Polixenes will disguise themselves and visit the shepherd to learn more.

Florizel appears in the play for the first time, and you probably guessed already that Florizel has been spending his time with Perdita. They are in love, and he asks for her hand in marriage. Her "father" (the shepherd who raised her) doesn't know who he really is, and he readily consents. Polixenes and Camillo, in disguise, overhear everything. Polixenes spoils the party and forbids the marriage.

Florizel won't give up, though. He plans to elope with Perdita and forsake his princely heritage. Camillo, always helping the underdog, tells him to travel to Sicilia. Leontes will treat them as friends, and Camillo will try to settle matters at home.

Polixenes's wrath extends to the shepherd and his son. He thinks that they were part of the conspiracy to wed a shepherdess with a prince. They want to clear their names by proving that Perdita is a foundling, not a blood relation, so they show the king the tokens and letter that they found with the baby.

Act 5

Florizel and Perdita arrive unexpectedly in Sicilia. Leontes welcomes them but can tell that something fishy is afoot because they arrive without warning and without fanfare. Leontes, of course, does not recognize Perdita. After all, she was a newborn when he ordered her abandonment.

SEE IT

On video

1981, BBC: Jane Howell director, David Burke as Camillo, Robert Stephens as Polixenes, and Jeremy Kemp as Leontes

Polixenes arrives in Sicilia soon after. Florizel assumes that Camillo betrayed him to his father, who now comes to fetch him home. The package that accompanied Perdita, though, changes everything. It proves that Perdita is Leontes's long-lost daughter. Now that she is of a station equal to Florizel, they can marry.

With one subplot concluded happily, the time has come to settle the other one. Paulina announces that she has commissioned a statue of Hermione — one so lifelike that it took 16 years to execute. The artist even took care to make the statue appear aged, the way Hermione would look 16 years after her death. The statue is so true to life that it seems to breathe. Surprise, surprise! It's not a statue, but the real Hermione. The Oracle had predicted that what was lost must be found, and Hermione has waited all these years to find her daughter. See? It's a comedy after all.

All's Well That Ends Well

Legend

♥	Falls in love	⚲	Woos a lover	T	Plays a trick
♠	Falls in love with the wrong person	⬦	Home run: Marries	·	Appears in scene
B	Betrays a friend	✚	Heals a sick person	"	Famous quote

Characters, in order of appearance

Act	1			2					3							4					5		
Scene	1	2	3	1	2	3	4	5	1	2	3	4	5	6	7	1	2	3	4	5	1	2	3
1 Countess of Rossillion, mother of Bertram																							
2 Bertram, Count of Rossillion																							
3 Lafew, an old lord																							
4 Helena, an orphan in love with Bertram																							
5 Parolles, a rogue and friend to Bertram																							
6 King of France																							
7 Lavatch, a clown in the employ of the Countess																							
8 Widow Capilet, an old widow of Florence																							
9 Diana, daughter of the widow																							
10 First French Lord																							
11 Second French Lord																							

As You Like It

Legend

Symbol	Meaning	Symbol	Meaning
♥	Falls in love	𝒢	Dons a disguise
♦	Home run: Marries	⊘	Removes a disguise
K	Strikeout: Rejected in love	↑	Sent to penalty box: Banished
		↓	Returns to game: Returns from banishment
		.	Appears in scene
		"	Famous quote

Characters, in order of appearance

	Act	1			2							3					4			5			
	Scene	1	2	3	1	2	3	4	5	6	7	1	2	3	4	5	1	2	3	1	2	3	4
1	Orlando de Boys																						
2	Adam, servant to Orlando																						
3	Oliver de Boys, brother of Orlando																						
4	Celia, daughter of Duke Frederick																						
5	Rosalind, daughter of Duke Senior																						
6	Touchstone, a fool																						
7	Duke Frederick																						
8	Duke Senior, brother of Duke Frederick																						
9	Amiens, lord attending Duke Senior																						
10	Corin, an old shepherd																						
11	Silvius, a young shepherd																						
12	Jaques, a lord attending Duke Senior																						
13	Phebe, a shepherdess																						
14	Audrey, a goatherder																						

The Comedy of Errors

Legend

♥	Falls in love
+	Reunited with long-lost kin
?	Mistaken for someone else

∞	Captured
⊘	Escapes
✗	Challenges to a duel

A	Arrested
·	Appears in scene
"	Famous quote

Characters, in order of appearance

	Act	1		2		3		4				5
	Scene	1	2	1	2	1	2	1	2	3	4	1
1	Egeon of Syracuse											
2	Duke of Ephesus											
3	Antipholus of Syracuse, son of Egeon											
4	Dromio of Syracuse, servant to Antipholus											
5	Dromio of Ephesus, servant to Antipholus											
6	Adriana, wife of Antipholus of Ephesus											
7	Luciana, sister of Adriana											
8	Antipholus of Ephesus											
9	Angelo, a goldsmith											
10	Balthasar, a merchant											
11	Courtesan											
12	Pinch, a schoolmaster											
13	Emilia, Abbess of Ephesus, wife of Egeon											

Cymbeline

Legend

+	Reunited with long-lost kin	✂	Dons a disguise	X	Ejected from game: Dies
☺	Victorious in battle	⊘	Removes a disguise	⚡	Visited by supernatural beings
☹	Defeated in battle	●X	Uses a potion or poison	.	Appears in scene
?	Mistaken for someone else	T	Plays a trick	"	Famous quote

Characters, in order of appearance

		Act	1							2					3							4				5				
		Scene	1	2	3	4	5	6	7	1	2	3	4	5	1	2	3	4	5	6	7	1	2	3	4	1	2	3	4	5
1	Queen																													
2	Posthumus, husband of Imogen																													
3	Imogen, daughter of Cymbeline by a former queen																													
4	King Cymbeline																													
5	Pisanio, servant to Posthumus																													
6	Cloten, son of the queen by a former husband																													
7	Iachimo, an Italian gentleman																													
8	Cornelius, a doctor																													
9	Caius Lucius, a Roman general																													
10	Belarius, a banished lord																													
11	Guiderius, son of Cymbeline																													
12	Arviragus, son of Cymbeline																													

Love's Labour's Lost

Legend

♠	Dons a disguise	♥	Falls in love	✗	Breaks an oath
⊘	Removes a disguise	⊠↑	Sends a letter	.	Appears in scene
⅟	Woos a lover	⊠↓	Receives a letter	"	Famous quote

Characters, in order of appearance

		Act	1	1	2	3	4	4	4	5	5
		Scene	1	2	1	1	1	2	3	1	2
1	King Ferdinand of Navarre										
2	Longaville, a lord attending the king										
3	Dumain, a lord attending the king										
4	Berowne, a lord attending the king										
5	Dull, a constable										
6	Costard, a clown										
7	Don Armado of Spain										
8	Jaquenetta, a country wench										
9	Boyet, a lord attending the princess										
10	Princess of France										
11	Maria, a lady attending the princess										
12	Katharine, a lady attending the princess										
13	Rosaline, a lady attending the princess										
14	Sir Nathaniel, a curate										
15	Holofernes, a schoolmaster										

Measure for Measure

Legend

Symbol	Meaning	Symbol	Meaning
K	Strikeout: Rejected in love	⚲	Woos a lover
A	Arrested	⚳	Agrees to an assignation
Ⓐ	Pardoned	◇4	Home run: Marries
!	Consummates a marriage		
·	Appears in scene		
"	Famous quote		

Characters, in order of appearance

Act	1				2				3		4						5
Scene	1	2	3	4	1	2	3	4	1	2	1	2	3	4	5	6	1
1 Vincentio, the duke																	
2 Escalus, an ancient lord																	
3 Angelo, a deputy																	
4 Lucio, a fantastic																	
5 Mistress Overdone, a bawd																	
6 Pompey, a clown																	
7 Claudio, a young gentleman																	
8 Juliet, beloved of Claudio																	
9 Provost																	
10 Isabel, sister of Claudio																	
11 Elbow, a simple constable																	
12 Mariana, betrothed to Angelo																	
13 Barnardine, a dissolute prisoner																	

The Merchant of Venice

Legend

Symbol	Meaning	Symbol	Meaning	Symbol	Meaning
↲	Woos a lover	Dons a disguise		Plays a clever legal trick	
◈	Home run: Marries	$	Borrows money	.	Appears in scene
E	Elopes		Picks a casket	"	Famous quote

Characters, in order of appearance

Act	1			2									3					4		5
Scene	1	2	3	1	2	3	4	5	6	7	8	9	1	2	3	4	5	1	2	1
1 Antonio, a merchant																				
2 Bassanio, friend of Antonio																				
3 Lorenzo, friend of Bassanio																				
4 Gratiano, friend of Bassanio																				
5 Portia, in love with Bassanio																				
6 Nerissa, waiting-woman to Portia																				
7 Shylock, a moneylender																				
8 Prince of Morocco																				
9 Launcelot Gobbo, a clown																				
10 Old Gobbo, father of Launcelot																				
11 Jessica, daughter of Shylock																				
12 Prince of Arragon																				
13 Tubal, friend of Shylock																				
14 Duke of Venice																				

The Merry Wives of Windsor

Legend

Symbol	Meaning	Symbol	Meaning	Symbol	Meaning
↑⊠	Sends a letter		Dons a disguise	◈	Marries the wrong person
⊠↓	Receives a letter	1	Woos a lover	.	Appears in scene
✗	Challenges to a duel	④	Home run: Marries	"	Famous quote

Characters, in order of appearance

Act		1				2			3					4						5				
Scene	1	2	3	4	1	2	3	1	2	3	4	5	1	2	3	4	5	6	1	2	3	4	5
1 Justice Shallow																							
2 Slender, kinsman of Shallow																							
3 Hugh Evans, a parson																							
4 Master Page																							
5 Sir John Falstaff																							
6 Bardolph, follower of Falstaff																							
7 Pistol, follower of Falstaff																							
8 Nym, follower of Falstaff																							
9 Ann Page, daughter of Page																							
10 Mistress Ford																							
11 Mistress Page																							
12 Host of the Garter																							
13 John Rugby, servant to Caius																							
14 Mistress Quickly, servant to Caius																							
15 Doctor Caius, suitor to Ann																							
16 Fenton, a young gentleman																							
17 Master Ford																							

A Midsummer Night's Dream

Legend

♥	Falls in love	ℳ	Turns into an animal	☠	Uses a potion or poison
♥	Falls in love with the wrong person	K	Strikeout: Rejected in love	.	Appears in scene
🐦	Falls in love with the wrong species	✎	Gets lost	"	Famous quote

Characters, in order of appearance

		Act 1		Act 2		Act 3		Act 4		Act 5
	Scene	1	2	1	2	1	2	1	2	1
1	Theseus, Duke of Athens									
2	Hippolyta, Queen of the Amazons									
3	Egeus, father of Hermia									
4	Hermia, in love with Lysander									
5	Lysander, in love with Hermia									
6	Demetrius, in love with Hermia and then Helena									
7	Helena, in love with Demetrius									
8	Peter Quince, a carpenter									
9	Bottom, a weaver									
10	Puck, or Robin Goodfellow, a fairy									
11	Oberon, King of the Fairies									
12	Titania, Queen of the Fairies									

Much Ado About Nothing

Legend

♥	Falls in love	T	Plays a trick
🍷	Woos a lover	K	Strikeout: Rejected in love
⬦	Home run: Marries	A	Arrested
		✗	Challenges to a duel
		.	Appears in scene
		"	Famous quote

Characters, in order of appearance

Act	1			2			3					4		5			
Scene	1	2	3	1	2	3	1	2	3	4	5	1	2	1	2	3	4
1 Leonato, Governor of Messina																	
2 Beatrice, niece of Leonato																	
3 Hero, daughter of Leonato																	
4 Don Pedro, Prince of Aragon																	
5 Benedick, a young lord																	
6 Don John, bastard brother of Don Pedro																	
7 Claudio, a young lord																	
8 Antonio, brother of Leonato																	
9 Conrade, follower of Don John																	
10 Borachio, follower of Don John																	
11 Margaret, gentlewoman attending Hero																	
12 Ursula, gentlewoman attending Hero																	
13 Dogberry, a constable																	
14 Verges																	
15 The Watch																	
16 Friar Francis																	
17 Sexton																	

Pericles

Legend

♥	Falls in love
◈	Home run: Marries
M	Goes mad
X	Ejected from game: Dies
+	Reunited with long-lost kin
S	Substitution
🦋	Sold into slavery
.	Appears in scene
"	Famous quote

Characters, in order of appearance

Act		1				2					3				4						5		
Scene		1	2	3	4	1	2	3	4	5	1	2	3	4	1	2	3	4	5	6	1	2	3
1	Antiochus, King of Antioch																						
2	Pericles, Prince of Tyre																						
3	Daughter of Antiochus																						
4	Thaliard, a lord of Antioch																						
5	Helicanus, a lord of Tyre																						
6	Cleon, Governor of Tarsus																						
7	Dionyza, wife of Cleon																						
8	Simonides, King of Pentapolis																						
9	Thaisa, daughter of Simonides																						
10	Escanes, a lord of Tyre																						
11	Lycorida, nurse to Marina																						
12	Cerimon, a lord of Ephesus																						
13	Leonine, servant to Dionyza																						
14	Marina, daughter of Pericles																						
15	Pandar																						
16	Boult																						
17	Lysimachus, Governor of Mytilene																						

The Taming of the Shrew

Legend

⚲	Solicits love		Home run: Marries
⚲	Meets a lover in private	T	Plays a trick
◈	Gets engaged	.	Dons a disguise
		,	Appears in scene
K	Strikeout: Rejected in love	"	Famous quote

Characters, in order of appearance

	Act	Induction		1	2			3	4				5	
	Scene	1	2	1	2	1	2	1	2	1	2	3	4	5	1	2
1	Christopher Sly														
2	Lord														
3	Lucentio, suitor of Bianca														
4	Tranio, servant to Lucentio														
5	Baptista, father of Katherina and Bianca														
6	Gremio, suitor of Bianca														
7	Katherina, shrewish daughter of Baptista														
8	Hortensio, suitor of Bianca														
9	Bianca, daughter of Baptista														
10	Biondello, servant to Lucentio														
11	Petruchio, a gentleman of Padua														
12	Grumio, servant to Petruchio														
13	Vincentio, father of Lucentio														

The Tempest

Legend

⚓	Shipwrecked	♪	Meets a lover in private	C	Involved in a conspiracy
♥	Falls in love	♫	Gets engaged	.	Appears in scene
½	Woos a lover	+	Reunited with long-lost kin	"	Famous quote

Characters, in order of appearance

	Act	1		2		3			4	5
	Scene	1	2	1	2	1	2	3	1	1
1	Boatswain									
2	Alonso, King of Naples									
3	Antonio, usurping Duke of Milan									
4	Gonzalo, advisor to Alonso									
5	Sebastian, brother of Alonso									
6	Miranda, daughter of Prospero									
7	Prospero, deposed Duke of Milan									
8	Ariel, a spirit									
9	Caliban, slave to Prospero									
10	Ferdinand, son of Alonso									
11	Trinculo, a jester									
12	Stephano, a drunken butler									

Troilus and Cressida

Legend

♥	Falls in love	K	Strikeout: Rejected in love	✗	Challenged to a duel
⅃	Solicits love	◇	Home run: Marries	·	Appears in scene
X	Ejected from game: Dies	F	Foul: Attacks someone	"	Famous quote

Characters, in order of appearance

		Act	1			2			3			4					5								
		Scene	1	2	3	1	2	3	1	2	3	1	2	3	4	5	1	2	3	4	5	6	7	8	9	10
1	Troilus, son of King Priam																									
2	Pandarus, uncle of Cressida																									
3	Cressida, daughter of Calchas																									
4	Agamemnon, a Greek general																									
5	Ulysses, a Greek commander																									
6	Aeneas, a Trojan commander																									
7	Ajax, a Greek commander																									
8	Thersites, servant to Ajax																									
9	Achilles, a Greek commander																									
10	Patroclus, servant to Achilles																									
11	Priam, King of Troy																									
12	Hector, son of Priam																									
13	Paris, son of Priam, lover of Helen																									
14	Diomedes, a Greek commander																									
15	Helen, abducted by Paris																									
16	Calchas, a Trojan defector to the Greeks																									

Twelfth Night

Legend

Symbol	Meaning	Symbol	Meaning
♥	Woos a lover	Falls in love	
⬦	Home run: Marries	Falls in love with the wrong person	
K	Strikeout: Rejected in love	Challenges to a duel	
⚓	Shipwrecked	Rescues or saves someones life	
ℰ	Dons a disguise		
+	Reunited with long-lost kin		
.	Appears in scene		
"	Famous quote		

Characters, in order of appearance

	Act	1					2					3				4			5
Scene		1	2	3	4	5	1	2	3	4	5	1	2	3	4	1	2	3	1
1 Orsino, Duke of Illyria																			
2 Viola																			
3 Sir Toby Belch, kinsman of Olivia																			
4 Maria, maid to Olivia																			
5 Sir Andrew Aguecheek, friend of Sir Toby																			
6 Feste, a clown																			
7 Olivia, a countess																			
8 Malvolio, steward to Olivia																			
9 Fabian																			
10 Sebastian, brother of Viola																			
11 Antonio, rescuer of Sebastian																			

The Two Gentlemen of Verona

Legend

Symbol	Meaning	Symbol	Meaning
♥	Falls in love	♀	Woos a lover
♥ (wrong)	Falls in love with the wrong person	🜨	Plans to elope
K	Strikeout: Rejected in love	B	Betrays a friend
♂	Dons a disguise		
.	Appears in scene		
"	Famous quote		

Characters, in order of appearance

		Act 1			Act 2							Act 3		Act 4				Act 5			
	Scene	1	2	3	1	2	3	4	5	6	7	1	2	1	2	3	4	1	2	3	4
1	Valentine, a gentleman																				
2	Proteus, a gentleman																				
3	Speed, servant to Valentine																				
4	Julia, in love with Proteus																				
5	Lucetta, maid to Julia																				
6	Antonio, father of Proteus																				
7	Panthino, servant to Antonio																				
8	Sylvia, in love with Valentine																				
9	Launce, servant to Proteus																				
10	Crab, Launce's dog																				
11	Thurio, suitor to Sylvia																				
12	Duke of Milan																				
13	Outlaws																				
14	Sir Eglamour, friend to Sylvia																				

The Two Noble Kinsmen

Legend

Symbol	Meaning	Symbol	Meaning	Symbol	Meaning
♥	Falls in love	✗ (crossed swords)	Challenges to a duel	M	Goes mad
X	Ejected from game: Dies	↑	Sent to penalty box: Banished	.	Appears in scene
☺	Victorious in battle	✍	Gets lost	"	Famous quote

Characters, in order of appearance

	Act	1					2						3						4			5			
	Scene	1	2	3	4	5	1	2	3	4	5	6	1	2	3	4	5	6	1	2	3	1	2	3	4
1	Theseus, Duke of Athens																								
2	Hippolyta, Queen of the Amazons, bride of Theseus																								
3	Emilia, sister of Hippolyta																								
4	Pirithous, friend to Theseus																								
5	Jailer																								
6	Wooer of the jailer's daughter																								
7	Jailer's daughter																								
8	Palamon, nephew of Creon																								
9	Arcite, brother of Palamon, nephew of Creon																								
10	Doctor																								

The Winter's Tale

Legend

♥	Falls in love	P	Makes a prophecy
◇4	Home run: Marries	T	Plays a trick
+	Reunited with long-lost kin	J	Jealous rage
		X	Ejected from game: Dies
		.	Appears in scene
		"	Famous quote

Characters, in order of appearance

		Act	1		2			3			4				5		
		Scene	1	2	1	2	3	1	2	3	1	2	3	4	1	2	3
1	Camillo, a lord of Sicilia																	
2	Polixenes, King of Bohemia																	
3	Leontes, King of Sicilia																	
4	Hermione, wife of Leontes																	
5	Mamillus, son of Leontes																	
6	Paulina, wife of Antigonus																	
7	Antigonus, a lord of Sicilia																	
8	Shepherd																	
9	Clown																	
10	Time																	
11	Autolycus, a rogue																	
12	Florizel, son of Polixenes																	
13	Perdita, lost daughter of Leontes																	

Chapter 14

Histories

· ·

In This Chapter

▶ Summaries of Shakespeare's history plays

▶ Interesting performances on videotape

· ·

This chapter summarizes Shakespeare's history plays about the kings of England. Most of the plays depict a tumultuous period in English history, from 1397 to 1485. Rebellion, war, intrigue, murder, and scandal fill these plays, and you need a scorecard to keep track of shifting loyalties, triumphs, and betrayals.

You can read or watch these plays in any order, but the action in eight of the plays moves smoothly from one play to the next. (Shakespeare didn't write them in that order, but it may help you to read them in chronological order.) The exceptions are the first, *King John,* and the last, *King Henry VIII.* You can treat the middle eight plays as a series, starting with *King Richard II* and ending with *King Richard III* (with a bunch of Henries in between). Call it *As the Globe Turns.*

When reading or watching the history plays, remember to treat them as entertainment, not as historical documentaries. Each play focuses on one or two key events in England's history. The title of the play tells you who is king at the time, but the story sometimes centers around someone else, often a contender for the throne.

How the BBC helps you keep track of who's who

The British Broadcasting Company (BBC) video series for the complete works of Shakespeare has a unique approach to help you keep track of who's who: The same actor plays the same character in every play in which that character appears. For example, David Gwillim plays Prince Hal in both parts of *King Henry IV* and plays the same character grown to adulthood — King Henry V — in *King Henry V.* Trevor Peacock, on the other hand, appears in many of the BBC productions, but in a different role each time.

For maximum fun, try to watch these videos in order. That way, you can see the progression of the characters from warring princes to warring kings to deposed kings.

King John

Key characters:

- John, King of England
- Arthur, John's nephew
- Eleanor, dowager Queen of England and John's mother
- Philip, King of France
- Hubert de Burgh, an Englishman
- Philip the Bastard, later Sir Richard, son of King Richard the Lionheart
- Cardinal Pandulph, a papal representative

Decisions, decisions. What do you want for supper? Which shirt will you wear today? Serve in heaven or rule in hell? Shakespeare shows two different approaches to decision-making in *King John.* The title character gives up an entire kingdom to save his skin. Philip Falcounbridge, on the other hand, gives up his inheritance and wealth in exchange for the dubious honor of bastardy.

King John ruled England from 1199 to 1216, taking the throne after the death of his elder brother, Richard the Lionheart. John first caused a rift with Pope Innocent III in 1206 over the choice of the Archbishop of Canterbury. Foreign affairs forced him to capitulate to the Pope in 1213; domestic affairs forced him to sign the Magna Carta in 1215; and he died in 1216. In typical fashion, Shakespeare ignores the passage of time and collapses the last decade of John's reign into five acts, which seem to take place over a matter of days or weeks.

The action in *King John* predates that in the other history plays by about a century, so think of this play as the preface to *As the Globe Turns,* not as part of the series proper.

Act 1

John is King of England, but his young nephew Arthur disputes John's claim. King Philip of France supports Arthur because he thinks that he can use Arthur to make a grab for John's territory in France. Not surprisingly, John defies Philip, and the stage is set for war between England and France.

Shakespeare quickly introduces a second plot. Robert Falcounbridge and his brother, Philip, disagree over their father's inheritance. Robert claims the entire inheritance, but Philip is the elder brother. Robert says that Philip is illegitimate and therefore cannot inherit. King John mediates the dispute with the help of the dowager Queen Eleanor, John's mother.

Philip has a tough choice: keep fighting for his claim or admit to being a bastard and thus give up any chance for a nice inheritance. He wouldn't be just any bastard, though. If his brother's accusations were true, Philip would be the son of the late King Richard the Lionheart. With no disrespect to the man who raised him, Philip accepts his illegitimate, noble heritage, saying, "Brother, you take my land, I'll take my chance" (1.1.151). He decides that a noble name is worth more than land and gold, even if that name requires him to accept the label of bastard. Robert gets the entire inheritance, but Philip makes out well enough when King John knights him with a new name — Sir Richard — in honor of his father.

Act 2

The next act introduces the characters in France. Philip is King of France, and his son Lewis is his heir. Arthur lives in France with his strong-willed mother, waiting for an opportunity to reclaim the throne of England, which he rightfully claims through his father, Geoffrey, John's elder brother.

The dispute between England and France takes place before the fortified town of Angiers. Both kings claim Angiers, but the townsfolk will have none of it. They swear allegiance to the King of England, but they're not sure who that is: Arthur or John. They choose the safest option and keep the doors closed "for neither, yet for both" armies (2.1.333). The town will wait to see who will win the coming battle.

The armies fight, but neither side gains an advantage. The newly knighted Sir Richard suggests a temporary truce. The armies, he says, should attack the town together. After recapturing Angiers, they can resume the original battle. Sir Richard clearly chose wisely when he gave up his inheritance and accepted bastardy. He went from insignificance to counseling kings on the art of war. Sometimes the risky choice is the better choice.

The kings like Richard's idea, but before they can begin their attack, the townsfolk propose a different solution: that Lewis marry Princess Blanche of Spain, John's niece. John agrees and delivers some of the disputed territory as Blanche's dowry. That's all Philip wants out of the war, so he happily gives up on Arthur. John mollifies Arthur by making him Duke of Brittany, Earl of Richmond, and Lord of Angiers, but that's a far cry from King of England.

Act 3

The plot twists unexpectedly with the arrival of Cardinal Pandulph, a papal legate. The Pope had appointed the Archbishop of Canterbury, the highest clerical position in England, but John didn't like the Pope's choice, so he defied the Pope and made his own choice. Now the Pope sends his hatchet man, Pandulph, to settle the problem. Pandulph excommunicates John and opens the John-hunting season by declaring that two wrongs make a right if it benefits the Pope and "is opposite to England's love" (3.1.180). Arthur's mother and Pandulph convince King Philip that right and might are on his side against England, so Philip goes to war with England.

John captures Arthur during the battle with the French and takes him back to England. Because some people still think that Arthur has a stronger claim to the English throne, John wants Arthur out of the way. He commands Hubert to take care of the matter.

Lewis lost his chance at adding England to his future inheritance, and now "life is as tedious as a twice-told tale" (3.3.108). Pandulph offers him hope, though. He convinces Lewis that John will probably kill Arthur, in which case Lewis should claim the English throne. With a little convincing, Lewis agrees to attack King John. When the English army pulls back to England, Lewis follows in eager pursuit.

Act 4

John thinks that his problems are behind him, and his lords agree. They see no reason to crown John again because he was the rightful king before. The Earl of Salisbury says:

To gild refined gold, to paint the lily, . . .

Is wasteful and ridiculous excess. (4.2.11–16)

What John doesn't know is that Hubert decided that loyalty to the king does not sanction murder. Hubert faces a difficult choice: He has the hot irons ready to blind and kill Arthur, but Arthur's gentle innocence persuades him not to carry out the deed. Instead, Hubert lies to John and pretends to have killed Arthur.

When Hubert delivers the news that Arthur is "dead," many English lords rebel against John. When Hubert learns this, he reveals the truth: that Arthur is actually alive. The news lifts John's hopes, and he orders Hubert to fetch Arthur at once and show him to the lords who think that he's dead.

Meanwhile, back at the prison, Arthur tries to escape. He makes his break by climbing a wall, but it's a long way down, and he falls to his death. The English lords find his body and accuse Hubert of having caused Arthur's death. Hubert is innocent, but he can't convince the lords. They defect to the French side. The moral here: Even if you make the right choice, the results aren't always what you expect.

SEE IT

On video

1984, BBC: David Giles director, Leonard Rossiter as King John. A decent performance of this rarely produced play.

Act 5

The French have landed in England, the English lords have turned against their king, and matters look bleak for John. He faces a difficult decision: yield to Philip or try to hang on and fight it out. He has a third option, though: He capitulates to the Pope on the matter of the Archbishop of Canterbury and also turns over the crown of England. The Pope, through his legate, Pandulph, allows John to rule England as the Pope's vassal. This "inglorious league" (5.1.65) will burn in the minds of the English for centuries to follow.

Pandulph thinks that he can stop the French army — after all, he thinks that he started the war by excommunicating John, so by bringing John back into the Church, he can stop the war. Needless to say, he fails.

Fortunately for John, French lords tell the rebellious English lords, "Lewis means to recompense the pains you take / By cutting off your heads" (5.4.15–16). After all, Lewis can't trust a lord who would betray his king. The lords go back to England's side. Seeing how matters stand, Lewis reconsiders Pandulph's offer and accepts peace. In the final scene, King John dies, poisoned by a monk. John's son becomes the new king, Henry III.

John's death is a fitting end (if historically inaccurate — it was more likely something he ate) for a king who traded his kingdom and all his subjects to protect his personal safety. Despite the ignominy of John's submission to the Pope, Shakespeare wrings a little patriotic fervor in Sir Richard's closing speech:

This England never did, nor never shall,

Lie at the proud foot of a conqueror. (5.7.112–13)

King Richard II

Key characters:

- ✔ Richard II, King of England
- ✔ Henry Bolingbroke, later King Henry IV, cousin of the king

> ✔ John of Gaunt, Duke of Lancaster, father of Henry Bolingbroke, and uncle of the king
>
> ✔ Edmund, Duke of York, brother of John of Gaunt, and uncle of the king
>
> ✔ Thomas Mowbray, Duke of Norfolk

The next episode of *As the Globe Turns* skips forward a century to the reign of King Richard II. This play begins a series of plays that take place more or less back to back. *Richard II* introduces a theme that reappears frequently: deposing your king for fun and profit. If you have trouble keeping track of the characters in this and the following plays, refer to your scorecards and to the genealogy in Figure 14-1. The figure shows those who appear in Shakespeare's plays or otherwise have a major role offstage.

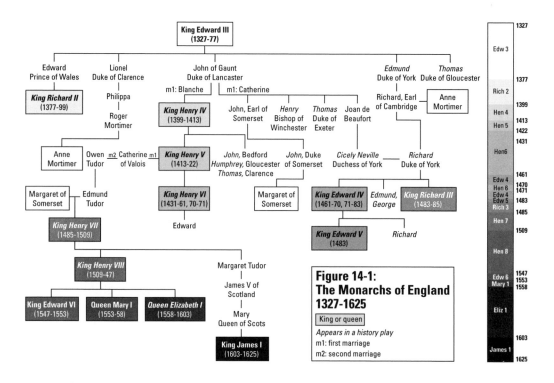

Figure 14-1: The Monarchs of England 1327-1625

King or queen
Appears in a history play
m1: first marriage
m2: second marriage

Act 1

Henry Bolingbroke accuses Thomas Mowbray of murdering the Duke of Gloucester (uncle of Henry and King Richard). Thomas denies the charges, and their dispute overheats until King Richard intervenes. Richard tries to settle the matter peaceably, but Bolingbroke and Thomas refuse to cooperate. Trial by combat is the only way to decide the matter, but at the last minute, Richard stops the duel. He banishes Bolingbroke and Thomas from England, Bolingbroke for six years and Thomas forever.

With that problem settled (or so he thinks), Richard turns to his next task: war against Ireland. To finance his campaign, he must raise taxes, especially on the wealthy nobility. Taxes were as unpopular then as they are now, so you can see that Richard is setting himself up for serious trouble.

Act 2

Henry Bolingbroke's father, the Duke of Lancaster, dies. Bolingbroke is in exile, though, so Richard seizes the opportunity to grab Lancaster's land and wealth, which Bolingbroke should inherit. Richard needs the money for his war against the Irish, and Bolingbroke isn't around to complain.

The Duke of York, another of Richard's uncles, objects to Richard's actions and warns him:

You pluck a thousand dangers on your head

You lose a thousand well-disposed hearts. (2.1.205–6)

But he is powerless to stop the king. Several lords are disturbed by these trends. After all, any one of them could be next. Bolingbroke doesn't take this illegal seizure lightly. He raises an army and returns to England to reclaim his title and inheritance.

The Duke of York sends word to Richard in Ireland about Bolingbroke's arrival. While waiting for Richard to return with his army, York musters what forces he can to resist Bolingbroke. Some lords remain loyal to King Richard, but "where one on his side fights, thousands will fly" (2.2.146) to the popular Bolingbroke.

King Richard and York have Welsh allies who will support the king, but the Welsh army grows impatient waiting for Richard to return from Ireland. Unable to wait any longer, they go home. Without the Welsh, Bolingbroke's victory is almost certain.

Act 3

King Richard returns to England to hear all the bad news: The populace is behind Bolingbroke, the Welsh army has disbanded, and Bolingbroke has executed several of Richard's loyal supporters. Richard can't take the strain. In a textbook example of manic-depressive syndrome, he vacillates between arrogance and despair while the news arrives. When he's upbeat, Richard believes that God is on his side and "heaven still guards the right" (3.2.62). (Read more about kings and their divine right to rule in Chapter 2.) He believes that the people will support their rightful king against the usurper, Bolingbroke. Then he learns the news of the Welsh army and falls back to weakness. He swings back and forth, regaining his faith only to learn that his loyal lords were captured and killed. He soon gives way to despair: "The worst is death, and death will have his day" (3.2.103).

Bolingbroke confronts Richard and demands the repeal of his banishment and the restoration of his title, lands, and full inheritance. Richard sees things differently. He sees a traitorous usurper who raised an army to combat his king. But Richard knows that he can't win. On the surface, Bolingbroke's demands seem reasonable, but will he want more?

Act 4

King Richard submits to the inevitable and yields the crown to Bolingbroke, who becomes King Henry IV. From king to commoner is a long way to fall. "For I must nothing be" (4.1.201), Richard says. He still has friends, though, and they plot against their new king.

Act 5

York is an honest, loyal man. He supported Richard even when Richard was wrong because he had sworn allegiance to his king. Now he has sworn loyalty to King Henry. So when York learns that his son is part of a conspiracy against Henry, he rushes to warn the king.

In a preview for the next two plays (the two parts of *King Henry IV*), the king hears news that his eldest son is stirring up a different kind of trouble. The young Prince Hal hangs out with the wrong crowd — thugs, delinquents, and "unrestrained loose companions" (5.3.7). Hal doesn't actually put in an appearance until the next play *(King Henry IV, Part 1)*.

The conspiracy against Henry's life falls apart. York's son goes to King Henry to seek the king's pardon because he hasn't done anything yet. His father, the Duke of York, arrives next and reports against his son. Finally, the Duchess pleads for mercy for her son. Henry agrees to pardon York's son but orders the capture of the other conspirators.

A former king is always a threat to a new king. The simplest solution is to execute the old king, but regicide is a terrible act, even for a king. Nonetheless, a knight thinks that Henry ordered him to kill Richard and does so. He thought that he had Henry's support, but the king disavows the deed. Henry promises to make a holy pilgrimage to atone for his role in the murder.

Has Henry finally quieted all rebellion in his kingdom? Will his son, Prince Hal, embarrass himself, his father, and the crown of England? Stay tuned for the next installment of *As the Globe Turns*, entitled *King Henry IV, Part 1*, to learn the answers to these and other questions.

SEE IT

On video

✔ 1990, English Shakespeare Company: Michael Bogdanov director. Not available in the U.S.

✔ 1978, BBC: David Giles director, Derek Jacobi as Richard II, Jon Finch as Henry Bolingbroke, and John Gielgud as John of Gaunt. A good production in a traditional setting.

✔ 1970, BBC: Richard Cottrell director, Ian McKellen as Richard II, Timothy West as Bolingbroke, and Paul Hardwick as John of Gaunt. A very good and clear production.

King Henry IV, Part 1

Key characters:

✔ Henry IV, King of England

✔ Prince Hal, son of King Henry

✔ Henry Percy, called Hotspur, son of the Earl of Northumberland

✔ Sir John Falstaff, a coward, thief, wit, and friend to Prince Hal

✔ Owen Glendower, a Welsh chieftain and rebel against King Henry

✔ Edmund Mortimer, a rebel against the king

✔ Earl of Douglas, a Scottish rebel against the king

In the previous episode of *As the Globe Turns,* Henry Bolingbroke deposed Richard II and became King Henry IV. Now he must defend his precarious position, at the same time trying to be a good father to his wayward son. Why can't his eldest son Hal be more like that nice boy, Hotspur, the son of the Earl of Northumberland? Learn the answers to these questions and more in *King Henry IV, Part 1.*

Act 1

The play opens with King Henry IV planning a holy crusade to Jerusalem to atone for the murder of King Richard II, but his plans are interrupted by reports of war on England's borders. Owen Glendower, a Welsh chieftain, has defeated an English army and captured its commander, Edmund Mortimer. Happier news arrives from Scotland, where the young Hotspur has the better hand against the Earl of Douglas, a great Scottish soldier.

Marring the king's Scottish victory is his eldest son's disreputable behavior. Prince Hal is about the same age as Hotspur, but while Hotspur defends England and wins fame and glory, Hal parties with the lowlifes of London, especially Sir John Falstaff, a fat, drunken, hedonistic coward.

It turns out that Hotspur is not quite as perfect as Henry imagines him to be. Hotspur violates custom by refusing to turn over to Henry his Scottish prisoners of war. Hotspur is angry that the king won't pay the ransom to release Edmund Mortimer, who is a prisoner of Owen Glendower. Mortimer is Hotspur's brother-in-law, so he naturally feels strongly about this issue.

The impulsive Hotpsur shows how he earned his name, ignoring his friends and relatives as they try to reason with him. Although Hotspur helped Henry gain the throne, he now believes that Mortimer is the rightful heir to the throne. He plans to return to Scotland, this time as an ally against Henry and England. His uncle will recruit the Welsh to their cause: "The game is afoot" (1.3.272), he says.

Act 2

Falstaff and other friends of Hal rob some pilgrims who are on their way to Canterbury. While enjoying their loot, Hal and another of his friends disguise themselves and set upon Falstaff and the others, who run away in fear. To Hal, it is all a game. He knows that Falstaff will exaggerate what took place, and he looks forward to having some fun at Falstaff's expense.

While Hal sports with his thieving friends, Hotspur prepares for war. He is all business. Even in his sleep, so his wife tells him, he cries, "Courage! To the field!" (2.3.50), and talks of battle. Hal and Hotspur are as different as any two people can be, but Hal has at least a hint of honor. He promises to repay the money that his friends stole from the pilgrims.

The king calls for Hal, and Hal must answer the royal summons. Falstaff asks him how he will answer his father. They play word games, and Falstaff asks Hal, when he is king, to treat Falstaff kindly, saying, "Banish not him thy Harry's company, banish plump Jack, and banish all the world" (2.4.472–74). Hal foreshadows the next play *(King Henry IV, Part II)* with his answer, "I do, I will" (2.4.475).

Act 3

The rebels count their chickens before the eggs are laid, let alone hatched. They have divided England into three parts: the west for Glendower and the Welsh, the south for Mortimer, and the north for Hotspur. Hotspur annoys Glendower by quibbling over the boundaries, but finally they come to a shaky agreement. The battle has not yet begun, but already they quarrel over the spoils.

Prince Hal reports to his father, who scolds him for his wanton behavior. At length, Henry rails against his son, compares him to the noble Hotspur, and carries on as fathers have done for centuries and will continue to do until the end of time. Hal apologizes and promises to show his true self on the battlefield, telling his father, "I will redeem all this on Percy's head" (3.2.132).

Act 4

The battle still has not begun, but the rebels already have trouble. The Earl of Northumberland, Hotspur's father, is ill and cannot march with the army. Glendower and the Welsh army are detained, and it will be another 14 days before they can join the main forces. The rebels also learn that King Henry has mobilized a large army, but Hotspur welcomes the coming fight.

Sir John Falstaff must lead others into battle, as must any knight. He has pressed into service 150 unlikely soldiers "with hearts in their bellies no bigger than pins' heads" (4.2.21–22). They are unfit for battle, but they are just as likely as Falstaff to turn and run, which is exactly what Falstaff looks for in his soldiers.

Following the forms of warfare and rebellion, the king sends an envoy to demand of Hotspur why he is rebelling against his king. Hotspur enumerates his grievances: Henry overstepped his bounds by deposing Richard and taking the throne himself; Henry refused to ransom Edmund Mortimer; and Hotspur thinks that Henry is unsuited to be King of England.

Act 5

Hotspur sends the Earl of Worcester as his representative to King Henry. Prince Hal offers a compromise instead of outright civil war: single combat between himself and Hotspur. Henry also offers to pardon the other lords and all who would fight against their king. Worcester, however, does not bring this offer back to Hotspur for fear that he would accept it. Worcester doesn't trust Henry's generous offer of amnesty. He fears that, in time, Henry would find ways to take revenge on the rebels. Instead, Worcester lies and tells Hotspur that the king wants to fight.

In the battle, many lords and knights dress as the king to confuse the rebels. Douglas kills several of them, each time thinking that he has killed the king. Prince Hal also distinguishes himself in battle. Although wounded and bleeding, he refuses to retire until the battle is won.

Finally, Douglas finds the real king and they fight. Douglas gets the upper hand, but Prince Hal rescues his father. Douglas retreats, but Hotspur enters, and Hal and Hotspur finally get the fight they both have longed for. Meanwhile, Falstaff and Douglas meet and fight until Falstaff falls over, pretending to be dead.

On video

✔ 1990, English Shakespeare Company: Michael Bogdanov director. Not available in the U.S.

✔ 1979, BBC: David Giles director, Anthony Quayle as Sir John Falstaff, Jon Finch as Henry IV, David Gwillim as Prince Hal, and Tim Pigott-Smith as Hotspur.

Hal kills Hotspur and goes to report his triumph. Falstaff gets up and sees Hotspur's body. He picks up the body and carries it back to the king so that he can claim to have killed Hotspur.

The new Hal is more than just a great soldier. In response to Falstaff's false claims, Hal explains the truth, but doesn't force the issue. If Falstaff would rather lie to assuage his ego, Hal will let him do so. As further evidence of his courtesy, Hal frees the Scottish prisoner, Douglas. The prodigal son has returned. Or has he? Will Falstaff further corrupt the young prince? For the answer to these and other questions, watch the next exciting episode of *As the Globe Turns*.

King Henry IV, Part 2

Key characters:

✔ Henry IV, King of England

✔ Prince Hal, son of King Henry IV, later King Henry V

✔ Prince John of Lancaster, brother of Hal

✔ Sir John Falstaff, friend to Hal

✔ Poins, friend to Hal

A king's work is never done. If it's not one rebellion, it's another. Prince Hal is back to his old tricks, too. This episode of *As the Globe Turns* opens with a unique prologue, given by the personification of Rumor. In the previous episode, *King Henry IV, Part 1,* King Henry triumphed over the rebels led by Hotspur, the son of the Earl of Northumberland. *King Henry IV, Part 2,* picks up immediately afterward, with rumors that Prince Hal died and that Hotspur and his Scottish ally Douglas conquered King Henry IV.

Act 1

The Earl of Northumberland waits for news from his son, Hotspur, and the other rebels. He hears that his son triumphed, then he hears that his son failed — Rumor has been busy — but he finally hears a firsthand account of how his son died at the hands of Prince Hal, and how the rebels' army was dispersed and vanquished. After the bad news comes the good news: The rebels lost a battle, but they have not given up the war. The Archbishop of York has raised his own army against the king. These tidings bring new hope to Northumberland and his followers.

The new rebels, under the leadership of the Archbishop of York, make their plans. They have a large army, larger than Hotspur had, and with the support of Northumberland, they will be unstoppable.

John Falstaff figures largely in this play, in more ways than one. When someone tells Falstaff that his financial "waste is great" (1.2.141), Falstaff replies that he wishes his "waist slenderer" (1.2.143). His girth is the subject of much humor, as are his gout, his predilection for booze, his dalliance with prostitutes, and his financial troubles.

Act 2

The innkeeper, Mistress Quickly, complains that Falstaff has "eaten me out of house and home" (2.1.74), so she hires officers to arrest him for non-payment of his considerable bar bill. Falstaff fights off the officers until the Chief Justice intervenes and orders Falstaff to pay the debt that he owes Mistress Quickly. Falstaff offers partial payment, which she accepts as being better than nothing. Meanwhile, the Chief Justice receives a letter. The king's army is on the move, and Falstaff must report for duty.

Northumberland plans to join the rebellion this time, but his wife and daughter-in-law persuade him otherwise. In an impassioned speech, Hotspur's widow at once berates Northumberland for not coming to Hotspur's aid and for trying to redress that wrong by going to war now. Hotspur's army was only half the size of the current one, so she argues that the archbishop has a large enough army without Northumberland. She counsels that he bide his time, and if the rebels prove stronger, he can bring up his armies "like a rib of steel / To make strength stronger" (2.3.55–56). If not, he can keep his head low in safety.

Prince Hal showed his mettle at the end of *King Henry IV, Part 1,* but now he's back in London and up to his old tricks, this time with his friend Poins, who has just as poor a reputation as Falstaff. Together, they dress as waiters and eavesdrop on Falstaff, who calls the prince a "shallow young fellow" (2.4.237). After taking in the insults, Hal and Poins drop their disguises and have their own go at Falstaff. A messenger interrupts their game with news from the king. The chastened prince hurries away. Falstaff, too, must head off to war.

Act 3

The king is sick. Feeling that his end is drawing near, he remembers the ups and downs of his reign — most recently downs. "Uneasy lies the head that wears a crown" (3.1.31), muses the king. Rumor is still busy, bringing exaggerated reports about the strength of the rebel army.

A local squire and justice of the peace, Shallow, remembers his younger days with Falstaff. Now that Falstaff is a knight and a close friend of the prince, Shallow hopes to renew his friendship and gain a friend in court. Falstaff has come in search of soldiers, and Shallow has lined up some unlikely candidates.

Falstaff examines the draftees. Those who can afford it buy their freedom, and those who cannot must march to war. Shallow plays up to Falstaff, but the old rogue is not fooled. Instead, Shallow's money lures him, and he plans to use his friendship with Prince Hal to take advantage of the naïve, doddering Shallow.

Act 4

Even though Northumberland will not join the rebels, their army is almost as big as the king's army. The rebel army is big enough to force the king to listen to their demands, which they present to the king's younger son, Prince John of Lancaster.

Prince John accepts the rebels' terms, giving his solemn word to redress all their grievances. He asks the rebels to disperse their army and likewise orders his army to return home, but John has a surprise planned. The rebel army leaves. John's army does not. John orders the arrest of the archbishop and the other rebel leaders. At first they feel betrayed, but John is earnest in saying that he will see that all their grievances are redressed. That does not excuse the king's sworn subjects from open rebellion, however. It's neither the first nor the last time a leader will say one thing and do another, defending himself by a strict interpretation of his words.

With peace in his kingdom, King Henry has one last job to finish before he dies. His eldest son is a big disappointment and doesn't seem ready to assume the responsibilities of kingship. Hal is eager to prove his critics wrong. He honestly repents his past life and wins back his father's affection. Seeing that the kingdom will be in good hands, the king dies.

Act 5

The king is dead, and a new king sits on England's throne. The chief justice remembers the riotous Prince Hal, who is now King Henry V. He often chastised the riotous young prince, and once even locked the prince in jail. Now he fears that the new king might seek revenge. He needn't have worried,

SEE IT

On video

✔ 1990, English Shakespeare Company: Michael Bogdanov director. Not available in the U.S.

✔ 1979, BBC: David Giles director, Anthony Quayle as Sir John Falstaff, Jon Finch as Henry IV, and David Gwillim as Prince Hal.

though. King Henry V struts his royal stuff and shows his true nobility. He thanks the chief justice for being honest and having the strength of will to jail him when he deserved it. Henry asks the chief justice to continue to watch over him as his closest advisor.

News reaches Falstaff that the king is dead, and Prince Hal is now King Henry V. Falstaff is elated. His "sweet boy" (5.5.43) is now king, and he expects to cash in on his friendship. He heads immediately to Westminster to get near the new king, but King Henry coldly repudiates him and orders his arrest. All of Hal's old friends must stay at least 10 miles from the king, on pain of death. The old Hal is like a dream, and now awake, King Henry V must forget his dreams. He is ready for his next challenge — France — as you discover in the next thrilling episode of *As the Globe Turns*.

King Henry V

Key characters:

✔ Henry V, King of England

✔ King Charles of France

✔ Princess Katherine, daughter of King Charles

✔ Fluellen, a Welsh captain

✔ Pistol, a rogue and friend to King Henry from his younger days

✔ Corporal Bardolph, friend to King Henry from his younger days

The prologue to *Henry V* is famous for its description of the Globe Theatre as "this wooden O" (Prologue.13) — that is, a circular theater. (Read more about the Globe Theatre in Chapter 2.) The prologue asks the audience to imagine 1,000 soldiers for each person onstage and to

Think, when we talk of horses, that you see them

Printing their proud hoofs i'th' receiving earth. (Prologue.26–27)

With modern films, you don't need to exercise your imagination in quite the same way, but even today the prologue remains a powerful testament to live theater.

Courtesy Two Cities

Figure 14-2:
Laurence
Olivier as
Henry V.

Act 1

The Archbishop of Canterbury is concerned about a bill before Parliament that would levy a heavy tax on the Church, stripping it of the lands, titles, and money that people have donated over the years. To fight this bill, the archbishop offers the king a bigger prize: all of France. He digs up an obscure point of law whereby Henry can lay claim to France. This suits the king well, especially when the dauphin insults Henry with a gift of tennis balls, implying that Henry should stick to games, not wars.

Act 2

Henry raises an army and prepares to invade France. Falstaff, Henry's disreputable companion in his wild youth, is sick and dying. His familiar sidekicks, Pistol and Bardolph, receive the grim news. Falstaff does not put in an appearance in this play, but dies offstage.

Henry shows his mettle when he confronts three would-be murderers. Three English noblemen, in the pay of France, plot against Henry. Henry could have had them quietly arrested and executed, but he confronts them in person, risking his life to do so. Contrast this with Shakespeare's depiction of the French, who are cautious and wary about the coming English army:

Let us fear

The native mightiness and fate of him. (2.4.63–64)

Act 3

The English army is now in France, attacking the city of Harfleur at the mouth of the Seine River. King Charles of France has tried to appease Henry, offering his daughter, Katherine, as bride and bribe, but Henry has refused the offer and now besieges the city. The city puts up a strong defense, but Henry urges his soldiers on with the rallying cry, "Once more unto the breach" (3.1.1). The city resists, expecting help from the dauphin, but when help doesn't arrive, the governor surrenders to Henry, who urges his generals to use mercy on the city's inhabitants.

In an amusing scene, Katherine prepares for the possible English victory: She asks her lady-in-waiting to teach her English. Her attendant actually teaches her Franglais — somewhere between French and English. Imagine an outrageous accent when you read "fingres" for fingers, "de nick" for neck, and so on.

The warring season is now over, and Henry plans to take the army to Calais and back to England before winter sets in. The French army, however, prepares to fight. They know that the English are sick and tired, and King Henry readily admits this to the French herald. He also says that the English army is more than ready to face the French. When the herald returns the news, the dauphin and the French generals are eager to begin the fight that they fully expect to win.

Henry may be invading France, but he's no barbarian. He issues strict orders to pay for the food that the army needs and not to take anything or harm anyone but soldiers. One of Falstaff's old friends, Bardolph, violates these orders and loots a church. Without hesitation, Henry orders Bardolph's execution. Remember Henry's sense of justice during the next act, when the French army is less honorable.

Act 4

During the night, Henry disguises himself as a soldier and wanders about the camp. Should the French capture him, he doesn't want the English to pay any ransom. The common soldiers are not convinced of his sincerity, but they are ready enough to engage the French in battle.

The French army is about five times larger than the English, but Henry finds the odds to his liking: "The fewer men, the greater share of honour" (4.3.22). He exhorts the troops with stories of how men at home in England will "hold their manhoods cheap" (4.3.66) that they were not present at the glorious battle in France.

Much to the surprise of the dauphin, the French are losing the battle. Even a coward such as Pistol succeeds in capturing a prisoner and holding him for ransom. The French army reassembles for an assault, and Henry orders his soldiers to kill their prisoners to prevent them from trying to rejoin their army. (Henry isn't entirely honorable, either.)

The French army has circled around the English and ransacked their camp. They attacked and killed the boys who watch the baggage, away from the main fray. This act of cowardice shows the desperate straits of the French army. In the confusion of battle, Henry is not sure who won the day, but the French herald tells him, "The day is yours" (4.7.85).

Henry has one bit of business to finish. While he roamed the camp in disguise, he exchanged strong words with a soldier who challenged him. Henry accepted the challenge, should they both survive the battle. Now is the time of reckoning, but Henry wants to have some fun. He gives the soldier's glove — the token of the challenge — to Fluellen, a Welsh captain. When the soldier sees Fluellen with the glove, he strikes Fluellen and renews the challenge. Fluellen is confused and confronts the challenger. Henry intervenes and explains the situation. He chastises the soldier for challenging the king, but the soldier responds that Henry was disguised. He would never take such a bold stance with the king, but only with a common soldier. Henry rewards the soldier's honesty and bravery.

The heralds count the number of the slain. The French have lost 1,500 lords, knights, and squires and 10,000 common soldiers. The English lost 3 noble lords and a total of 25 men. Shakespeare's numbers exaggerate the truth, but the battle of Agincourt was an English high point in the long-running war with the French.

Act 5

Pistol is still a swaggering, boasting coward. He has words with Fluellen, who returns strong words with strong blows. Ever resourceful, Pistol plans to return to England and pretend that the scars he received from Fluellen he actually received from the French.

Henry has defeated the French in war, and now it is time to turn to love. To cement the peace treaty between the countries, he asks for the hand of Princess Katherine. She has learned only a little English, and Henry speaks even less French. Nonetheless, he woos her and wins her. She will become Queen Katherine of England, and Henry will become the heir to the French throne.

On video

- ✔ 1990, English Shakespeare Company: Michael Bogdanov director. Not available in the U.S.

- ✔ 1989, Renaissance Films: Kenneth Branagh director and as Henry V, Derek Jacobi as the Chorus, and Emma Thompson as Katherine. An exciting production that takes some liberties with the script.

- ✔ 1979, BBC: David Giles director, Jocelyne Boisseau as Katherine, David Gwillim as Henry V, and Alec McCowan as the Chorus.

- ✔ 1944, Two Cities Film: Laurence Olivier director and as Henry V. A classic.

England and France unite in peace, but how long will it last? Stay tuned for the next thrilling episode of *As the Globe Turns,* when you will see the fate of Henry V's alliance and how the son of Henry and Katherine manages the kingdom in *King Henry VI, Part 1.*

King Henry VI, Part 1

Key characters:

- ✔ Henry VI, King of England
- ✔ Charles, the Dauphin of France
- ✔ Talbot, leader of the English army, later Earl of Shrewsbury
- ✔ Joan la Pucelle, also called Joan of Arc
- ✔ Duke of Gloucester ("GLAW-ster"), uncle of King Henry
- ✔ Richard Plantagenet ("plan-TAJ-eh-net"), of the House of York
- ✔ Duke of Somerset, of the House of Lancaster
- ✔ Bishop of Winchester, later Cardinal, great-uncle of the king
- ✔ Reignier ("RAIN-yay"), Duke of Anjou and King of Naples
- ✔ Margaret, daughter of Reignier, later married to King Henry

King Henry VI, Part 1 begins the series of plays that cover the Wars of the Roses, a civil war in England that pitted the House of Lancaster against the House of York. Refer to Figure 14-1 to trace the rival houses and their claims to the English throne. The next three episodes of the ongoing saga *As the*

Globe Turns cover the reign of Henry VI, son of Henry V. This play also presents an English perspective on the subject of Joan of Arc.

Act 1

The play begins with the funeral of King Henry V and the foreshadowing plea of the Duke of Bedford:

Henry the Fifth, thy ghost I invoke:

Prosper this realm, keep it from civil broils. (1.1.52–53)

France seeks to reclaim the territory it lost to Henry V, but England's biggest threats come from within, not from France. Henry's son, also named Henry, is still young, and his uncles and other English lords seek power through young Henry or despite him.

The English army besieges the town of Orleans, and the French army besieges the English. The English are caught between the French in the town with the French army surrounding them. The English general, Talbot, valiantly leads the English army against the French, but he is vastly outnumbered. The French leaders marvel at the tenacity, ferocity, and bravery of the English. It's everything you expect from a play written by an Englishman.

The hope for the French is a girl, a shepherdess: Joan la Pucelle, whom we know as Joan of Arc. (*Pucelle* is French for maiden.) She claims divine inspiration to free the French from their English overlords. Charles, the dauphin, is skeptical, but Joan offers to fight him to prove her mettle. They fight and she wins, convincing Charles that she can help, regardless of whether her strength is divinely inspired.

Back in England, the "civil broils" (1.1.53) are getting out of hand. The Duke of Gloucester and the Bishop of Winchester even brawl in the streets of London before the mayor breaks up the fight.

Joan launches her attack at Orleans, sweeping away the English army. The act ends with the French celebrating their victory, crying that "Joan de Pucelle shall be France's saint" (1.6.29), which is amazingly prophetic. Centuries later, in 1920, Pope Benedict XV canonized her as Saint Joan.

Act 2

Don't give up on the English yet! They sneak up on Orleans at night, climb over the walls, and take the French by surprise. The French leaders don't even have time to dress as they flee the town. The French are worse off than when they started, but Joan is undaunted. She commands that the army reassemble to attack again.

Shakespeare throws in a couple of scenes that help establish the character of Talbot without advancing the plot. The Countess of Auvergne tries to trick Talbot and capture him, but she traps only "Talbot's shadow" (2.3.45). His true substance — what makes him the feared enemy of France — is his army. He spotted the trap and brought his soldiers with him, outsmarting the countess, but Talbot does not take her prisoner. All he asks for is wine and food for his soldiers, which she graciously offers.

The next scene plants the seed of what will blossom into civil war. Richard Plantagenet (of the House of York) and the Duke of Somerset (of the House of Lancaster) have a minor disagreement over a subtle point of law. Shakespeare never tells what the disagreement actually is because it doesn't matter. Richard and Somerset ask others to arbitrate, but no one wants to get involved at first. Finally, Richard plucks a white rose from the garden and asks that anyone who believes he is right also pluck a white rose. Somerset plucks a red rose and asks that others pluck a red rose to show their support. Thus you see the emblems for the Wars of the Roses, pitting the white rose of York against the red rose of Lancaster.

Richard Plantagenet visits his aging uncle, Edmund Mortimer, who explains why the Yorks have a stronger claim to the throne than Henry does. Richard's mother, Anne Mortimer, descends from King Edward III's third son, Lionel, but Henry descends from Edward's fourth son, John. Shakespeare makes a few mistakes in recounting the details, but you can see the Yorkist claim in the genealogical table back in Figure 14-1.

Act 3

In England, Winchester and Gloucester continue to feud. Henry tries to patch up their differences and makes them promise to be friends. He then bestows on Richard the title of Duke of York, which was his father's title. Despite the outward appearance of friendship, deep divisions remain among the peers of England — divisions that will be England's undoing.

In France, Joan is a busy girl. She sneaks into Rouen, and the French army takes the town from the English. The English, undaunted, attack and retake the town from the French. After settling the further defense of the city, Talbot and the Duke of Burgundy plan to travel to Paris, where Henry will be crowned King Henry VI.

Joan tries to keep up the spirits of the French lords. She hatches a new plan: to entice Burgundy to switch sides from the English to the French. She stops Burgundy as he travels to Paris and asks for a parley. He grants the request and listens to her passionate plea on behalf of the French people. She pleads, "Strike those that hurt, and hurt not those that help" (3.3.54), and convinces him to join the French army.

Act 4

In Paris, Henry grants the title Earl of Shrewsbury to Talbot. They learn the news of Burgundy, and Talbot proposes to march immediately against him. The newly crowned King Henry VI asks York (Richard Plantagenet) and Somerset to strengthen the English army, but their feuding continues unabated. Talbot attacks the town of Bordeaux but is trapped by the French army. He needs reinforcements from York and Somerset, but they bicker like children. York blames his delay on Somerset. Somerset blames it on York. All the while, English soldiers die in the battlefield. Talbot fights on, but without reinforcements he is doomed. He dies, but still the English spirit lives on.

Act 5

Gloucester tries to cement a peace treaty between England and France by suggesting that King Henry marry the daughter of the Earl of Armagnac, a French lord who is a close relative of the French king, Charles VII. Gloucester easily convinces Henry to agree to the match.

Somerset and York have patched up their differences, at least to the degree of mounting a joint army against the French. Joan calls upon her divine spirits, but they no longer help her. The Duke of York captures her and will later execute her.

Just when you think that everything is going smoothly for the English, the Earl of Suffolk meets Margaret, the daughter of Reignier, who is the French Duke of Anjou. Reignier also claims the title of King of Naples, which makes Margaret a princess and a suitable match for a king. Suffolk is enamored of Margaret, but he is already married. He hatches a plan that will let him stay near Margaret and win favor with his king.

Suffolk convinces Henry to marry Margaret. Margaret becomes Queen of England, and her father gets full control over the duchies of Maine and Anjou. Henry elevates Suffolk from an earl to a duke. Gloucester, however, is incensed that Henry would back out of the deal with Armagnac, risking further war with France.

Suffolk hopes to stay near Margaret and control her, and through her control the king, and therefore England. Will he succeed? Will the Duke of Gloucester get the king to see reason? Stay tuned for the next exciting episode of *As the Globe Turns*.

SEE IT

On video

✔ 1990, English Shakespeare Company: Michael Bogdanov director. Not available in the U.S. The three parts of *Henry VI* are combined into two videotapes: *Henry VI: House of Lancaster* and *Henry VI: House of York.*

✔ 1983, BBC: Jane Howell director, Peter Benson as Henry VI, Julia Foster as Margaret, Brenda Blethyn as Joan la Pucelle, and Trevor Peacock as Talbot. A nice performance from Brenda Blethyn as Joan of Arc.

King Henry VI, Part 2

Key characters:

✔ Henry VI, King of England

✔ Margaret, later Queen of England

✔ Duke of Suffolk

✔ Humphrey, Duke of Gloucester ("GLAW-ster"), uncle of the king

✔ Richard Plantagenet ("plan-TAJ-e-net"), Duke of York

✔ Cardinal Beaufort, Bishop of Winchester, great-uncle of the king

✔ Earl of Warwick

✔ Jack Cade, a peasant rebel

In the previous episode of *As the Globe Turns,* Suffolk was smitten with Margaret, daughter of the Duke of Anjou. Suffolk convinced King Henry VI to marry Margaret and hoped to control Margaret, Henry, and the throne of England. *King Henry VI, Part 2,* picks up with Suffolk's return to England, bringing Margaret to the king.

Act 1

With great ceremony, Suffolk introduces Margaret to King Henry, who rewards him by elevating him to Duke of Suffolk (which is how *King Henry IV, Part 1,* ended). The king's uncle, Humphrey, the Duke of Gloucester, reads the marriage contract, but stops in shock when he learns that Margaret brings no dowry and that England has given up two duchies in France to Margaret's father. The custom of the time was for the bride's father to pay

Figure 14-3:
Peggy
Ashcroft
as Queen
Margaret.

Shakespeare Centre Library

the bridegroom handsomely, especially in a royal marriage, not the other way around. Nonetheless, the king is pleased and leads away his new bride. Gloucester is unhappy with this arrangement and sees that Suffolk is plotting against the king. Some of the English lords agree with him, but they distrust Gloucester more than Suffolk.

Gloucester's problem is that he is an honest man and a loyal supporter of the king. The king's numerous enemies go after Gloucester first so that they can more easily get to the king. Cardinal Beaufort is at the top of the I-hate-Gloucester list, so he allies himself with Suffolk to topple Gloucester.

Somerset and Buckingham can't stand the "haughty Cardinal" (1.1.173), but they also dislike Gloucester, so they pretend to like the Cardinal, but only until they can bring down Gloucester. Warwick and his father support Gloucester but are more concerned with France, so they aren't much help to him. Finally, Richard, Duke of York, can't forget his argument with Somerset and that the king sides with Somerset (of the House of Lancaster). The loss of the duchies in France further angers him because he means to steal the throne, and he wants all of France, too.

To make matters worse, Gloucester has domestic problems. His wife is ambitious and wants her husband to seize the throne. Gloucester will have none of it and chastises his wife for her ambition. He doesn't know that she is consulting witches and spirits "rais'd from depth of under ground" (1.2.78) to further her goals. She doesn't know that Suffolk has hired her spiritual advisor to steer her wrong. Even with a scorecard, keeping track of who is for or against whom in this play can be difficult.

The act ends with Gloucester's wife and the witch. The witch conjures a spirit who makes direful but confusing predictions. York and Buckingham interrupt the proceedings and arrest everyone, including the Duchess of Gloucester.

Act 2

Buckingham reports the capture of the witch to the king. Gloucester is present when Buckingham makes the report, and he learns his wife is also a prisoner. The witch and her accomplices are condemned to death for witchcraft. The duchess is banished to the Isle of Man. Lacking frequent flights from London, the Isle of Man was a remote destination at the time. Gloucester is saddened, but he supports the rule of law. Even when his retainers offer to rescue his wife, he stops them. She must face her just punishment for her crime. She tries to warn him against the conspirators in the king's court, but he knows that he is "loyal, true, and crimeless" (2.4.63) and naively believes that it offers him protection.

York convinces Warwick and his father of York's rightful claim to the throne. His heritage is from the third son of King Edward III (Lionel), but King Henry's claim is through the fourth son (John), and in England the elder son rules before the younger. Figure 14-1 shows the royal family tree, where you can trace York's ancestry.

The king summons Gloucester to appear before the king's Parliament. By convention, the king would notify him beforehand and ask his consent. That the king surprised Gloucester with the summons does not bode well.

Act 3

Gloucester's enemies invent numerous false charges, but he disproves them all. Finally, Suffolk resorts to the childish trick of saying that Gloucester committed other crimes, but he doesn't say what they are, so of course Gloucester cannot refute them. The king asks that Gloucester receive a fair trial. That's all he can do against so many enemies. Even a king has limits.

The conspirators know that Gloucester is completely innocent of any crime they can imagine and that they could never manufacture a false accusation that would stick. Instead, they must murder him, and the Cardinal will "provide the executioner" (3.1.276). During their discussions, a messenger arrives with news that Ireland is revolting against England's rule. The Cardinal asks that York take an army to put down the rebellion.

York sees the opportunity presented. He has already hired an upstart, Jack Cade, to lead a peasant revolt in England. Cade will be his substitute in England, trying to rouse the populace against the king and in support of York. If the attempt fails, York loses nothing. If it succeeds, however, he can return from Ireland at the head of an army, redirect the army against Henry, and take the throne of England by force.

Gloucester is murdered in his sleep. The king suspects Suffolk, whom the queen defends. The townsfolk quickly learn of Gloucester's death and cry foul play. They also blame the murder on Suffolk and demand his punishment. Warwick and his father quiet the crowd but confront Suffolk. They fight, but the king interrupts and orders Suffolk's banishment. The queen is distraught at the thought of losing Suffolk. Suffolk's plan to manipulate the king through Margaret failed, but he succeeded in manipulating Margaret, and she tries to change Henry's mind. When she fails, she and Suffolk exchange a tender good-bye.

Act 4

Suffolk was banished, but en route to France, pirates capture his ship. The pirates demand a ransom for their prisoners, but when they learn of Suffolk's identity, they demand his death and will not accept ransom. They blame him for the murder of Gloucester.

In England, Jack Cade rouses the peasants in a cultural revolution. A peasant cries, "The first thing we do, let's kill all the lawyers" (4.2.74). Cade agrees and condemns a man to death for the penalty of knowing how to read and write. He fights ferociously and marches on London. The king flees for a safer haven, but Margaret is preoccupied with Suffolk's death. One of the pirate's released prisoners has delivered Suffolk's body and head to the queen, and she carries and cradles the head in disregard for propriety or her dire situation.

Cade has mowed down the English army until now. Finally, Buckingham raises an army large enough to confront Cade. He offers a pardon to all rebels who would leave Cade peacefully. Cade tries to persuade them to stay with him. The people are still sheep, but Cade is no longer the chief ram. He realizes his predicament and runs for his life.

He runs for five days without food. He bravely enters a private garden in search of food. The owner confronts him and they fight. Due to his weakened condition, Cade loses and dies. The owner learns of Cade's identity and goes to claim the reward that King Henry offered for Cade's head.

SEE IT

On video

✔ 1990, English Shakespeare Company: Michael Bogdanov director. Not available in the U.S. The three parts of *Henry VI* are combined into two videotapes: *Henry VI: House of Lancaster* and *Henry VI: House of York.*

✔ 1983, BBC: Jane Howell director, Peter Benson as Henry VI, David Burke as Gloucester, Bernard Hill as York, and Trevor Peacock as Jack Cade.

Act 5

York has returned from Ireland at the head of an army. His attempt at rebellion failed, so he goes to Plan B. He sends a command to the king to imprison Somerset. Buckingham reports that the king has done so, but the queen parades Somerset before York to entice and enrage him.

York claims the crown of England and calls Warwick and his father as his allies against King Henry. In the ensuing battle, York's son Richard kills Somerset, giving you a taste of things to come. (Richard will reach his height of infamy as King Richard III.) The king and queen flee for their lives. York wins the day, but to learn how matters turn out, you must wait for Part 3 in the ongoing story of *As the Globe Turns.*

King Henry VI, Part 3

Key characters:

✔ Henry VI, King of England

✔ Margaret, Queen of England

✔ Edward, Prince of Wales, son of Henry and Margaret

✔ Richard Plantagenet, Duke of York

✔ Edward, son of the Duke of York, later King Edward IV

✔ Richard, son of the Duke of York, brother of Edward

✔ Earl of Warwick

In action, *King Henry VI, Part 3,* follows immediately after the second part. In the preceding episode of *As the Globe Turns,* the Duke of York defeated Henry's army. Will York seize the throne? Will Henry retaliate? Keep your scorecard close at hand, because the shifting loyalties can be hard to follow.

Act 1

York and his allies triumphed in battle and followed King Henry VI to London. In the Parliament House, York sits on the throne. Henry enters and confronts York, and the battle lines are drawn. Some English lords support Henry, and others support York. To avoid another bloody battle, Henry proposes a compromise: He will rule as king for the rest of his life, but upon his death, York and his sons will inherit the crown. York accepts the offer, but Henry's supporters, especially Queen Margaret, are upset. Her son, the Prince of Wales, should be the next King of England.

The sons of York are impatient, though. They are not content to wait until the natural death of King Henry. Richard, York's third son, convinces his father to break his vow to Henry. Soon after, they learn that Margaret has raised an army and is marching on York. Although outnumbered, they are not afraid of a woman general. Much to their surprise, they lose the battle. A lord in Margaret's army kills York's youngest son, who is just a child. (Leaving York with three sons: Edward, George, and Richard. They figure prominently in *King Richard III.*) The lord and Margaret also kill the Duke of York and proudly display his head on the city walls. (She has a thing about heads. In the *King Henry VI, Part 2,* she wanders around, carrying her lover's severed head in her arms.)

Act 2

The queen, in triumph, marches against the remaining sons of York. The furious fight rages, but Henry waits on the sidelines. He is not a warrior and does not revel in bloody combat. While he watches, he grieves for his subjects — "sad-hearted men" (2.5.123) who are dying in both armies. In the end, the sons of York triumph and Margaret flees, towing Henry with her.

Edward is the eldest son of the late Duke of York, and so claims the kingship of England. He appoints his brother George as Duke of Clarence and Richard as Duke of Gloucester. The Earl of Warwick proposes marrying Edward to Lady Bona, sister-in-law of the King of France. The marriage will ally England and France. Thus Edward would have a strong enough army that he would never fear Henry again.

Act 3

Margaret and Henry have fled in separate directions, Henry to Scotland and Margaret home to France. Margaret wants to convince the King of France to come to Henry's aid. While Margaret is in France, Henry secretly returns to England, his homeland that he loves too much to leave. In England, he is captured and taken to Edward, now King Edward IV.

Edward seems to have forgotten about Warwick and Lady Bona. His eyes fall upon Lady Elizabeth Grey, a recent widow. She refuses his affections until he offers to marry her. His character is laid plainly before the reader, as is that of Richard. Richard is younger than Edward and Clarence, and so sits farthest from the throne. That deters him not a whit; he is crippled in body, and to Shakespeare's audience that meant that he was also crippled in mind. (Read more about the attitudes toward body and mind in Chapter 2.) His ambition is not tempered by mercy, pity, or loyalty. As he puts it, "I can smile, and murder whiles I smile" (3.2.182). He appears to remain loyal to Edward only to gain further advantage.

Meanwhile, in France, Margaret pleads her case before Lewis, King of France. She convinces him to help Henry, but then Warwick arrives. Lewis changes his mind and decides to ally himself with the victor in England, namely Edward IV. News then arrives from England, telling of Edward's marriage to Lady Grey. Lewis is angry that Edward would spurn his sister-in-law and switches back to Margaret's side. Warwick also switches sides to support Margaret and "to seek revenge on Edward's mockery" (3.3.265).

Act 4

Edward hands favors out to his followers, but not to his brothers. Edward's brother, George, Duke of Clarence, is upset and promises to join Warwick. The two great armies prepare for battle, but Warwick sneaks into Edward's camp and captures him. Warwick turns Edward over to the Archbishop of York for safekeeping. Thus they have retaken England without need for a bloody battle. They free Henry from the Tower of London and set him back on the throne, ruling once again as King Henry VI.

The archbishop keeps Edward under too light a guard, and Richard easily rescues him. Together, they seek allies, quickly raise an army, and once again proclaim Edward as King Edward IV of England.

SEE IT

On video

✔ 1990, English Shakespeare Company: Michael Bogdanov director. Not available in the U.S. The three parts of *Henry VI* are combined into two videotapes: *Henry VI: House of Lancaster* and *Henry VI: House of York.*

✔ 1983, BBC: Jane Howell director, Peter Benson as Henry VI, Bernard Hill as York, Ron Cook as Richard, Duke of Gloucester, Julia Foster as Margaret, and Brian Protheroe as Edward IV.

Act 5

Warwick collects his armies, but Clarence returns to fight alongside his brother. Nonetheless, the Lancastrian supporters bring their armies to strengthen Warwick's.

The battle is joined, and Edward wins the day and kills Warwick. Margaret brings a power from France. Against the odds, Margaret and her son incite their troops to valor and glory, but it's too late. Edward triumphs and captures the queen and her son. All three sons of York kill the prince. King Edward shows mercy to Margaret, though, and does not kill her.

Richard knows that Edward will also be merciful to Henry, so he takes matters into his own hands. He rides off to the Tower of London, where Henry is a prisoner. Shakespeare foreshadows the next play in the series, *King Richard III,* by having Henry prophesy that "many a thousand . . . shall rue the hour that ever thou wast born" (5.6.37–43). Richard doesn't want to hear it and kills Henry.

The play ends with Edward IV sitting on the throne and Richard plotting Edward's demise from the sidelines. Stay tuned for the thrilling conclusion of the Wars of the Roses.

King Richard III

Key characters:

✔ Edward IV, King of England

✔ George, Duke of Clarence, brother of King Edward

✔ Richard, Duke of Gloucester, brother of Edward, later King Richard III

- Elizabeth, Queen of England, wife of Edward IV
- Duke of Buckingham, allied with Richard
- Lady Anne, widow of Edward (Prince of Wales, son of Henry and Margaret), later wife of Richard
- Margaret, widow of Henry VI, former Queen of England
- Earl of Richmond, later King Henry VII

In the preceding episode of *As the Globe Turns,* Edward IV usurped the throne from Henry VI. Richard was already plotting against his brother's life. In the final thrilling episode of the Wars of the Roses, learn Richard's fate as one of Shakespeare's most totally wicked characters.

The real Richard III was nothing like Shakespeare's depiction of him, but Shakespeare was merely reflecting the attitudes of his time. King Henry VII (the grandfather of Queen Elizabeth I) defeated Richard at Bosworth Field, and the victors get to write the history books.

Figure 14-4:
Al Pacino as Richard III in the film *Looking for Richard.*

Everett Collection

Act 1

The play opens with Richard bemoaning:

Now is the winter of our discontent

Made glorious summer by this son of York. (1.1.1–2)

Richard is referring to his brother, Edward, who is now King Edward IV. Lacking beauty and grace, Richard is out of place in peacetime. He feels that he has no recourse but villainy, so he lays plans against his brothers. Edward thinks that his brother, George, Duke of Clarence, plots against his life, so he confines Clarence to the Tower of London. Richard promises to help Clarence, but in truth, Richard planted the false story about Clarence and turned his brothers against each other.

Richard's plots go farther than his brothers, though. Henry VI is not yet buried, and already Richard sets his eyes on Henry's widowed daughter-in-law, Anne. Richard plans to marry Anne to further his nefarious plans. (It's not clear why he must marry Anne, but a marriage to Anne ties him to the House of Lancaster, which might appease some of his family's traditional enemies.)

The king is sick, and his loyal followers fret over his welfare. Rumors abound of who loves or hates whom. Richard puts on his best, dissembling face and claims goodwill toward his brother and everyone. The queen, in particular, is Richard's enemy. Richard publicly blames the queen for setting Edward against Clarence. She knows nothing about the accusation because Richard made it all up. She denies everything, but Richard succeeds in sowing discontent among the English lords, half mistrusting the other half. The Duke of Buckingham comes down squarely on Richard's side, and he will be a staunch ally.

Margaret, the widow of Henry VI, vents her spleen against Richard and his friends. With colorful curses, such as "Thou elvish-mark'd, abortive, rooting hog" (1.3.228), and dire predictions, she prophesies doom for Richard, Buckingham, and the other lords who follow Richard. Pay attention to what she says, because all her predictions will come true.

Richard doesn't trust Edward to follow through on the imprisonment of their brother Clarence, so he hires two murderers to finish the deed.

Act 2

The king, although still grievously ill, tries to patch up the differences caused by Richard when the court learns of Clarence's death. The news is more than he can bear, and Edward dies, leaving the queen distraught.

The heir to the throne is Edward's son, also named Edward, but he is still a child. Richard moves quickly and imprisons some of Edward's loyal lords. The queen sees that she and her children are in danger and runs to sanctuary, taking her youngest child with her.

Act 3

Richard has custody of the young Prince Edward, although he is too young and naive to fully understand his position. For his "protection," Richard invites Edward to sleep in the Tower of London, which also serves as a prison.

Richard executes his prisoners: the lords who were loyal to Edward. Not content with those few, he extends his reach to others who might stand in his way. Richard is Protector of England until young Edward comes of age, and as protector, he wields power as though he were already king.

Richard's next step is to declare Edward's children bastards. He points out that Edward reneged on his original promise to marry Lady Bona of France before he married Lady Grey. Even prior to that, though, he was engaged to someone else. These arguments are weak and convince no one except his hired help. Buckingham, in a staged show, publicly denies the legitimacy of Edward's children and offers the crown to Richard, who, in a false show of modesty, declines. Buckingham insists, and Richard relents.

Act 4

The queen and the Duchess of York (Edward IV's and Richard's mother) learn that Richard will proclaim himself King of England. Further, they are denied access to the young prince and his brother, who are now prisoners in the tower. The duchess sees that Richard will bring only misery for himself and for England: "Bloody thou art; bloody will be thy end" (4.4.195). The only way she can see to stop her "damned son" (4.4.134) is to seek help from the Earl of Richmond.

Richard needs to cement his hold on the throne. As long as Prince Edward lives, some people will believe that Edward has a greater claim to the throne than Richard, so Richard asks Buckingham to take care of the problem. Until this moment, Buckingham has done whatever Richard requested, but now he hesitates. Furious, Richard turns to a common murderer and asks him to do the deed. Richard doesn't forgive Buckingham. When Buckingham asks Richard for the title and lands that Richard promised, he gets nothing as payment for his loyal service because Richard is "not in the giving vein today" (4.2.116). Fortune's wheel turns quickly in this play.

To further consolidate his power, Richard proposes to marry his niece, the daughter of the late King Edward. Such a move would help cement his hold on the throne. Richard has already taken care of his previous wife, Anne. Shakespeare doesn't tell exactly how she died, but given Richard's track record, it's a safe bet that he had her murdered. Of course, the queen resists, but Richard wears her down as he did Anne, and she pretends to give in. In truth, she promised her daughter to the Earl of Richmond.

Richmond has raised an army and is crossing the English Channel to attack Richard. Buckingham has joined Richmond, and many in England are rising against the newly crowned King Richard. Then Richard gets some good news: Buckingham's army was dispersed by floodwaters. The winds blow against Richmond, and his ships are scattered. Richard still has allies, and he prepares his army to defend his throne.

Act 5

Richmond manages to land his army, and at Bosworth Field, the two opposing sides meet. Richard is confident of success because his army is several times the size of Richmond's. During the night, though, the ghost of Henry VI visits both sides, vilifying Richard and inspiring Richmond. Richard is disturbed by other spirits: ghosts of those he murdered.

The battle turns against Richard. Unhorsed, he desperately tries to find another, offering "my kingdom for a horse!" (5.4.7). In the end, Richmond wins the day and kills Richard. Richmond will marry Elizabeth, the daughter of Edward IV, and ascend the throne as King Henry VII. The Earl of Richmond, Henry Tudor, is the grandson of the Duke of Somerset, which is his claim to the throne.

Thus ends the Wars of the Roses and begins the rise of the House of Tudor. Henry's reign will be peaceful, and his son and granddaughter will reign as two of the greatest monarchs that England will ever know. His daughter Margaret will marry King James IV of Scotland. Their great-grandson will succeed Elizabeth and rule over England and Scotland as King James I.

SEE IT

On video

- ✔ 1995, United Artists: Richard Loncraine director and Ian McKellen as Richard III. The script modernizes Shakespeare's English, which makes it easier for modern audiences to understand. The setting is the early 20th century. Overall, an excellent production.

- ✔ 1990, English Shakespeare Company: Michael Bogdanov director. Not available in the U.S.

- ✔ 1983, BBC: Jane Howell director and Ron Cook as Richard III.

- ✔ 1956, London Films: Laurence Olivier director and as Richard III, Ralph Richardson as Buckingham, John Gielgud as Clarence, and Claire Bloom as Lady Anne. The classic version.

King Henry VIII

Key characters:

- ✔ Henry VIII, King of England
- ✔ Katherine, Queen of England
- ✔ Anne Bullen, later Queen of England
- ✔ Cardinal Wolsey
- ✔ Gardiner, Wolsey's secretary
- ✔ Cardinal Cranmer

How many wives is enough? King Henry VIII managed to go through six, beheading or divorcing most of them. The final episode of *As the Globe Turns,* like *King John,* is separate from the main series. It touches on just a few events in Henry's life: mostly the rise and fall of Cardinal Wolsey and Henry's marriage to Anne Boleyn (spelled Bullen in this play). The play ends with the birth of Anne's daughter, Princess Elizabeth, who would later become Queen Elizabeth I. It skips lightly over Henry's divorce from his first wife, Katherine of Aragon, and the religious contention between Catholics and Protestants.

Act 1

Like modern film scripts, plays in Shakespeare's day may have undergone large-scale rewriting. *King Henry VIII* shows evidence of this kind of manhandling. The play begins with a prologue, albeit a muddled one. The prologue announces a sad play, but the play ends with the christening of Elizabeth, hardly a sad event. It's probably best to ignore the prologue and jump right into the play. The Duke of Buckingham learns about a grand spectacle where the Kings of England and France met. The historic event is known as the Field of the Cloth of Gold, referring to the sumptuous trappings of the gathering. The story is interrupted when Cardinal Wolsey orders the imprisonment of Buckingham. He has done nothing wrong, but Wolsey is that most dangerous type of enemy: powerful and nasty.

King Henry VIII is set to hear the charges against Buckingham, but Queen Katherine interrupts the proceedings with her own charges against Wolsey. She reports that the common people are upset about onerous taxes levied by Wolsey without the king's knowledge. Wolsey weasels out of the situation, promising to lift the tax without acknowledging that he did anything wrong. Wolsey tells his servant to order the tax removed but privately amends the order to tell the populace that Wolsey ordered the tax relief.

Buckingham's surveyor appears before the king to accuse his master of treason. The queen points out that Buckingham fired his surveyor after tenants complained about him. This certainly colors his testimony, and she cautions him to be careful about his accusations. The king believes the false charges, though, and orders that Buckingham be brought to trial.

Cardinal Wolsey is hosting a party, having invited the ladies and gentlemen of the court. The lords and ladies are enchanted by Wolsey's bounty. To them, Wolsey appears to have "a bounteous mind indeed, / A hand as fruitful as the land that feeds" (1.2.54–55) them. The king crashes the party and is enchanted by one of the queen's ladies-in-waiting, Anne Bullen.

Act 2

Based on the false testimony of his ex-surveyor, Buckingham is condemned to death. In contrast to the scene at the end of Act 1, the common folk hate Cardinal Wolsey — they "hate him perniciously" (2.1.50). They "love and dote on" (2.1.52) the honest Duke of Buckingham and accuse Wolsey of complicity in his death. Buckingham's death is bad enough, but rumors abound that the king will divorce his queen, although they have been married for 20 years, and the Church of Rome does not allow divorce. The word on the street is that Wolsey instigated the matter to revenge himself on Katherine's nephew, Charles V, the emperor of the Holy Roman Empire, who has denied Wolsey an archbishopric.

Wolsey pushes the lords too far. They witness how Wolsey could take down an honest man, so they all fear that they could be next. They try to bring the matter before the king, but he will have none of it. He is concerned solely with the impending divorce.

The queen claims that she is lawfully married to the king and that no one on earth has the power to separate a marriage duly contracted before God. Nonetheless, Wolsey has asked the Pope to send a representative to adjudicate the matter.

Act 3

Wolsey appeals to the queen to participate in the divorce proceedings. She knows that he is evil and not to be trusted, but he persists. The queen mourns not only for herself but also for her attendants. If the divorce becomes official, they may be left without succor in a hateful court. Wolsey ignores her arguments and continues to protest his goodwill. In the end, Katherine relents, knowing that she is defeated.

The English lords who oppose Wolsey receive some unexpected good news. One of the cardinal's messages went awry and fell into the king's hands. The message shows how Wolsey is trying to arrange the divorce proceedings to his personal benefit. The Pope's envoy has returned to Rome without rendering a verdict in the divorce case. All of Wolsey's plans are crumbling.

Wolsey tries to appease the king but goofs again. He accidentally included in his letters a list of all the property he owns: "piles of wealth" (3.2.107) that amount to much more than befits a cardinal. Wolsey intended for his wealth to pave the way to his becoming Pope, but through a minor slip, he is utterly undone.

Act 4

Even without a judgment from Rome, Henry has divorced Katherine and married Anne. Now Anne is on her way to her coronation, to be crowned the Queen of England.

Katherine is now the princess dowager, instead of queen, and is in poor health. She hears news of Wolsey's death. He died full of repentance for his evil life, but Katherine has difficulty forgiving his cruelty to her. A servant points out that even Wolsey had good points and accomplished much to benefit England.

Act 5

One more plot besets the English court. Wolsey's secretary, Gardiner, now sits on the king's council, where he tries to match his old master's ruthlessness. The new Archbishop of Canterbury is Cranmer, a close friend to the king. Gardiner wants to bring down Cranmer, much the way that Wolsey brought down Buckingham. This time, though, the king is more vigilant and is careful to see that Cranmer gets true justice.

Meanwhile, Queen Anne is in labor. She delivers a girl: Elizabeth.

The king's council meets to attempt to convict Cranmer on trumped-up charges. He tries to reason with them, but to no avail. Finally, he shows the king's ring, a token that the king supports Cranmer, not the council. The king intervenes because the council works "more out of malice than integrity" (5.2.179). He orders his councilors to love each other and work together.

SEE IT

On video

1979, BBC: Kevin Billington director, John Stride as King Henry VIII, Claire Bloom as Queen Katherine, and Timothy West as Cardinal Wolsey

The populace supports their new queen and princess. They throng to the christening, breaking through the outer gates and crowding the palace. Cranmer christens the new princess, Elizabeth, and makes a thrilling prophecy: that the princess will become a great ruler over England and that England will prosper under her rule. Further, he prophesies that her successor will likewise rule in great fame and that

peace, plenty, love, truth, terror,

That were the servants to this chosen infant. (5.5.47–48)

Elizabeth will likewise serve her successor (whom Shakespeare's audience knew to be their ruling king, James).

Any working person in Shakespeare's day knew the importance of pleasing the reigning monarchs, but his paean to Elizabeth and James is a work of unparalleled histrionics, which brings a close to *As the Globe Turns*.

Bring down the house

The first performance of *King Henry VIII* brought down the house. Literally. In Act 1, scene 4, King Henry makes a royal entrance at Cardinal Wolsey's party. A stage direction says, "Drum and trumpet; chambers discharged." In other words, drums, trumpets, and cannons announced the royal entrance.

On opening day, June 29, 1613, when the chambers discharged, a small piece of wadding must have landed on the thatched roof of the Globe Theatre. The ensuing fire engulfed the entire structure (sprinklers and fire extinguishers being rather more recent inventions).

Fortunately, no one was hurt. One unlucky patron's britches caught fire, but a quick-witted bystander extinguished the flames with a bottle of ale. History does not relate whether the bystander magnanimously sacrificed his own ale for the rescue.

King John

Legend

X	Ejected from game: Dies	☺	Victorious in battle	G	Grovels
A	Arrested	☹	Defeated in battle	.	Appears in scene
/	Knighted	◇	Home run: Marries	"	Famous quote

Characters, in order of appearance

		Act	1	2			3				4			5						
		Scene	1	1	2	3	1	2	3	4	1	2	3	1	2	3	4	5	6	7
1	King John																			
2	Chatillon, ambassador from France																			
3	Queen Eleanor, mother of King John																			
4	Philip the Bastard, later Sir Richard																			
5	Lewis, the Dauphin of France																			
6	Philip, King of France																			
7	Arthur, nephew of King John																			
8	Constance, mother of Arthur																			
9	Blanche, niece of King John																			
10	Hubert																			
11	Earl of Salisbury																			
12	Cardinal Pandulph																			
13	Earl of Pembroke																			
14	Melun, a French lord																			
15	Prince Henry, son of King John																			

King Richard II

Legend

↑	Sent to penalty box: Banished
↓	Returns to game: Returns from banishment
X	Ejected from game: Dies
☺	Victorious in battle
☹	Defeated in battle
F	Foul: Attacks someone
⊗	Deposed
·	Appears in scene
"	Famous quote

Characters, in order of appearance

	Act	1	1	1	1	2	2	2	3	3	3	3	4	5	5	5	5	5
	Scene	1	2	3	4	1	2	3	1	2	3	4	1	1	2	3	4	5
1	King Richard II																	
2	John of Gaunt, uncle of the King																	
3	Henry Bolingbroke, son of John of Gaunt																	
4	Thomas Mowbray, Duke of Norfolk																	
5	Duke of Aumerle																	
6	Sir Henry Greene																	
7	Sir John Bushy																	
8	Sir John Bagot																	
9	Duke of York																	
10	Queen Isabel																	
11	Lord Ross																	
12	Lord Willoughby																	
13	Henry Percy, Earl of Northumberland																	
14	Henry Percy, called Hotspur, son of Northumberland																	
15	Bishop of Carlisle																	
16	Duchess of York																	
17	Sir Piers Exton																	

King Henry IV, Part 1

Legend

S	Sacked: Victim of an attack	X	Ejected from game: Dies	C	Involved in a conspiracy
F	Foul: Attacks someone	☺	Victorious in battle	.	Appears in scene
F$	Robs someone	☹	Defeated in battle	"	Famous quote

Characters, in order of appearance

	Act	1			2				3			4			5				
	Scene	1	2	3	1	2	3	4	1	2	3	1	2	3	1	2	3	4	5
1	King Henry IV																		
2	Earl of Westmoreland																		
3	Prince John of Lancaster																		
4	Sir John Falstaff																		
5	Prince Hal																		
6	Poins, friend to Hal																		
7	Thomas Percy, Earl of Worcester																		
8	Henry Percy, Earl of Northumberland																		
9	Hotspur, son of Northumberland																		
10	Sir Walter Blunt																		
11	Bardolph, follower of Falstaff																		
12	Lady Percy, wife of Hotspur																		
13	Edmund Mortimer, Earl of March																		
14	Owen Glendower																		
15	Earl of Douglas																		
16	Archbishop of York																		

King Henry IV, Part 2

Legend

F	Foul: Attacks someone	☺	Victorious in battle	⊘	Rejected by a friend	
S	Sacked: Victim of an attack	☹	Defeated in battle	.	Appears in scene	
T	Plays a trick	👑	Crowned king	"	Famous quote	

Characters, in order of appearance

	Act	1			2				3		4					5				
	Scene	1	2	3	1	2	3	4	1	2	1	2	3	4	5	1	2	3	4	5
1	Lord Bardolph																			
2	Henry Percy, Earl of Northumberland																			
3	Sir John Falstaff																			
4	Lord Chief Justice																			
5	Archbishop of York																			
6	Thomas Mowbray																			
7	Hostess Quickly																			
8	Prince Hal																			
9	Poins, friend of Hal																			
10	Bardolph, follower of Falstaff																			
11	Lady Northumberland																			
12	Lady Percy, widow of Hotspur																			
13	Doll Tearsheet																			
14	Pistol, a rogue																			
15	Earl of Warwick																			
16	Justice Shallow																			
17	Earl of Westmoreland																			

King Henry V

Legend

☺	Victorious in battle	⅃	Woos a lover	B	Betrays a friend
☹	Defeated in battle	✑	Dons a disguise	.	Appears in scene
X	Ejected from game: Dies	✑	Removes a disguise	"	Famous quote

Characters, in order of appearance

	Act	1		2				3						4								5	
	Scene	1	2	1	2	3	4	1	2	3	4	5	6	1	2	3	4	5	6	7	8	1	2
1	Archbishop of Canterbury																						
2	King Henry V																						
3	Duke of Exeter, uncle of the King																						
4	Earl of Westmoreland																						
5	Bardolph, former friend to Falstaff and Hal																						
6	Pistol, former friend to Falstaff and Hal																						
7	Duke of Bedford, brother of the King																						
8	Henry, Lord Scroop of Masham																						
9	Richard, Earl of Cambridge																						
10	Sir Thomas Grey																						
11	Captain Fluellen																						
12	King Charles VI of France																						
13	Louis, the Dauphin, son of King Charles																						
14	Constable of France																						
15	Katherine, Princess of France																						
16	Montjoy, the French herald																						
17	Duke of Orléans																						

England (characters 1–11)

France (characters 12–17)

King Henry VI, Part 1

Legend

☺	Victorious in battle	X	Ejected from game: Dies	B	Betrays a friend
☹	Defeated in battle	T	Plays a trick	.	Appears in scene
○	Starts a pointless argument	TT	Plays a counter-trick	"	Famous quote

Characters, in order of appearance

Act	1						2					3				4							5				
Scene	1	2	3	4	5	6	1	2	3	4	5	1	2	3	4	1	2	3	4	5	6	7	1	2	3	4	5
England																											
1 Duke of Bedford, uncle of the King																											
2 Duke of Gloucester, uncle of the King																											
3 Bishop of Winchester																											
4 Earl of Salisbury																											
5 Lord Talbot																											
6 Duke of Burgundy																											
7 Richard Plantagenet																											
8 Earl of Suffolk																											
9 Duke of Somerset																											
10 Earl of Warwick																											
11 King Henry VI																											
12 John Talbot, son of Lord Talbot																											
France																											
13 Charles, Dauphin																											
14 Duke of Alenon																											
15 Bastard of Orlans																											
16 Joan la Pucelle																											
17 Countess of Auvergne																											
18 Margaret of Anjou																											

King Henry VI, Part 2

Legend

X	Ejected from game: Dies	⚡	Visited by supernatural beings
F	Foul: Attacks someone	☺	Victorious in battle
C	Conspiracy	☹	Defeated in battle
		☹	The peasants are revolting
		.	Appears in scene
		"	Famous quote

Characters, in order of appearance

	Act	1				2				3			4										5		
	Scene	1	2	3	4	1	2	3	4	1	2	3	1	2	3	4	5	6	7	8	9	10	1	2	3
1	Duke of Suffolk																								
2	King Henry VI																								
3	Queen Margaret																								
4	Humphrey, Duke of Gloucester																								
5	Cardinal Beaufort																								
6	Earl of Salisbury																								
7	Earl of Warwick																								
8	Richard Plantagenet, Duke of York																								
9	Duke of Somerset																								
10	Duke of Buckingham																								
11	Eleanor, Duchess of Gloucester																								
12	Margery Jourdain, a witch																								
13	Murderers																								
14	Jack Cade, a rebel																								
15	Sir Humphrey Stafford																								
16	Lord Say																								
17	Lord Clifford																								
18	Alexander Iden																								

King Henry VI, Part 3

Legend

½	Woos a lover
⌂	Home run: Marries
B	Betrays a friend
☺	Victorious in battle
☹	Defeated in battle
S	Sacked: Victim of an attack
P	Makes a prophecy
.	Appears in scene
"	Famous quote

Characters, in order of appearance

Act	1				2						3			4								5						
Scene	1	2	3	4	1	2	3	4	5	6	1	2	3	1	2	3	4	5	6	7	8	1	2	3	4	5	6	7
1 Earl of Warwick																												
2 Duke of York																												
3 Edward, later King Edward IV																												
4 Richard, later Duke of Gloucester																												
5 King Henry VI																												
6 Earl of Northumberland																												
7 Lord Clifford																												
8 Earl of Westmoreland																												
9 Duke of Exeter																												
10 Queen Margaret																												
11 Edward, Prince of Wales																												
12 Edmund, Earl of Rutland																												
13 George, Duke of Clarence																												
14 Lady Elizabeth Gray, later Queen																												
15 King Lewis of France																												
16 Earl of Oxford																												

King Richard III

Legend

F	Foul: Attacks someone	X	Ejected from game: Dies	◈	Home run: Marries
☺	Victorious in battle	✔	Visited by supernatural beings	.	Appears in scene
☹	Defeated in battle	P	Makes a prophecy	"	Famous quote

Characters, in order of appearance

Act	1				2				3							4					5				
Scene	1	2	3	4	1	2	3	4	1	2	3	4	5	6	7	1	2	3	4	5	1	2	3	4	5
1 Richard, later King Richard III																									
2 Clarence, brother of King Edward IV																									
3 Lord Hastings																									
4 Lady Anne																									
5 Elizabeth, wife of Edward IV																									
6 Lord Rivers																									
7 Lord Grey																									
8 Duke of Buckingham																									
9 Margaret, widow of Henry VI																									
10 Sir William Catesby																									
11 Murderers																									
12 Duchess of York																									
13 Prince Edward, son of Edward IV																									
14 Duke of York, son of Edward IV																									
15 Sir James Tyrrel																									
16 Earl of Richmond, later King Henry VII																									
17 Ghost of King Henry VI																									

King Henry VIII

Legend

X	Ejected from game: Dies	♫	Woos a lover	K	Strikeout: Divorces
B	Betrays a friend	◇	Home run: Marries	·	Appears in scene
A	Arrested	C	Involved in a conspiracy	"	Famous quote

Characters, in order of appearance

		Act	1				2				3				4			5			
		Scene	1	2	3	4	1	2	3	4	1	2	3	4	1	2	1	2	3	4	
1	Duke of Buckingham																				
2	Duke of Norfolk																				
3	Cardinal Wolsey																				
4	King Henry VIII																				
5	Queen Katherine of Aragon																				
6	Buckingham's surveyor																				
7	Duke of Suffolk																				
8	Cardinal Campeius																				
9	Gardiner, Bishop of Winchester																				
10	Anne Bullen, later Queen																				
11	Lord Surrey																				
12	Cromwell, servant to Wolsey																				
13	Cranmer, Archbishop of Canterbury																				

Chapter 15

Tragedies

. . . .

In This Chapter

▶ Summaries of Shakespeare's tragic plays

▶ Interesting performances on videotape

. . . .

*T*his chapter completes the summaries of Shakespeare's plays. The organization is the same as in the comedies chapter, listing all the tragedies in alphabetical order.

Many of the tragedies are set in ancient times throughout the western world, from Egypt to England and points in between. To help you understand the setting, some of the play summaries begin with a synopsis of the true history or political background.

Antony and Cleopatra

Key characters:

> ✔ Mark Antony, Cleopatra's lover, a Roman general who rules the eastern part of the Roman Empire
>
> ✔ Octavius Caesar, ruler of the western part of the Roman Empire
>
> ✔ Lepidus, ruler of the southern part of the Roman Empire
>
> ✔ Cleopatra, Antony's lover, Queen of Egypt
>
> ✔ Octavia, sister of Octavius, later wife of Mark Antony
>
> ✔ Pompey, enemy of Antony, Octavius, and Lepidus

Think of *Antony and Cleopatra* as the sequel to *Julius Caesar* (a summary of which appears later in this chapter). Their love — or obsession — for each other forms the center of this tragedy, around which Shakespeare weaves stories of war, intrigue, and conquest.

After the assassination of Julius Caesar in 44 B.C.E., Mark Antony, Marcus Æmilius Lepidus, and Octavius Caesar jointly ruled the Roman Empire. Antony's portion was the east, including Egypt, where Antony lived the high life and enjoyed the company of Cleopatra, the mesmerizing Queen of Egypt. The historical events took place about 41 to 30 B.C.E., but Shakespeare didn't bother with such details as exact dates. Instead of occupying a decade, the events in this play seem to take place in just a few weeks. He was more interested in entertainment than in history.

Act 1

Mark Antony is a great soldier and an experienced general. He's seen the world and conquered much of it. Back home, he has a wife and kids. He's the last person you'd expect to see panting after another woman, but here he is in Egypt, having a wild midlife fling with Cleopatra. He spends all his time with her, completely ignoring his day job, which is ruling the eastern Roman Empire. One of his friends calls him

The triple pillar of the world transformed

Into a strumpet's fool. (1.1.12–13)

In a desperate plea for attention, his abandoned wife raises her own army and wages a small war — first against Antony's brother and later against Rome. That would attract the notice of almost any husband, but Antony remains enchanted by Cleopatra, and no one else can rouse him.

Rome's enemies are not so idle. Without Mark Antony, Rome's army is considerably weaker, exposing the empire to threats from its traditional enemies. The Parthians expand their control of Asia, and closer to home, Pompey and his navy challenge Rome on the Mediterranean Sea. Ever the soldier, Antony starts to feel the effect of his dotage. Then a messenger brings news that Antony's wife has died. The news of his wife's death and the threats of war against Rome's empire finally shock Antony out of his stupor, and he prepares to return to Rome.

Lepidus and Octavius Caesar's biggest concern is Pompey's threat against Rome. The two rail against Antony in his absence for neglecting his duties as a Roman general. Octavius fondly recalls the good old days, when Antony was a soldier's soldier, a real man. Now Rome needs his help, but he's off dallying in Egypt while Pompey and his pirate friends control the sea, and no port in Italy is safe.

Act 2

Pompey is planning his attack when his pirate allies bring news that Octavius Caesar and Lepidus have raised their armies and are advancing on Pompey. A messenger arrives with more news: Antony is on his way to Rome. Surprise! Pompey expected Antony to stay in Egypt, but now he must face the full, combined force of the Roman armies.

In Rome, Octavius Caesar greets Antony coolly. He naturally feels some anger at Antony's disregard for Rome's safety, but Antony says that he repents his past behavior and promises to atone for his negligence. To guarantee his renewed support for Caesar, Antony agrees to marry Octavia, Caesar's sister. Caesar agrees to the arrangement, thinking that the marriage will cement the ties between Antony and Caesar. But in truth, Antony can never escape from Cleopatra's bonds.

A messenger brings Cleopatra the news of Antony's marriage to Octavia. She responds by trying to kill the messenger, who flees from her wrath. She manages to calm down a little and recalls the messenger, promising not to hurt him. She can't believe that Antony would betray her that way, but the messenger repeats that the two are married. Cleopatra retreats to her chamber, devastated.

Pompey also has problems. Now that the Romans have their act together, they are more than Pompey can handle. He capitulates without a fight.

Act 3

Cleopatra has calmed down and can now hear the messenger's full report of Antony's marriage to Caesar's sister. The messenger has wised up and lies — saying that Octavia is ugly and ungainly — to please Cleopatra.

Caesar is ungrateful for the help he got from Lepidus and Antony. He wages new wars with Pompey and refuses to give Antony credit for helping Rome, so Antony responds the only way he knows how: with his sword. Octavia tries to bring peace between the two parties, suggesting to Antony that she reconcile her brother with her husband. Antony agrees, and Octavia goes to talk with Caesar. Antony, however, uses this opportunity to escape to Egypt and Cleopatra. Caesar breaks the bad news to his sister that Antony secretly left her, and furthermore, that Antony is raising a huge army to challenge Rome.

Cleopatra wants to join Antony in the battle that is to come. Antony's aids try to convince him not to engage Caesar at sea but to draw him onto land, where Antony's army is stronger. Antony will not listen, heeding only Cleopatra and her insistence that her 60 Egyptian ships are sound and strong. Mark Antony was once Rome's greatest general, but when the general takes orders from his lover, the bookies lay the odds on the other side.

Antony commands his navy well at first. He is on the brink of victory, but Cleopatra can't take any more of the battle and orders her personal ship to leave the fray. This in itself wouldn't be a problem, but Antony plays the lover, not the general, and orders his ship to follow hers. Without its general, the Egyptian navy falls to the Romans. Antony curses himself for having run from the fight, but what's done is done. He offers to surrender to Caesar on the condition that he can live out his days in peace with Cleopatra. Caesar denies the offer, but he says that he will allow Cleopatra to rule as Queen of Egypt — if she kills Antony. Cleopatra will not obey Caesar's wishes, spurring Antony to fight anew. Antony sends a challenge to Caesar to meet in single combat.

Act 4

Caesar ignores Antony's request for single combat. He has the upper hand in battle and intends to use it. Antony meets Caesar's army on land, where he triumphs, driving Caesar back. That night, Antony celebrates and plans for the next day's battle.

The next day, Antony and Caesar meet at sea, but the Egyptian navy mutinies and surrenders to Rome. Antony accuses Cleopatra of treachery. He rails against her until she retreats to safety. Her servants lie, telling Antony that she killed herself, which calms him down instantly. The line between obsession and madness is a thin one, and Cleopatra's apparent death pushes Antony over that line. He hails Cleopatra's courage to take her own life but falters in his attempt to do the same. Antony stabs himself but misses the vital organs, which leaves him to linger for quite some time before finally succumbing. Before he dies, his soldiers bear him before Cleopatra — who is still very much alive — where they make their final farewells.

Act 5

Octavius Caesar respects Antony although they were rivals, but now he must turn his attention to Cleopatra. Caesar sends messengers to her offering peace. He intends to make of her a war trophy and lead her in humiliation through the streets of Rome. He knows that she can stall his plans by killing herself, so he dissembles by saying that she can still rule as Egypt's queen.

Cleopatra is not fooled. She knows exactly what she must do: commit suicide for real. A countryman brings her poisonous snakes, which she allows to bite her. Her devoted attendants die with her. Caesar beholds the bodies and recognizes how Cleopatra saw through him. Having triumphed over Antony and Egypt, Caesar can afford to be generous, and he orders that Antony and Cleopatra be buried together.

On video

1981, BBC: Jonathan Miller director, Colin Blakely as Antony, and Jane Lapotaire as Cleopatra. A good production in a traditional setting.

Coriolanus

Key characters:

- ✔ Caius Martius, later called Coriolanus, a Roman general

- ✔ Cominius, Roman consul and general

- ✔ Menenius Agrippa, friend to Coriolanus

- ✔ Volumnia, mother of Coriolanus

- ✔ Tullus Aufidius, Volscian general, enemy to Coriolanus

The setting for *Coriolanus* is ancient Italy — about 490 B.C.E. — before the rise of the Roman Empire, well before the time of Caesar, and shortly after the events in Shakespeare's narrative poem *The Rape of Lucrece* (which you can read about in Chapter 17) take place. At this time in Rome's history, two elected consuls led the Roman government, but the true power of the government resided in the Senate — 300 members of the aristocracy. Tribunes represented the common people in the Senate. The tribunes could veto measures passed by the Senate, but they held little real power. When the play begins, Rome has one consul, Cominius, and no tribunes.

Act 1

Eat your vegetables. Clean your room. Listen to your mother. Be a hero. Cover yourself in blood and glory to defend Rome from its enemies. Caius Martius always does what his mother tells him to do.

Now Martius must fight Rome's traditional enemies, the Volsces, who are led by his longtime foe, Tullus Aufidius. But first he must put down a peasant uprising. Against his wishes, the government negotiates with the rioters and grants them a voice in government: five elected tribunes. Martius would rather send the whole mob packing. He doesn't like their petty whining; they don't like his attitude. Nonetheless, the people need Martius because he is their best warrior and general.

Figure 15-1:
Kenneth
Branagh as
Coriolanus.

The consul, Cominius, will lead the army against the Volsces, with
Martius under his command. Despite Rome's need for Martius and his
martial abilities, two of the new tribunes envy Martius. They call him
"proud" because he disdains the common people; they don't want to
acknowledge his importance to Rome's safety, and they discount his
past accomplishments.

Aufidius knows Martius well — they have often faced each other in battle,
and each time Martius got the better of him. He will lead the army against
Rome, but Rome might send its own army against the Volscian city of
Corioli.

While part of the Roman army (led by Cominius) meets Aufidius in the field,
the rest of the army (led by Martius) attacks Corioli. The Volsces beat back
the Roman attack, and Martius rails against the troops for their cowardice in
running from the Volsces. He leads a new attack but is caught alone inside
the city gates, which close behind him. He single-handedly faces the
Volscian army. The rest of the Roman troops run from the city, thinking that
they witnessed the end of their general. That shows how little they understand him. Martius is no ordinary soldier. Shakespeare doesn't tell you
exactly what happens, but Martius emerges from the city, hurt but very much
alive, and the Roman soldiers rush through the city gates to loot the city
that Martius single-handedly won for them. Won't Mom be proud of her son?

While the Roman soldiers loot and spoil the city of Corioli, Martius heads out to join the other part of the Roman army and find Aufidius. The two want nothing more than to face each other in combat, which they do, but several Volsces come to the aid of Aufidius and rescue him.

Rome triumphs on all fronts, thanks to Caius Martius. The consul Cominius awards Martius with the new name Coriolanus, in honor of his triumph at the city of Corioli.

Act 2

Rome awaits news from the battle. The tribunes and Menenius discuss Martius: The tribunes call him proud and boastful, and Menenius calls the tribunes "unmeriting, proud, violent, testy magistrates (alias fools)" (2.1.44). When the good news arrives, Volumnia is glad to hear of her son's triumph and his new wounds: "Oh, he is wounded; I thank the gods for't" (2.1.120). It's not what most mothers want from their sons, but Volumnia is no ordinary mother, and Coriolanus is no ordinary son.

Cominius leads the Roman army in its triumphant procession and announces the new title for Coriolanus. It's clear that Coriolanus is in line to be elected the next consul, to rule with Cominius. The populace doesn't like Coriolanus's attitude, but they can't ignore his military prowess and unselfish dedication to Rome. The tribunes, however, cannot endorse his new popularity and seek to thwart him.

Coriolanus bemoans a system that rewards insincere flattery over honest merit. He knows that he deserves the consulship — for his dedicated service to Rome — even if he doesn't make a false show of fawning over the people whose lives he saved and whose homes he protected. The tribunes are the opposite. The cowards never defended Rome or received wounds. Their power and position rely solely on flattery and political machinations. They're good at it, though. To them, Coriolanus is a threat that must be stopped. With twisted words, outright lies, and shrewd propaganda, they turn the people against Coriolanus.

Act 3

Coriolanus and his friends think that they have convinced the populace to support him as consul. They don't yet know about the work of the tribunes, who have whipped up the crowds into a frenzy against Coriolanus. His friends try to reason with the tribunes and ask to speak to the people. Coriolanus, on the other hand, doesn't believe in negotiating with rioters. They must be governed, not coddled. He goes so far as to say that the tribunes should be removed from office because Rome has no more need for them. To the tribunes this is treason, and they call for their guards. They want to put Coriolanus to death.

A mere crowd is no match for the warrior Coriolanus, and he and his friends beat back the tribunes' guards. Volumnia tries to reason with her son. She explains that using sweet words to calm and reassure the populace is just like using peaceful words to convince a town to surrender without bloodshed. Coriolanus does as his mother tells him and returns to the mob to beg their pardon. The tribunes are ready for him, though. They know him well and know which buttons to press. When he tries to speak calmly, they needle him with outrageous accusations, inciting him to anger and defiance. Coriolanus falls into their trap. When he rails against the tribunes, they banish him from Rome. Their power over the people is so strong that they all think they have banished their enemy.

Act 4

Aufidius and the Volsces prepare to renew their attack on Rome, this time starting from Antium. Coriolanus, nurturing his hatred toward the Rome that banished him, makes his way to Antium, where he presents himself before Aufidius. The two who were once mortal enemies become allies. Aufidius turns over half his army to Coriolanus's command.

In Rome, the tribunes pat themselves on their backs for a job well done. Before they can organize their victory parties, news arrives that the Volsces are arming for war. The tribunes don't want to believe the reports. Then they hear that Coriolanus sides with the Volsces and leads half the army against Rome. The tribunes are in deep denial. The Senate and all of Rome tremble before the expected onslaught.

The Volsces march readily through the Roman Empire. Coriolanus is popular among the Volscian soldiers, eclipsing even Aufidius. Coriolanus, who is equal in rank to Aufidius, treats him more as an underling than an equal. Aufidius needs him for the attack on Rome, but after that, Coriolanus will no longer be useful and will instead be a threat. Aufidius, who is no fool, makes plans for the long term.

Act 5

Coriolanus leads the Volscian army to the gates of Rome. All of Rome cowers against the coming onslaught. One after another, Coriolanus's past friends try to reason with him, but he refuses even to hear them speak. Not even his wife and child get through to him. Rome's fate rests in the hands of one person: Mom.

Volumnia reminds Coriolanus that he is about to attack his own city, his home, and his honor. She finally convinces him to negotiate a peace settlement between Rome and Volsce.

SEE IT

On video

1984, BBC: Elijah Moshinsky director, Alan Howard as Coriolanus, Joss Ackland as Menenius, and Irene Worth as Volumnia. Set in the 17th century.

Everyone is happy except Aufidius and the Volscian soldiers, who expected to loot and pillage Rome as part of their pay. Now Aufidius must deal with the discontented army. Aufidius tells the Volscian leaders how Coriolanus dishonored them by giving up without a fight, saying that "he sold the blood and labour / Of our great action" (5.6.47–48). Aufidius and several others set on Coriolanus and kill him, teaching him his final lesson: You don't always get what you deserve.

Hamlet

Key characters:

- Hamlet, Prince of Denmark
- Claudius, King of Denmark and Hamlet's uncle
- Gertrude, Queen of Denmark, Hamlet's mother, and wife of Claudius
- Polonius, advisor to Claudius
- Ophelia, Polonius's daughter and beloved by Hamlet
- Laertes, Polonius's son
- Fortinbras, Prince of Norway
- Horatio, close friend to Hamlet
- Rosencrantz, disloyal friend to Hamlet
- Guildenstern, disloyal friend to Hamlet

Your first impression when reading *Hamlet* may be that it's just a bunch of famous quotes strung together. And you're right. But Shakespeare manages to fit a lot of play around the famous quotes, making *Hamlet* one of his longest plays. The role of Hamlet has the most lines of any character in his plays. Of special interest are Hamlet's several soliloquies — his speeches to himself and to the audience, taking you inside his mind and revealing his thoughts and feelings. Hamlet has more soliloquies than most other characters, which tells you much about him. Hamlet is more than the great Dane; he's also the great

Brain — thinking, analyzing, plotting, and planning. As you'll find out, though, life requires more than great ideas; it also requires action, something that Hamlet figures out too late.

Act 1

When the play opens, you learn that a ghost is bothering the night watch, Prince Fortinbras and his Norwegian army are bothering Denmark, and Hamlet's Uncle Claudius is bothering Hamlet. You see, Hamlet should have succeeded his late father to Denmark's throne, but Claudius intervened and took the crown for himself. To make matters worse, he married Gertrude, Hamlet's mother. Hamlet is displeased with both matters and doesn't try to hide it.

You also meet the king's advisor, the bumbling Polonius, and his children, Laertes and Ophelia. Laertes dropped in for a visit and to celebrate the new king's coronation and wedding. Now he is returning to school. His father overflows with advice to his son, some of which is helpful today:

Neither a borrower nor a lender be,

For loan oft loses both itself and friend. (1.3.75–76)

It turns out that the ghost is Hamlet's late father, once King of Denmark, also named Hamlet. Old Hamlet tells a sordid tale of how Claudius murdered him to get the throne. Even worse, the murder prevented Old Hamlet from receiving the last rites. Hence his current predicament — being a ghost. Instead of going straight to heaven, he must remain in purgatory, haunting the Earth by night and suffering fiery privations by day.

The ghost of Old Hamlet demands revenge. Young Hamlet vows to get even with his uncle. Already his active mind starts its work. He isn't exactly sure what he'll do, but his plan is to pretend to be crazy. It doesn't seem like much of a plan, but it distracts his enemies and gives him time to think and plan.

Act 2

Polonius is always meddling in the affairs of others. He even sends a spy to check out how his son is behaving. Suddenly, his daughter Ophelia interrupts him. She reports that Hamlet is acting peculiar — he burst into her chamber, grabbed her, and stared at her without saying anything. This isn't what princes are supposed to do, so Polonius runs off to report this news to the king, Claudius. Polonius is quick to offer advice to others but never heeds his own words, especially "brevity is the soul of wit" (2.2.90).

Meanwhile, Claudius has called for two of Hamlet's school chums, Rosencrantz and Guildenstern. He wants them to speak to Hamlet and try to understand the root of his apparent madness. Polonius thinks that he already knows: unrequited love for Ophelia. To Polonius's thinking, that explains Hamlet's strange behavior in Ophelia's chamber.

Polonius wants to prove his contention to Claudius and Gertrude. He proposes that they hide while he accosts Hamlet to sound him out. Hamlet continues to act up, but even Polonius figures out that there's more to Hamlet's madness than meets the eye.

Polonius brings news to Hamlet: Itinerant actors have arrived. Polonius hopes that the diversion will take Hamlet's mind off whatever is bothering him. Hamlet welcomes the actors and invites them to perform a play, *The Murder of Gonzago,* for the court, but with some small modifications that he will supply. His plan is for the play to unmask the murderer:

The play's the thing

Wherein I'll catch the conscience of the King. (2.2.606–7)

Act 3

In his famous "To be, or not to be" soliloquy (3.1.56–89), Hamlet wonders whether he might have been better off if he simply hadn't been born. Perhaps he would be better off killing himself, but the church expressly forbids suicide. Besides, death — "the undiscovered country" (3.1.79) — may well be worse than life.

In public, Hamlet continues to act crazy. He insults Ophelia, which seems to argue against Polonius's theory about unrequited love. Hamlet's big plan, though, is the play. He asks his friend Horatio to pay particular attention to the king. Hamlet has modified the play to reenact his father's murder. His plan works, and the play strikes home. The guilt-ridden Claudius runs from the room, crying for light.

Hamlet has the proof that he needs, but still he hesitates. He sees Claudius praying, but he doesn't strike because he wants Claudius's soul to suffer as his father has suffered. He wants Claudius to die unshriven, so he passes up the opportunity.

Hamlet reveals his father's murder to his mother, but in an overeager manner, saying, "I must be cruel only to be kind" (3.4.180). Polonius, hiding behind a curtain, cries for help. Hamlet kills him, taking definite action for the first time, hoping that it is the king. Gertrude is horrified by all she witnesses but doesn't know what to do. Suddenly, Hamlet acts even more peculiar than usual. He sees and hears the ghost, but she cannot. The ghost chides Hamlet for his lack of action, but to Gertrude, it seems that Hamlet speaks to thin air.

Gertrude reports Hamlet's actions to the king: the murder of Polonius and his bizarre behavior. Claudius ships Hamlet off to England; perhaps a sea voyage will do him some good. Rosencrantz and Guildenstern accompany him.

Act 4

It's Ophelia's turn to go crazy. Grief for her father's death and for Hamlet's madness has taken a toll on her young mind. Her brother, Laertes, returns. He received the news of his father's death and now wants to kill Hamlet in revenge. His grief doubles when he sees his sister's madness.

News comes that Hamlet has returned from England. Claudius is surprised and disturbed, but he doesn't explain why. He and Laertes prepare for Hamlet's return by plotting against his life. In the midst of their machinations, Gertrude brings sad news: Ophelia, in her madness, has drowned herself.

Act 5

Hamlet meets his friend Horatio and explains the circumstances of his return from England. On board the ship, he learned that Rosencrantz and Guildenstern carried a letter to the King of England, asking him to kill Hamlet. Hamlet altered the letter to have the king kill Rosencrantz and Guildenstern instead. Hamlet escaped and made his way back to Denmark.

Hamlet and Horatio are interrupted by Ophelia's burial. Hamlet and Laertes have a mourning contest, vying to see who loved her and misses her more. Laertes challenges Hamlet to a duel. Horatio cautions Hamlet that Laertes is a skilled fencer. Hamlet feels ready to face Laertes. More important, he has comes to terms with life, the universe, and everything. If his destiny is to die, so be it, for he will die someday no matter what. Hamlet theorizes, "If it be not now, yet it will come. The readiness is all" (5.2.220–21). This is Hamlet's tragic lesson: Life is what happens when you're busy making plans. He spent the entire play making plans, and it didn't do him any good. Now is the time to stop planning and just get on with life. Or death. Whatever.

What Hamlet doesn't know is that Laertes plans on cheating. The fencing match is to be a sporting match with bated (dull) blades. Laertes, though, secretly substitutes a sharp blade. Just to be safe, he poisons the tip of his blade. To be extra, extra sure, Claudius has his own poison for Hamlet.

Laertes's plans go awry when he is unable to score any touch on Hamlet. Finally, in desperation, he attacks Hamlet during a break. Hamlet feels the sharp point and forces Laertes to swap rapiers. Using the poisoned rapier, Hamlet attacks Laertes. (Hamlet doesn't know about the poison yet; he just thinks that the rapier is illegally sharpened.)

SEE IT

On video

- 1996, Castle Rock: Kenneth Branagh director and as Hamlet, Derek Jacobi as Claudius, and Kate Winslet as Ophelia. This uncut video runs four hours, so pop plenty of popcorn. If you want to see the scenes that other directors omit, this is the one for you. The 19th-century setting works well.

- 1990, Warner Bros.: Franco Zeffirelli director, Mel Gibson as Hamlet, Glenn Close as Gertrude, and Helena Bonham Carter as Ophelia. Mel Gibson clearly enjoys the role, which makes this an enjoyable performance. Many people appreciate the length, which is half that of Branagh's *Hamlet.*

- 1980, BBC: Rodney Bennett director, Derek Jacobi as Hamlet, and Patrick Stewart as Claudius. A good production in a traditional setting.

- 1948, Two Cities Film: Laurence Olivier director and as Hamlet, Eileen Herlie as Gertrude, and Jean Simmons as Ophelia. A classic in black and white, but some people prefer the more recent productions.

Claudius has poisoned Hamlet's drink, but Gertrude accidentally drinks it instead. Gertrude dies from the poison, identifying the drink as the source. Laertes falls and succumbs to the poisoned blade. As he dies, he accuses the king. Now that Hamlet knows that the rapier is poisoned, he stabs the king with it and, just to be sure, forces Claudius to drink the poisoned drink, too. The poison from Laertes's rapier slowly works its way through Hamlet's system, and he dies in Horatio's arms.

The English ambassadors arrive to report that Denmark's wishes have been fulfilled and that Rosencrantz and Guildenstern are dead. Fortinbras also shows up, returning from Poland. The ruling family of Denmark is dead, which leaves Fortinbras of Norway in charge. He takes over, restoring proper order to the throne of Denmark. As Hamlet says, "The rest is silence" (5.2.365).

Julius Caesar

Key characters:

- Julius Caesar, elected ruler of Rome
- Mark Antony, friend of Caesar, co-ruler of Rome after Caesar's death

- Marcus Brutus, conspirator against Caesar
- Cassius, conspirator against Caesar
- Calphurnia ("kal-PUR-nee-ah"), wife of Caesar
- Octavius Caesar, nephew of Caesar, co-ruler of Rome after Caesar's death
- Lepidus, co-ruler of Rome after Caesar's death

Julius Caesar is not so much a tragedy about the title figure as it is about Marcus Brutus and how a good person can do bad things. When the play starts, Julius Caesar is already a military and political hero, loved by the people but hated by his political rivals. Politics in ancient Rome were notoriously corrupt. Caesar labored for many years trying to clean things up; as a result, he had many enemies in government.

Historically, the assassination took place in 44 B.C.E. The events in the rest of the play took place over two years, but as he often does, Shakespeare compresses that time into five short acts.

Figure 15-2:
Marlon
Brando as
Mark
Antony in a
1953 film of
*Julius
Caesar.*

Courtesy MGM

Act 1

It's party time in ancient Rome as the people celebrate the Feast of the Lupercal (February 15), a time of purification and renewal. They decorate Caesar's statues throughout Rome, but two tribunes interrupt the celebrations and scold the people for leaving their jobs. The party-poopers send the people home and tear the decorations off the statues. The tribunes, and many other Roman politicians, are wary of Caesar and his popularity. They worry that he will try to make himself King of Rome, taking power from the elected government.

In the marketplace, Mark Antony tries three times to crown Caesar symbolically, but Caesar refuses the crown each time. His refusal pleases the populace. They, too, are wary of kings, despite their support for Caesar. Later, a fortune-teller accosts Caesar and warns him to "beware the ides of March" (1.2.18) — that is, March 15. Caesar ignores the fortune-teller. Instead, he has his eyes on Cassius. He warns Mark Antony that "lean and hungry" Cassius (1.2.191) is to be feared.

Cassius is especially concerned about Caesar's popularity and his political ambitions. He feels that he must convince Marcus Brutus to help stop Caesar before it's too late. Cassius has already enlisted the support of other conspirators, but he needs Brutus, who is known for his honor and integrity. If Cassius can win Brutus to his side, the conspiracy against Caesar will have a clean facade. So Cassius disguises his handwriting and sends notes to Brutus, commending Brutus and indirectly asking him to intervene and stop Caesar's ambition.

Fast-forward a month. The night before the conspirators are to act against Caesar, a violent storm overtakes Rome. As always in Shakespeare's plays, a great storm portends great deeds. Cassius relishes the storm.

Act 2

The storm keeps Brutus awake at night while he considers his options. He reads the letters that appear to come from average citizens of Rome, but that actually were written by Cassius. The letters tell him to "Speak, strike, redress!" (2.1.47). He doesn't want to see Caesar crown himself king, but the only prevention seems to be assassination. Cassius and the other conspirators meet with Brutus to finalize their plans. Cassius wants to add Mark Antony to the hit list, but Brutus objects. To Brutus, killing Caesar is a noble act, necessary to defend Rome from a would-be king, but killing Mark Antony is different. Antony is a close friend of Caesar, but Brutus thinks that he will pose no threat once Caesar is dead. Brutus prevails, and the conspirators agree to kill only Caesar.

In the morning, Caesar's wife, Calphurnia, warns him not to go to the Senate as he plans. The wild storms are an ill omen, and she dreamt horrible, portentous dreams in the night. "The heavens themselves blaze forth the death of princes" (2.2.31), she tells her husband. Storms and dreams don't bother Caesar, but finally he gives in to Calphurnia's entreaties.

One of the conspirators arrives to escort Caesar to the Senate. When he learns of Caesar's decision, he offers a different interpretation of Calphurnia's dream. He tells Caesar that the Senate intends to offer him the crown, but it might withdraw the offer if he doesn't show up. Caesar changes his mind again and agrees to go to the Senate as originally planned.

Act 3

The day is still March 15, the ides of March. Caesar is marching to the Senate when someone tries to pass a message to him, warning of the conspiracy. Caesar promises to read it soon but will handle affairs of state before handling personal affairs. The fortune-teller warns Caesar again, but he marches on to the Senate.

The conspirators gather around Caesar in the Senate and stab him. They try to calm the senators, telling them that Rome is free and that the senators are safe, but everyone flees from the blood-drenched murderers. Now it's time for the spin doctors to do their work.

Mark Antony asks for safe passage to speak with the conspirators, and Brutus grants it. Antony asks only that he be allowed to carry Caesar's body to the marketplace and there address the crowd for Caesar's funeral. Brutus will speak first, giving the conspirators' reasons for their actions, and Antony can speak next, provided that he does not speak against the conspirators, but only in Caesar's praise. Cassius thinks only of his personal safety and doesn't want Antony to speak to the public. Brutus thinks only of honor and knows that allowing Antony, Caesar's friend, to deliver a eulogy is the right thing to do.

Brutus addresses the crowd and gives the conspirators' reasons for killing Caesar. He points out that Antony wanted to crown Caesar and make him king, against the will of the public. The conspirators killed Caesar for the good of Rome. His oratory wins the people's hearts, and they want to give Brutus the honors that they recently gave to Caesar. He stops the crowd and tells them to heed Antony's eulogy.

Mark Antony delivers the famous "friends, Romans, countrymen" speech (3.2.74–108). True to his word, he does not speak out against the conspirators, except obliquely. He asks whether Caesar was ambitious and reminds the crowd that Caesar refused the crown. He reveals Caesar's will, in which he bequeaths money to every Roman citizen and turns over some of his private land for a public park. Mark Antony's stirring speech turns the fickle crowd once more, from Brutus back to Caesar. They build a pyre for Caesar and take brands to burn down the homes of the conspirators. The populace runs Cassius and Brutus out of town.

The public is out of control. A marauding crowd happens upon Cinna the poet. He shares a name with one of the conspirators, but nothing else. That's enough for the crowd, who attack him merely because his given name happens to be the same as one of the conspirators'.

Act 4

Antony meets with Lepidus and Octavius, the nephew of Julius Caesar. The three seize control of Rome and viciously eliminate anyone standing in their way, especially the conspirators and their allies. Brutus and Cassius have raised armies to attack Rome, and the three prepare to defend themselves and the city.

Brutus and Cassius are linked by their joint guilt in Caesar's murder, but their differences interfere in their present enterprise. Brutus accuses Cassius of accepting bribes in exchange for officerships. He further charges Cassius of not meeting his financial obligations so that Brutus can pay his soldiers. Cassius denies that he withheld payment, although he doesn't deny the other charges. The differences between the two stand out clearly. Cassius takes bribes because he needs the money; Brutus is short on money because he refuses to accept bribes. Eventually, they work out their differences and show a united front to the armies and their commanders.

Act 5

Brutus faces Octavius. Cassius faces Antony. The armies meet, and Brutus's forces initially gain the upper hand. Cassius is not so lucky. He sees no hope for himself or his army. Aided by his bondsman, Cassius falls on his sword and kills himself.

In the end, Brutus cannot resist the armies of Octavius and Antony. When it becomes clear that he has lost, he too falls on his sword and kills himself rather than face the humiliation of being led captive back to Rome.

Antony honors the death of Brutus, "the noblest Roman of them all" (5.5.68). He recognizes that Brutus acted out of honor as he saw it. The other conspirators were envious of Caesar, but Brutus truly believed that he was helping Rome.

On video

- 1979, BBC: Herbert Wise director, Charles Gray as Caesar, Keith Michell as Mark Antony, and Richard Pasco as Brutus. A decent performance in a traditional Roman setting.

- 1970, Commonwealth: Stuart Burge director, Charlton Heston as Mark Antony, Jason Robards as Brutus, and John Gielgud as Julius Caesar.

- 1953, Metro G.M.: Joseph L. Mankiewicz director, Louis Calhern as Julius Caesar, James Mason as Brutus, Marlon Brando as Mark Antony, and John Gielgud as Cassius.

King Lear

Key characters:

- Lear, King of Britain
- Goneril, Lear's daughter
- Regan, Lear's daughter
- Cordelia, Lear's daughter
- Duke of Albany, husband of Goneril
- Duke of Cornwall, husband of Regan
- Earl of Gloucester ("GLAW-ster"), loyal friend to King Lear
- Edgar, Gloucester's son
- Edmund, Gloucester's bastard son
- Earl of Kent, loyal friend to King Lear
- Lear's Fool

King Lear takes sibling rivalry to new heights (or depths, depending on your point of view). The main story is about King Lear and his three daughters, but Shakespeare mixes in a second story about the Earl of Gloucester and his two sons. Lear succumbs to false flattery, Gloucester to false malice. The result is the same regardless of the cause: chaos, ruin, and death. This play is full of fools and foolish behavior. How many fools can you find? (Read more about fools and similar characters in Chapter 8.)

Act 1

King Lear rules over Britain in a mythical past. Being of unsound mind, he wants to divide his inheritance according to which of his three daughters loves him the most. Fool number 1! Goneril gushes with insincere flattery, saying that she loves him more than anything, even life itself. Regan tops her sister by professing that she loves her father so much that she forgoes all other pleasure. The hollow flattery pleases Lear, and he doles out one-third of his kingdom to each daughter. He saves the best part for his favorite daughter, Cordelia. Poor Cordelia can't lie the way her sisters can. She answers that she loves her father as a daughter should, but that she cannot give him all her love, lest she have nothing left for her husband. That's not what her father wants to hear. He disinherits Cordelia and divides his kingdom between Goneril and Regan. Is Cordelia being foolish, or is Lear?

The Earl of Kent, Lear's close friend and advisor, tries to reason with Lear but only makes him angrier, and Lear banishes Kent from the kingdom. Immediately after Kent leaves, the King of France enters. Although disinherited, Cordelia isn't alone. The King of France is happy to marry Cordelia, who is "most rich being poor" (1.1.252).

Meanwhile, in a subplot, the Earl of Gloucester has two sons: Edgar and Edmund. Edgar is the elder son, and Edmund is a bastard. To the Elizabethan audience, Edmund's illegitimacy meant that he was up to no good. Gloucester's legitimate son, Edgar, stands to inherit everything, but Edmund has other ideas. He forges a letter that seems to be in Edgar's handwriting and urges Edmund to help Edgar kill their father so that they can get their hands on the land and wealth immediately. Gloucester falls for the trick and thinks that Edgar is out to kill him. Have you spotted the fool in this scene? (We have trouble keeping Edgar and Edmund straight, so we use the following aid: Ed*g*ar is *g*ood, and Ed*m*und is *m*ean.)

Kent was banished, but he has not left England. He disguises himself and enters Lear's service. A Fool also attends Lear, and this Fool wisely sees that his master is more foolish than he.

The deal that Lear proposes to Regan and Goneril is that each daughter gets half the kingdom, and in exchange, Lear will live for one month at a time with one daughter and then the other, attended by 100 knights. His daughters aren't content with the arrangement and seek to strip their father of everything he has. Goneril breaks the bargain and wants her father to dismiss half his attendants. Lear laments:

How sharper than a serpent's tooth it is

To have a thankless child. (1.4.280–81)

Lear decides to stay with Regan, thinking that she will offer him the comfort that Goneril withholds. Secretly, Goneril writes to Regan, telling her what passed between her and their father and urging Regan to do the same.

Act 2

Edmund continues plotting against Edgar, taking advantage of his foolish honesty. Edmund warns Edgar that their father is out to get him and counsels him to run away. Edmund even cuts himself with his own sword and tells his father that Edgar did it. Gloucester again falls for Edmund's trick and sends out an all-points bulletin calling for Edgar's capture.

Regan and her husband, the Duke of Cornwall, visit the Earl of Gloucester just so that they won't be home when Lear visits. Kent discovers a servant of Goneril's and sees immediately that Goneril is dispatching messages to Regan so that they can work together against Lear. He draws his sword on the servant and attacks him. Cornwall interrupts the fight and orders Kent be placed in the stocks, a punishment typically reserved for common thieves, not for a king's attendant.

King Lear follows Regan to Gloucester's castle, only to find Kent in the stocks. Lear is incensed at this mistreatment of his follower, so Cornwall releases Kent. Lear also rails against Goneril's mistreatment of him and his attendants and asks Regan to take them in, but she refuses. Goneril arrives and the tag-team match begins in earnest. The daughters team up and tell Lear to dismiss all his servants and attendants, making him entirely dependent on them, but he will not. A storm brews, which in Shakespeare's plays is always an omen for momentous events to follow. Lear and the Fool withdraw into the stormy night.

Act 3

Kent learns that the King of France is landing an army in England to rescue Lear. Kent tries to bring this news to Lear, but the stress has taken its toll on Lear. It's more than his old mind can bear, and he cracks under the pressure. He competes with the storm to see who can rage the most: "Blow winds and crack your cheeks! Rage, blow!" (3.2.1). His Fool is his only company while Kent tries to find shelter for them. He finds a hovel that he thinks is abandoned, but that's where Edgar is hiding from his own father. (Remember from Act 2 that Edmund fooled Edgar into thinking that their father was after Edgar.) Edgar calls himself poor Tom and acts almost as crazily as Lear. Together, the Fool, the foolish King, and the playacting fool wait out the storm.

Gloucester is sorry for the mistreatment of his king. The next morning, he sends Lear, Kent, and the Fool to Dover, where they will meet Cordelia and the French army. He doesn't recognize "poor Tom" as his son Edgar.

Gloucester confides in Edmund, whom he thinks is his loyal son. Edmund, however, betrays his father to the Duke of Cornwall. As punishment, Cornwall blinds Gloucester. A servant rebels against this mistreatment of an innocent, harmless man and attacks Cornwall. Regan kills the servant, but not before Cornwall receives a fatal wound. Although wounded, Cornwall manages to finish his bloody job before dying. Regan thrusts the blind Gloucester from his home and tells him to make his own way to Dover.

Act 4

Edgar, still pretending to be poor Tom, meets his blind father. Gloucester now realizes that Edgar is his true and loyal son, but Edgar does not reveal himself to his father yet. Instead, as poor Tom, he agrees to lead Gloucester to Dover.

Edmund has risen high in the esteem of Goneril and Regan. Goneril's husband, the Duke of Albany, doesn't like the cruel treatment that the daughters have inflicted on their father. He then hears the news of Gloucester's eyes. Albany fumes at this mistreatment of the king and Gloucester. Goneril is angry because Albany is not as bloodthirsty as she. She prefers Edmund. But Regan, now a widow and free to marry, also has eyes for Edmund.

The scene shifts to Dover, where Cordelia and her army prepare for attack. Kent brings Lear to Cordelia. Edgar leads his father to Dover, where they meet Lear, who doesn't recognize them. They also run into Goneril's servant, whom Edgar kills. The servant has a letter from Goneril, entreating Edmund to kill her husband and marry her. Edgar now has the means to prove Edmund's treachery.

Act 5

Regan, now a widow, looks favorably on Edmund. Goneril wants to be a widow and also looks favorably on Edmund. Albany still doesn't fully appreciate the villainy of his wife and her sister, but he joins his army with Goneril's to defend England from the French invasion.

The English army wins. King Lear and Cordelia are taken prisoner, and Edmund secretly gives the order to hang them. Albany asks that they be brought before him, but Edmund refuses to comply, saying that it would be better to wait. Regan wants to marry Edmund but feels strangely sick and must retire to her tent.

SEE IT

On video

- 1997, BBC: Richard Eyre director, and Ian Holm as King Lear. A good production in a somewhat stark setting.

- 1984, Granada: Michael Elliott director, Laurence Olivier as King Lear, Diana Rigg as Regan, and John Hurt as the Fool.

A good performance, even if it isn't Olivier's best.

- 1982, BBC: Jonathan Miller director, Michael Hordern as King Lear, and Frank Middlemass as the Fool.

Albany also has business with Edmund, accusing him of treason. Edgar challenges Edmund to a duel, and Edgar wins. Goneril claims that the fight isn't fair, but her husband shows her the letter that Edgar found, which clearly accuses Goneril of plotting to murder Albany. She storms away.

Edgar reveals himself to his dying brother and tells how their father died when he learned who Edgar really was. A soldier enters with more bad news: Regan and Goneril are dead. Regan wasn't really sick, but poisoned. Goneril poisoned her sister, hoping to win Edmund for herself. When she saw Edmund receive his mortal wound and her guilt was exposed, she rushed off to kill herself. Edmund sees the wreck that he caused and hopes to remedy it at least in some small part. He hastily sends a message to stop the secret murder of Lear and Cordelia.

Too late — Cordelia is hanged at Edmund's order. Lear killed the hangman and now bears Cordelia's body onstage. Grief piles upon grief until he can stand no more and dies. Albany turns over England to Kent and Edgar, but Kent follows his master, leaving Edgar in charge.

With families like these, who needs enemies?

Macbeth

Key characters:

- Duncan, King of Scotland

- Malcolm, Duncan's elder son

- Donalbain, Duncan's younger son

- Macbeth, Thane of Glamis, later King of Scotland

- Lady Macbeth, Macbeth's wife, later Queen of Scotland

✔ Banquo, Macbeth's friend

✔ Fleance, Banquo's son

✔ Macduff, a Scottish lord, loyal to Duncan

Macbeth was a real king of Scotland: He murdered King Duncan in 1040 C.E. and reigned for about 17 years before Duncan's son Malcolm killed Macbeth. Shakespeare wrote his play using the sources that were available to him, and he felt free to modify them, compress time, and add witches and whatnot to suit his whim. The result is an exciting play, but one that bears little resemblance to history.

In this play more than any other, Shakespeare explores the nature of free will: Is Macbeth the master of his fate, or is it the other way around?

Doo-dee-doo-doo. Doo-dee-doo-doo.

There is a fifth dimension, beyond space and time, a place where past, present, and future collide, a place of magic, ghosts, and madness. You are about to enter . . . The Shakespeare Zone.

Doo-dee-doo-doo. Doo-dee-doo-doo.

Act 1

Macbeth, the Thane of Glamis, has successfully quelled a rebellion against his king, Duncan. (*Thane* is the Scottish equivalent of an English earl.) He and his sidekick Banquo return in triumph when three witches stop them. The witches greet Macbeth three times: using his current title, Thane of Glamis, as Thane of Cawdor, and as "King hereafter" (1.3.50). Macbeth marvels at the greeting because Cawdor is not his title, and certainly king is beyond his reach. Messengers from King Duncan arrive and tell Macbeth that he is now Thane of Cawdor. Score one for the witches. Doo-dee-doo-doo.

Banquo asks the witches if they can prophesy his future. They answer enigmatically, saying that he will not be king but will father kings.

The witches were right about Cawdor; perhaps they will be right about king, too. Macbeth tells his wife about the witches and their prediction. To Lady Macbeth, the prediction is almost a command, and she thinks immediately of seizing the throne by force. She fears that her husband "is too full o'th' milk of human kindness" (1.5.16) for such a deed.

For Macbeth to be king, they must get rid of Duncan and his two sons, Malcolm and Donalbain. Their best opportunity will be that very night because Duncan will stay with Macbeth on his way home. To prepare for the bloody task, Lady Macbeth calls upon the spirits:

Fill me, from the crown to the toe, top-full

Of direst cruelty. (1.5.40–41)

Macbeth is reluctant to follow through on his plans. Duncan is a good king; Macbeth cannot rationalize his murder. Lady Macbeth has no such inhibitions. She urges her husband to do the job, saying, "When you durst do it, then you were a man" (1.7.49). She will ply Duncan's bodyguards with wine and give Macbeth the opportunity to kill the unguarded Duncan. They will then frame the guards for the murder. His wife finally sways him, and Macbeth is resolved to carry out the deed.

Act 2

Banquo and his son, Fleance, are up and about in the middle of the night. They meet Macbeth, and Banquo delivers gifts from Duncan, including a rich diamond for Lady Macbeth. Banquo reminds Macbeth about the three witches, but Macbeth pretends that he hasn't thought about them. After Banquo and Fleance leave, Macbeth imagines that he sees a dagger hovering in the air in front of him. Doo-dee-doo-doo. Suddenly the dagger has bloodstains on it. Is this a warning? The apparition unsettles him, but not enough to dissuade him from his bloody job.

Lady Macbeth has done her job: to make the guards drunk. She takes their daggers, which Macbeth uses to kill Duncan. When he stabs Duncan, he thinks he hears a voice chiding and accusing him. He refuses to enter the room again, so Lady Macbeth must plant the daggers and smear Duncan's blood on the guards.

Macduff discovers Duncan's body and cries out. Macbeth blames the guards and kills them, ostensibly out of rage and anguish over his king's death. The outcry awakens the household, including Duncan's sons. They don't believe the story about the guards being the murderers and know that the murderer is still at large. Their lives are at risk, so they flee during the night: Malcolm to England and Donalbain to Ireland. To the Scottish lords, the sons' hasty flight smacks of guilt. They think that the sons hired the guards to murder Duncan. They crown Macbeth as King of Scotland. The witches' prophecy has come true, and Act 3 hasn't even started yet. Doo-dee-doo-doo.

Act 3

Banquo sees that the prophecy has come true but suspects Macbeth's foul play in achieving it. Macbeth sees that Banquo suspects him, so he hires assassins to kill Banquo and Banquo's son. According to the witches,

Banquo's destiny is to father kings, but Macbeth wants to thwart that prophecy by killing Banquo and Fleance. The astute viewer sees that Macbeth's situation is hopeless. The prophecy will come true, and anything Macbeth tries to do is the means by which the prophecy will be fulfilled. Doo-dee-doo-doo.

King Macbeth and his wife, now queen, prepare for a banquet. Macbeth is fearful and nervous, and his wife tries to calm him down, saying that "what's done is done" (3.2.12). They must present a fair face to the Scottish lords and pretend that they have nothing to hide.

The murderers that Macbeth hired accost and kill Banquo, but Fleance escapes. At dinner, Macbeth invites his guests to sit down, but Banquo's ghost arrives uninvited and takes Macbeth's seat. Doo-dee-doo-doo. Macbeth is the only person who can see Banquo's ghost. If Macbeth was nervous before, he is tormented now; his mind is "full of scorpions" (3.2.36). Lady Macbeth tries to cover for her husband and explain that this happens sometimes, and with a little rest, he'll be all right. She shoos the lords from the room with her apologies.

Fleance escaped the assassins, but now the rumors are that he killed his father, just as everyone thinks that Malcolm and Donalbain killed Duncan. The lord Macduff, however, does not believe Macbeth to be innocent. He follows Malcolm to England and incites the English king (Edward the Confessor) to lend his strength and attack Scotland and Macbeth.

Act 4

Macbeth prepares for war and visits the three witches to learn what outcome to expect. They give him news that he thinks is good news: He will not die, except at the hand of one who was not born of woman. His army will not be overthrown until Birnam Wood moves to Dunsinane Hill. Both prospects seem impossible, so Macbeth is confident of success. Doo-dee-doo-doo.

Like so many fictional murderers, Macbeth can't seem to get out of the habit of killing. When he learns of Macduff's flight to England, he seeks revenge by murdering Macduff's wife, children, and servants. In England, Malcolm is at first reluctant to side with Macduff. Malcolm mistrusts him until he tests the degree to which Macduff is loyal to the late Duncan and disloyal to Macbeth. Macduff passes the test, and together they plan their attack on Scotland.

Another Scottish lord tells Macduff the bad news about his family. Macbeth's tyranny is evident, and Macduff realizes that for the good of Scotland, he must be deposed.

Act 5

Lady Macbeth has been driven mad by her sins. She stays in her bed, rising only to sleepwalk and sleepwash, as it were. In her sleep, she washes her hands over and over, crying "Out, damned spot! out, I say!" (5.1.36). She talks to herself, and within earshot of her maid and a doctor, she reveals her complicity in the murders.

Macduff and Malcolm, with the English army, gather at Birnam Wood. Other Scottish lords join them to fight Macbeth's tyranny. Those who stay with Macbeth do so only because of Macbeth's command, not out of love for the tyrannical, murderous king.

Macbeth disregards the news of the opposing army. He learns that his wife is dead, too, probably driven to take her own life. Nonetheless, Macbeth is resolute. He is confident that the forest cannot move, and that every man must be born of woman, so he thinks that he has nothing to worry about. Malcolm orders his soldiers to cut boughs from the forest to camouflage themselves and obscure their numbers. Carrying the boughs before them, they march toward Macbeth's army, which sits on Dunsinane Hill. The scouts report this to Macbeth, who immediately sees how this affects the prophecy. Birnam Wood is coming to Dunsinane Hill. Macbeth raises the alarm and prepares to fight a battle that he now knows he will lose.

One prophecy remains unfulfilled: Macbeth cannot die except at the hands of one who was not born of woman. He remains confident until he faces Macduff, who reveals he was not born normally, but was "Untimely ripped from his mother's womb" (5.8.15–16) — a Caesarian delivery when such procedures were uncommon and considered unnatural. Macbeth valiantly tries to defy the prophecy, but he cannot. Macduff kills him and proclaims Malcolm King of Scotland. So Macbeth's destiny is fulfilled. The witches are never wrong. Doo-dee-doo-doo.

On video

- 1983, BBC: Jack Gold director, Nicol Williamson as Macbeth.

- 1979, Thames Television and the RSC: Trevor Nunn director, Ian McKellen as Macbeth, and Judi Dench as Lady Macbeth. A wonderful production. Not available in the U.S.

- 1971, Playboy Productions: Roman Polanski director, Jon Finch as Macbeth, and Francesca Annis as Lady Macbeth. A popular production, but with graphic violence.

- 1948, Mercury: Orson Welles director and as Macbeth, and Jeanette Nolan as Lady Macbeth. A classic in black and white. Hear Orson Welles with a Scottish accent.

Othello

Key characters:

- ✔ Othello the Moor, a Venetian general
- ✔ Desdemona, daughter of Brabantio and Othello's wife
- ✔ Iago, a villain, third in command to Othello
- ✔ Cassio, second in command to Othello
- ✔ Roderigo, a Venetian gentleman, duped by Iago
- ✔ Emilia, Iago's wife, attending Desdemona

Atypically, *Othello* has no kings, armies, battles, or ghosts — only a minor officer as a villain. But what a villain. Iago is implacable, unshakable, and entirely evil. What makes Iago such an effective villain is that he has so many willing, even eager, victims. Without victims, even the greatest of villains would be a nobody.

Figure 15-3: Edmund Kean in his most famous role as Othello, which he performed hundreds of times in the early 19th century.

V+A Picture Library

Act 1

Iago lost the big promotion to Cassio. Iago thought that he was next in line, but their boss, Othello, doesn't play by the old rules. Iago decides to get even. He knows that Othello eloped with Desdemona, which is sure to cause a scandal when the news becomes known. Although he is a great general and is popular in Venice, Othello is a Moor. A broad-minded Venetian might invite a Moor to his house, but he wouldn't want his daughter to marry one. (You can read more about Moors and Shakespeare's society in Chapter 8.) Desdemona's father is no exception, so when Iago and a friend, Roderigo, wake him in the middle of the night with the news, he immediately rushes off to rescue his daughter.

Iago warns Othello about Desdemona's angry father, but Othello is not concerned because they are in love. Besides, Venice needs Othello's good will because he is their best general. As evidence, Cassio enters with a summons from the duke, who calls for Othello to defend Cyprus from the Turks.

The duke straightaway dispatches Othello to Cyprus, but Desdemona's father interrupts to bring his accusations against Othello. The duke summons Desdemona to hear her side of the story. While they wait for her to appear, Othello recounts the tale of how he visited Desdemona and her father, who encouraged him to tell the story of his life. She fell in love with the exotic Moor for the many dangers he faced, and he loved her because "she did pity them" (1.3.169). It's not the strongest foundation for a relationship, so don't be surprised if they have some marital problems down the road. Desdemona arrives and confirms all that Othello said.

Othello has to be off to Cyprus to fight the Turks, and Desdemona insists on accompanying him. Othello appoints "Honest Iago" (1.3.296) to escort her to Cyprus. Emilia, Iago's wife, will also travel with them.

Iago's plans run deep. He seeks to supplant Cassio as Othello's lieutenant, and will do so by convincing Othello that Cassio is sleeping with Desdemona. To help him, Iago recruits Roderigo, a former suitor of Desdemona. Iago dupes Roderigo into bankrolling their conspiracy by convincing him that he can help Roderigo win back Desdemona.

Act 2

To the relief of the people of Cyprus, a great storm destroys most of the Turkish fleet, and Othello takes care of the remaining ships. Cassio has already landed in Cyprus with the news. The ship carrying Iago and Desdemona arrives next, and they greet Cassio. Iago notes the easy friendship between Desdemona and Cassio (and later uses it to his advantage). Finally, Othello lands in Cyprus, happy to find his wife already present.

Iago's hatred for Othello consumes him, and it's time to put his plan in motion. He tells Roderigo to start a quarrel with Cassio. The people of Cyprus will not tolerate street brawling and will demand that Othello dismiss Cassio.

Iago gets Cassio drunk in celebration of the victory over the Turks. Iago then lies to the governor of Cyprus, saying that Cassio drinks to excess every night. Roderigo accosts Cassio, who responds violently, beating Roderigo.

Othello demands to know what the disturbance was all about. Iago hesitates to answer, pretending that he doesn't want to say who started the fight. The governor of Cyprus forces him to speak, and reluctantly (or so it seems), Iago tells how Cassio threw the first punch. Othello dismisses Cassio as his lieutenant, which falls right in line with Iago's plan.

Roderigo seems to be getting the raw end of Iago's trick. Cassio beat him; he is out of money, having given it to Iago; and he is no closer to winning Desdemona. Iago encourages him by pointing out that the blows Roderigo received worked to drive Cassio away from Othello. Roderigo must have patience and wait for the plan's fruition, Iago says.

Act 3

Cassio asks Desdemona to take up his cause before Othello. Iago leads Othello to where he can see the two talking and plants the seed that they are talking of love. Iago warns Othello to watch his wife closely, especially in her relationship with Cassio. He reminds Othello that she deceived her father when she eloped — surely she can deceive again. Iago manipulates Othello with consummate skill. He disingenuously warns Othello:

O beware, my lord, of jealousy!

It is the green-eyed monster, which doth mock

That meat it feeds on. (3.3.167–69)

With a few well-placed lies, Iago further works on Othello's mind. Then fortune hands Iago another tool to use against Othello.

Desdemona drops a handkerchief, and Emilia picks it up. Iago has often asked her to steal it, but she never before had the opportunity. She doesn't know why Iago wants it, but her plan is to make a copy and give him the copy. That way, she can make her husband happy without betraying her mistress. Before she can take away the handkerchief, though, Iago finds her and takes it from her. Emilia is puzzled but has no reason to suspect that Iago is up to no good.

Iago has plans for the handkerchief. He makes up a story about Cassio dreaming of Desdemona. He also says that he saw Desdemona's handkerchief in Cassio's hand. That's all the proof Othello needs, and he orders Iago to kill Cassio. Iago agrees but then urges Othello not to harm Desdemona, which has the opposite effect — driving Othello to want to kill her all the more — which is exactly what Iago hopes for.

Othello asks Desdemona for the handkerchief. She says that she lost it earlier and has been looking for it, but she doesn't know where it is. Naturally, she can't give it to him. She thinks that the handkerchief is unimportant and wants to talk about Cassio.

Cassio finds the handkerchief, which Iago planted in his room. He doesn't know where it came from or whose it is, but he's certain the owner will inquire about it soon enough. He likes the design, so he gives it to a friend to copy.

Act 4

Iago's masterful manipulation of Othello is almost complete. He tells Othello to hide while he confronts Cassio about Desdemona. Actually, Iago and Cassio talk about a courtesan, the one Cassio asked to copy the handkerchief. They laugh together and poke fun at her; all the while, Othello thinks that they are talking about Desdemona. The courtesan returns the handkerchief to Cassio. She can tell that it is a woman's handkerchief and probably a love token, so she wants nothing to do with it. Othello recognizes the handkerchief. He assumes that Desdemona gave it to Cassio, who gave it to the courtesan.

Othello finally confronts Desdemona, but it's too late for her to plead innocent. He's convinced that she slept with Cassio, and nothing she says can convince him otherwise. Emilia protests on Desdemona's behalf, but to no avail. Iago promises Desdemona and Emilia that he will try to calm Othello.

Emilia helps Desdemona prepare for bed. Desdemona tries to imagine why a woman would be unfaithful to her husband. She asks Emilia if she would be unfaithful "for all the world" (4.3.67). Emilia answers that the world is a huge price for a small deed. Desdemona, on the other hand, would not be unfaithful, even for the whole world.

Act 5

Iago convinces Roderigo to kill Cassio, but Cassio proves the better swordsman and wounds Roderigo. Iago sneaks up on Cassio but only manages to wound him in the leg. The tumult alerts others, who rush to the scene. Iago sees that Roderigo is still alive and kills him, ostensibly for attacking Cassio but actually so that he won't squeal.

Othello confronts Desdemona and accuses her of infidelity. She denies the charge, of course. She begs him not to kill her but to banish her, or at least wait one night or even half an hour before killing her. She asks for time "but while I say one prayer!" (5.2.82), but he refuses and suffocates her in her bed. Emilia brings news that Roderigo is dead and Cassio attacked. Othello hopes that Cassio is dead, as Iago promised, but is chagrined to learn that Cassio is merely wounded. Emilia is horrified to find Desdemona dead at Othello's hands. She learns that Othello obtained his evidence from Iago and suspects Othello of making up accusations against her husband, whom she believes to be honest.

Iago and others enter to witness Othello's deed. Emilia reveals the truth about the handkerchief, which uncovers Iago's dishonesty. Iago cannot quiet his wife, so he kills her.

On Roderigo's body were letters that further expose Iago's role in matters. Othello now learns the whole truth: that Desdemona was faithful, that Iago was dishonest, and that he was a jealous fool for believing Iago's lies. Othello finishes his final act of victimization and kills himself. Iago is taken prisoner, and his punishment — "the time, the place, the torture" (5.2.369) — is left for Cassio to decide.

SEE IT

On video

- ✔ 1995, Castle Rock: Oliver Parker director, Laurence Fishburne as Othello, Irène Jacob as Desdemona, and Kenneth Branagh as Iago. A good production, but we prefer Burge's film.

- ✔ 1981, BBC: Jonathan Miller director, Anthony Hopkins as Othello, Bob Hoskins as Iago, and Penelope Wilton as Desdemona. A good production in a traditional setting.

- ✔ 1965, Warner Bros.: Stuart Burge director, Laurence Olivier as Othello, Frank Finlay as Iago, and Maggie Smith as Desdemona. An excellent production in a traditional setting.

- ✔ 1952, Mercury: Orson Welles director and as Othello. The original film was lost for several decades and was rediscovered in 1992.

Romeo and Juliet

Key characters:

- ✔ Romeo Montague, young lover of Juliet
- ✔ Juliet Capulet, young lover of Romeo
- ✔ Juliet's nurse
- ✔ Tybalt, cousin of Juliet
- ✔ Mercutio, friend to Romeo
- ✔ Friar Laurence, confidant to the lovers
- ✔ Count Paris, a nobleman in love with Juliet

Romeo and Juliet is one of Shakespeare's best-known plays, and many people consider it his finest love story. It's a terrific story, but don't lose sight of the tragedy. The lovers die in the final act, and that's not how most of us want our love affairs to end.

Act 1

The play opens with a brawl, pitting the Montague family against the Capulets. Shakespeare makes it clear that the fighting has been going on for many years and shows no sign of lessening. The Prince of Verona puts his foot down and decrees that anyone who starts another fight will face the death penalty.

Romeo Montague missed the fight, though. He was too busy mooning over his latest love, Rosaline (who doesn't appear in the play). His friends, Benvolio and Mercutio, poke fun at him for his youthful love.

Juliet Capulet is now old enough to be married (14 years old), and her parents want her to marry the Count Paris. Juliet hasn't given marriage much thought, but she promises to keep an open mind.

The act ends with a costume party at the Capulets' home, which Romeo and his friends crash. Romeo goes because he thinks that he'll see Rosaline, but when he arrives, he sees Juliet and completely forgets what's-her-name. He falls madly in love with Juliet. Juliet, in turn, falls in love with the strange man who woos her at the party, only to learn too late that he is of the rival family, the Montagues. For this play to make any sense, you must believe in love at first sight (as explained in Chapter 7) — if not in real life, at least for the duration of the play.

So the stage is set. Romeo Montague loves Juliet Capulet, and Juliet loves Romeo. Neither is a free agent; the two cannot change teams without the owners' consent. You know that won't happen. In the modern era, their respective lawyers would meet to iron things out, but this is a Shakespearean tragedy. The only way to resolve this problem is through bloodshed and mayhem.

Act 2

The famous balcony scene defines the fundamental problem in the play. Juliet asks, "O Romeo, Romeo, wherefore art thou Romeo?" (2.2.33), or "Why is your name Romeo?" The only obstacle to their love is their names. If they had different names, they could marry and have kids, the play would be over before intermission, and everyone could go home early.

The young lovers pledge their undying love to each other, and Romeo hastens off to Friar Laurence to arrange the lovers' elopement. Friar Laurence hasn't heard the news yet, so he thinks that Romeo is still pining for what's-her-name. Romeo says that he is in love with Juliet, and the friar remarks that "young men's love lies / Not in their hearts but in their eyes" (2.3.63–64). Romeo convinces the friar that he is in earnest. The friar thinks that this new love might be just the ticket to patch things up between the Capulets and the Montagues, even though no one, not even the prince, has been able to end it.

Meanwhile, Tybalt is annoyed that Romeo and his friends crashed his uncle's party, so he's on the warpath. Romeo has more pressing things to deal with — namely, how to elope with Juliet. He works out the details with Juliet's nurse, and the act closes with Romeo meeting Juliet, ready to be married by the friar.

Act 3

Soon after Romeo and Juliet's clandestine marriage, Tybalt catches up to Romeo and challenges him. Now that Tybalt is related to Romeo by marriage, Romeo declines to fight. Mercutio steps into the breach, and Tybalt kills him when Romeo tries to break up the fight.

Romeo, seeing his friend slain, is understandably more than a little upset. He hunts down Tybalt and revenges his friend's death by killing Tybalt. By now, the prince has heard about the violations of his strict edicts. Romeo has already carried out the death sentence that should have fallen on Tybalt for slaying Mercutio, but the Prince frowns on Romeo's act of vigilantism, so he banishes Romeo from Verona.

Romeo runs to the friar, who still hopes that one day, he will be able to reveal the secret marriage and that somehow this news will reverse all those years of bitter, bloody fighting. Shakespeare doesn't say, but apparently, the friar lives on a different planet than the rest of us.

Juliet has conflicting feelings. Her cousin is dead, but at her husband's hands. On the other hand, her cousin killed her husband's friend. In the end, she sides with her husband, and they consummate their marriage.

Meanwhile, Juliet's parents decide to hasten the forced marriage of their daughter to Paris. Juliet resists her parents' wishes, but she is powerless to stop them.

Act 4

The friar tries to slow down the Capulets' wedding plans. After all, he already married Juliet to Romeo, and he can hardly keep his vows if he then marries her off to Paris, too. He tells Juliet that the situation "strains me past the compass of my wits" (4.1.47).

With Juliet, the friar hatches a desperate plan. He provides a powerful drug. When Juliet takes it, everyone will think that she's dead, but she won't be *completely* dead. After she's put to rest, the friar will break into the tomb and rescue her. He sends a letter to Romeo telling him of the plan so that Romeo can take Juliet away.

Juliet takes the drug. The next morning, her family finds her, apparently dead. They carry her to the family tomb.

Act 5

Unfortunately, the friar's letter never reaches Romeo. Instead, Romeo hears the news that Juliet is dead. He buys some poison and plans to kill himself next to Juliet's body, and he hastens back to Verona.

The friar learns that his letter did not reach Romeo, so he heads to the Capulet tomb to take Juliet with him until he can reach Romeo.

As you might expect, the timing just doesn't work out right. Romeo gets to the tomb before the friar. He encounters Paris, mourning for Juliet. They fight, and Romeo kills Paris. Romeo breaks into the tomb and takes the poison at Juliet's side:

O true apothecary,

Thy drugs are quick. Thus with a kiss I die. (5.3.119–20)

SEE IT

On video

- 1996, Fox: Baz Luhrmann director, Leonardo DiCaprio as Romeo, and Claire Danes as Juliet. A contemporary setting, but surprisingly faithful to Shakespeare's text. This is a good choice to get teenagers interested in Shakespeare's plays.

- 1978, BBC: Alvin Rakoff director, Patrick Ryecart as Romeo, and Rebecca Saire as Juliet.

- 1968, Paramount: Franco Zeffirelli director, Leonard Whiting as Romeo, Olivia Hussey as Juliet. A classic film in a traditional setting.

Juliet's drug wears off just as the friar arrives. He tries to hasten Juliet away, but she sees the dead bodies around her and refuses to follow. He gets scared and runs off. Juliet takes Romeo's dagger and stabs herself, thus following Romeo in death.

The prince arrives, and the friar spills the beans. With the whole truth out and dead bodies littering the stage, the families finally reconcile and end their feud. It turns out that Juliet was right after all: "That which we call a rose by any other word would smell as sweet" (2.2.43–44). The problem is that nobody believes her until it's too late.

Timon of Athens

Key characters:

- Timon, a noble Athenian
- Apemantus ("AH-pay-MAHN-tuss"), a churlish philosopher
- Alcibiades ("AL-kib-EYE-ah-daze"), an Athenian captain
- Flavius, Timon's faithful steward

A spot of trouble is all you need to separate your fair-weather friends from your true friends. In this play, Timon learns this lesson the hard way.

Donald Cooper/Photostage

Figure 15-4:
David Suchet (better known for his role of Hercule Poirot) plays Timon.

Act 1

Timon is a party animal. Everyone loves Timon and his parties, which is hardly surprising because he is free with his money. Poets, painters, merchants, and jewelers flock to Timon and bestow gifts and praises on him. In return, Timon lavishes his riches on his guests. His generosity knows no bounds. A messenger, for example, brings word that his master is in jail, unable to repay a debt of five talents (thousands of dollars). Timon doesn't hesitate to pay off the debt on his behalf. Timon's servant, Lucilius, woos the daughter of an Athenian gentleman. The father wants Timon to forbid the match, but instead Timon offers to pay the servant enough money to bring him up to the standing of a gentleman and therefore be a suitable match for the man's daughter.

Apemantus is the only guest who doesn't fawn over Timon, flatter him, or gush with praise. Apemantus speaks bluntly and bitterly to everyone, and he warns Timon against flatterers and false friends. He refuses anything that Timon offers and rails against all the Athenians for their falsehood and duplicity, even to their so-called friends. Timon doesn't heed Apemantus, but continues to spread his cheer and wealth.

Timon's steward, Flavius, tries to stop his master's free-spending ways, but to no avail. (The steward would like to cut up Timon's credit cards, but they haven't been invented yet.) When the money runs out, Timon will learn who his true friends are.

Act 2

Timon's debts start to mount, and the collection agencies are on his tail. Flavius tries to delay the debt collectors, but they push their way to Timon and importune him to repay the loans. Timon confronts Flavius, who explains the situation: Every time Flavius broached the matter, Timon pushed him away. Flavius did his best to manage, selling or mortgaging land until finally he could do no more. Timon is bankrupt.

Timon dispatches servants to entreat his friends for help. The noble Athenians who so often dined with Timon, on whom Timon showered gifts — surely they will remember with gratitude all that Timon did for them, or so he thinks. The Athenian Senate, which owes him so much, can afford to loan him 1,000 talents, but Flavius has already tried them. Everyone makes up excuses, and no one agrees to help Timon.

Act 3

One by one, Timon's servants present their master's suit to the gentlemen of Athens. One by one, the fair-weather friends refuse, each with a different excuse. Enraged, Timon drives the debt collectors from his house. He tells his servants to invite his friends to one more party. Flavius is puzzled because Timon has no more money, but Timon insists.

The Athenian lords gather for the party, trying to guess what Timon is up to. Maybe Timon was playing a trick on them to sound out who his true friends are. If that's the case, the lords need to figure out how to get back on Timon's good side. They hope the party demonstrates that all is forgiven. Timon invites them to dine, but when they sit down, they discover that the only dish is warm water. Timon assails his false friends and all of mankind.

Alcibiades, the Athenian captain, has his own problems: The Senate condemns one of his soldiers to death. It seems that the soldier got into a quarrel over words and defended his honor with his sword. The Senate views this not as a matter of honor, but as murder. Alcibiades pleads for his soldier's life, offering as testimony the soldier's loyalty, honor, and courage when he risked his life in Athens's wars, but nothing sways the Senate. Alcibiades persists, angering the senators, who banish him from Athens. Alcibiades accepts, and even relishes the banishment because it gives him ample cause to turn his army against Athens.

Act 4

Timon is out of money and out of his mind. He leaves Athens, and outside the city, he rails against the world. He has nothing, not even food, so he digs for roots to eat. While digging, he uncovers buried treasure — gold, gold, and more gold. Gold is useless to him because he can't eat it, but he isn't so mad that he forgets the value of gold, so when someone approaches, he hides the treasure.

Alcibiades and his army march against Athens. He has heard about Timon's afflictions and offers friendship to him, but Timon now hates all people. Alcibiades offers money, but Timon refuses. Instead, Timon offers gold to Alcibiades. He wants to pay Alcibiades to "be as a planetary plague" (4.3.110) and kill everyone he meets. Alcibiades takes the gold to pay his troops, and then he heads off to conquer Athens.

Bandits have heard of Timon's wealth, and they want to rob him. In a surprise role reversal, Timon freely gives them gold and encourages them to keep stealing, to defy the law. Timon wants everyone else to be as miserable as he is. He wants the bandits to go to Athens and "cut throats" (4.3.447) and "break open shops" (4.3.449). His words move them, but with an opposite effect. They accept the gold but will no longer be bandits.

Flavius finds Timon and tries to help him. Timon refuses at first, but relents and accepts that he has one loyal friend in the world. Nonetheless, Timon gives Flavius gold and encourages him to leave.

Act 5

Once again, Athens needs Timon, this time to defend the city from Alcibiades and his army. From Timon's point of view, no one in Athens is worth saving, but he offers one bit of advice. He has a tree that will help them. He invites any Athenian who wants to escape from Alcibiades's wrath to visit the tree and there to hang himself.

Athens has no choice but to surrender to Alcibiades. They beg for peace and lenience. To save their skins, the senators offer to turn over all the false dealers and enemies of Alcibiades and Timon. Alcibiades accepts the offer, fulfilling the dramatic need to restore order and punish the wrongdoers. It wouldn't be a true tragedy if the protagonist didn't die at the end of the play, so a soldier brings news that Timon is dead.

SEE IT

On video

1981, BBC: Jonathan Miller director, Jonathan Pryce as Timon. Not one of the BBC's best productions, but notable because it's the only performance of *Timon of Athens* available on videotape.

Titus Andronicus

Key characters:

- ✔ Titus Andronicus, a Roman general
- ✔ Saturninus, Emperor of Rome
- ✔ Bassianus, Saturninus's brother, in love with Lavinia
- ✔ Lavinia Andronicus, daughter of Titus
- ✔ Lucius Andronicus, son of Titus
- ✔ Tamora, Queen of the Goths, later Empress of Rome
- ✔ Demetrius, son of Tamora
- ✔ Chiron, son of Tamora
- ✔ Aaron, a Moor, lover of Tamora

Call it the *Roman Chainsaw Massacre*. In almost every act of this play, someone kills, rapes, or slices body parts off of someone else. Every tragedy features a few deaths, but *Titus Andronicus* is totally gross — the most gruesome play that Shakespeare wrote.

Act 1

Following the usual pattern for Shakespeare's plays, the first act introduces the heroes and villains. Titus Andronicus, being the title character, is the tragic hero. His children are also heroes, and all but one will die by the end of the play. Titus bemoans the 21 sons he lost in battle, but four remain alive, as does his only daughter, Lavinia. She greets him in his triumphant return to Rome after conquering the Goths (the villains). Also on the heroes' side are Bassianus, the younger son of the late emperor, and Marcus Andronicus, Titus's brother.

For the villains, Shakespeare offers Saturninus, elder son of the late emperor. The really nasty villains, though, are Tamora, queen of the Goths, and Aaron, her lover. Tamora has raised her three sons — Alarbus, Demetrius, and Chiron — so they follow the family traditions of rape, murder, and mayhem.

The first act starts quickly: The people of Rome want Titus to be their new emperor, but he makes Saturninus the Emperor of Rome to preserve the natural order. (See Chapter 2 for more on natural order in Shakespeare's universe.) Saturninus is a sore winner, though, and continues to feud with his younger brother, Bassianus. Saturninus tries to take Lavinia (Titus's daughter) from Bassianus, but he fails. Titus sides with Saturninus against the rest of his family, killing one of his sons in the skirmish. The Andronicus family reconciles by the end of the act, however.

Tamora, the evil Gothic queen, gets off the starting block quickly and seduces newly made Emperor Saturninus. Titus brought Tamora and the other Goths to Rome as prisoners, but Saturninus frees them and then marries Tamora. Thus she rises from prisoner to Empress of Rome, and the first act isn't even over yet. Despite her newfound status, she remembers her humiliation as Titus's prisoner and vows revenge on him and his family. Remember, this is a tragedy — many bodies will fall, but you can rest assured that she and the other Goths will get their just desserts in the end.

The body-count score at the end of the act is 1 to 1: The heroes sacrificed Tamora's eldest son, but the villains incited the rift in the Andronicus family (over Lavinia), which resulted in one son's death.

Act 2

Aaron and Tamora's remaining sons, Chiron and Demetrius, get an early start on their troublemaking. They kill Bassianus and drag off his new wife, Lavinia, to ravish her. Not content with rape, Chiron and Demetrius also cut out Lavinia's tongue so that she can't tell anyone what happened. They cut off her hands so that she can't write anything, either.

Aaron shows himself to be a master trickster. He frames two of Titus's sons for the murder of Bassianus. Saturninus forgets his past differences with his brother and sentences Titus's sons to death. The score: Heroes, 1, Villains, 4 (plus two hands).

Act 3

Titus tries in vain to free his two condemned sons. The last son tries to rescue his siblings but fails. He is banished from Rome as punishment. Titus and his banished son meet Titus's brother, Marcus, who found Lavinia. Naturally, they are upset when they see Lavinia without her tongue or hands.

Figure 15-5:
Brian Cox
and Peter
Polycarpou
in *Titus
Andronicus.*

Aaron has another trick up his sleeve. He announces that the emperor will spare the lives of the two condemned sons if Titus or any other relative will chop off one of his own hands. Aaron chops off Titus's hand, but you quickly learn that it was just a trick. A messenger returns Titus's hand and delivers the severed heads of Titus's two sons. Out of 25 sons, 24 are dead and one is banished. His daughter is in sorry shape, so it's no wonder that Titus goes a little crazy.

The score becomes more lopsided: Heroes, 1, Villains, 6 (plus three hands).

Act 4

Without a tongue or hands, Lavinia has trouble communicating. She opens a book to a story that tells of a girl who is raped, thus revealing her terrible ordeal. By grasping a stick in her mouth, she writes two names in the dirt: Chiron and Demetrius. Titus plots revenge, but he is clearly off his rocker. He shoots arrows at the emperor's palace and behaves erratically, adding a comic element to an otherwise grim play.

To keep the body count as high as possible, Shakespeare arranges for a few more deaths. Tamora gives birth to a child, but the father is Aaron, not Saturninus. Aaron takes custody of the child, but not before he kills

Tamora's nurse to preserve the secret. An innocent fool happens to wander into the wrong scene at the wrong time, and Saturninus executes him. The official score still stands at Heroes, 1, Villains, 6 (plus three hands) because the two people killed in this act were neutral characters, not from the heroes' team.

Act 5

The last son of Titus, Lucius Andronicus, has been busy. After he was banished from Rome, he returned to the Goths and raised an army. He is now leading the army against Rome to seek revenge against Saturninus.

Everyone thinks that Titus is totally mad, but he's also crafty. Tamora is working her plans of revenge, but she underestimates Titus. Titus tricks and captures Tamora's sons. He kills them, cooks them for dinner, and serves them as the main course at a banquet he holds for the emperor and empress.

Titus publicly kills his daughter Lavinia. She has suffered a fate worse than death, so this is a mercy killing. Titus then announces who the main course was. Before Tamora can react, however, he kills her. This upsets Saturninus, who kills Titus. Lucius sees his father cut down and kills Saturninus. Lucius is his only remaining son, so the people of Rome crown him emperor. He sentences Aaron to a grisly death, and the curtain falls on a stage littered with bodies.

The final score: Heroes, 4, Villains, 7. But the heroes win anyway because they are the only ones alive at the end.

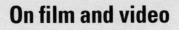

On film and video

✔ 1999, Clear Blue Sky Productions: Julie Taymor director and Anthony Hopkins as Titus. Look for this film in late 1999.

✔ 1985, BBC: Jane Howell director, Trevor Peacock as Titus, Anna Calder-Marshall as Lavinia, and Edward Hardwicke as Marcus.

Antony and Cleopatra

Legend

⬦	Home run: Marries	⊗	Deposed	⊗	Own goal: Commits suicide
☺	Victorious in battle	B	Betrays a friend	.	Appears in scene
☹	Defeated in battle	P	Makes a prophecy	"	Famous quote

Characters, in order of appearance

Act						1								2							3														4															5	
Scene	1	2	3	4	5	1	2	3	4	5	6	7	1	2	3	4	5	6	7	1	2	3	4	5	6	7	8	9	10	11	12	13	1	2	3	4	5	6	7	8	9	10	11	12	13	14	15	1	2
1 Cleopatra, Queen of Egypt																																																	
2 Mark Antony, Triumvir of Rome																																																	
3 Charmian, servant to Cleopatra																																																	
4 Soothsayer																																																	
5 Iras, servant to Cleopatra																																																	
6 Mardian, a eunuch attending Cleopatra																																																	
7 Enobarbus, follower of Antony																																																	
8 Octavius Caesar, Triumvir of Rome																																																	
9 Lepidus, Triumvir of Rome																																																	

Coriolanus

Legend

☺	Victorious in battle	F	Foul: Attacks someone	↑	Sent to penalty box: Banished
☹	Defeated in battle	S	Sacked: Victim of an attack	.	Appears in scene
C	Involved in a conspiracy	X	Ejected from game: Dies	"	Famous quote

Characters, in order of appearance

Act	1										2			3			4							5					
Scene	1	2	3	4	5	6	7	8	9	10	1	2	3	1	2	3	1	2	3	4	5	6	7	1	2	3	4	5	6
1 Menenius Agrippa																													
2 Caius Martius — Coriolanus																													
3 Cominius, a general																													
4 Lartius, a Roman general																													
5 Sicinius, a tribune																													
6 Brutus, a tribune																													
7 Tullus Aufidius																													
8 Volumnia, mother of Coriolanus																													
9 Virgilia, wife of Coriolanus																													

Hamlet

Legend

⊗	Own goal: Commits suicide	X	Ejected from game: Dies	⋔	Crowned king
F	Foul: Attacks someone	K	Strikeout: Rejected in love	✂	Challenges to a duel
S	Sacked: Victim of an attack	⊗✗	Uses a potion or poison	.	Appears in scene
M	Goes mad	✗	Visited by supernatural beings	"	Famous quote

Characters, in order of appearance

	Act	1					2		3				4						5	
	Scene	1	2	3	4	5	1	2	1	2	3	4	1	2	3	4	5	6	7	1	2
1	Horatio, friend to Hamlet																				
2	Ghost of Old Hamlet																				
3	King Claudius, uncle of Hamlet																				
4	Laertes, son of Polonius																				
5	Polonius, advisor to the king																				
6	Hamlet, Prince of Denmark																				
7	Queen Gertrude, mother of Hamlet																				
8	Ophelia, daughter of Polonius																				
9	Rosencrantz, friend to Hamlet																				
10	Guildenstern, friend to Hamlet																				
11	Players																				
12	Fortinbras, Prince of Norway																				

Julius Caesar

Legend

P	Makes a prophecy
F	Foul: Attacks someone
S	Sacked: Victim of an attack
C	Involved in a conspiracy
☺	Victorious in battle
☹	Defeated in battle
⚡	Visited by supernatural beings
·	Appears in scene
"	Famous quote

Characters, in order of appearance

Act	1			2				3			4			5				
Scene	1	2	3	1	2	3	4	1	2	3	1	2	3	1	2	3	4	5
1 Julius Caesar																		
2 Casca, a conspirator																		
3 Calphurnia, wife of Caesar																		
4 Mark Antony																		
5 Soothsayer																		
6 Marcus Brutus, a conspirator																		
7 Cassius, a conspirator																		
8 Cicero, a senator																		
9 Cinna, a conspirator																		
10 Metellus, a conspirator																		
11 Trebonius, a conspirator																		
12 Decius Brutus, a conspirator																		
13 Portia, wife of Brutus																		
14 Cinna, a poet																		
15 Octavius Caesar																		
16 Lepidus																		

King Lear

Legend

F	Foul: Attacks someone	M	Goes mad	⚔	Challenges to a duel
S	Sacked: Victim of an attack	X	Ejected from game: Dies	.	Appears in scene
♥	Woos a lover	B	Betrays a friend	"	Famous quote

Characters, in order of appearance

Act		1					2				3							4							5		
	Scene	1	2	3	4	5	1	2	3	4	1	2	3	4	5	6	7	1	2	3	4	5	6	7	1	2	3
1	Earl of Kent																										
2	Earl of Gloucester																										
3	Edmund, son of Gloucester																										
4	King Lear																										
5	Goneril, daughter of Lear																										
6	Cordelia, daughter of Lear																										
7	Regan, daughter of Lear																										
8	Duke of Cornwall, husband of Regan																										
9	Duke of Albany, husband of Goneril																										
10	King of France																										
11	Edgar, son of Gloucester																										
12	Oswald, steward to Goneril																										
13	Fool, attendant to King Lear																										

Macbeth

Legend

✦	Visited by supernatural beings	☺	Victorious in battle	F	Foul: Attacks someone
⌒	Crowned king	☹	Defeated in battle	.	Appears in scene
X	Ejected from game: Dies	M	Goes mad	"	Famous quote

Characters, in order of appearance

	Act																																		
		1							2				3						4			5							
	Scene	1	2	3	4	5	6	7	1	2	3	4	1	2	3	4	5	6	1	2	3	1	2	3	4	5	6	7	8	9
1	Witches																													
2	Duncan, King of Scotland																													
3	Malcolm, son of Duncan																													
4	Lenox, a Scottish lord																													
5	Rosse, a Scottish lord																													
6	Donalbain, son of Duncan																													
7	Macbeth, a Scottish general																													
8	Banquo, a Scottish general																													
9	Lady Macbeth																													
10	Fleance, son of Banquo																													
11	Porter																													
12	Macduff, a Scottish lord																													
13	Murderers																													
14	Lady Macduff																													
15	Siward, Earl of Northumberland																													

Othello

Legend

♥	Falls in love	☺	Victorious in battle	F	Foul: Attacks someone
♠	Falls out of love	☹	Defeated in battle	⊗	Own goal: Commits suicide
◇	Home run: Marries	X	Ejected from game: Dies	.	Appears in scene
J	Jealous rage	B	Betrays a friend	"	Famous quote

Characters, in order of appearance

	Act	1			2			3				4			5	
	Scene	1	2	3	1	2	3	1	2	3	4	1	2	3	1	2
1	Roderigo, duped friend to Iago															
2	Iago, Othello's ensign															
3	Brabantio, father of Desdemona															
4	Othello, the Moor															
5	Cassio, Othello's lieutenant															
6	Duke of Venice															
7	Desdemona, wife of Othello															
8	Montano, Governor of Cyprus															
9	Emilia, wife of Iago															
10	Clown															
11	Bianca, a courtesan															
12	Lodovico, kinsman of Desdemona															
13	Gratiano, kinsman of Desdemona															

Romeo and Juliet

Legend

♥	Falls in love	↑		Sent to penalty box: Banished
⟨A⟩	Home run: Marries	X		Ejected from game: Dies
!	Consummates a marriage	T		Plays a trick: Fakes own death

⊗		Own goal: Commits suicide
·		Appears in scene
"		Famous quote

Characters, in order of appearance

	Act	1					2						3					4					5		
	Scene	1	2	3	4	5	1	2	3	4	5	6	1	2	3	4	5	1	2	3	4	5	1	2	3
1 Sampson, a servant																									
2 Gregory, a servant																									
3 Tybalt, nephew of wife of Capulet																									
4 Old Capulet																									
5 Wife of Capulet																									
6 Count Paris, kinsman of the Prince																									
7 Nurse to Juliet																									
8 Juliet, daughter of Capulet																									
9 Abram, servant to Montague																									
10 Benvolio, nephew of Montague																									
11 Old Montague																									
12 Wife of Montague																									
13 Romeo, son of Montague																									
14 Mercutio, friend of Romeo																									
15 Escalus, Prince of Verona																									
16 Friar Laurence																									

Capulets (rows 1–8)
Montagues (rows 9–16)

Timon of Athens

Legend

↑$	Gives gifts, jewels, and gold	?	Seeks help
⊗	Goes bankrupt	⊘	Rejects help
M	Goes mad	X	Ejected from game: Dies
B	Betrays a friend		
.	Appears in scene		
"	Famous quote		

Characters, in order of appearance

		Act	1		2		3						4			5			
		Scene	1	2	1	2	1	2	3	4	5	6	1	2	3	1	2	3	4
1	Poet																		
2	Painter																		
3	Timon																		
4	Apemantus, a churlish philosopher																		
5	Alcibiades, an Athenian captain																		
6	Ventidius, a false friend																		
7	Lucullus, a false friend																		
8	Steward to Timon																		
9	Fool																		
10	Flaminius, servant to Timon																		
11	Lucius, a false friend																		
12	Sempronius, a false friend																		
13	Bandits																		

Titus Andronicus

Legend

X	Ejected from game: Dies	F	Foul: Attacks someone	↑	Sent to penalty box: Banished
K	Strikeout: Rejected in love	S	Sacked: Victim of an attack	↓	Returns to game: Returns from banishment
◇	Home run: Marries	⚜	Crowned emperor or empress	·	Appears in scene
⌐	Dons a disguise	◉	Shake 'n' Bake-speare	"	Famous quote

Characters, in order of appearance

		Act	1			2				3			4				5		
		Scene	1	1	2	3	4	1	2	3	4	1	2	3	4	1	2	3
1	Saturninus, son of late Emperor of Rome																	
2	Bassianus, brother of Saturninus, in love with Lavinia																	
3	Marcus Andronicus, tribune of the people, brother of Titus																	
4	Titus Andronicus, a general against the Goths																	
5	Lucius Andronicus, son of Titus																	
6	Alarbus, son of Tamora																	
7	Tamora, Queen of the Goths																	
8	Chiron, son of Tamora																	
9	Demetrius, son of Tamora																	
10	Lavinia, daughter of Titus																	
11	Mutius Andronicus, son of Titus																	
12	Martius Andronicus, son of Titus																	
13	Quintus Andronicus, son of Titus																	
14	Aaron, lover of Tamora																	
15	Nurse																	
16	Clown																	

Part V
The Other Poems

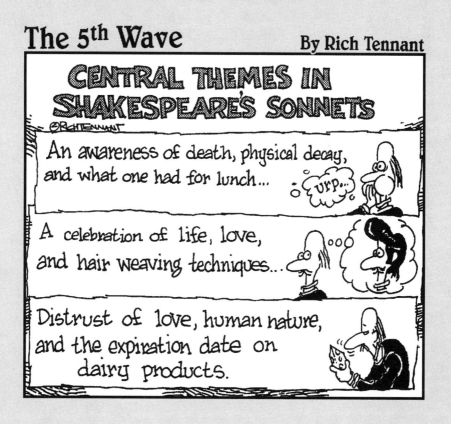

The 5th Wave   By Rich Tennant

CENTRAL THEMES IN SHAKESPEARE'S SONNETS

An awareness of death, physical decay, and what one had for lunch...   urp...

A celebration of life, love, and hair weaving techniques...

Distrust of love, human nature, and the expiration date on dairy products.

In this part . . .

Shakespeare is best known for his plays, which are a form of poetry — but he wrote other poetry, too. He borrowed the sonnet, an Italian form of love poetry, and reshaped it for the English language. He also wrote narrative poems, telling the story of Venus and her crush on Adonis and the tale of Lucrece from ancient Rome. This part tells you all about Shakespeare's "other" poetry.

Chapter 16

All About the Sonnets

A *sonnet* is a poem of 14 lines that rhyme in a particular pattern. Shakespeare used sonnets within some of his plays (especially *Love's Labour's Lost*), but his sonnets are best known as a series of 154 poems that tell a story about a young aristocrat and a mysterious mistress. This chapter tells you about the sonnets and the mysteries that surround them.

The sonnet form is one of the most difficult for a poet. The restricted pattern forces the poet to capture the maximum passion within those 14 lines. In his plays, Shakespeare was free to add subplots, use long speeches, vary the rhyme scheme, and mix prose and verse. But in the sonnets, you meet Shakespeare the master poet.

Italian and English Sonnets

The Italian poets of the Renaissance invented the sonnet form. The most famous sonneteer before Shakespeare was Petrarch, who lived in the 14th century. He wrote a series of sonnets as a kind of love story. In Petrarch's sonnets, the first eight lines describe a picture, emotion, or other complete thought. The final six lines deliver a summary or commentary on that thought or emotion.

The sonnet form was wildly popular and spread through France to England. The English sonnet flourished in the 1500s — once the sonneteers figured out how to make them rhyme. In Italian, every word ends in a vowel, which makes it easy to find rhymes. (See the section "Rhyme and Reason" for more information about rhyming in the sonnets.)

The Italian sonnet form used rhymes in the pattern *abba abba,* followed by two or three rhymes without any particular pattern. At first, the English poets tried to copy the Italian rhyme pattern, but rhyming in English is harder than rhyming in Italian. The English poets experimented with different forms and finally developed the *abab cdcd efef gg* rhyme pattern that is now known as a Shakespearean sonnet.

Shakespeare's Sonnets

Shakespeare didn't invent the style named after him, but he perfected it. One of the hallmarks of Shakespeare's sonnets is his use of the final *couplet* (two adjacent lines that rhyme), either to summarize the rest of the sonnet in two neat lines or to throw you a surprise ending. For example, Sonnet 19 bemoans the advance of "devouring time," and the poet asks time to "carve not with thy hours my love's fair brow." The surprise ending comes in the last two lines:

Yet do thy worst, old Time, despite thy wrong,

My love shall in my verse ever live young.

He used the same sonnet style when he included sonnets in his plays and in his series of 154 sonnets published in 1609. The sonnets in the series are not titled and are referred to by number. We don't know whether Shakespeare determined the order and numbering of the sonnets. You can read more about the questions surrounding the sonnets in the section "The Mystery of the Sonnets," later in this chapter.

Shakespeare the poet is also Shakespeare the playwright and vice versa. Even in the sonnets, Shakespeare cannot escape his ties to the theater. In some of the sonnets, he uses theatrical metaphors, such as the start of Sonnet 23:

As an unperfect actor on the stage,

Who with his fear is put besides his part;

Rhyme and Reason

Unlike Shakespeare's plays, which are mostly in *blank* — or unrhymed — verse, the sonnets follow a specific rhyme pattern, represented as *abab cdcd efef gg.* (The standard way to show a rhyme pattern in a poem is to use letters, where each letter represents a different rhyme at the end of a line.)

Each line follows the same rhythmic pattern that Shakespeare used in his plays — dah-DUM dah-DUM dah-DUM dah-DUM dah-DUM — called *iambic pentameter*. The rhythm of the sonnets is more striking than the rhythm usually found in his plays. That doesn't mean that you need to read the poems with a heavy beat, but you should feel the beat and how it carries you through each line. (You can read about Shakespeare's use of rhythm in Chapter 6.) Read each poem out loud to fully appreciate its beauty.

Sonnet 18 is typical of Shakespeare's sonnets:

Shall I compare thee to a summer's day?

Thou art more lovely and more temperate:

Rough winds do shake the darling buds of May,

And summer's lease hath all too short a date:

Sometime too hot the eye of heaven shines,

And often is his gold complexion dimmed;

And every fair from fair sometime declines,

By chance, or nature's changing course, untrimmed:

But thy eternal summer shall not fade,

Nor lose possession of that fair thou ow'st,

Nor shall death brag thou wander'st in his shade

When in eternal lines to time thou grow'st:

 So long as men can breathe or eyes can see,

 So long lives this, and this gives life to thee.

The first line rhymes with the third, and the second rhymes with the fourth, giving the pattern *abab*. The next set of four lines follows the same pattern, but the rhymes are different from those in the first four lines, so the pattern is *cdcd*. The third set of four lines also rhymes in the same pattern, giving *efef*. The last two lines rhyme as a couplet: *gg*.

Almost all of Shakespeare's sonnets follow this same rhyme pattern: *abab cdcd efef gg*. Only a few sonnets have different patterns — for example, Sonnet 126 has 12 lines in 6 couplets. (You can read about the rhyme patterns that Shakespeare used in his other poems in Chapter 17.)

Sometimes the lines don't really rhyme, at least to our modern ears. For example, the words *temperate* and *date* don't quite rhyme. Other sonnets contain examples of near-misses, such as the end of Sonnet 71:

O if (I say) you look upon this verse,

When I, perhaps, compounded am with clay,

Do not so much as my poor name rehearse,

But let your love even with my life decay;

    Lest the wise world should look into your moan,

    And mock you with me after I am gone.

In modern English, *moan* and *gone* do not rhyme. Scholars call this *assonance,* which is just a fancy way of saying that the words sound similar enough to use them as rhymes in a poem, even though they don't really rhyme. We don't know how Shakespeare and his contemporaries pronounced these words, but these lines give us a clue. They probably sounded much more similar 400 years ago.

The Story of the Sonnets

Shakespeare's collection of sonnets reveals a story. Most of the poems speak to a handsome young lord: advising him, admonishing him, praising him, and nagging him. The last several poems are about the poet's mistress, who apparently also became the young lord's mistress. The poet in the sonnets is not necessarily Shakespeare himself. One of the mysteries of the sonnets — which you can read more about later in this chapter — is whether they are autobiographical. Either way, you can enjoy the story and the poetry of the sonnets separately from the mystery.

The series starts with several poems that encourage the lord to settle down and have children. His youthful beauty will not last forever, and the poet urges the lord to have children so that the lord's beauty can live in his children.

The first 17 sonnets repeat this same message. Sonnet 2 is an example:

When forty winters shall besiege thy brow,

And dig deep trenches in thy beauty's field,

Thy youth's proud livery, so gazed on now,

Will be a tattered weed of small worth held:

Then being asked, where all thy beauty lies,

Where all the treasure of thy lusty days,

To say, within thine own deep-sunken eyes,

Were an all-eating shame and thriftless praise.

How much more praise deserved thy beauty's use

If thou couldst answer, 'This fair child of mine

Shall sum my count, and make my old excuse',

Proving his beauty by succession thine:

> This were to be new made when thou art old,

> And see thy blood warm when thou feel'st it cold.

Many of the early sonnets sing the praises of the young lord and express the poet's love and admiration for him. Shakespeare used *love* in this context to mean a deep friendship without any sexual connotation, as you can read in Sonnet 26, which begins like this:

Lord of my love, to whom in vassalage

Thy merit hath my duty strongly knit:

To thee I send this written embassage,

To witness duty, not to show my wit;

The story turns sour — the lord steals the poet's mistress, or maybe the mistress seduces the poet's friend. The friends contend for her, but in the end, the poet gives her up to the lord:

That thou hast her it is not all my grief,

And yet it may be said I loved her dearly;

That she hath thee is of my wailing chief,

A loss in love that touches me more nearly. (Sonnet 42)

Another crisis arises when the lord becomes patron to a rival poet. In the end, though, the young lord and poet are reconciled:

For if you were by my unkindness shaken,

As I by yours, you've passed a hell of time,

And I, a tyrant, have no leisure taken

To weigh how once I suffered in your crime.

. . .

> But that your trespass now becomes a fee;

> Mine ransoms yours, and yours must ransom me. (Sonnet 120)

Sonnets 1 through 126 tell the story of the young lord. Sonnet 127 begins a new section, this one focusing on the poet's mistress. The poet describes her as "black," which doesn't literally mean black, but darker than the standard of beauty at the time: pale and blond. The poet's description of his mistress is most interesting in Sonnet 130, which pokes fun at the exaggerations of conventional love poetry:

My mistress' eyes are nothing like the sun;

Coral is far more red than her lips' red;

If snow be white, why then her breasts are dun;

If hairs be wires, black wires grow on her head;

I have seen roses damasked, red and white,

But no such roses see I in her cheeks;

And in some perfumes is there more delight

Than in the breath that from my mistress reeks.

I love to hear her speak, yet well I know

That music hath a far more pleasing sound;

I grant I never saw a goddess go;

My mistress when she walks treads on the ground.

>   And yet, by heaven, I think my love as rare

>   As any she belied with false compare.

As you know from the first part of the sonnets, the poet loses his mistress to the young lord. He struggles with his competing interests, but it's clear which way his preferences tend:

Two loves I have, of comfort and despair,

Which, like two spirits, do suggest me still:

The better angel is a man right fair,

The worser spirit a woman coloured ill.

To win me soon to hell my female evil

Tempteth my better angel from my side,

And would corrupt my saint to be a devil,

Wooing his purity with her foul pride;

And whether that my angel be turned fiend

Suspect I may, yet not directly tell;

But being both from me both to each friend,

I guess one angel in another's hell:

>   Yet this shall I ne'er know, but live in doubt,

>   Till my bad angel fire my good one out. (Sonnet 144)

The Mystery of the Sonnets

Over the centuries, scholars have debated furiously over the identity of the lord and the mistress in the sonnets. When the sonnets were published in 1609, the dedication on the cover page addresses someone whose initials are W. H. Who is W. H.? Is he the young lord of the sonnets? Equally mysterious is whether the narrator of the sonnets is meant to be William Shakespeare — that is, did he write the sonnets as deliberate autobiography or as fiction and pure poetry?

Bootlegged poetry?

The first mystery is whether Shakespeare approved the publication of his sonnets. The first few sonnets appeared in 1599 in a volume entitled *The Passionate Pilgrim*. The publisher stole poems from several different poets, including Shakespeare, and most likely none of the poets gave their permission. In 1609, the full collection of Shakespeare's 154 poems was published by Thomas Thorpe. (Also in the same book is *A Lover's Complaint*, which you can read about in Chapter 17.)

The dedication to the sonnets reads, "To the only begetter of these ensuing sonnets. Mr. W. H." Shakespeare's name does not appear at all. Some people believe that Shakespeare wrote the sonnets as private messages and as poems to be shared among friends, and that he never intended them to be published or read by the general public. The sonnets feel intimate and private. No names are ever mentioned (except in Sonnets 135 and 136, which contain puns on the name Will). Reading the sonnets, you feel as though you are intruding on a private conversation, albeit a one-sided conversation in rhymed verse.

Other scholars believe that Shakespeare approved the publication of the sonnets. Many poets published their own series of sonnets, telling stories of love won and love refused. The sonnet as a poetical form reached its height of popularity in England around the middle of the 1590s, which is when Shakespeare was writing his sonnets. Shakespeare was a poet as well as a playwright, so it's natural that he would want to show off his skill at sonnet writing.

Most likely, Shakespeare approved the printing of his sonnets and determined the order in which the sonnets appear. For the most part, the sonnets tell a coherent story, which tends to indicate the author's involvement in their printing.

Who are they?

The identities of the patron, W. H., the young lord, and the mistress remain unknown. W. H. might even be a typographical error for W. S. — that is, the printer dedicated the book to the author, William Shakespeare. The two most likely candidates for W. H. are William Herbert, Earl of Pembroke, and Henry Wriothesley (probably pronounced "RIZE-ly"), Earl of Southampton.

✔ The First Folio, published in 1623, was dedicated to William Herbert. He was an avid supporter of the theater and of Shakespeare, so he might be the W. H. of the sonnets.

✔ In 1593 and 1594, Shakespeare dedicated his narrative poems (*Venus and Adonis* and *Lucrece,* which you can read about in Chapter 17) to Henry Wriothesley. Wriothesley was a generous patron of Shakespeare and other poets. With a simple reversal of the initials, he could be W. H.

Knowing the identity of W. H. is one thing, but figuring out the identity of the young lord is more difficult. First of all, is W. H. the young lord, or are they separate people? William Herbert and Henry Wriothesley had scandalous affairs, not unlike the young lord of the sonnets. Herbert's mistress was Mary Fitton. She had many lovers and illegitimate children. Despite her social position as the daughter of a knight and maid of honor to Queen Elizabeth, she carried on with men of all ranks, above and below her in social standing. Some people believe that she is also the dark mistress of the sonnets, the mistress the young lord (perhaps William Herbert) stole from the poet.

Henry Wriothesley had his own scandal when Elizabeth Vernon became pregnant by him. He was forced to marry her, which they did in secret. When Queen Elizabeth learned of the affair, she ordered the couple imprisoned for a short time. If Wriothesley is the lord mentioned in the sonnets, the identity of the dark lady is unknown. Elizabeth Vernon was no Mary Fitton and was not likely anyone's mistress — except Wriothesley's.

The third possibility is that the sonnets are not strictly autobiographical, and that the young lord is not a specific person. Shakespeare did not pay close attention to true history when writing his history plays, and it stands to reason that he took artistic license when writing the sonnets, too. We expect poetry to be artistic and free, not constrained to actual people and events, and perhaps it's best to give Shakespeare the same freedom we allow other poets. If you love a good mystery, it's fun to try to track down the dark lady and the young lord of the sonnets, but you can also read and appreciate the sonnets on their own terms.

Chapter 17
Narrative and Other Poems

- -

In This Chapter

▶ *Venus and Adonis* tells a tale from classical mythology

▶ *The Rape of Lucrece* tells a story from ancient Rome

▶ Other poems talk about love

- -

Shakespeare the poet is best known for his sonnets, but he wrote other nondramatic poetry, too. In particular, he wrote and published two long, narrative poems: *Venus and Adonis* and *The Rape of Lucrece* (also known simply as *Lucrece*). The stories for these poems come from ancient Greece and Rome; Shakespeare's interest in the classics is evident in his poems and plays. He also wrote two other poems about love: love gone awry *(A Lover's Complaint)* and love among the birds *(The Phoenix and Turtle)*. This chapter summarizes the long poems and tells you about each of the nondramatic poems.

Shakespeare the Poet

The first published work to identify William Shakespeare as the author was *Venus and Adonis,* in 1593. A year later, Shakespeare published his second narrative poem, *The Rape of Lucrece.* He dedicated these poems to Henry Wriothesley (probably pronounced "RIZE-ly"), Earl of Southampton. (Read more about Wriothesley and his possible connection to the sonnets in Chapter 16.)

Another narrative poem, *A Lover's Complaint,* was published in 1609 with Shakespeare's sonnets, and *The Phoenix and Turtle* was published in 1601 as part of *Love's Martyr,* by Robert Chester, who included poems by several poets.

Shakespeare also included poems and songs in his plays. *Love's Labour's Lost,* for example, includes several sonnets worked into the dialogue and as separate poems in love letters that the characters write to each other.

The distinction between a poet and a playwright was not as clear-cut for Shakespeare as it is today. Most plays were written in verse, and before Shakespeare's day, plays often used rhymed verse instead of blank verse. In other words, a play was a kind of poem.

In Shakespeare's day (and today), the public didn't flock to poetry readings. As a playwright, Shakespeare had a steady job, writing about two plays every year. He later became part-owner of the Globe Theatre. Small outbreaks of the plague sometimes closed the theaters in London, and during one of those times, Shakespeare wrote *Venus and Adonis,* possibly while living at home in Stratford-upon-Avon. When the theaters opened again, he was hard at work on his plays. After publishing *Lucrece,* he probably didn't have time for his nondramatic work. His plays paid the bills in a way that his other poetry never could.

Venus and Adonis

The story of *Venus and Adonis* comes from classical mythology, although Shakespeare modified the tale to suit his needs. The poem is more than 1,000 lines long, written in stanzas of 6 lines that rhyme in the pattern *ababcc.* (Each letter represents a line. In other words, alternating lines rhyme in the first four lines of each stanza, and the last two lines rhyme as a couplet.)

Venus, the goddess of love, falls in love with Adonis, a mortal. She dotes on him, but he does not return her love. He tries to ride away on his horse, but his horse smells a nearby mare and runs away with its own thoughts of love. Venus continues to implore Adonis, who continues to resist. In despair, Venus falls over, apparently dead. Adonis tries to revive her; when he kisses her, she comes to. She misinterprets his kiss and falls all over him, but he leaves her to go hunting. She urges him not to hunt ferocious and dangerous creatures, such as bears and boars. He loves the hunt as much as Venus loves him, so he goes off to hunt boars anyway. A boar kills him, and Venus mourns over his body. His body dissolves away, replaced by a beautiful, sweet-smelling flower.

The poetry is rich and ornate, full of emotion and erotic imagery. For example:

Even as an empty eagle, sharp by fast,

Tires with her beak on feathers, flesh and bone,

Shaking her wings, devouring all in haste,

Till either gorge be stuff'd or prey be gone:

    Even so she kissed his brow, his cheek, his chin,

    And where she ends she doth anew begin.

Forc'd to content, but never to obey,

Panting he lies and breatheth in her face.

She feedeth on the steam as on a prey,

And calls it heavenly moisture, air of grace,

> Wishing her cheeks were gardens full of flowers,

> So they were dew'd with such distilling showers. (55–66)

Shakespeare was clearly aware that the unbridled, lusty nature of *Venus and Adonis* would raise eyebrows in some circles. In the dedication, he wrote that he would "take advantage of all idle hours" to produce "some graver labour." His atonement was to write *The Rape of Lucrece*.

The Rape of Lucrece

The poem *The Rape of Lucrece* tells a story from ancient Rome. It takes place shortly before the story of *Coriolanus* (see the summary in Chapter 15), well before the time of Julius Caesar. The poem is almost 2,000 lines long, written in stanzas of seven lines, with the rhyme scheme of *ababbcc,* called *rhyme royal.*

The poem begins with a prose "argument" that sets the stage. Lucretia is the wife of Collatinus (Collatine), a Roman lord. Sextus Tarquinius (Tarquin) is the son of the king of Rome. Tarquin and his pals decide to attack the town of Ardea, and one night during the siege, they sit around the fire and discuss their wives. Each one claims to have the best, most virtuous wife. They decide on a test. They head back to Rome and check up on their wives. Only Lucretia is at home, dutifully working. The other wives are dancing and carousing. The men congratulate Collatine and hand him the victory. Tarquin, however, is jealous of Collatine and his beautiful, virtuous wife. He makes his excuses and heads back to Rome with evil intentions. That's where the actual poem starts.

Tarquin visits Lucretia, who invites him in — knowing that he's the son of the king and a friend of her husband. He makes up an excuse for his being there and spends the evening regaling her with stories of Collatine and his bravery. The night closes in, and Lucrece asks the servants to prepare a bed for Tarquin.

In the middle of the night, Tarquin goes to Lucrece's room and ogles her beauty. He debates his base lust versus her virtue, but in the end lust wins. He decides that he must have her. He wakes her up, and she demands to know what he's doing. He explains that he means to rape her. If she resists, he will kill her and a servant, tossing the servant's body into her bed. He would then claim to have seen them in bed together.

She pleads for mercy, for pity, for decency, but to no avail. He rapes her and leaves. Needless to say, Lucrece is distraught. The act dishonors her, but it also dishonors her husband, the innocent Collatine. Her first inclination is to kill herself, but she realizes the importance of telling her husband the truth of what happened. She dispatches a message to summon immediately her husband, her father, and others.

Her husband and the others arrive to find Lucrece dressed in mourning. She tells them what happened but does not yet say who did it. First, she asks for an oath of revenge, which they all readily swear. She reveals the perpetrator and then kills herself. They bear her body through Rome, telling the story of her rape, until all of Rome rises against Tarquin.

The poem ends there. This event drove Tarquin out of Rome, wresting control from his family and ending the reign of kings.

Where *Venus and Adonis* treats love romantically, *Lucrece* treats it tragically. The language is no less rich, but it has a decidedly different tone. You can see the difference, for example, when the poem describes Lucrece asleep in her bed:

Without the bed her other fair hand was,

On the green coverlet; whose perfect white

Show'd like an April daisy on the grass,

With pearly sweat resembling dew of night.

Her eyes like marigolds had sheathed their light,

    And canopied in darkness sweetly lay,

      Till they might open to adorn the day.

Her hair like golden threads play'd with her breath:

O modest wantons, wanton modesty!

Showing life's triumph in the map of death,

And death's dim look in life's mortality.

Each in her sleep themselves so beautify,

    As if between them twain there were no strife,

      But that life liv'd in death and death in life. (393–406)

The dark mood is reminiscent of Shakespeare's great tragedies. You can imagine how Shakespeare might have written a play about Lucrece to add to his other Roman tragedies: *Antony and Cleopatra, Coriolanus, Julius Caesar,* and *Titus Andronicus.*

The Phoenix and Turtle

This strange poem has no title, so modern scholars usually call it *The Phoenix and Turtle,* where *Turtle* is a turtledove, not a reptile with a hard shell. The poem appears in a collection of poems printed in 1601 under the title *Love's Martyr.* The book includes poems from several authors, including this one of Shakespeare's. The poem is written in four-line stanzas that rhyme *abab* (called *quatrains*) and ends with five three-line stanzas that rhyme *aaa.* Each line has only eight syllables, with the stress on the first syllable, making the poem sound more like a song.

The poem describes the love between a phoenix and a turtledove. (A *phoenix* is a mythical bird that dies a fiery death every 500 years, only to be reborn from its ashes.) Even in death, the phoenix and turtledove were together — consumed by the flame of the phoenix. It's a strange poem, with an unusual verse form and subject matter.

Hearts remote, yet not asunder;

Distance and no space was seen

'Twixt the Turtle and his queen:

But in them it were a wonder.

So between them love did shine

That the Turtle saw his right

Flaming in the Phoenix' sight;

Either was the other's mine. (29–36)

The latter part of the poem is entitled *Threnos,* or funeral song. It has a different verse structure than the earlier part of the poem:

To this urn let those repair

That are either true or fair:

For these dead birds sigh a prayer. (64–66)

Shakespeare wrote several songs in his plays, but *The Phoenix and Turtle* is the only one that stands alone. It shows us a glimpse of Shakespeare the poet separate from Shakespeare the playwright.

Shakespeare or not Shakespeare?

The only works that Shakespeare published deliberately seem to be *Venus and Adonis* and *The Rape of Lucrece*. He may have published his sonnets, but that's less clear. As you can read in Chapter 12, scholars aren't always sure which plays he wrote. The difficulty, 400 years after the fact, is to sift through the historical evidence and try to determine which plays and poems are truly Shakespeare's work and which are not.

Modern scholars rely on two kinds of evidence: internal and external. Internal evidence means examining the actual texts for clues about the author; external evidence includes everything other than the actual text of the play or poem.

Shakespearean scholars piece together many clues to come to their conclusions. Many papers have been lost to fire and time, but many other records have survived. In particular, the Stationers' Register records many publication details that are helpful to modern literary detectives. The Stationers' Company was the guild of printers and publishers. They held a monopoly on the printing business in London, and their Register recorded all the works they published. Sometimes, the Register also recorded performances of plays.

Other people wrote letters, diaries, essays, and other works that give additional clues. For example, Thomas Heywood objected to the inclusion of some of his poems in *The Passionate*

Pilgrim. He wrote about the "manifest injury" done to him. His argument lends credence to the belief that the printer also took Shakespeare's work without permission.

For internal evidence, scholars examine the words, meter, rhyme, subject matter, and more. For example, scholars have analyzed all the poems in *The Passionate Pilgrim*. Some are clearly Shakespeare's — stolen from his sonnets or from *Love's Labour's Lost*. Other poems are the work of other poets, but we don't know the authors of those remaining poems. By examining the poetry, you can see clearly that Shakespeare is not the author. For example, poem 15 starts

> It was a lordling's daughter, the fairest one of three,
>
> That liked of her master as well as well might be,
>
> Till looking on an Englishman, the fairest that eye could see,
>
>> Her fancy fell a-turning.

The verse is clumsy and clearly not Shakespeare's work. Other works are not so easy to classify. If you want to know more about the debates surrounding Shakespeare's authorship, read the notes that accompany your edition of his plays and poetry. Different editors have different opinions, but they all discuss the controversies and disputes that surround Shakespeare's works.

A Lover's Complaint

A Lover's Complaint appeared in the same volume as the sonnets. (You can read about the sonnets in Chapter 16.) Just as we are not sure whether Shakespeare approved the publication of the sonnets, we cannot be sure about *A Lover's Complaint*. Unlike the sonnets, however, Shakespeare had no reason to refrain from publishing this poem.

The poem is shorter than the other narrative poems, at slightly more than 300 lines. It uses the same structure as *The Rape of Lucrece* — that is, seven-line stanzas that rhyme *ababbcc* (*known as rhyme royal*).

The poet tells the story from his own point of view. He happens on a disheveled girl who is tearing papers and breaking rings and things and casting them away. She was once beautiful, but sorrow has erased most — but not all — of her former self. She tells her story to the poet: the story of a handsome young man.

The young man flirted with all the maids. Unlike many of her friends, the girl telling the story did not fall prey to his charm. He pursued her, plying her with gifts, fair words, promises, and even tears. In the end, he won her over. Once he triumphed over her chastity, he left her. She laments how, once burned, she would again fall for the same fair-seeming words, false protestations, and insincere promises:

'O, that infected moisture of his eye!

O, that false fire which in his cheek so glowed!

O, that forced thunder from his heart did fly!

O, that sad breath his spongy lungs bestowed!

O, all that borrowed motion, seeming owed,

Would yet again betray the fore-betrayed,

And new pervert a reconciled maid.' (323–29)

Some scholars doubted that Shakespeare wrote *A Lover's Complaint,* but the recent consensus is that Shakespeare wrote the poem and agreed to its publication.

The Passionate Pilgrim

The Passionate Pilgrim is a book of collected poems from many authors, including Shakespeare. The printer claimed that the poems were written by "W. Shakespeare," but only 5 of the 20 were Shakespeare's. Thomas Heywood complained about the inclusion of his poems, and most likely, the printer misappropriated all the poems.

The printer apparently took two sonnets and another poem from privately circulating copies of *Love's Labour's Lost.* Two other poems are similar to Sonnets 138 and 144. He took Nathaniel's sonnet, which begins like this:

If love make me forsworn, how shall I swear to love?

Ah! never faith could hold, if not to beauty vow'd;

Though to myself forsworn, to thee I'll faithful prove:

Those thoughts to me were oaks, to thee like osiers bow'd. (*Love's Labour's Lost,* 4.2.106–9)

The printer also used Longaville's sonnet to Maria and Dumain's poem to Katharine, both from Act 4, scene 3.

Part VI
The Part of Tens

The 5th Wave   By Rich Tennant

"I know you're all classically trained actors, but I don't think the public's ready for Titus Andronicus performed by the cast of Stomp."

In this part . . .

Nay, it is ten times strange! (*Measure for Measure* 5.1.45)

*I*f you've read this book from the start, it's time for a break. If you prefer, you can jump straight into the strange part of Shakespeare: the fun and funky lists. Find out about innovative adaptations of Shakespeare's plays, discover Shakespeare's birthplace . . . in Japan, or pop back through history and discover the top Shakespearean actors of all time.

Chapter 18

The Ten Best Places to Watch Shakespeare's Plays

. . . .

S hakespeare wrote plays for performance, not literature for silent study. So now that you're all fired up and ready to watch some Shakespeare, where do you go? This chapter lists (in no particular order) the best places to watch Shakespeare's (and others') plays.

The Royal Shakespeare Company, Stratford-upon-Avon

You can't discuss Shakespeare without mentioning the Royal Shakespeare Company. What is now the RSC started as the Shakespeare Memorial Theatre in Stratford-upon-Avon in 1879. The theater burned down in 1926, and a new building opened in 1932. It was improved in 1945 and soon saw a series of top-notch artists and plays. In 1961, the Shakespeare Memorial Theatre became the Royal Shakespeare Company, under the direction of Peter Hall.

The RSC built two additional theaters in Stratford, so you can now enjoy plays at any of the following venues:

- ✔ **The Royal Shakespeare Theatre** is the new name for the Shakespeare Memorial Theatre. This large, conventional theater is home to many of the greatest performances of Shakespeare's plays in modern times.

- ✔ **The Swan Theatre** opened in 1986 at the location of the original Memorial Theatre. The design is similar to that of an Elizabethan theater, but with the advantage of having a roof to protect the actors and audience from the weather. The name comes from the original Swan Theatre, which was one of the Globe's competitors. In keeping with this spirit, at the new Swan Theatre, the RSC often performs plays written by Shakespeare's contemporaries.

✔ **The Other Place** is a small space best known for its ground-breaking productions of new work and classical texts. In 1974, the RSC performed risky and experimental plays at a small theater in London called The Place. Naturally, when they opened an experimental theater in Stratford, they named it The Other Place.

The company aims to put together the very best of British theater talent, producing a large number of plays in the repertoire each year. The RSC also tours throughout the United Kingdom and abroad, even performing Shakespeare in Pakistan.

If you visit, be sure to take a backstage tour or listen to a post-show talk. Stratford-upon-Avon has other attractions and excellent dining facilities as well.

Note: The Royal Shakespeare Company is distinct from the National Theatre, which is a theater in London founded by Sir Laurence Olivier.

The New Globe Theatre, London

It took an American actor, Sam Wanamaker, to found the Shakespeare Globe Trust in 1970 and lead the effort to build a replica of the Globe Theatre (see Figure 18-1) near the location of the original. His performances in Shakespeare's plays were famous in the United States and the United Kingdom. When he visited London in 1949, he was disappointed that he could not find a suitable memorial to England's greatest playwright, so he arranged to have one built himself.

Wanamaker's efforts to build a replica of the Globe Theatre were greatly enhanced in 1989 when construction workers accidentally discovered the foundation of the original Globe Theatres. (There were two Globe Theatres. Shakespeare used the first one, which burned down in 1613. It was rebuilt soon after and used for several decades before being torn down in a fit of Puritanical excess in 1644.) Construction on the replica began in 1993, but Wanamaker died before he could see the final fruition of his dream. In 1997, the New Globe Theatre opened with *King Henry V,* which is believed to have been the opening play for the original Globe Theatre.

The Trust now supports the International Shakespeare Globe Centre, near the site of the original Globe Theatre. The Centre comprises three ventures, all supporting education and the enjoyment of the works of Shakespeare and his contemporaries:

Figure 18-1:
The replica
of the Globe
Theatre,
near the
site of the
original.

- ✔ **The Globe Theatre** is the replica of Shakespeare's theater. It hosts a summer season of plays by Shakespeare, his contemporaries, and others, including plays commissioned expressly for performance in this unique setting.

- ✔ **Globe Education** works with students of all ages, exploring Shakespeare's plays and their relationship to the stages for which he wrote them.

- ✔ **The Globe Exhibition** is a continuation of the Bear Gardens museum, which Wanamaker opened in 1972 as a theatrical museum devoted to Shakespeare and his contemporaries.

Also on the site is an indoor theater built to a design by Inigo Jones, who was an architect and scene designer in Shakespeare's day. The indoor theater seats about 300, and the design is probably similar to that of the Blackfriars, for which Shakespeare wrote some of his later plays. The theater temporarily houses the Globe Exhibition. The Shakespeare Globe Trust is still raising money to complete the interior and open the theater for performances.

The New York Shakespeare Festival

Because New York City is well-known for its high cost of living, especially for theater tickets, you may be surprised to learn that its Shakespeare Festival is free! Joseph Papp started the Shakespeare Workshop in 1954 with the goal of promoting interest in Shakespeare. In 1962, the city built the Delacorte Theater in Central Park as a permanent home for the newly renamed New York Shakespeare Festival. In 1967, the city built the Public Theater as a year-round home. The Public Theater has hosted many different kinds of plays, but the highlight for many theater-goers is still Shakespeare, often called Shakespeare in Central Park.

Papp felt that it was important to bring the highest quality theater to as broad a public as possible, so the festival has always been free, with tickets given out the day of the performance on a first-come, first-served basis. The season for Shakespeare in Central Park is June through August and includes plays by Shakespeare and others.

The festival has often lived up to Papp's dream, drawing top performers and directors, including Michelle Pfeiffer as Olivia and Jeff Goldblum as Malvolio in a recent production of *Twelfth Night* and Patrick Stewart as Prospero in *The Tempest*.

The Stratford Shakespeare Festival, Stratford, Ontario, Canada

If you live in a town called Stratford, it's natural to think of Shakespeare, even if that town is in Canada. In 1953, the founder of the Stratford Shakespeare Festival (in Ontario), Tom Patterson, invited Tyrone Guthrie to direct *King Richard III*. Alec Guiness played the title role, and the stage was set for success. A permanent theater was built in 1957 and renovated in 1997, with seating for almost 2,000 people. The productions continued to bring in stars for the major roles while training and building an ensemble of local talent who later took on the major roles themselves, including Christopher Plummer as Henry V.

The festival continued to grow and added plays by other playwrights. It also took plays on tours across Canada. In 1963, it opened a second theater, the Avon, which seats 1,100 people. And in 1971, it opened a small, experimental theater that it renamed in 1991 in honor of Patterson. By 1978, the festival had produced Shakespeare's entire canon.

The Stratford Shakespeare Festival recorded some of its recent stage productions. It's difficult to find the videotapes outside of Canada, but you can find *Romeo and Juliet* and several comedies if you search hard enough.

The Open Air Theatre, Regent's Park, London

The Open Air Theatre has operated for more than 60 years in Regent's Park, London. In 1963, operation of the theater changed hands, and the company adopted its new name, The New Shakespeare Company. An outdoor theater in London means that you must contend with rain, but it also means that you get to watch top Shakespearean actors and directors. The early days saw Vivien Leigh, Deborah Kerr, and Jessica Tandy; more recently, Ralph Fiennes played Lysander in *A Midsummer Night's Dream*.

The theater is a sweeping amphitheater similar to a Greek outdoor theater. It has a main seating block, going off to grassy banks on the sides where you can even enjoy a bottle of wine while watching a performance. With both banks full, it can seat more than 1,200 people, making it one of the largest theaters in London.

The season usually includes at least one of the more popular plays, one of the less-performed of Shakespeare's plays, and also a musical (not necessarily influenced by Shakespeare). The season runs from late May to early September. Get your tickets well in advance, because the shows are extremely popular and very much a part of the London summer season.

The Oregon Shakespeare Festival, Ashland, Oregon

Angus Bowmer started the Oregon Shakespeare Festival in 1935. Except for a break during World War II, this festival has been running every year since. Every year, the festival produces four or five of Shakespeare's plays and has expanded to include other playwrights and plays. Every play of Shakespeare's has been performed at the festival at least three times.

There are three theaters at the site:

✔ **The Elizabethan Stage** is an outdoor theater, built in 1950 as a replica of the Fortune Theatre. (The Fortune was one of the Globe's competitors. The original contract for its construction has survived and is the model for several modern re-creations.) The theater seats about 1,200. Performances are in the evening, using modern theatrical lighting. The festival uses the Elizabethan Stage primarily for Shakespeare's works.

✔ **The Angus Bowmer Theater** opened in 1970. It's an indoor theater seating about 600. Performances include plays of all kinds, including Shakespeare's. Some plays premiere in the Bowmer Theater.

✔ **The Black Swan** is a tiny theater seating about 120. It's home to experimental and risky productions, including occasional performances of Shakespeare's plays adapted for the small setting.

The Oregon Shakespeare Festival has earned an international reputation for the excellence of its productions. The emphasis is on ensemble acting, without relying on big-name stars. The season runs from February through October. The Elizabethan stage is open only during the summer, however. Contrary to Oregon's popular image as a wet and rainy locale, hot, dry weather is the norm during the summer (but if you go, be prepared for anything).

Plan your trips to Ashland well in advance. During the summer, most shows are sold out. Travel agents can arrange packages of tickets, travel, and lodging. Ashland is far from any population center, but it's close to many other exciting destinations, including towering redwood forests, white-water rafting, skiing (for the early season), and the ocean.

Japan

Shakespeare has universal appeal, and you can find Shakespeare theaters and festivals throughout the United States, Europe, and the world. Japan has a particular fondness for the Bard.

Not far from Tokyo, at the end of the Boso Peninsula, is the Shakespeare Country Park. This theme park features replicas of several buildings in Stratford-upon-Avon. Julian Bicknell, who has overseen the restoration of numerous historic sites in England, designed the buildings in the park.

The park's features include

✔ New Place, which was Shakespeare's home in Stratford after he retired from the stage. The historic New Place was destroyed in the 18th century, so the reconstruction is conjectural.

✔ A faithful reproduction of Shakespeare's birthplace in Stratford.

✔ A replica of the home of Shakespeare's mother (Mary Arden), who lived near Stratford-upon-Avon. You can visit her restored home in England.

The park grounds are styled after Elizabethan landscaping, with an herb garden. The building construction uses historic techniques and timber imported from England.

The Tsubouchi Memorial Theatre Museum at Waseda University, Tokyo, is modeled on the Fortune Theatre, albeit built to modern earthquake standards. The museum encompasses all of theater history — Japanese and non-Japanese, including Shakespeare. Performances and lectures at the museum include Shakespeare plays performed by local actors and touring companies.

Your Local Theater

Shakespeare's plays are a staple of school, community, amateur, and professional theaters everywhere. You shouldn't expect the likes of Laurence Olivier in a community production, but that doesn't mean that you have to settle for bad productions. Many schools and community theaters perform simply and honestly, which is more important than stars and special effects.

If you want to discover the true meaning within Shakespeare's plays, get involved. Show up at the auditions for the next Shakespeare play, and maybe you'll get a part. Don't worry about not having experience. Remember that Shakespeare's plays are about passion and human relations, which are universal. Relate the play to your own, everyday life. Make sure that you understand the words before you read them. Then speak the words clearly, simply, and honestly.

Some community theaters hold open play readings. You don't need to audition or perform in public. Just show up and read a play out loud in a friendly, relaxed setting. Bring your copy of the play, if you have one.

A short drive away, you can probably find a regional Shakespeare festival. These festivals cover the globe, from Australia to Austria to Austin. The seasons, theaters, and performances are as varied as the locales, but you're never too far from Shakespeare.

The Cinema

Every year sees new releases of films based on Shakespeare's plays. In recent years, Kenneth Branagh has helped spark a revival of Shakespeare on the big screen with *Much Ado About Nothing, Henry V,* and *Hamlet* (all available on videotape).

Most film versions of the plays are edited to make the plays shorter. Film is a highly visual medium, quite different from Shakespeare's bare stage at the Globe. Directors and writers often edit the scripts to make the best use of the film medium. Different directors and writers choose to omit or highlight different parts of the plays, so two different movies of, say, *Romeo and Juliet* can be wildly different. Just watch Franco Zeffirelli's lavish film from 1968 and compare it to Baz Lurhmann's modern version from 1996.

Chapter 19
Ten Everyday Phrases from Shakespeare

- -

S hakespeare influenced the English language more than any other individual. He invented new words and phrases, used old words in new ways, and helped shape the language that we speak today. Many expressions that we use every day originated in Shakespeare's plays. This chapter lists ten such phrases. As you read the plays, see if you can find others.

Brave New World

Miranda. How beauteous mankind is! O brave new world,

That has such people in 't! (*The Tempest* 5.1.183–84)

Fair Play

Troilus. When many times the captive Grecian falls

Even in the fan and wind of your fair sword,

You bid them rise, and live.

Hector.   O, 'tis fair play. (*Troilus and Cressida* 5.3.40–43)

Foregone Conclusion

Iago. Nay, this was but his dream.

Othello. But this denoted a foregone conclusion. (*Othello* 3.3.429–30)

Foul Play

Gloucester. Good my friends, consider; you are my guests.

Do me no foul play, friends. (*King Lear* 3.7.30–31)

Into Thin Air

Prospero. Our revels now are ended. These our actors,

As I foretold you, were all spirits, and

Are melted into air, into thin air. (*The Tempest* 4.1.148–50)

It Was Greek to Me

Casca. But those that understood him smil'd at one another, and shook their heads; but for mine own part, it was Greek to me. (*Julius Caesar* 1.2.278–80)

The Livelong Day

Marullus. Knew you not Pompey? Many a time and oft

Have you climb'd up to walls and battlements,

To towers and windows, yea, to chimney-tops,

Your infants in your arms, and there have sat

The livelong day, with patient expectation,

To see great Pompey pass the streets of Rome. (*Julius Caesar* 1.1.38–43)

One Fell Swoop

Macduff. Did you say all? — O Hell-kite! — All?

What, all my pretty chickens, and their dam,

At one fell swoop? (*Macbeth* 4.3.217–19)

Rhyme and Reason

Falstaff. And these are not fairies? I was three or four times in the thought they were not fairies; and yet the guiltiness of my mind, the sudden surprise of my powers, drove the grossness of the foppery into a received belief, in despite of the teeth of all rhyme and reason, that they were fairies. (*Merry Wives of Windsor* 5.5.122–27)

Too Much of a Good Thing

Rosalind. Why then, can one desire too much of a good thing? Come sister, you shall be the priest and marry us. (*As You Like It* 4.1.116–18)

Chapter 20

The Ten Greatest Shakespearean Performers

● ●

Comparing Shakespearean performers to find the top ten is akin to comparing Apple computers with orange paint. It's a fruitless exercise. Nonetheless, a few actors and actresses have performed so notably that they clearly deserve a place among the top ten.

Richard Burbage

Richard Burbage was the resident tragedian in Shakespeare's acting company. Shakespeare wrote his greatest roles for Burbage: Richard III, Hamlet, King Lear, and others. Burbage's acting ability was acclaimed in his day, and his reputation survived his death in 1619. Shakespeare's great tragic roles are also his most difficult for the actor. For him to have written these roles knowing that Burbage would play them is itself a testament to Burbage's skills as an actor.

David Garrick

David Garrick lived from 1717 to 1779. When he started acting, actors were still considered vagabonds, but he raised the profile of acting as an art and as a profession. His acting style drew lavish praise in part for his naturalness. Unlike many of his contemporaries, Garrick did not use a leading role as a vehicle for self-aggrandizement, but worked with the other actors onstage to create believable, artistic scenes.

When Garrick took over management of the Drury Lane Theatre in 1747, he enforced his own acting style on all the actors, raising the standards of performance and creating an ensemble of talented actors.

Sarah Siddons

Born Sarah Kemble, Sarah Siddons lived from 1755 to 1831. Her stage debut was at the age of 12, when she played Ariel in *The Tempest*. She was an acting prodigy whose fame spread quickly throughout England. David Garrick brought her to the Drury Lane Theatre in 1775 to play Portia in *The Merchant of Venice*. The London critics did not take kindly to the young Mrs. Siddons, but she performed to wide acclaim elsewhere in England, tackling Shakespeare's toughest roles, including Lady Macbeth.

In 1781, Siddons returned to Drury Lane, and this time the critics were more agreeable. She stayed at Drury Lane until 1790, performing non-Shakespearean and Shakespearean roles, including Ophelia and Queen Gertrude in *Hamlet* and Constance in *King John*. After she left Drury Lane, she continued to act, especially in her most popular roles, in particular Lady Macbeth.

Edwin Booth

Edwin Booth (1833–1893) was one of the finest Shakespearean actors in America. He was the middle son of Junius Brutus Booth, also a noted actor. Edwin achieved fame in Philadelphia and New York for Hamlet and other roles. In *Julius Caesar*, he played opposite his brothers for the first and only time. He built his own theater in 1869, which opened with *Romeo and Juliet*, in which he played Romeo. The theater was not a financial success, and he returned to touring in the United States, England, and Germany.

Despite Edwin's talent, the Booth family is best known for its youngest son. John Wilkes Booth was also an actor, but he lived in Edwin's shadow until 1865, when he earned everlasting infamy by assassinating President Abraham Lincoln.

The Drew-Barrymore Family

The name Barrymore is synonymous with acting in the United States, but the family's roots go back further, to the Drew family. John Drew (1827–1862) was a popular Irish actor whose performances in America included Andrew Aguecheek in *Twelfth Night* and Dromio in *The Comedy of Errors*. He married Louisa Lane (1820–1897), an accomplished actress since childhood. She performed Lady Macbeth at only 16 years old. John Drew briefly managed the Arch Street Theater in Philadelphia before Mrs. Drew took over. She managed this theater successfully for more than 30 years.

John and Louisa had two children who also took up acting, under strict guidance from their mother. John (1853–1927) earned acclaim in London for his performance as Petruchio in *The Taming of the Shrew*. Their other child, Georgina (1856–1893), was a popular comic actress who married Maurice Barrymore (1847–1905). He played supporting roles in various shows and is remembered not for his acting but for his name. Their children — Lionel, Ethel, and John — all became famous actors, with famous children of their own.

The eldest, Lionel (1878–1954), is best known for his film career, although he also played Macbeth onstage in 1921. Ethel (1879–1959) performed in a variety of roles, including Ophelia in *Hamlet* and Portia in *The Merchant of Venice*. In 1928, she opened and managed her own theater in New York. John (1882–1942) achieved the greatest success with his performance of Hamlet, which he performed in 1922 in New York and in 1925 in England.

Dame Ellen Terry

Born in 1847, Ellen Terry came from a family of actors and is the great-aunt of Sir John Gielgud. As a child, she played Mamillius in *The Winter's Tale* and other child roles. By 1862, she tackled Titania in *A Midsummer Night's Dream*. She married several times and acted on and off over the years. From about 1878 to 1902, she traveled with Henry Irving — who was the first actor to be knighted — performing in the United States eight times in Shakespeare's greatest female roles, including Beatrice in *Much Ado About Nothing*, Desdemona in *Othello*, and Lady Macbeth.

In 1903, she managed the Imperial Theatre in Westminster with critical success. She continued to travel and act and often went on lecture tours. Her last performance was in 1925, the same year she was made Dame of the British Empire. She died in 1928.

Dame Peggy Ashcroft

Peggy Ashcroft (1907–1991) was one of the finest actresses of her day. Her stage career began in 1926, but her first role in a Shakespeare play was as Desdemona in 1930, with Paul Robeson (the famous American actor) as Othello. Her career advanced, and she played many of Shakespeare's great roles, including Juliet, Portia in *The Merchant of Venice*, Imogen in *Cymbeline*, Titania in *A Midsummer Night's Dream*, Cleopatra, and many others. Her most acclaimed role was Queen Margaret in the Royal Shakespeare Company's *War of the Roses* (*King Henry VI*, Parts 1, 2, and 3, and *King Richard III*).

Nobody spoke the verse better than she. She made this extraordinary language so easy to understand. She was also a founding member of the Royal Shakespeare Company and became a director in 1968. She was made Dame of the British Empire in 1956.

Lord Laurence Olivier

Laurence Olivier (1907–1989) began his stage career in 1924 and quickly became a leading actor on the London stage. In 1935, he alternated the roles of Romeo and Mercutio with John Gielgud. In 1946, he directed and starred in *King Henry V,* which broke new ground in movie-making. Some consider his *Hamlet* of 1948 and his *King Richard III* of 1956 to be the finest modern versions of these plays.

His performance as Othello shocked many for its physical and sensual interpretation of the role. He was famous for adding muscle to Shakespeare. He later played the same role in a film version, which is still available on videotape.

Not just an actor and director, Olivier was the artistic director for the Chichester Festival Theatre, which was the forerunner to the Royal National Theatre, which he founded and helped run until 1973. He was knighted in 1947 and elevated to Baron in 1970.

Sir John Gielgud

John Gielgud, born in 1904, made his stage debut in *King Henry V.* His talent was immediately evident, and he went on to perform in many of Shakespeare's plays. In 1935, he and Laurence Olivier performed in *Romeo and Juliet,* alternating the roles of Romeo and Mercutio. Many critics consider him to be the finest Shakespearean performer of the 20th century. He received a knighthood in 1953.

Gielgud's credits include numerous stage performances in London, the United Kingdom, Europe, the United States, and throughout the world, including an acclaimed performance as Prospero in *The Tempest.* He performed in films from 1932, and his film roles include King Henry IV in Orson Welles's *Chimes at Midnight* and Prospero in Peter Greenaway's *Prospero's Books.*

His one-man television show, *The Ages of Man,* and an audio recording of the same name reveal the passion and power that come from speaking Shakespeare's words. His audio recordings include *King Lear* in 1994.

Many Others

The modern stage is blessed with many excellent actors and actresses. Some are best known for comedy, and others for tragedy. Picking one person as the best is a job for future historians. Instead, we leave you with a list of some of the foremost Shakespearean performers today:

✔ **Kenneth Branagh** made his stage debut in London in 1982. He went on to perform in and direct several of Shakespeare's plays. He also helped spark a renewed interest in Shakespeare with his films, starting with *Henry V* in 1989 and later with *Much Ado About Nothing* in 1993. He continues to act in and direct Shakespeare films and formed a film company in 1998 to bring more of Shakespeare's plays to the cinema.

✔ **Dame Judi Dench** started her illustrious Shakespearean career as Ophelia in 1957. She has performed in numerous plays — Shakespeare's and others — including a terrific performance as Viola in *Twelfth Night* in 1969, and as Cleopatra with Anthony Hopkins as Antony in 1987 (see Figure 20-1). Primarily a stage actress, Dench has also performed in film and on television. American audiences may know her best as "M" in the latest James Bond movies, but she also played Mistress Quickly in *Henry V* and Queen Elizabeth in *Shakespeare in Love* (for which she won an Academy Award). She was made Dame of the British Empire in 1988.

Figure 20-1:
Anthony
Hopkins as
Antony and
Judi Dench
as
Cleopatra.

Donald Cooper/Photstage

- **Sir Anthony Hopkins** earned acclaim for his performance with Judi Dench in *Antony and Cleopatra* (refer to Figure 20-1). His long and varied career includes a performance as Audrey in an all-male production of *As You Like It.* His television and film career includes Othello in 1981 and the title role in the film *Titus* in 1999.

- **Sir Derek Jacobi** performed the title role in *Hamlet* for the National Youth Theatre in 1955. He joined the National Theatre Company in London in 1963, playing Laertes in *Hamlet.* He performed often in London, Scandinavia, Australia, Japan, China, and the United States. In 1982, he played Benedick in *Much Ado About Nothing* for the Royal Shakespeare Company. He is best known for his work on the London stage, but he has performed often on television and in film, including the role of the Chorus in Kenneth Branagh's *Henry V.*

- **Sir Ian McKellen** played Aufidius in *Coriolanus* in 1963, and soon after earned acclaim for roles including Claudio in *Much Ado About Nothing* for the National Theatre Company in 1965. He played many roles in Shakespearean and other plays, including tours in England, Scotland, and the United States. His one-man show, *Acting Shakespeare,* toured Europe and the United States from 1980 to 1987. He recently worked with Richard Loncraine on a film adaptation of *King Richard III.*

- **Helen Mirren** is widely known for her film and television appearances, but she began her career with the National Youth Theatre, which quickly led to a stint with the Royal Shakespeare Company. Her varied stage career includes notable performances as Cleopatra, Lady Macbeth, and Queen Margaret.

- **Paul Scofield's** illustrious career has included the title roles in most of Shakespeare's great plays. He has performed with the Royal Shakespeare Company, the Shakespeare Memorial Theatre, the National Theatre, and other companies in England and throughout the world.

- **Patrick Stewart,** best known to American audiences as Jean-Luc Picard in *Star Trek: The Next Generation,* is also a classical actor whose roles have included many performances with the Royal Shakespeare Company and as Prospero at the New York Shakespeare Festival in 1995.

Chapter 21

Ten Films and Shows Based on Shakespeare's Plays

Since the 1600s, actors and directors have been rewriting, revamping, and retelling Shakespeare's plays. Sometimes, the result is an entirely new work that merely borrows Shakespeare's plots and characters — much the same way that Shakespeare borrowed other stories and used his own words and poetry. Some works keep parts of Shakespeare's script but modify it: shorten it for television, modernize it, or use excerpts from Shakespeare's script in an otherwise modern script. A few productions are noteworthy not for their scripts themselves but for their novel interpretations of Shakespeare's text. This chapter lists ten of the most popular and interesting performances of and variations on Shakespeare's plays.

West Side Story

Borrowing the basic story of *Romeo and Juliet, West Side Story* sets the story on the mean streets of New York City. Gang conflicts substitute for feuding families. Instead of Romeo, you see Tony, a member of the Jets. Juliet is Maria, whose brother is head of the rival Sharks. The musical emphasizes the noise, the sordidness, and the toughness of tenement life, its lyricism confined to the love story and to the passions of much of Leonard Bernstein's score. The lyrics represented the Broadway debut of Stephen Sondheim. Choreography by Jerome Robbins captured the tense feelings and action of the gang war.

The immense success of the musical on Broadway and in London led to a film version of the musical in 1961 (see Figure 21-1), which also enjoyed raves and awards.

Figure 21-1:
West Side Story is a popular musical based on *Romeo and Juliet*.

Everett Collection

Verdi's Falstaff

Several operas are based on Shakespeare's plays. Giuseppe Verdi borrowed from Shakespeare several times. One of his most famous operas is *Falstaff*, based on *The Merry Wives of Windsor*. His other Shakespearean operas are *Otello* and *Macbetto*. These great operas are among the staples for opera companies worldwide, and you can find some excellent performances on videotape.

Prokofiev's Romeo and Juliet

Shakespeare's plays inspired other composers as well. Sergei Prokofiev composed a score for *Romeo and Juliet* as a ballet. The ballet has seen numerous performances, including a 1988 production by the American Ballet Theatre at Lincoln Center.

Chimes at Midnight

Orson Welles wrote, directed, and starred in this 1966 film about Falstaff by taking excerpts from both parts of *Henry IV, Henry V,* and *The Merry Wives of Windsor*. The title is a quote from *Henry IV, Part 2*. Some people consider *Chimes at Midnight* to be among Welles's finest work, and others consider it ridiculous or worse. A newly restored version is now available on videotape.

Rosencrantz and Guildenstern Are Dead

This play, written by Tom Stoppard, shows us *Hamlet* from the point of view of Rosencrantz and Guildenstern. Hamlet's two hapless college buddies find themselves hopelessly out of their depths while the world spins out of control around them. In 1990, Stoppard made a film from his play, starring Tim Roth and Gary Oldman.

Looking for Richard

This 1996 documentary shows Al Pacino trying to create a film of *Richard III* in New York. Like many similar documentaries, this movie intersperses scenes from the play with commentary about the difficulties of adapting Shakespeare to film, acting Shakespeare, coming to grips with the language, and so on. The film is available on videotape.

Peter Brook's A Midsummer Night's Dream

Peter Brook changed forever how we approach Shakespeare's plays, especially *A Midsummer Night's Dream*. His 1970 stage production involved trapezes and acrobatics. He required the audience to use their imaginations — which is exactly what must have happened in Shakespeare's time. Set within the confines of a white box designed by Sally Jacobs, the production starred Alan Howard as Oberon and Sara Kestelman as Titania.

His production has become known as "Brook's Dream," and it was indeed just that. It was a total release from naturalism and a forerunner to the countless imaginative productions that we have seen since. Somehow, the bravery of the production perfectly matches the stature of the language.

Trevor Nunn's Macbeth

As artistic director for the Royal Shakespeare Company, Trevor Nunn directed many notable shows, but his most groundbreaking production was *Macbeth* in 1976, starring Ian McKellen and Judi Dench. It started at The Other Place in Stratford and then transferred to the Donmar as part of the London season.

A dark space with a circle of wooden boxes was the environment for a small company to tell the story. There were no theatrical tricks, and Shakespeare's text was allowed to shine in all its passionate and terrifying glory. The production was filmed for television in 1978 and released on video in 1979. The video may never quite allow you to enter into the dark theatrical world that Nunn so brilliantly created, but it's still one of the most successful Shakespeare plays on tape. Unfortunately, the videotape is not available in the United States.

Return to the Forbidden Planet

The Forbidden Planet is a 1956 movie whose story is a science-fiction version of *The Tempest,* in which a distant planet substitutes for the island. *Return to the Forbidden Planet* pays homage to the first film but tells its own rock-and-roll story of Doctor Prospero, his daughter Miranda, and the space-bound hero Captain Tempest. Unlike the film, the show includes lines from Shakespeare's *The Tempest,* and you can spend the evening playing "find the quote."

The show started as a late-night piece of entertainment in the tent of the "Bubble," a theater company that toured London's parks. In the 1980s, director and writer Bob Carlton developed the idea into a full-length show. He brought the show to London's West End, where it won the coveted Olivier Award in 1990. It has since played Broadway and throughout the world. Look for it. It's a lot of fun and a great way to bring your kids to the Bard.

Kurosawa's Throne of Blood

Shakespeare is popular in many countries. The famous Japanese film director Akira Kurosawa adapted several plays to the Japanese cinema. *Throne of Blood* (*Kumonosu-Djo,* or *Spider Web Castle*) is his 1957 film adaptation of *Macbeth,* starring Toshiro Mifune as Lord Toho. Kurosawa follows *Macbeth* closely, albeit setting the film in medieval Japan rather than in Scotland.

Kurosawa also adapted *Hamlet* and *King Lear* for the Japanese cinema. His 1963 film *The Bad Sleep Well* sets *Hamlet* in modern-day Japan. In his 1985 film *Ran (Chaos),* Kurosawa freely adapts Shakespeare's *King Lear* to medieval Japan. King Lear is Hidetora Ichimonji, who divides his kingdom among his three sons.

Index

• L •

• M •

IDG BOOKS WORLDWIDE BOOK REGISTRATION

Register This Book and Win!

We want to hear from you!

Visit **http://my2cents.dummies.com** to register this book and tell us how you liked it!

- ✔ Get entered in our monthly prize giveaway.

- ✔ Give us feedback about this book — tell us what you like best, what you like least, or maybe what you'd like to ask the author and us to change!

- ✔ Let us know any other *...For Dummies®* topics that interest you.

Your feedback helps us determine what books to publish, tells us what coverage to add as we revise our books, and lets us know whether we're meeting your needs as a *...For Dummies* reader. You're our most valuable resource, and what you have to say is important to us!

Not on the Web yet? It's easy to get started with *Dummies 101®: The Internet For Windows® 98* or *The Internet For Dummies®*, 5th Edition, at local retailers everywhere.

Or let us know what you think by sending us a letter at the following address:

...For Dummies Book Registration
Dummies Press
7260 Shadeland Station, Suite 100
Indianapolis, IN 46256-3917
Fax 317-596-5498

BESTSELLING BOOK SERIES